LONDON RECORD SOCIETY
PUBLICATIONS

VOLUME LVIII

THE BREWERS' BOOK
PART 1, 1418–25

An Edition of the
Minute Book of William Porlond,
Clerk of the Brewers' Company

EDITED BY

CAROLINE ANNE METCALFE

LONDON RECORD SOCIETY
THE BOYDELL PRESS
2023

First published 2024

A London Record Society publication
Published by The Boydell Press
an imprint of Boydell & Brewer Ltd
PO Box 9, Woodbridge, Suffolk IP12 3DF, UK
and of Boydell & Brewer Inc.
668 Mt Hope Avenue, Rochester, NY 14620–2731, USA
website: www.boydellandbrewer.com

ISBN 978-0-900952-08-1

A CIP catalogue record for this book is available
from the British Library

The publisher has no responsibility for the continued existence or
accuracy of URLs for external or third-party internet websites referred to
in this book, and does not guarantee that any content
on such websites is, or will remain, accurate or appropriate

This publication is printed on acid-free paper

Printed and bound in Great Britain by TJ Books Limited, Padstow, Cornwall

CONTENTS

v

This book is published with the generous assistance of grants from the Brewers' Company and from The Yorkist History Trust.

ILLUSTRATIONS

FIGURES

PLATES

1 The Brewers' funeral pall dating from the late fifteenth century.
   © The Brewers' Company.
2 The Brewers' funeral pall: detail showing how the attributes of
   St Thomas were altered during the Reformation. © The Brewers'
   Company.

The editor, contributors and publisher are grateful to all the institutions and persons listed for permission to reproduce the materials in which they hold copyright. Every effort has been made to trace the copyright holders; apologies are offered for any omission, and the publisher will be pleased to add any necessary acknowledgement in subsequent editions.

ACKNOWLEDGEMENTS

I am most grateful to the Clerk of the Worshipful Company of Brewers for his kind permission to work on this manuscript, and to both the former Archivist, Jerome Farrell, and the present Archivist, Hannah Dunmow, for their enthusiasm and support.

I am very grateful to Professor Caroline Barron for suggesting that I might work on this remarkable manuscript, and for all her help with the final stages of this edition. Professor Clive Burgess, as the Honorary General Editor, was working with me until his untimely death. I will always remember his kindness, gentle guidance and wisdom. I am also very grateful to Professor Martha Carlin, Stuart Forbes, Stephen Freeth, Dr Stephen O'Connor, Dr John Oldland and Giles Darkes at the Historic Towns Atlas, for all their help. My husband, Steve Metcalfe, has been truly supportive throughout.

ABBREVIATIONS

Barron, *London in the Later Middle Ages*   C. M. Barron, *London in the Later Middle Ages: Government and People, 1200–1500* (Oxford, 2004)

Bowtell, Elsyngspital   A. Bowtell, 'A Medieval London Hospital: Elsyngspital 1330–1536' (unpublished PhD thesis, Royal Holloway, University of London, 2010)

Cal. Letter-Books   *Calendar of Letter-Books Preserved Among the Archives of the Corporation of the City of London, at the Guildhall*, 11 Volumes, ed. R. R. Sharpe (London, 1899–1912)

CPMR 1364–81   *Calendar of Plea and Memoranda Rolls preserved among the archives of the Corporation of the City of London at the Guildhall, 1364–81*, ed. A. H. Thomas (Cambridge, 1929)

CPMR 1413–37   *Calendar of Plea and Memoranda Rolls of the City of London, 1413–37*, ed. A. H. Thomas (Cambridge, 1943)

Chambers and Daunt, *London English*   *A Book of London English: 1384–1425*, ed. R. W. Chambers and M. Daunt (Oxford, 1931)

DMLBS   *Dictionary of Medieval Latin from British Sources*

GL   Guildhall Library

GL MS 5440   William Porlond's Minute Book, Being an Account and Memorandum Book, compiled by William Porlond, clerk to the Brewers' Company, 1418–40, now CLC/L/BF/A/021/MS05440

Harben, Dictionary	H. A. Harben, *A Dictionary of London: being notes topographical and historical relating to the principal buildings in the city of London* (London, 1918)
Harvey, *Mediaeval Architects*	J. Harvey, *English Mediaeval Architects: A Biographical Dictionary down to 1550* (Gloucester, 1984)
Hennessy, *London Clergy*	G. L. Hennessy, *Novum Repertorium Ecclesiasticum Parochiale Londinense* (London, 1898)
History of Parliament	*The History of Parliament: The House of Commons 1386–1421*, 4 vols., ed. J. S. Roskell, L. Clark, C. Rawcliffe (Stroud, 1993)
LMA	London Metropolitan Archives
Map of Tudor London	*Tudor London: The City and Southwark in 1520* (second edition 2022, published by The Historic Towns Trust)
ODNB	*Oxford Dictionary of National Biography*, ed. D. Cannadine and others (Oxford, 2004)
Trans LAMAS	*Transactions of the London and Middlesex Archaeological Society*

INTRODUCTION

'William Porlond's Minute Book, Being an Account and Memorandum Book, compiled by William Porlond, clerk to the Brewers' Company, 1418–40', is a remarkable book and a rare survival.[1] It was compiled as the personal memorandum book of the clerk to the Worshipful Company of Brewers of London, for the years 1418–40, with a gap in the records from 1425 to 1429.[2] It survives not as an official set of minutes and memoranda but as an informal record of matters of concern to the Brewers, gathered by their clerk, William Porlond, in his own working volume of draft materials. On the very first page he recorded, in Norman French, his appointment as clerk to the mistery and fraternity of Brewers of London on 14 February 1418 and that he, the said William, 'ordained this book, to have cognizance of all the things done in the mistery and fraternity abovesaid, for all the time that the said William should be clerk of the said Brewers' [1]. This book, with its collection of more personal proceedings, affords a valuable insight into the clerk's ways of working and into those matters that he considered significant.

HISTORIOGRAPHY

William Porlond created his memorandum book during his time as clerk to the craft and fraternity of Brewers, 1418–40. No books compiled by his predecessor, John Morey, or Porlond's successor, Robert Coket, have survived. Indeed, no further Brewers' clerks can be identified from Coket, who began his term in 1440, until John Bowgham in 1554.[3] Porlond's book was rescued from the Great Fire of London in 1666, over 200 years after its compilation, and it also survived the destruction of the seventeenth-century Brewers' Hall in December 1940. One of

---

[1] This book, along with other items in the Brewers' archive, is lodged in the Guildhall Library, London; previously GL MS 5440, it is now catalogued as CLC/L/BF/A/021/ MS05440. The Guildhall Library originally catalogued the manuscript with the name 'Porland', which appears in gold letters on the spine of the book. This spelling, however, is never used in the book, where his name appears as Purlond, Purland and Purlang, but most frequently as Porlond – the version used in this Introduction and in footnotes.

[2] This edition of the Brewers' Book covers folios 1–156v and ends in 1425. The second part, covering the years 1429–40, is currently in preparation and will be published by the London Record Society within the next few years.

[3] M. Ball, *The Worshipful Company of Brewers: A Short History* (London, 1977), 126.

Porlond's successors, William Vines, the Brewers' clerk 1824–48, clearly worked through the whole manuscript identifying damaged and missing pages **[92] [165]**. During 1830–1, the antiquary W. H. Black compiled an unpublished manuscript volume, The Brewers' Company Extract of Minutes 1418–40, in which he commented briefly on the contents of the Brewers' Book.[4]

But, from the early decades of the twentieth century, the Brewers' Book has been the subject of a more varied scrutiny. George Unwin drew upon material within the Book for his work on the guilds and companies of London, and he went so far as to include a photograph and translation of the invaluable list of London crafts on folio iiv **[26]**.[5] In *A Book of London English*, published in 1931, R. W. Chambers and Marjorie Daunt transcribed extracts that Porlond had written – notably – in English, taken from fifty folios in the first part of the manuscript, up to 1425 (folios 69v–121r) **[217–376]**.[6] The work of Chambers and Daunt, more than any other, highlighted the linguistic significance of Porlond's book and, memorably, they described him as a 'new broom' who 'continued dutifully to keep up his sweeping' and who was 'a chatty man as well as a good secretary'.[7] Mia Ball, who compiled *The Worshipful Company of Brewers: A Short History* in 1977, was more concerned to use extracts from Porlond's book to illustrate the history of the craft in the early fifteenth century.[8] But, more recently, historians such as Malcolm Vale and Judith Bennett have begun to exploit the potential of the materials contained within the book in earnest. Following the lead of Chambers and Daunt, Malcolm Vale has explored the impact that Henry V's professed preference for using English in the conduct of domestic affairs had on the choice of language that a man such as Porlond made when compiling certain sections of his book – which is to say that the Brewers' clerk chose to use English as a working language, discernibly in accordance with Henry's directives.[9] Judith Bennett, by contrast, has in recent years made extensive use of the materials compiled by Porlond to derive an unprecedentedly detailed understanding of ale production within London and, most valuably, highlight the importance of the role played

4   GL MS 5441. This book of sixty single-sided hand-written folios is also kept at the Guildhall Library; on Black, see B. Nurse, 'Black, William Henry, 1808–72', in *ODNB*.
5   G. Unwin, *The Gilds and Companies of London* (London, 1908), 167, 374; this list of crafts is discussed more fully below.
6   *A Book of London English: 1384–1425*, ed. R. W. Chambers and M. Daunt (Oxford, 1931), 138–91.
7   Chambers and Daunt, *London English*, 138.
8   M. Ball, *Brewers: Short History*.
9   M. Vale, *Henry V: The Conscience of a King* (New Haven and London, 2016), chapter 3, especially 109–11.

by women brewsters in the day-to-day practice of the craft.[10] She also analysed the fraternity quarterage lists and livery lists in the Brewers' Book in pursuit of women who, whether married, widowed or single, brewed ale and joined the fraternity of the Brewers of London in their own right.[11] Porlond's record, while redolent of experience in the lower and middle reaches of society – and, if differing in outlook from those who shaped the city's directives, nevertheless also reveals the impact of royal decrees – constitutes a unique resource shedding light on social and economic mores within the city at a formative time.

THE MANUSCRIPT

The manuscript consists of 328 folios, mounted and bound within a later cover. Some folios are damaged, others are torn, and some have been cut out at some time. Arabic numerals have been added later in the top right-hand corner of the recto pages as folio numbers. Occasional pencil notes were added by William Vines, who dated his brief notes 1830–1 and was the Brewers' clerk, 1824–48. The folios measure 30.4 × 22.0 cm and, with the cover, the whole is 32.7 × 24.4 cm.

Writings in three languages – Norman French, Latin and English – within the manuscript show that all three were currently in use for company record-keeping (see Figures 7, 9, 10). The very first folio was written in Norman French and this language was used interchangeably with Latin and some English passages (although these may be later insertions, c.1424–5) until folio 24v [65]. This last passage in Norman French was a copy of an ordinance about the production and sale of ale and takes its place in materials compiled during the quarrel with Richard Whittington at the time of his last mayoralty (1419–20). After that, there are three sentences in French on folio 35v (about regulations governing the sale of grain) [95] and four lists of food for dinners, in 1422 and 1423, on folios 41v [112–13], 52v [148–9], 57v–58v [167–72] and 79v–80v [253–8]. The last two ordinances for a dinner were written in a mixture of French, English and Latin.[12] From folio 24v onwards, however, Latin was used predominantly, with some English insertions, until folio 69v [216].

10 J. M. Bennett, *Ale, Beer and Brewsters: Women's Work in a Changing World, 1300–1600* (New York and Oxford, 1996).

11 J. M. Bennett, 'Women and Men in the Brewers' Gild of London, circa 1420', in *The Salt of Common Life: Individuality and Choice in the Medieval Town, Countryside, Nation and Church: Essays Presented to J. Ambrose Raftis*, ed. E. De Windt (Kalamazoo, Michigan, 1995), 181–232 (200–25).

12 On folios 57v and 79v there are the English names for pike, herring, oysters, swan, chicken, and words such as taps, pots, and coarse flour, amongst the French, whilst the money totals have the Latin word '*summa*'.

Then, in 1422, the clerk declared, in Latin, his intention to use English in future, to emulate the example of Henry V, who used English in his letters from France to the people of England [216].[13] Porlond wrote that, while many brewers could understand and write in English, they could not understand French and Latin. After this declaration, there were longer sections in English from 83v to 107r [265–334] and 113r to 152v [357–452], although Latin was still in use for two more sections, 107v to 112r [334–56], and indeed, this part of Porlond's book ended with the accounts recorded in Latin, in 1425 [453–66].

The use of Latin, French and English and the record of the clerk's decision to use English for the better understanding of many of the brewers give the book a linguistic significance and show that the use of language was evolving, not only at the court of Henry V but also within the less elevated confines of the Brewers' company. As a result, this book contains some of the first surviving company records to be kept in English and notably, whilst within the book copies of ordinances were variously entered in Latin or French, copies of petitions were written in English [48, 61, 166, 187, 248–9]. Payments to professional clerks for translating documents include 'Item to John Stafford of the Guildhall for drawing of a bill out of English into French and for the writing of the said bill, 2s.' c.1424–5 [433]. But, significantly, all three languages were used within this book.

If one turns to consider how the book was compiled, throughout its first section, up to and including folio 156v, in 1425, pages were crossed right through, from corner to corner, presumably after the accounts had been read to the masters at the annual feast. This practice ceased from folio 157r, when Porlond's detailed records were resumed (and after the hiatus in the surviving record) in the year 1429. The writing on folio 157 repeats some of the material on the very first folio, but in English, not French, referring to mayor Sevenoke, and records how the masters stood for two years at a time until 1429, after which they were to stand for only one year. The records then continue from the year 1429, but it seems likely that any other pages, covering the years 1425–9, have been lost.

Chronology within this book is not straightforward, partly because formerly blank pages were sometimes filled in later; but later additions have been left uncrossed, which makes it easier to identify them. One striking example of this is found amongst records for 1420, where there is a section of a draft petition about servants, with the phrase 'by Coket' [111]. Robert Coket was Porlond's assistant and successor, but his name did not occur again in the book until c.1433–4, so Coket clearly added an entry some fourteen years after the original text was written on that page.[14] Another example of a chronological leap occurred with a list

13 See Figure 9. Vale, *Henry V*, 107, 122–5.
14 GL MS 5440, f. 241r, in the second part of the Brewers' Book.

of repayments to some brewers dated 1438, yet which appeared just after the quarterage list for 1424–5 **[401]**. In both cases, a scribe used a previously blank space, out of date order, but still within Porlond's book. A third example followed lists of brewers infringing regulations during the mayoralty of William Walderne (1422–3). Underneath the last section of these lists, a sentence in English introduced a copy (in Latin) of the charter of the Fishmongers of London, which would have been useful to the Brewers of London as an 'enformer', that is as an example for them when they came to make their own charter. The clerk gave the Fishmongers' charter its date, 8 February 1433, but did not record when he wrote out this copy.[15] The Brewers of London gained their own royal charter on 22 February 1438.[16] This entry therefore must have been made between 1433 and 1438, yet it is to be found in records for 1422–3.

The clerk once acknowledged that his records were not in the correct date order when, after the account of the funeral procession for Henry V in November 1422 in the city of London, he noted:

'Here should be written the costs of a dinner made at the Conversion of St Paul [25 January], in the time of the said William Walderne being mayor of London [1422–3], in the first year of the reign of Henry VI [1422–3] … the which parcels, seek, and you shall find them written on the thirty-first leaf of this paper before this leaf' **[226]**.

The costs of the dinner can indeed be found thirty-one pages earlier **[112]**. Recording the death of Henry V, and the role played at this time by the city crafts, disrupted the usual pattern of the clerk's records and perhaps made him fill up previously blank pages. Paper and parchment were expensive and were used sparingly. In 1425 Porlond recorded 4s. spent on paper, parchment and ink over the preceding two years **[466]**.

To an extent, the interest of this book lies in the manner of its compilation as well as in its content. It should be noted, for instance, that Porlond's lists of names were usually grouped by Christian name, so that those called Henry, John, Robert, Thomas or William were recorded together, regardless of their surnames, as can be seen in the quarterage list for 1424–5 during Michell's mayoralty **[396–400]**. Porlond also grouped together widows or unmarried women, and left spaces between the groups of names so that he could make later additions. Overall, it also seems likely that he had draft lists of his own which he could copy into this book when convenient or necessary. But, equally, it must be remembered that Porlond's book is but one fragment of a once larger collection of company records and accounts, most of which have been lost – as applies, for instance, to the list of names that the clerk referred

15 The Charter of the Fishmongers, dated 8 February 1433, is kept at the Fishmongers' Hall amongst the Books of Ordinances and Transcripts. See P. Metcalf, *The Halls of the Fishmongers' Company: an architectural history of a riverside site* (London and Chichester, 1977), 13 (n.20).
16 Guildhall Library GL MS 5425 (CLC/L/BF/A/001/MS05425)

to as being on a roll of parchment hanging in a purse of leather attached to his book [287].

William Porlond's memorandum book does, however, include information written by several other people and differing handwriting certainly appears within the book. Some Latin headings, such as the top section of folio 69v, or the title pages for the accounts, are written in a large script that is quite different from the smaller script often used for passages in English [216]. Once, Porlond wrote a copy of a petition 'of less matter and shorter y made' suggesting that he wrote this passage himself [61].[17] Frequent corrections between the lines suggest that Porlond checked entries made by others. The only assistant clerk ever named in the book was Robert Coket, who emerges from c.1433 onwards but who, as mentioned, interpolated one signed entry in the first part, using up a blank space [111]. Another scribe used a distinctive ornate hand, beginning on folio 11v (c.1421–2), with a listing of London's crafts in three columns; this script can be found up to folio 81v (c.1423–4), but not again after that [26].[18] The list of crafts is, however, of great interest to historians – as discussed below.

WILLIAM PORLOND AND THE ROLE OF THE CLERK

William Porlond's creation of this book can play a part in fleshing out our understanding of the developing role of the company clerks in the fifteenth century. Matthew Davies has described these clerks as 'recorders of company practice', and pointed out that they were 'responsible for the institutional memory of the guilds'; he also noted that these clerks, by their documentation of procedures and events, helped to establish and perpetuate them within the mores of their respective companies.[19]

Porlond was appointed clerk to the craft and fraternity of Brewers between 1418 and 1419 and he served conscientiously until his death, probably in spring 1440. He stated on the first page of his book that he succeeded John Morey, clerk, just four days after Morey's death [1]. Nothing more about John Morey has emerged, nor do we have any details of how Porlond secured this role or what he did before 1418.

---

[17]   See Figure 8.
[18]   Simon Horobin has identified this ornate hand with that of the C text of *Piers Plowman* as found in Oxford Bodleian Library Manuscript Digby 102 and suggests that this may have been the hand of Robert Lynford; see S. Horobin, 'The Scribe of Bodleian Library MS Digby 102 and the Circulation of the C Text of *Piers Plowman*', *Yearbook of Langland Studies* 24 (2010), 89–112. Whilst Lynford became a resident almsman at Brewers' Hall from 1423, there is nothing to suggest that he worked as a literary scribe or as a clerk assisting with Porlond's book.
[19]   M. P. Davies, '"Monuments of Honour": Clerks, Histories and Heroes in the London Livery Companies', ed. H. Kleineke, *Parliament, Personalities and Power: Papers presented to Linda S. Clark*, The Fifteenth Century 10 (2011) 143–63 (147, 150).

From within his book a very brief outline of his career can be traced: he began with a salary of 40*s*. annually, which was doubled to £4 in 1423, because he was 'profitable and besy to do the common profit of the craft' **[330]**. Porlond joined the fraternity as the Brewers' clerk, but was not, himself, a brewer and never became a freeman of the craft **[44]**. He was granted free and quiet dwelling within Brewers' Hall, for his wife, any children, and his servants, with the use of a chamber, utensils and necessaries pertaining to the hall **[38]**. His wife, Dionysia or Denise, first appeared in the fraternity membership list for 1420–1 and was alive in 1440, so they were married for at least twenty years **[134]**.²⁰ Porlond made no provision for any children in his will, and did not even request prayers for any deceased children, so we may assume that there were none to share his furnished accommodation within Brewers' Hall.²¹ Mention of two female servants, Rose and Alison, tells us a little about his household. In this first part of the book his servant Rose was mentioned three times: she helped to collect money to pay John Pekker, the carpenter, when he began work on the hall; she had 5*s*. worth of livery cloth for one yard of green cloth for a hood; and later a house 'sometime of Rose' within the almshouse was repainted during repairs 1424–5 **[243]** **[307]** **[420]**. Alison featured in the second part of the book.²² Porlond's death may be deduced from a payment of a 40*s*. pension to Dionysia Porlond, in 1440, an entry presumably written by his assistant and successor, Robert Coket.²³

Beyond Porlond's life and work at Brewers' Hall, a few biographical facts can be established. One William Purlonde was a member of the fraternity of St Nicholas for Parish Clerks and was listed on the bede roll amongst clerks who had died before 1454.²⁴ Porlond bequeathed 20*s*. to this fraternity, conditional upon the wardens keeping four torches and four candles burning around his body before burial, paying wages to the torch-bearers and having two small torches burning continuously until his burial.²⁵ The records of the parish fraternity of the Holy Trinity and Saints Fabian and Sebastian, moreover, show that Porlond was involved in property transactions concerning the Falcon on the Hoop brewhouse, which eventually passed into the possession of the Brewers' fraternity. Further, in the will of John Mason, brewer, in 1431, Porlond was appointed as an executor, to be paid 40*s*. and given five

20 GL MS 5440, f. 324r.
21 William Porlond's will, LMA, DL/C/B/003/MS09171/004, f. 40.
22 GL MS 5440, f. 218v.
23 GL MS 5440, f. 324r. For discussion of Porlond's friends and associates, see C. Metcalfe, 'William Porlond, Clerk to the Craft and Fraternity of Brewers of London, 1418–1440', *Trans. London and Middlesex Archaeological Society* 64 (2013), 267–84 (278–80).
24 *The Bede Roll of the Fraternity of St Nicholas*, ed. N. W. and V. A. James, London Record Society 39, 2 vols (2004), i, 34.
25 LMA, DL/C/B/003/MS09171/004, f. 40.

yards of black cloth costing 4*s.* a yard, 'for counsel only'.[26] These brief occurrences of his name amongst the surviving records of two London fraternities nevertheless suggest that Porlond was a man with connections extending beyond Brewers' Hall.

While we can assemble a profile for William Porlond within the city, the book that he compiled between 1418–19 and 1440, when serving as clerk to the craft and fraternity of Brewers of London, inevitably stands as his main memorial. Indeed, this book was important to him for, right at the very end of his own will, which he had made in 1439–40, Porlond included a clause about his books. The place of this clause, after all the other instructions both to his wife and to his executor, John Neel, master of the hospital of St Thomas Acre, concerning his burial, his exequies, the disposal of his goods and his bequests to friends, suggests that he attached a personal value to his books.[27] Having bequeathed his furred red cloak with his hood of 'musterdevillers' to his assistant, Robert Coket, clerk, he finally added:

> [*Latin*] I leave to the abovesaid Robert Coket each and all those books made by me, of whatever kind, concerning ordinances and regulations for the government of the Brewers of London, always with the specific proviso that I wish that after the death of the said Robert, that all the books shall remain to the said craft of Brewers completely and perpetually.

Any other books made by Porlond are now lost. He referred to his own old missal, which was to be given to the church of St Mary Fenchurch, and to his first primer, 'in quires and not bound', which he bequeathed to Thomas Clerk. This man may have been the scrivener who received payment for writing the 'deed of feoffment' and the testament of demise of land to the craft, which secured possession of Brewers' Hall for the craft in 1439–40.[28] Porlond did not, however, refer to any literary works that he had collected or copied; by contrast, we know that another clerk, Porlond's near contemporary, John Brynchele, the first known clerk to the Taylors and who made his will in 1421, bequeathed, among other books in Latin and French, a copy of the 'Talys of Caunterbury', in the earliest recorded bequest of this book.[29]

Whilst there is nothing within the Brewers' Book to support the idea that Porlond himself copied literary manuscripts for payment, his presentation of lengthy petitions and the vivid account of the Brewers' quarrel with Whittington in 1422 (discussed below) suggest an easy proficiency

[26]   *Parish Fraternity Register, Fraternity of the Holy Trinity and Ss. Fabian and Sebastian in the Parish of St Botolph without Aldersgate*, ed. P. Basing, London Record Society 18 (1982), 118–20, 122–4, 125.
[27]   LMA, DL/C/B/003/MS09171/004, f. 40.
[28]   GL MS 5440, f. 304v.
[29]   Davies, 'Monuments of Honour', 148.

in English **[48] [217–19]**. Malcolm Vale described Porlond's account of
the funeral ceremonies for Henry V as forming 'an extended piece of
English narrative prose worthy of a chronicler' **[220–5]**.[30] Whether or
not the clerk owned or copied works of literature, his compilation of the
account of the funeral of Henry V and his resolve to write his book in
English from c.1422 certainly link Porlond with the literary movement
in London in the early fifteenth century, and to the growing interest in
English literary works amongst London citizens.[31]

CONSOLIDATING THE BREWERS' COMPANY IN THE EARLY FIFTEENTH CENTURY

Ale brewing was an ancient art. Possibly the earliest written reference to
the existence of brewers as a body of citizens of London can be found
in the City of London *Letter-Book C* in 1292, when Edward I required
the Brewers' complaints against the London sheriffs to be heard and for
the Brewers to enjoy 'such liberties and customs as they ought, and such
as their predecessors used to enjoy'.[32] By 1364 the Brewers were able to
contribute £14 6*s*. 8*d*. towards a gift for Edward III.[33] The existence of a
mistery of Brewers of London was established by 1376, when they first
returned four members to the common council: Thomas Potesgrave, John
Cook, John Chipstede and William Strode.[34] Then, on 13 October 1406,
an important development took place when freemen of the mistery of
Brewers petitioned to choose four wardens and four masters, two of each
from east and west of Walbrook, to rule the mistery and exercise search,
assay and survey over all who were brewing ale within the city, whether
selling wholesale or retail.[35] The petition was granted, with the proviso
that if the masters and wardens 'should do anything hurtful', the mayor,
with the consent of the aldermen, should govern and punish offenders
in the mistery as before. The mayor and aldermen had delegated to the
Brewers the supervision of their craft (as had already been granted to
other crafts) but retained the right to rescind this privilege. Porlond wrote
out a copy of this ordinance and called it 'le bon ordeignance' of mayor
John Woodcock, because of its importance **[62]**.[36] Then, reflecting this

---

30 Vale, *Henry V*, III (n.78).

31 For further discussion on this theme, see L. R. Mooney and E. Stubbs, *Scribes and the City: London Guildhall Clerks and the Dissemination of Middle English* (York, 2013), 121.

32 *Calendar of the Letter-Books of the City of London A L*, ed. R. R. Sharpe, II vols (London, 1899–1912) [hereinafter *Cal. Letter-Book*], C, 7.

33 *Cal. Letter-Book*, G, 172.

34 *Cal. Letter-Book*, H, 43.

35 *Cal. Letter-Book*, I, 50.

36 The process whereby the mayor and aldermen delegated responsibility for the quality and price of ale and beer to the Brewers should be viewed in the context of the overall control that the mayor and aldermen still retained over food-pricing within the city; see

important step forward in the craft's history, the names of the masters and wardens of the Brewers for 1406 were recorded in the City *Letter-Book* for the first time.[37] The masters were: Nicholas Stratton, Thomas Bristowe, Peter Hayforde and Richard Rowdone, whilst the wardens were: John More, John Davy, John Wyghtmore and William atte Wode.

Greater power to regulate their craft, even with the caveat that this privilege could still be removed, was a significant step forward for the Brewers' craft and marks their rise in importance amongst London guilds. Thirty-two years later, the Brewers acquired their royal charter from Henry VI on 22 February 1438.[38] William Porlond recorded much administrative work, with many payments to officials, to secure this in the second half of his book (1429–40). Having a charter not only enhanced the standing of the Brewers within the city but also granted them the rights associated with incorporation, allowing them to hold property, to develop spiritual and charitable practices, and also to draw up their own rules for the administration of their craft.[39]

When William Porlond began writing his book in 1418, he and the Brewers were beginning to establish company practice. In a lengthy passage in Latin, he noted in 1418–19 that 'By an oath to observe the wise profit and constitution of the company it was agreed to inspect the great table of the fraternity which specifies our brothers and sisters of that same fraternity, for evidence **[9]**.' Members of the fraternity were listed on a table, probably mounted upon the wall, so that their names could be read aloud and they could be prayed for in life and after death. The Expenses c.1423 included 'Item to a text-writer for the writing of names of the brethren and sisters in the table, 6*d.*' and 'Item to a limner for the illuminating of the letters in the same table, 2*d.*' **[322]**.

It transpired that many listed as fraternity members in this table in 1418–19 had not paid their quarterage. So Porlond improved the standard of record-keeping, writing long lists in his book showing who had paid and who had not paid. He also recorded that, for every freeman admitted to the craft, the masters paid the sum of 6*s.* 8*d.* to the commonalty of the Brewers; similarly, for each man admitted to the fraternity, they paid 3*s.* 4*d.* **[41]**. This was an ancient custom approved unanimously by the brothers and he noted that it appeared in an ancient paper with a red calf-skin binding – sadly no longer extant. Another important part of the craft's life was established during Whittington's last mayoralty (1419–20), whereby the masters and other members of the craft would meet at Brewers' Hall every Monday (except when certain religious

C. M. Barron, *London in the Later Middle Ages: Government and People, 1200–1500* (Oxford, 2004), 57–8.
37 *Cal. Letter-Book, I*, 51.
38 GL MS 5425.
39 On the city crafts' pursuit of incorporation, and the many benefits that resulted, see Barron, *London in the Later Middle Ages*, 209–10.

festivals fell on that day) 'to consider whatsoever necessaries of the craft were to be inquired of, scrutinised and executed' by the masters [66]. Porlond recorded and helped to formalize these evolving practices.

THE BREWERS' FRATERNITY

The Brewers' fraternity developed from a small fraternity founded by John Enefield, brewer, and six others, including a whitetawyer, a chandler and an attorney at law, in 1342, at the church of All Hallows London Wall. Originally these men intended to repair a chapel there, in honour of Jesus, the Virgin Mary and the saints, and they funded a taper to burn before the cross in a chapel at All Hallows. Of the seven, only Enefield survived the plague, so he 'assembled other good men of the Brewers of London' to maintain the light in that church, and this became the fraternity for that craft.[40] When Enefield died in 1361, he bequeathed a tenement in West Smithfield to the fraternity and, in 1383, the four wardens purchased a rent in order to generate income to pay a chaplain. One of the earliest examples of this fraternity's existence can be found in the will of John London, brewer, dated 11 May 1361, who left a bequest to the fraternity of Brewers in the church of All Hallows London Wall.[41]

Between 1342 and 1389, this brotherhood had developed into the fraternity of the craft of Brewers, as seen in its return made to the court of chancery in 1388–9. During the reign of Richard II (1377–99), the parliament at Cambridge in 1388 petitioned for the abolition of all guilds and fraternities and their common chests, amidst 'a climate of concern in government about the aims and purposes of the proliferating religious and craft associations in late fourteenth-century England'.[42] A government enquiry was set up and sheriffs proclaimed that masters and wardens of guilds and fraternities were to bring information about the foundation, organization and funds of their fraternity to chancery. The fraternity of All Hallows London Wall, had by this time developed into a craft fraternity for the Brewers of London, as is shown by one clause in their ordinance returned to chancery in 1389: it stipulated that no member of the fraternity should receive the servant of another member unless he had left in a good manner and with his master's goodwill, whilst another prescribed that if a member placed his son or daughter with someone else to learn the craft, the brethren were to help to ensure

40 C. M. Barron, 'The Parish Fraternities of Medieval London', in *The Church in Pre-Reformation Society: Essays in Honour of F. R. H. Du Boulay*, ed. C. M. Barron and C. Harper-Bill (Woodbridge, 1985), 13–37 (15–16).
41 *Calendar of Wills Proved and Enrolled in the Court of Husting, London 1258–1688*, ed. R. Sharpe, 2 vols (London, 1889–90), ii, 26.
42 Davies, 'Monuments of Honour', 143–65 (146); C. M. Barron and L. Wright, 'The London Middle English Guild Certificates of 1388–89', *Nottingham Medieval Studies* 49 (1995), 108–45 (108).

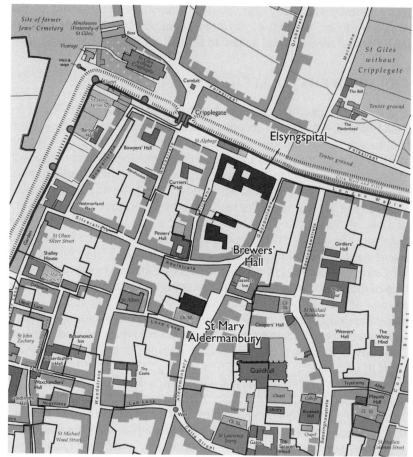

Figure 1. Map showing the location of Brewers' Hall and the parish church of St Mary Aldermanbury. © The Historic Towns Trust. Map by Giles Darkes.

that the terms of the indenture were carried out.[43] These are not parish fraternity requirements, rather a trade guild's rules.

The association of the Brewers with All Hallows London Wall, persisted until 1438 but, in that year, the clerk recorded that during preparations for gaining their charter, mayor William Estfeld had asked that the Brewers should make their parish church of St Mary Aldermanbury into their fraternity church as well, as he 'said it was most convenient ... for to have our priest there ... because our hall standeth in the same parish'.[44]

After this, the association with All Hallows church lapsed. As a result, within the first part of the Brewers' Book, annual payments were made to the rector and parish clerk of St Mary Aldermanbury, as well as to

[43]   Barron, 'Fraternities', 15–16.
[44]   GL MS 5440, ff. 290v, 305.

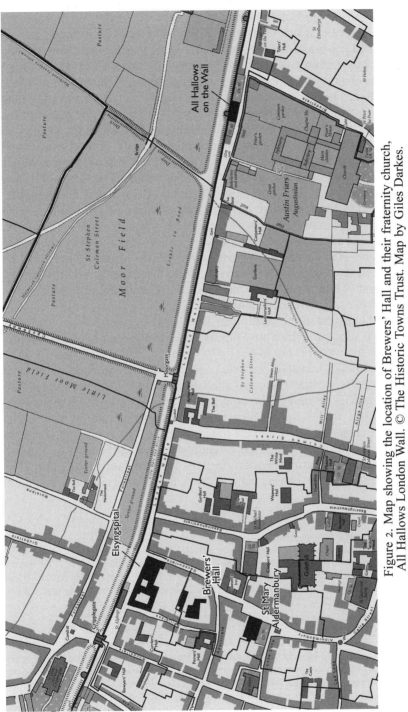

Figure 2. Map showing the location of Brewers' Hall and their fraternity church, All Hallows London Wall. © The Historic Towns Trust. Map by Giles Darkes.

the parish clerk at All Hallows London Wall **[46] [184] [352] [463]**.
Moreover, Adam Dalton, rector of All Hallows London Wall, from 1417
until his death in 1430, was a guest at the Brewers' feast three times, in
1421–2, 1423–4 and 1424–5 **[175] [261] [412]**.⁴⁵ After 1438, however, no
further payments to All Hallows were recorded within Porlond's book.⁴⁶

The clerk referred only rarely to the dedication of the fraternity. Twice
he referred to it as the fraternity of the Holy Trinity, and once he called
it the fraternity of All Hallows 'also the Holy Trinity', and another time
'Holy Trinity' was scored and 'All Hallows' was added above the line
[177] [334] [234] [150]. Possibly the fraternity's devotion changed from
one to the other over time. By the second part of the book, the fraternity's
annual feast was usually held in November, probably because of the long
connection with All Hallows, celebrated on 1 November. Several other
companies had more than one fraternity, such as the cordwainers, who
had an additional fraternity by 1423 for the yeomen of the cordwainers,
for young men newly free of apprenticeship, and this fraternity hired
Brewers' Hall twice c.1423 **[267] [336]**.⁴⁷ But it seems unlikely that the
Brewers had two separate fraternities; had there been another fraternity,
Porlond would surely have made lists for that as well. The dedication
of a fraternity could be enlarged and altered over time, which seems to
have happened in the case of the Brewers.⁴⁸

Two successive fraternity priests were mentioned in this first section
of the manuscript. During 1418–19, payment of 53s. 4d. was made to
'Sir Edmund', chaplain, for one quarter of a year and eight weeks, and
reference was made to a room called 'Sir Edmond's chamber', suggesting
that the priest, Edmund, sometimes used, or stayed in, a room at Brewers'
Hall **[45] [192]**.⁴⁹ Robert Steynton, his successor, featured early in the
book, paying 6s. 8d. to join the fraternity in 1418–19, receiving four yards
of coloured livery cloth, and attending the fraternity feast as a guest,
as well as appearing regularly in lists **[3] [16] [36] [463] [466]**. The
fraternity paid its own chaplain to provide spiritual guidance throughout

45 Hennessy, *London Clergy*, 82.
46 The churchwardens' accounts for All Hallows London Wall – calendared in
   *The Churchwardens' Accounts of the Parish of All Hallows, London Wall, 33 Henry VI
   to 27 Henry VIII (AD 1455–AD 1536)*, ed. C. Welch (London, 1912) – survive only from
   1455, too late for any correspondence with Porlond's work, as he died in 1440. Church
   records for St Mary Aldermanbury survive only from 1538.
47 Barron, *London in the Later Middle Ages*, 214.
48 It was not unusual for a parish fraternity to change its dedication over time, as in
   St Andrew Hubbard, Eastcheap; see C. Burgess, 'London Parishioners in Times of
   Change: St Andrew Hubbard, Eastcheap, c. 1450–1570', *Journal of Ecclesiastical History*
   53 (2002), 38–63 (51–2 and n.64). Similarly, the London parish churches of St Botolph,
   Billingsgate, St Sepulchre, Newgate and St Michael Cornhill all had fraternities whose
   dedications evolved over time. I am grateful to Clive Burgess for this reference.
49 Priests were customarily honoured with the title Sir, a flattering translation of the Latin
   Dominus; such a title did not denote any other social status.

the time of Porlond's book. In addition, the rector of the fraternity church, All Hallows London Wall, was Adam Dalton, who was invited to the Brewers' feasts as a guest, entered the Brewers' fraternity, paid quarterage three times from 1422–3 onwards, and received a hood of green with a livery gown from the Brewers [273] [262] [364] [396] [236] [380]. In addition to their fraternity chaplain and the rector of the fraternity church, the Brewers had another priest to provide spiritual support at their parish church, St Mary Aldermanbury. This church had been appropriated to the Augustinian house of Elsyngspital in 1331 and the bishop of London had required Elsyngspital to provide a parish priest for St Mary Aldermanbury.[50] Payments to the rector of St Mary Aldermanbury were recorded, although he was not named. John Fuller, one of the Augustinian canons at Elsyngspital, may have filled this role from 1418–25.[51] The curate or rector for St Mary Aldermanbury church was paid 6s. 8d. for his oblations for two years in 1425 and annually in the preceding accounts [352] [463] [184] [46]. There were clearly spiritual links between the Brewers' fraternity, All Hallows London Wall, St Mary Aldermanbury parish church and the Augustinian canons at Elsyngspital.

Until the Reformation, Thomas Becket was the Brewers' patron saint, although the reasons for this are unclear. The Worshipful Company of Brewers possess a funeral pall, thought to date from the late fifteenth century.[52]

The attributes thereon of St Thomas Becket, archbishop of Canterbury, who had of course defied royal authority, had to be altered at the time of the Reformation, being made to represent the much less controversial St William Fitz Herbert, archbishop of York, who died in 1154.[53]

Porlond always wrote separate lists of names of those entering the freedom of the craft and those joining the fraternity [2] [3] [43] [44] [98–9] [100] [179] [180] [267–8] [269–71] [339–40] [442–3] [456–7]. Sometimes he listed those who joined both at the same time. The two groups overlapped but remained distinct. In 1423, the Brewers allowed many new admissions to their fraternity, consisting of seventy-seven men with thirty-seven wives and Katherine Wirgeyn, who was a brewster in her own right [267] [271–4]. The entry fees and subsequent quarterage payments from these new members naturally generated more income for the fraternity. The timing of this increase in membership, just after the significant expenses incurred by the Brewers during their tussle with Whittington (as discussed below), suggests a deliberate response both to increase funds and create a larger, perhaps more resilient, fraternity.

---

50   Bowtell, Elsyngspital, III, 264.
51   Bowtell, Elsyngspital, 119, 306.
52   The pall was examined by Lisa Monnas, Kay Staniland, Dr Jenny Stratford and Poppy Singer (see Plates 1 and 2).
53   D. H. Farmer, *The Oxford Dictionary of Saints* (Oxford, 1978), 406.

BREWERS' HALL

By the time that William Porlond began writing his book in 1418, the Brewers had their own company hall, within Cripplegate ward in the north-west part of the city and in the parish of St Mary Aldermanbury. Brewers' Hall stood south of Elsyngspital (the hospital of St Mary Cripplegate), and Addle Street ran east–west between Brewers' Hall and the parish church of St Mary Aldermanbury.

Brewers' Hall still stands today upon the same site in the city of London, in Aldermanbury Square, 'in the rounded angle of Addle Street and Aldermanbury'.[54] Brewers' Hall, as William Porlond knew it, was destroyed in the Great Fire of London in 1666. The rebuilt seventeenth-century Brewers' Hall was, in turn, destroyed by enemy action on 29 December 1940. Brewers' Hall was subsequently rebuilt in 1960 and has recently been extended by the addition of an upper floor.

The only authoritative plan of the seventeenth-century hall is in the City of London volume of the Historical Monuments Commission.[55] W. F. Grimes recorded that, during excavation in 1958, it became clear that 'in rebuilding their hall after the Great Fire, the company had pursued a policy of economy by following the original lines and no doubt utilising as far as possible the existing structures on the east side of the site'.[56] The original complex had been 'a typically medieval layout', including the main body of the hall laid out on a regular recti-linear plan with an extension for domestic offices to the north, a garden of irregular outline beyond and, to the north-east, a courtyard with a staircase along the eastern side. There were three levels of walls, made of stone, brick and chalk, and those walls were left rough and unfaced on the east side, but had been faced on the west side of the complex. There was evidence of a cellar, with a window opening near the north-east corner. These details provide hints of the buildings that Porlond knew and referred to in his book.

The earliest surviving deed for the site of Brewers' Hall is dated 1291–2, in which a rent of 2s. and a rose garland were due annually to Walter of Fychingfield and his heirs, at Midsummer Day or the Feast of the Nativity of John the Baptist (24 June).[57] Regular annual costs for a rose garland 'for quitrent of our hall' were recorded in Porlond's

---

[54] W. F. Grimes, *The Excavation of Roman and Medieval London* (London, 1968), 171.

[55] *An Inventory of the Historical Monuments in London*, vol. 4, The City (London, HMSO, 1929), 94. (See Figure 4.)

[56] Grimes, *Excavation of Roman and Medieval London*, 171–2.

[57] I am grateful to Jerome Farrell, the former archivist to the Brewers of London, for sharing his unpublished research on the deeds of Brewers' Hall. He examined CLC/L/ BF/G/143/MS05503, 1–14 and CLC/L/BF/G/144/MS06809, 1–14. The earliest deed is CLC/L/BF/G/143/MS05503 [sub number 1]. See also *A Survey of Documentary Sources for Property Holding in London before the Great Fire*, ed. D. Keene and V. Harding, London Record Society 22 (1985), 14.

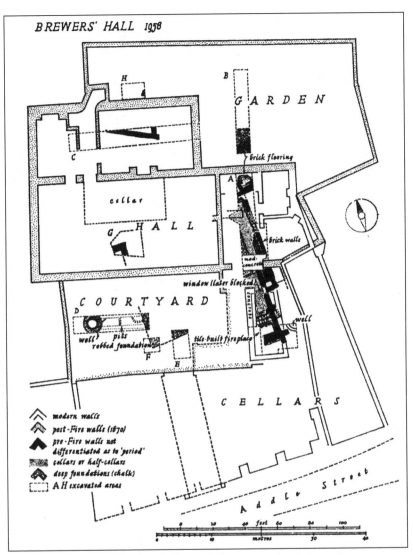

Figure 3. Archaeological Plan of Brewers' Hall, 1958.
W. F. Grimes, *The Excavation of Roman and Medieval
London* (London, 1968), 171. Copyright (© 1968) by Imprint.
Reproduced by permission of Taylor & Francis Group.

book from 1418–25 in his lists of 'customary payments' [46] [184] [352]
[463]. The first such payment listed was for 1*d*. for one wreath or rose
garland and thereafter the payments were for 4*d*., 5*d*., or 5½*d*., for two
rose garlands over two years. The rose garland evidently resembled a
symbolic 'peppercorn rent' although, oddly, Porlond never referred in his
book to its accompanying rent of 2*s*. amongst the customary payments.
There is, however, on the dorse of the 1291–2 deed, a note suggesting

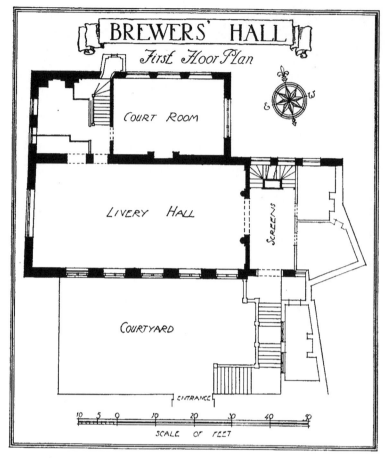

Figure 4. Brewers' Hall, destroyed in 1940, first floor plan.
An Inventory of the Historical Monuments in London,
vol. 4, The City (London: HMSO, 1929), 94.

that it refers to the capital tenement now called 'Brewershalle and
Pykedhacche', with the sum of 2*s*. now being given to 'le almeshouse
pandaxatorum' (the Brewers' almshouse). This almshouse (as discussed
below) was created in 1423, so the note on the dorse of the deed must
have post-dated this.

In attempting to establish the origins of property on which the Brewers
sited their hall, it is important to include a deed dated 23 November
1402, which recorded a gift from William Betele, citizen and mercer
of London, to John Hore, brewer and citizen of London, of land and
tenements in Ade Lane (Addle Street).

[*Latin*] The property lies between the tenement belonging to
the house of St Paul's, London, on the east, and to the west the
tenement of St Mary called Elsyngspital, the tenement formerly

of John Makenheues, goldsmith, and the tenement and gardens of the said St Paul's. Extending the other way, it lies between the tenement formerly of Stephen de Bradle (and previously of Thomas Dallyng) to the north, and the lane called Ade Lane to the south.⁵⁸

Then, on 11 October 1403, John Hore, citizen and brewer of London, gave all the lands, tenements and appurtenances, as above, to four men: Master Walter Cook, Master Thomas Lovent, William Wynwyk, and Henry Jolypas, all clerks.⁵⁹ Five years later, on 16 February 1408, a deed recorded that Cook, Lovent and Wynwyk had passed their rights in the property from John Hore to Jolypas, by a deed of 5 February 1407, and that Jolypas now gave the property to ten men, all citizens of London. Of these ten, John Staunton was a brewer, and another, William atte Wode, appeared regularly in Porlond's lists, and was one of the wardens of the Brewers' craft recorded in 1406 in the City of London *Letter-Book*, whilst John Chapman was once recorded as a maltman [3] [5] [23] [356] [410] [458].⁶⁰ Nicholas Stratton was one of the four masters of the Brewers' craft recorded in the City of London *Letter-Book* in 1406, and Agnes Stratton, his widow, was included in Porlond's quarterage lists from 1418 until 1423–4 [4] [131] [364].⁶¹ William Smalsho was one of the witnesses in 1402 and again in 1408, so he, too, may have been a brewer, as he featured regularly in lists in Porlond's book from 1418 until the record of a trental for him in 1424–5 [8] [466].⁶²

This appears to be the genesis of Brewers' Hall, with the transactions from 1402–3 leading to the gift of lands and tenements in the parish of St Mary Aldermanbury from John Hore to the ten feoffees, at least three of whom were brewers and one was linked to the brewing trade, in 1407–8.

John Hore made two wills. The first, recorded in the court of husting on 3 March 1412, referred only to property in the parish of St Alphage, just north of Brewers' Hall, and made no reference to his former property in St Mary Aldermanbury, presumably because he had already transferred that property to the ten feoffees in 1408.⁶³ In the Husting will he left all his lands and tenements in the parish of St Alphage to his wife, Alice, so that she might keep an obit for his soul and that of his first

⁵⁸ CLC/L/BF/G/MS05503 [sub number 3].
⁵⁹ CLC/L/BF/G/MS05503 [sub number 4].
⁶⁰ CLC/L/BF/G/MS05503 [sub number 5].
⁶¹ *Cal. Letter-Book, I*, 51.
⁶² Mia Ball's suggestion that the Brewers only leased the site from the Dean and Chapter of St Paul's cannot be subtantiated. Ball, *Worshipful Company of Brewers*, 46. I am grateful to the archivist of St Paul's Cathedral, Sarah Radford, for advice on this point.
⁶³ *Calendar of Wills proved and enrolled in the Court of Husting, London, preserved among the archives of the Corporation of the City of London at the Guildhall*, ed. R. R. Sharpe, 2 vols (London, 1889–90), ii, 400. Hustings Roll 141/68.

wife, Isabella, with the reversion of these properties to be sold in his wife's lifetime with her consent and their proceeds devoted to pious and charitable causes. John Hore's second will of 1413 was registered in the commissary court in 1413 with probate granted on 2 July 1413.[64] It repeated the terms of the first will, but also issued precise instructions for bequests to the mendicant orders and to prisoners in London. There was a small bequest of 'seven or eight pence' to the fraternity of the Brewers of London, echoing his link with this craft and fraternity, but no mention of the building and land that had become their hall.[65]

John Hore's name only appeared twice in William Porlond's Brewers' Book in two references to William Cardell 'living in the house where John Hore used to dwell', in the parish of St Alphage at Cripplegate [119] [120]. Alice Hore, presumably John's widow, featured regularly in the quarterage lists, paying her annual contribution of 12d., from 1418–19 to 1424–5 [4] [195] [209] [262] [364] [396]. In 1418–19 the clerk recorded that she had paid her quarterage but did not have livery cloth of the fraternity that year, whilst in 1419–20, during Whittington's third mayoralty, when particularly careful records were kept, she was listed as a widow [20] [131]. The entries are unremarkable and do not specifically acknowledge her as the wife of the man who passed the land and property to the Brewers for their company hall and its surroundings. Alice did not feature in the second part of the book, for the years 1429–40.

Nevertheless, John Hore's gift was effectively the foundation of Brewers' Hall, through the gift to Jolypas and the other clerks. Ten years after Jolypas had passed the property to ten feoffees, including at least three brewers, William Porlond began compiling his book, recording the annual provision of a rose garland as a symbolic quitrent for the hall, and listing the hiring of the hall, or rooms within it, to other crafts and fraternities for occasions such as the feast days of those crafts. As a result of Hore's gift, Brewers' Hall and the lands and other buildings within the complex were well established by 1418–19 when Porlond was appointed as clerk.

Thanks to the bequest of John Hore, the Brewers had their own hall by 1418. They occasionally raised income by hiring the hall, or rooms within the complex, to other companies without a hall of their own at that time. Such 'hirings' were recorded in the accounts from 1418–25 [43] [178] [267] [336] [454]. Crafts hiring Brewers' Hall included the Haberdashers for their feast day and the Coopers, Point-makers, Barbers, Cooks, Waxchandlers and Cutlers [178] [454]. Other groups listed included a meeting of the wardmote inquest and, on three occasions,

64 LMA, DL/C/B/004/MS09171/002, f. 252v. The will of John Hore, citizen and brewer.
65 On John Hore see R. A. Wood, 'Life and Death: A Study of the Wills and Testaments of Men and Women in London and Bury St Edmunds in the Late Fourteenth and Early Fifteenth Centuries' (unpub. PhD thesis, Royal Holloway, University of London, 2012), 192, 215, 271, 280.

Plate 1. The Brewers' funeral pall dating from the late fifteenth century. © The Brewers' Company

Plate 2. The Brewers' funeral pall: detail showing how the attributes of St Thomas were altered during the Reformation. © The Brewers' Company

'the football players' [267] [336] [454]. Clearly Brewers' Hall was sufficiently commodious for other groups to wish to hire it. The payments
varied, perhaps according to the number of chambers reserved, and
whether food, drink, furnishings or servants were included.

The contingency of hiring out the hall to supplement income had the
perhaps unintended effect of creating a memorandum, now one of the
best-known features of the Brewers' Book. On folio 11v, a list of London
crafts practised 'then and of old' was created, in the hope that, if any of
those crafts hired Brewers' Hall, then this might profit the hall or the
craft [26]. The list is dated 1421–2 and consists of 112 crafts or groups
in three columns, but it is not clear whether the clerk deliberately listed
the city crafts in order of rank or not. Oddly, the writer included crafts
such as burlesters and basket makers, which lacked any formal organization, but omitted some well-organized crafts including the Coopers and
Fusters.[66] The Coopers, however, regularly hired the hall, and paid 4s. 6d.
for the years 1423–5, so the Brewers certainly had contact with them
[454]. The way in which this list was composed is puzzling, although its
purpose was to generate income for the craft. Hiring out their hall was a
useful source of income for the Brewers, and it is referred to regularly
in the accounts from 1418–25, and once more when the Brewers gave
the Girdlers' beadle 12d. for 'his help in procuring various crafts to the
profit of the hall' [43] [178] [267] [336] [454] [194].[67]

If the hall was to be serviceable, or even lucrative, then it was
imperative that the building should be maintained or, if possible,
improved. In the course of building work on the hall, the clerk recorded
that the Brewers wished to have a bay window like that at the 'rent of
the Charterhouse in Cornhill' and when this proved unreasonable, they
asked for a window like that of the inn of the earl of Warwick [303]
[306].[68] On another occasion they paid a glazier to set an image of a
greyhound in a glass window [434]. The clerk not only accounted for
expenditure on repairs and building work at the hall but, from 1423,
also for the craftsmen employed in building and then maintaining
the almshouse – as revealed in the longest list of works from 1423–5
[417–33] [436–41]. The details of the tasks, materials used, and even
equipment such as a 'ferne' or crane, together with the craftsmen and
labourers employed, provide a remarkable insight into building work in
the city in the early fifteenth century [308]. During the construction of
the almshouse, John Croxton, the master mason who had been employed
on the works at nearby Guildhall from 1411, supplied four feet of hard
stone for the foot of the almshouse door, and he was paid 20d. for

66 Barron, *London in the Later Middle Ages*, 229–30.
67 The hand in which the list is written was probably not Porlond's own, but attempts to
   identify the scribe have so far proved inconclusive; see above n.18.
68 Warwick Inn, the Earl's London townhouse, stood just to the south of Newgate, on the
   west side of Warwick Lane.

oversight of works on Brewers' Hall itself, 'for it was yn poynte at þis tyme to have falle don yn defawte of reparation' [289] [302] [315].[69] By contrast, their employment of John Pekker, carpenter, of Cambridge, was unsatisfactory. The indenture between the masters and Pekker was copied into the Brewers' Book, but Pekker proved to be unreliable and expensive and 'the same John Pekker, carpenter made no work of carpentry beside his covenant at Brewers' Hall, but only the pentice that is on the side of the said hall, notwithstanding all the parcels of money that he received' in addition to the terms of the covenant [302–5] [309].

From 1424, John Houghton, carpenter, was frequently employed at Brewers' Hall for repairs, first for six days, then for twelve and a half days, and he earned 2d. for acting as porter at the gate for the Brewers' feast, which suggests that the Brewers trusted him [408] [418] [450].

THE BREWERS' ALMSHOUSE

The responsibilities incumbent upon a fraternity such as the Brewers included caring for poorer members. There are records within this book of alms payments to Stephen Lalleford, Robert Lynford, Johanna Cole and Johanna Cook, before the almshouse was created [176] [45] [184]. In 1423, the property known as 'the tenement near the great gate' at Brewers' Hall, which may have been part of John Hore's gift, was 'made and ordeyned to been an almeshouse for ye powre brethren and sustren' of their craft and fraternity, and this decision was made by the four masters with nine others who had been masters before [266]. Hitherto, the Brewers had received rent from tenants in this property, and the reasons for their decision to establish an almshouse at this time were never disclosed. Nevertheless, the Brewers were one of the first four London companies known to have established an almshouse for poorer members.[70] The Tailors were the first, using the bequest of John Chircheman, who died in 1413, followed by the Skinners in 1416 and the Cutlers in 1422. In 1424, Whittington's executors set about establishing his almshouse, with the intention that it should be administered by his company, the Mercers.[71]

It is not clear which Brewers' property was used for the almshouse and the name 'Pykedhacche', found on the dorse of the deed of 1291–2, never appeared in Porlond's book. It is clear, however, that Brewers' Hall and the almshouse were linked by a 'tresance' or cloister, revealing that the almshouse stood within the Brewers' Hall complex [296]. Robert Smyth, one of the masters, was able to give the considerable sum of £10 towards the almshouse works, with 2s. 6½d. borne by 'the common

---

[69] Harvey, *Mediaeval Architects*, 76.

[70] Barron, *London in the Later Middle Ages*, 299.

[71] J. Imray, *The Charity of Richard Whittington: A History of the Trust Administered by the Mercers' Company 1424–1966* (London, 1960), 10, 16–20.

cost of the craft' [266]. Another master, John Philippe, provided wood for a hen coop in the yard and the Brewers paid 27*s*. 9*d*. for labour and materials for this [300].

Porlond's book gives us brief glimpses of the earliest resident Brewers' almsfolk from 1423. There are no records setting out criteria for the selection of almsfolk, nor are there any signs of ordinances directing their behaviour.[72] For the almspeople mentioned in this book, this may be their only memorial. Robert Lynford and his wife, Margaret, had chambers in the almshouse, for which a lock, staple, keys, and a catch were recorded, with three keys to the chamber door of Robert and a new clicket (door latch) for his wife [291]. It is difficult to tell from such entries whether husbands and wives were accommodated together or in separate chambers, but clearly both men and women resided within this almshouse. On one occasion Margaret Lynford provided a cloth to cover the dresser at the Brewers' feast and was given 1*d*. [328]. Robert once swept the cloister and yard with Porlond and was rewarded with ale [296] [300]. Robert Lynford may, indeed, have been the first warden or steward of the almshouse.[73] Although we may not know why he was admitted to the almshouse, Lynford had already been in receipt of alms and of assistance with his livery costs from the Brewers before construction of the almshouse [176] [162] [252]. Lynford may have been a brewer, or his wife a brewster, as malt was confiscated from his house, the Horse Head in Poultry, c.1420, before they became residents of the almshouse [95] [96]. And while both Robert and Margaret belonged to the Brewers' fraternity, his quarterage payments were consistently late or incomplete: he paid only 15*d*. of the 2*s*. joint quarterage subscription in 1418–19 and paid it on the day after the masters' accounts; he was in arrears in 1420–1, and paid only 9*d*. out of 12*d*. in 1421–2, whilst his wife was unable to pay 'because of poverty' [7] [136] [196] [197].

John Turvey and his wife Margaret were another resident couple. A loft was made for the chamber of John Turvey [427] [437]. Margaret appeared earlier in quarterage lists with her husband and was later listed as an almswoman after John's death [34].[74] Other almsfolk mentioned include Johanna Awmbele, later described as 'widow and almswoman by many years in our craft', whose 'house', either within Brewers' Hall or the almshouse, needed repairs and whose chamber received a coal bin [291] [292].[75] Old Stephen, 'sometime brewersman' whose surname was probably Lalleford, received alms from the Brewers and carried out tasks for small payments, but it is not recorded whether he lived in a chamber

---

72 Indeed, the regulations directing the behaviour of Whittington's almspeople (given in Imray, *The Charity of Richard Whittington*, Appendix I) seem to have been the exception rather than the rule at this time.

73 I am grateful to Caroline Barron for this suggestion.

74 GL MS 5440, f. 289r.

75 GL MS 5440, f. 224v.

in the almshouse, within Brewers' Hall, or elsewhere [176] [320]. Jonette Bromle, for whom a lock and keys to her door were noted, was recorded as a tenant, rather than an almswoman [427]. Jonette Brygham's walls were lime washed by the Brewers but, again, it is not clear whether she was a neighbour, a tenant or an almswoman [323]. John Moyne, to whose window the Brewers fitted a padlock, and Johnette Moyne, to whom the Brewers paid 2d. for a stool 'that was lost', may similarly have been almsfolk or tenants [408] [422]. Thomas Draycote, broiderer, moved into an almshouse chamber, but with no obvious connection to the Brewers' craft or fraternity; he, too, may have been a tenant rather than an almsman [421] [439]. These names give us some impression of the community within Brewers' Hall in Porlond's day, in the early days of their almshouse; and, clearly, the almshouse was occupied both by men and women for at least seventeen years after 1423.[76]

FEASTS AT BREWERS' HALL

In his book, the Brewers' clerk included records of company feasts and occasional company breakfasts held at Brewers' Hall. On 7 September 1419 there was a lavish feast, for which he recorded the menu, expenses in the pantry, buttery and kitchen and for poultry, butchery, spices and grocery, with rewards given for service, and 'necessaries' such as eight burdens of rushes with carriage [28–33]. This was followed by a list of those brothers and sisters of the fraternity who attended, and how much each paid, with lists of the absentees and of the guests [34–6]. After burdensome expenses sustained by the craft during Richard Whittington's third mayoralty (1419–20) the Brewers decided to deny themselves a feast and livery cloth for the year 1420 and to have new livery only every two years [139]. There were company breakfasts on 13 February 1420 and 20 May 1421 [38] [143]. Five more feasts were recorded in this first part of the book, one in 1421–2, another in 1423–4, one on 29 August 1424, then two undated lists, perhaps from 1425 [167] [253] [327] [402] [452]. Preparations for the feast once included the hire of trestles and tables and the employment of John Houghton, carpenter, for six days [407]. Hired staff included 'Hugh Sharpe for his travail in the buttery' and payments were made to the cook, usually John Hardy [407] [148]. Four minstrels and three players were paid in 1423–4 [261]. Some of the fraternity members present included Agnes Bugge, Katherine Wirgeyn and Johanna Ambewell, who were each excused 4d. of the cost. More exalted guests included the prior and the provincial of the Austin Friars, Adam Dalton, parson of All Hallows London Wall, William Goodswayne,

---

[76] Pykkedhacche, which may have been the almshouse building, was purchased by the prior of Elsyngspital in 1533, shortly before the dissolution of this house; see Bowtell, *Elsyngspital*, 213.

the rector of St Mary Woolnoth, and Robert Steynton, the fraternity priest, and once, Henry Somer, the Chancellor of the Exchequer [261] [413]. The records of these occasions provide information about the food and drink served at the time, but they also give us a cross-section of the life and connections of this London craft in the years 1418–40.

THE PURCHASE OF LIVERY

Another recurrent expense for the craft and fraternity was the purchase of new livery cloth, from which to make gowns and hoods for its members, in an outward and visible sign of membership and status. The first livery list recorded by Porlond is dated 1418–19 when the Brewers took ray cloth, which was striped, and green cloth [10–20]. This list contains much crossing out and is very untidy, suggesting that Porlond was inexperienced in recording livery costs and distribution at the start of his career with the Brewers. Porlond listed those who sold cloth to the Brewers and accounted for the material purchased. He made long lists of the amounts of cloth supplied to individuals and how much they were charged. In his first list, he recorded the numbers of rays for each member, but rarely specified the coloured cloth needed by individuals, which might also suggest unfamiliarity with the process of livery distribution. The second list for the year 1419–20 records the purchase and dispersal of rays and blue cloth [150–62]. Then, following expenses incurred during Richard Whittington's last mayoralty (1419–20), the Brewers decided to have new livery only every two years [139]. The next list is therefore for the year 1422–3, when the cloth was ray cloth and green cloth [234–47]. The last list in this part of the book is for 1424–5, when the livery was of rays and murrey cloth [377–93].[77] The processes involved in preparing the cloth for cutting and tailoring included fulling, shearing, and dyeing. The payments from each recipient probably included a charge for tailoring, too.[78]

The lists of names and amounts of cloth are predominantly for men, but the masters' wives were given livery of the craft, and some men bought livery cloth for their wives, whilst occasionally some women, possibly single or widowed, were recorded as buying cloth for a hood: the total of murrey engrained cloth for John Broke, one of the masters from 1424–5, included murrey for a hood for his wife; William Eyre bought rays and murrey for himself and a yard of murrey for his wife, whilst Agnes Carleton bought a yard of murrey in her own right, and Elizabeth Colbrook bought a yard of superior murrey engrained cloth in 1424–5 [382] [377] [380]. Porlond himself was granted cloth of colour

---

77 Murrey denotes a purple-red colour, like that of the mulberry.
78 I am grateful to Dr John Oldland for discussing the livery lists with me; see J. Oldland, *The English Woollen Industry, c.1200–c.1500* (London and New York, 2020).

without any rays, which denoted his status as the clerk of the fraternity, but not a freeman of the craft [159]. The fraternity chaplain, Robert Steynton, also received blue cloth without rays in 1419–20 [157]. Others received concessions for the cost of their livery, with the sums ranging from ½*d*., for Hugh Glene and William Bacon, to 14*s*., for John Yver, in 1422–3 [250–1]. Glene later became one of the masters, and Bacon was a butcher who sometimes supplied meat for the feasts, but it is not clear why Yver deserved so large a concession for his livery costs.[79] The four livery lists provide information about the use of cloth, but also much detail about the membership of this craft and fraternity.

RELATIONS WITH THE CITY

The making and selling of ale had been subject to regulation since at least 1215, when Clause 35 in Magna Carta stipulated one standard measure for ale.[80] The assizes of weights and measures and of victuals were a general code which grew up in medieval England, standardizing weights and measures for vital commodities, and, by them, governing the quality and quantity of food.[81] The assize of bread and ale was introduced in 1267, whereby civic authorities fixed the prices of these essential commodities, according to local prices of wheat and malt.[82] Ale was an important staple in people's diets and because the water used to make it was boiled, ale was safer to drink than water which, drawn from wells and open-conduits, could easily be contaminated. Ale was deemed 'as necessary to the poor as bread', in an ordinance of 1381–2, which required bread to be sold in loaves for a farthing (a quarter of a penny) and measures of ale to be sold for a farthing, 'the mayor and aldermen deeming it [ale] equally necessary to the poor as in the case of bread'.[83]

While the Brewers' Book yields scant information as to the brewing process, limited to the occasional purchase of vats, tubs and brooms at Brewers' Hall [325], it provides more on malt, the main ingredient of ale [61] [166] [187] [248–9]. Although some brewers purchased their malt, others began by malting their grain, which could be barley or oats or wheat and 'dredge' (a mixture of oats and barley).[84] Malting the grain involved soaking it for several days, draining it, piling it into a 'couch' where it would germinate, then curing it in a kiln. Coarsely ground

---

79 GL MS 5440, f. 157v.
80 *English Historical Documents*, Vol. 3, 1189–1327, ed. H. Rothwell (London, 1975), 320.
81 J. T. Rosenthal, 'The Assizes of Weights and Measures in Medieval England', *The Western Political Quarterly* 17:3 (1964), 409–522 (409).
82 *Cal. Letter-Book, A*, 216.
83 *Cal. Letter-Book, H*, 183. For further discussion of the regulations and penalties prescribed for the ale trade, see C. Metcalfe, 'Richard Whittington and the Brewers of London, 1419–22', *Trans LAMAS* 72 (2021), 221–41 (224–5).
84 Bennett, *Ale, Beer and Brewsters*, 32–3.

malt was then mixed with boiled water, and the 'wort' was drawn off and mixed with yeast and herbs. Several worts, in diminishing strength, might be drawn from the malt mix.

Prices had been regulated by an ordinance of 1354 and a subsequent proclamation fixing the price of ale at 1½*d.* a gallon.[85] From 1360 ale was to be sold only in gallons, pottles (half gallons) and quarts (quarter gallons), with the measures assayed and marked by a deputy of the chamberlain, whereas this had before been the duty of the aldermen of each ward. Aldermen were, however, still required to survey brewers in their wards to enforce the rules.[86] By 1388, brewers were required to sell their ale in sealed measures and not by hanaps – that is, unregulated measures. Ale tasters or ale conners were appointed in each ward from 1377 to test the quality and enforce regulations.[87] Gilbert the ale taster (presumably for Cripplegate ward) featured several times in William Porlond's book: he was invited to the company breakfast in 1420 as a guest, received 6*s.* worth of livery, was a guest at the feast in 1423–4, and again in 1424–5 with his wife, and was granted 8*s.* worth of livery in 1424–5, consisting of eight rays, half a yard and one nail of murrey cloth [115] [252] [261] [413] [380]. These entries suggest that the Brewers wanted to keep this important official on their side. The Brewers also seem to have enjoyed a good relationship with William Pethin, another 'aletaker', who joined their fraternity in 1418–19, featured regularly in livery lists and indeed was given a hood and a reward of 4*s.* 9*d.* in 1424–5, as well as being a guest at the last Brewers' feast in this section of Porlond's book [25] [354] [466] [413].

Regulations concerning the production and sale of ale in the early fifteenth century were recorded in the City *Letter-Books* and Porlond copied some of these into his book. He referred to 'le bon ordeignance' of John Woodcock, mayor 1405–6, which granted a petition submitted by the Brewers, so that they could now appoint their own wardens and masters to survey all ale-brewers in the city, and survey all barley brought to the city for sale to ensure its quality [62].[88] Further regulation was needed during the mayoralty of William Staundon, 1407–8, in response to complaints of dishonest measures, so now all barrels were to be marked at the Guildhall by the chamberlain's deputy, so that the amount within could be certified [57].[89] In 1411, mayor Robert Chichele ordained that those allowed to sell ale at their houses must use pewter pots of gallon, pottle or quart size, marked with the seal of the chamber, rather than tankards, hanaps, or other vessels of random sizes.[90]

---

[85]   *Cal. Letter-Book*, *G*, 33.
[86]   *Cal. Letter-Book*, *G*, 124, and *H*, 373.
[87]   *Cal. Letter-Book*, *H*, 71.
[88]   *Cal. Letter-Book*, *I*, 50.
[89]   *Cal. Letter-Book*, *I*, 63.
[90]   *Cal. Letter-Book*, *I*, 97–8.

By the time of Porlond's book, the Brewers of London had obtained an increased power to regulate the making, quality and sale of their ale, but the city still retained ultimate control. As a result, by the early fifteenth century, those allowed to sell ale were brewers and brewsters, cooks, pie bakers and hostelers. Selling to hucksters (who resold the ale at a higher price) had been prohibited in 1388, but the practice evidently continued, as Porlond reveals, when Whittington demanded a list of hucksters in 1420, and in listings of offenders against ale regulations, which included both women and men identified as hucksters [81] [79].[91]

Porlond's book, moreover, includes copies of several petitions drafted on behalf of the Brewers concerning the quality and price of malt, as this too was clearly contentious. The petitions complain about unclean malt that was unripe, 'wynnel eaten', and contained 'drawke, darnel and kerlok seed' and small stones and congealed earth, forcing brewers to buy a greater quantity and wash out the filth [61] [166] [187] [248–9]. But, in 1422, Whittington accused the Brewers of inflating the price of malt, claiming that they rode into the country buying up or 'forestalling' malt, creating a scarcity and forcing the price up to 9s. a quarter, when malt could be bought more cheaply for 4s. a quarter, although the Brewers argued that they could not make good ale from such malt [217–18].

Copies of ordinances were written in this book in Latin or French [49–50] [57]. The draft petitions about malt were written in English. There are also copies of draft petitions complaining about Brewers' servants demanding weekly wages instead of a fixed annual salary and forming a 'confederacy', illustrating some of the economic consequences of the Black Death and the greater bargaining power of the skilled worker [51] [54] [395]. Other petitions complained about charges for tolls and customs on malt, which the Brewers, as victuallers, providing vital sustenance for citizens, claimed they should not have to pay, according to the terms of ordinances passed in 1402–3 [49–51] [53] [394].[92] The Brewers apparently faced increased costs, yet their prices were closely regulated. We know from the City of London *Letter-Books* that a long petition was submitted by the Brewers to mayor Whittington on 18 January 1420, and that the mayor and aldermen gave their consent to two articles but refused to allow the sale of ale both inside and outside at 2d. a gallon, insisting that ale sold outside must still be sold at 1½d. the gallon.[93]

[91] *Cal. Letter-Book, H*, 337.
[92] One draft petition was clearly a later addition: written during John Michell's mayoralty (1424–5), it was inserted much earlier in the book [48]. Other petitions are undated and uncrossed, whereas the rest of the content of those pages has been crossed, so the copies of petitions are probably later additions, too, filling up blank spaces. All are written in English.
[93] *Cal. Letter-Book, I*, 235–7.

ALE AND BEER

Ale remained the predominant beverage in London and England during the period of this book. Perhaps the earliest mention of 'beere' in civic records is the record of Henry Vandale buying four barrels of beer from John Westle in the Pool of London on 14 August 1372, in order to 'forestall' it, but the barrels were forfeited to the sheriffs.[94] Vandale was possibly Flemish and in this entry he was importing the beer, but Flemish or 'Duche' immigrants also produced beer to sell in the city during the early fifteenth century.[95] Ale was made with malt, yeast and water, whereas beer, made with the addition of hops, lasted for longer and travelled better than ale. Both beer and ale were supplied to the English army at Rouen in 1418: 200 tuns (casks or barrels) of ale at 30*s.* each and 300 tuns of beer at 13*s.* 4*d.* each, which suggests that beer was cheaper than and, perhaps, considered inferior to ale.[96]

Porlond referred in his book in 1424–5 to 'foreign beer brewers' brewing in the city, who were not of the craft and who retailed their beer 'to the great harm of Brewers' craft', whilst other entries referred to 'aliens', from elsewhere, not of the city, doing the same **[48] [51] [394]**. A few 'beer brewers' such as Matys Adrianesson, 'beerman', joined the craft and fraternity of Brewers **[268] [270]**. Not all London beer brewers became members of the craft or fraternity, meaning that the production and sale of beer posed something of a threat to the ale trade. Nevertheless, ordinances passed during 1418–25 concerning ale production made no distinction between ale and beer.[97]

QUARRELS WITH RICHARD WHITTINGTON

The Brewers of London had a protracted quarrel with Richard Whittington during and after his third mayoralty of 1419–20.[98] Two ordinances were passed concerning the brewing and selling of ale: first the ordinance of 1406–7 was reissued, ordering ale to be sold at 2*d.* the gallon when served inside an inn or tavern, and at 1½*d.* the gallon when served outside.[99] Vessels were to be marked by a deputy of the chamberlain to

---

94 *CPMR 1364–81*, 147.
95 See M. Pajic, '"Ale for an Englishman is a Natural Drink": the Dutch and the Origins of Beer Brewing in Late Medieval England', *Journal of Medieval History* 45:3 (2019), 285–300.
96 *Memorials of London and London Life in the Thirteenth, Fourteenth and Fifteenth Centuries*, ed. H. T. Riley (London, 1868), 666; and *Cal. Letter-Book, I*, 200, which recorded that one thousand pipes of ale and beer were dispatched to the army on 8 September 1418.
97 *Cal. Letter-Book, I*, 63, 97–8, 232, 233, 236.
98 For a fuller discussion of the quarrel, see Metcalfe, 'Whittington and the Brewers of London', 227–34.
99 *Cal. Letter-Book, I*, 232.

show their capacity. Then a second ordinance of 27 January 1420 laid down that a cooper should now mark all barrels and kilderkins with their own mark, and that all coopers' marks were to be registered at the Guildhall within fourteen days. A heavy penalty of 40s. was to be imposed upon those selling barrels or kilderkins that were not properly marked with a cooper's mark, or not full of good clear ale.[100]

Porlond recorded that Whittington began to criticize the Brewers early on in his third mayoralty (1419–20), complaining of the 'unlicensed fat swans' at their feasts and 'vestments and furs in the style of their superiors' [56]. Whittington clearly believed that the Brewers were rising above their station and was concerned that their wealth was all too obviously being made at the expense of poorer Londoners. Whittington and his mayoral household visited five brewhouses and forced those brewers to sell their ale at the lower price of only 1d. a gallon for the whole day, instead of 2d. inside and 1½d. outside [55]. These intimidating visits to the five brewhouses were evidently intended to be punitive, since three of the brewers can be identified in Porlond's lists of offenders: William Herry and Richard Sherwod had both been fined for incorrect measure, and William Payne, who had rebelled against the masters, refused to contribute ale for the king in France, then refused to pay a fine or buy his new livery, but redeemed himself by providing a swan for the masters' breakfast, and was then fined again for not selling malt in the open market [55] [78] [39–40] [96]. The clerk also recorded that William Herry at Long Entry beside the Stocks had twelve or sixteen large vessels full of ale, so Herry must have lost money on that day when the price was forcibly lowered [55]. As a result, Porlond noted that 'caution was to be used towards the mayor' [55].

Whittington then issued the order that the names of 'all those called in English hucksters' in the city (those who bought ale to sell on at a higher price) should be recorded, with the names of the brewers who supplied them and the prices paid. Furthermore, he demanded payment of a £20 bond or recognisance into which he claimed that the Brewers had entered, to be paid for their perceived transgressions [81]. The Brewers denied ever agreeing to such a bond and asked to see a copy; when none could be found to give them, John Carpenter, the common clerk, read aloud the bond in the mayor's court – presumably from a registered copy – although unfortunately we do not know in what language he read it [83].

In response, the Brewers collected a voluntary taxation to offer a gift to Whittington in an attempt to placate him, effectively with a bribe or gift, and to have the heavy 40s. penalty (prescribed in his ordinance of 27 January 1420) modified [67–9]. The list of those contributing and the amounts they paid, ranging from 12*d*. to 20*s*., survives in the book, affording us an invaluable insight into those involved in making and selling ale in the city c.1419–20. The account of how the money was distributed reveals the Brewers' perception of the workings of government at this time: payments were made to John Carpenter, the common clerk, and to the recorder of London, and to Whittington's butler, presumably for the mayor's household **[70]**. Whittington himself was not, however, amenable to bribes, so this tactic failed and the money 'did not lessen the anger of the mayor' **[56]**. The masters and representatives of the Brewers were summoned to the mayor's court six times between July and October 1420, but never paid the £20 bond **[81–90]**. They eventually did pay this sum, but just after Whittington had retired from office **[89]**.[101]

Even after the end of his mayoralty, Whittington kept a close watch on the Brewers. An account by William Porlond outlined the unusual occasion on 30 July 1422 when twelve of the worthiest men of the Brewers' craft were summoned to the Guildhall and accused by Whittington of stockpiling malt, thereby inflating the price **[217]**. As a result, Whittington demanded a further £20 fine and the twelve men were to remain in the ward of the chamberlain at the Guildhall until they had paid this sum or found surety for it. In the evening, the Brewers asked what they should do. Then John Carpenter, who was Whittington's friend and executor:

> Dede comaunde hem to goon home to her houses and so John Carpenter behight hem atte þat tyme þat þei sholde nomore harme haue neyþer of prisonement of her bodies ne of losse of xx li for well þei wysten and knewen that all ye forsaid Juggement of the Mair and Aldremen was not done at þat tyme bot for to plese Richard Whityngtone for he was cause of alle the forsaid Juggement **[219]**.

The description of this episode in Porlond's book is our only surviving account, and that English was used for the record reveals its significance for the craft at the time.[102] Through it we see the civic government at work, with the aldermen, mayor Chichele and the chamberlain all apparently supportive of Whittington's position, and the resulting threat of another large fine, until John Carpenter defused the situation.

Whittington's criticisms of the Brewers appear to have encouraged Porlond to keep very detailed lists of those fined and the reasons, sometimes with a note of their dwelling place as well. In 1419–20 Porlond filled four folios with a list of those not selling ale in the correct measures **[73–80]**. Other lists for that year and until 1424–5 recorded:

---

[101]   The pages which contained the list of contributors to this sum have been cut out, as was noted on 30 November 1830 by William Vines, the Brewers' clerk at the time **[92]**.

[102]   Vale, *Henry V*, III.

those selling defective malt, or not selling it at the malt market in Gracechurch, or those using unsealed barrels and kilderkins, or barrels not marked with a cooper's mark [93–6] [108–9] [118–26] [140–2] [200–7] [228–30] [358–61] [371–5].

Whittington was clearly angry with the Brewers, and spoke to them harshly, repeatedly summoning them to his court [82]. Nevertheless, it can be argued that Whittington was trying to enforce agreed food-pricing by, in this case, upholding proper measures and fair prices of ale in the city. We do well to remember that, 'The mayor represented the king's person within the municipalities and was expected to act for the peace, good ruling and advantage of the town, and especially the assize of beer and ale and of other victuals.'[103] Whittington clearly saw fit to monitor and control the Brewers, doing so for the good of the inhabitants of the city and to keep the peace; but Porlond's personal account reveals the bitterness of the ensuing quarrel in a way that civic records do not.

After the problems that the Brewers had experienced with Whittington, it comes as no surprise that earning and maintaining the goodwill of subsequent mayors had become a priority for craft members, and Porlond's writings convey something of the understandable desire to make up the lost ground with mayors who succeeded Whittington, up to 1425. This very unusual record, shedding light on the behaviour that craft members might adopt to ingratiate themselves with those in positions of influence – again improving our grasp of the reactions of those on the receiving end of authority – is clearly of great interest. Following Whittington's mayoralty, we are told that his successor, grocer William Cambrigge (1420–1) 'behaved wisely and discreetly' towards the Brewers 'in all the freedoms, customs and things incumbent upon the craft', and asked them to behave well towards the commons of the city – again displaying a concern for the common good. He also required the craft's wardens and searchers 'to keep diligent watch, make arrests and presentations'. Although he still insisted upon the full payment of the £20 bond demanded by Whittington, he allowed the Brewers to pay £10 at first and the rest when it could be collected without grievance to the craft [139] [88]. Mayor Robert Chichele (1421–2), another grocer, at first 'behaved well and honestly towards our craft of Brewers', and was 'pleasantly disposed', urging that 'no complaints about their pots should come to his notice' [199]. However, Whittington's last encounter with the Brewers took place in 1422, during Chichele's mayoralty, suggesting that issues pertaining to the Brewers were still of concern to Whittington [217]. Chichele, too, imposed heavy fines of 40s. for the use of vessels without a cooper's mark, just as Whittington had done [199]. When no defaulters were

---

[103] Rosenthal, 'The Assizes of Weights and Measures', 416.

presented, Chichele reduced the fine to 20*d.* for an unmarked barrel and 10*d.* for an unmarked kilderkin. Porlond then recorded several pages of offenders' names, showing that the Brewers were prepared to acquiesce, fining members of their craft, when the penalties were reasonable [200–7].

Mayor William Walderne (1422–3), a mercer, sent for the masters of the Brewers' craft and asked them to make good ale, to give neither lords nor commons cause for complaint [222]. Porlond recorded that Walderne had received forty complaints about the craft of Brewers, and a scored note said that with all those complaints, 'he would have been right well advised what to do.' Knowing of the 'mischief and disease' of Whittington towards the Brewers, Walderne licensed them 'to brew and live so that they might hold their own', but he became unfriendly towards them three weeks before the end of his mayoralty, prompting the Brewers to give him a 20*s.* boar and 17*s.* ox, 'to soften his sinister intentions' and pacify him for the remainder of his time in office [227].

The mayor of whom Porlond approved most was the draper, William Crowmer (1423–4), 'a good man and loving to the craft of Brewers', who 'did no disease' to the craft. He would not take any gifts from them yet thanked them for the offer and promised 'to be a good friend to them during all his year, and so he was' [337]. Mayor John Michell (1424–5), stockfishmonger, received gifts from the Brewers of an ox, price 21*s.* 2*d.* and a boar, price 30*s.* 1*d.* 'so that he did not harm the Brewers' and he, too, advised them to make good ale so that he would have no complaints against them [372]. We know, therefore, that at least two mayors, William Walderne (1422–3) and John Michell (1424–5) accepted gifts from the Brewers, unlike Whittington.[104] Whittington's predecessor, the grocer William Sevenoke (1418–19), was only mentioned on the first folio and again on the first folio of the second part of Porlond's book, but without any assessment of his character [1].[105]

The first part of Porlond's book, concerned with the years 1418–25, saw the Brewers facing serious challenges from Whittington until 1422, before the latter's death on 14 March 1423.[106] The comments upon the five mayors after Whittington and the records of gifts to some suggest that the years 1418–25 saw the Brewers having to defend their right to regulate their craft and, with the extensive lists of fines – that is, showing a willingness, when necessary, to punish their own members – demonstrating that they could be trusted to proceed openly and with fairness and in the interests of the common good.

---

[104] See Metcalfe, 'Whittington and the Brewers', 235–6.
[105] GL MS 5440, f. 157r.
[106] *The Brut or the Chronicle of England*, ed. F. W. D. Brie (London, 1908), 449.

THE NATIONAL CONTEXT

The duties incumbent on crafts to act for the common good are reflected in the account of the Brewers' contribution to the destruction of fish weirs in the Thames, as ordered by Henry V in parliament in 1421 [348]. Two men from each of twenty-six London crafts were required to go with the mayor on this business. The Brewers' representatives joined those from the crafts of Girdlers, Salters, Barbers, Dyers and Tallow Chandlers, and those of the Fletchers should have been in the same barge. The Fletchers, however, excused themselves from this duty since they were occupied in preparing artillery for the king, obliging them to find substitutes and make a payment instead [164]. The costs of sending Thomas Grene and Roger Swannefeld in one barge from London to Staines, and John Mason and Robert Carpenter in another from London to Gravesend to achieve this, came to at least £4 16s. for the Brewers, and the burden was shared by many members of the craft [287] [282–86].[107]

Porlond's book also discloses a good deal about the city and national events. Some Brewers supplied ale for the household of Queen Katherine (1421–2) and the repayments due to them were carefully listed, minus a small deduction, presumably for transaction costs [72]. The Brewers also supplied ale for the return of Henry V from France in 1421 and the coronation of Queen Katherine on 23 February that year [130]. In 1422 the clerk recorded that Henry V 'passed out of this world' in France, on the last day of August 1422 [220]. In the book there is a valuable account of the funeral procession for Henry V and the ceremonial role played by the crafts of the city from 5–7 November 1422, for which the Brewers provided eight of the 200 torches used by the crafts [221] [223–5]. This account, perhaps appropriately in the circumstances, was written in English.[108] The impact of the French wars during the reigns of Henry V and Henry VI can be deduced from a payment made to a 'taker of the king's' to allow the carpenters working at Brewers' Hall to continue their work there rather than being either conscripted into the army or assigned to work on royal projects [317].

---

107 The Taylors paid over £20, whilst the Grocers and Mercers each contributed over £10. See C. M. Barron, 'The Government of London and its relations with the Crown: 1400–1450' (unpub. PhD thesis, University of London, 1970), 357–65.
108 Vale, *Henry V*, III, 246–7.

EDITORIAL METHOD

The aim throughout has been to provide an accessible edition of William Porlond's Brewers' Book that is close to the original.

Passages in Latin or French are indicated [*Latin*] or [*French*] and have been calendared. The English in some of the lengthy, repetitive passages has been streamlined.

For the list of crafts, the Latin names have been retained, with a suggested translation in the footnotes, whilst the names of crafts that were written in English have been copied as the clerk wrote them in 1421–2 [26–7]. George Unwin deserves great respect for being amongst the first to consider the trades and guilds of London, but a few of his interpretations are open to question: he interpreted *Bladesmyths* as *Blacksmiths*, and *Setters* as *Potters*, whilst what he saw as *Brothmakers* could equally be *Brochemakers*, and he translated *Cementarii* as plasterers, although this word can also mean masons.[1] He also omitted *Bokelermakers* just above *Botelmakers*, which gives us a list of 112 trades, not 111 as he stated. It seems right to present this list as the clerk wrote it, as far as possible, for future discussion, without a layer of interpretation.

Place names and the names of parishes have been modernised where possible. Where dwelling places or names of brewhouses were given, the entry 'atte Swan' has been translated as 'at the Swan'. Henry Harben, *A Dictionary of London*, has been a great help, as has the map *Tudor London: The City and Southwark in 1520*.[2]

Surnames have been left as Porlond or other clerks wrote them, with the various versions shown in the Index. First names have been modernized unless they are unusual, such as Idonea, or have no obvious modern equivalent, such as Weveyne.

Money has been converted from Roman numerals to Arabic – i.e. xij*d.* to 12*d.*

The accounting has been left as Porlond recorded it and corrections have not been added. Frequently the amounts are correct. Sometimes, however, the accounting does not add up and there must have been other factors at play, recorded elsewhere, known to Porlond at the time, but lost to us.

---

[1]   G. Unwin, *The Gilds and Companies of London* (London, 1908), 371.

[2]   H. Harben, *A Dictionary of London* (London, 1918); *Tudor London: The City and Southwark in 1520* (second edition 2022, published by The Historic Towns Trust).

Round brackets ( ) show a repeated and unnecessary word or phrase in the text.

Square brackets [ ] indicate an editorial insertion.

Passages printed in bold indicate titles and sections written in darker ink and larger letters in the original manuscript.

Regnal dates are taken from *A Handbook of Dates for Students of British History* edited by C. R. Cheney, revised by Michael Jones (Cambridge, 2000).

Dates falling within 1 January–24 March have been silently modernised.

Mayoral dates are taken from C. M. Barron, *London in the Later Middle Ages: Government and People 1200–1500* (Oxford, 2004), 336–42.

Dictionary definitions are taken from the *Oxford English Dictionary* online <http://www.oed.com>, the *Dictionary of Medieval Latin from British Sources* <http://www.dmlbs.ox.ac.uk> and the *Anglo-Norman Dictionary* <https://anglo-norman.net>.

Paragraph numbers such as [1] have been inserted to make it easier to locate references to people and places, or particular items of interest. Paragraph numbers, rather than folio numbers, have been used in the indexes and in footnotes.

The Index applies to the text only and not to the Introduction.

THE BREWERS' BOOK,
PART 1, 1418–25

[1] [f. 1r]

[*French*] **This paper,**[1] **first written in the month of November, in the sixth year** [1418–19][2] **of the reign of King [*Henry*] the fifth after the conquest of England, makes full remembrance of all the receipts and expenses made by the Masters for the time being of the fraternity and mistery of the Brewers of the city of London, founded in the parish church of All Hallows in London Wall: William Sevenoke then being mayor of the same city, John Perneys and [*Ralph*] Barton sheriffs of the same city, [1418–19] and William atte Wode, William Edrich, William Ferrour, and John Reyner being the Masters of the aforesaid fraternity. And in this year John Morey, then clerk of the same Brewers, died, to wit on the 10th day of the month of February, in the sixth year, abovesaid. And on the 14th day of the same month of February, William Porlond was received into the same office, to be clerk of the said Brewers, and the said William ordained this book, to have cognizance of all the things done in the mistery and fraternity abovesaid, for all the time that the said William should be clerk of the said Brewers.**[3]

[2]

Received for the creation of freemen of the Mistery [*Mainly French*]

First, received from William Hillying at the Cock in the parish of St Margaret Pattens	13s. 4d.
Item from Thomas Webbe for his franchise and to become a brother of the fraternity	20s.
[Margin note: at George in Thames Street [*in*] St Dunstan [*in the East*]]	
Item from Roger Blissote at the Swan in the parish of St Nicholas Shambles	13s. 4d.
Item from Henry Grene at Long Entry in the parish of St Mary Woolchurch	16s. 8d.
Item from John Frost at the Hartshorn in the parish of St Sepulchre	15s.
Item from Gilbert Boton at the Harp in the parish of St Giles without Cripplegate	13s. 4d.

---

[1] This folio is badly damaged (see Figure 5). This first paragraph draws upon a translation from French by W. H. Black in his manuscript volume, The Brewers' Company Extract of Minutes 1418–40, GL MS 5441, compiled in 1831.

[2] November 1418. Sevenoke was the mayor 1418–19.

[3] 10 and 14 February 1419. In fact Henry V's 6th regnal year began on 21 March 1418. Either Porlond had helped Morey before being appointed clerk, or this is a mistake and should be the fifth year, February 1418.

Figure 5. GL MS 5440 The Brewers' Book. The first page
of the Brewers' Book. © The Brewers' Company.

Item from William Knot at the Swan in Coleman Street	18s. 4d.
Item from William Gros at the Swan in the parish of St Nicholas Cole Abbey	13s. 4d.
Item from Morys Tranaill at the Ship beside London Wall in the parish of St Alphage	13s. 4d.
Item from William Rikherst at the Key on Basing Lane in the parish of [*St Mary*] Aldermary church	6s. 8d.
Item from John Farman at the Dragon without Bishopsgate	10s.
Item from Bechamp, maltman of Barnet	26s. 8d.
Item from John Cheseman [*above the line*: at the Garland without Bishopsgate]	11s. 8d.
[*scored*: who has paid 52s. for 12 years of missing payments at [.] p.a.]	
Item from Stephen Clean at the Bell beside Aldersgate in the parish of St Anne	11s. 8d.
Item from John Ivor at the Pannier in Paternoster Row in the parish of St Michael le Querne	23s. 4d.
Item from Robert Stapill, [*above the line*: clerk of St Swithin in Candlewick Street]	11s. 9d.
[*Line scored*: at the Chequer in East Cheap in the parish of St Clement]	
Item from Dederik Claysson, *Ducheman*, with Weveyn his wife, for his franchise and for his admission to be a brother of the said fraternity,	£4.

Sum total £ [15 18s.] 8d.

Which remains as profit to the Masters, that is, William atte Wode and his fellow
Masters of the craft, William Ederich, William Ferrour, John Reyner
And a memorandum that the aforesaid Robert Stapill lately in Wood Street
[*damaged*]
William atte Wode and his fellows the Masters of the same craft [*damaged*] for the
freedom [*damaged*].

[3] [f. 1v]
Men enfranchised […] without paying
Henry Forteyn enfranchised at the request of the mayor
John Laurence enfranchised at the request of John Stantonne, brewer.

Received for the creation of new brothers of the fraternity

First received from John Lumbard at the Cock beside Dowgate in the parish of All Hallows the Great	6s. 8d.
Item from Michael Tregononne at the Red Lion in the parish of St Botolph without Aldersgate	5s.
Item from John Basset at the Crown outside the Friars Minor in the parish of St Audoen	3s. 4d.
Item from William Gros at the Swan in the parish of St Nicholas Cole Abbey	6s. 8d.
Item from Morys Tranaill at the Ship beside London Wall in the parish of St Alphage	6s. 8d.
Item from Sir Robert Steynton,⁴ chaplain of the craft and fraternity at that time	6s. 8d.

---

4   Robert Steynton was the fraternity chaplain c.1418–29. Dominus or Sir was a courtesy
title for clergy.

Item from William Purland, common clerk of the said craft and fraternity as appears	6s. 8d.
Item from Walter Glyn at the Rose in Aldersgate Street	6s. 8d.
Item from John Laurence at the Hart in the same Aldersgate Street	3s. 4d.
Item from Roger Blissote at the Swan in St Nicholas Shambles	3s. 4d.
Item from Nicholas Agomnaylok at the Swan in Wall Street in the parish of St Michael Huggin Lane	5s.
Item from Thomas Hancok at the Swan in the parish of St Michael in Cornhill	6s. 8d.
Item from John Aleyn, baker, lately at the Swan, Wood Street	5s.
Item from William Illying at the Cock in the parish of St Margaret Pattens	6s. 8d.
Item from Walter Copseye, shearman, at the Pannier in Paternoster Row in the parish of St Michael le Querne	6s. 8d.
Item from William Baily at Leaden Porch in Smithfield	6s. 8d.
[*scored*: Item from Thomas Botiller]	
Item from John Cock at the Crown beside Horsepool in Smithfield	6s. 8d.
Item from William Boteler at the Cock in the parish of St Andrew Cornhill	6s. 8d.
[*scored*: from Alan John	6s. 8d.]
from William Termeday at the Peahen without Bishopsgate	3s. 4d.
Item from Robert Walram at the Cock in the parish of St Michael Queenhithe	6s. 8d.
Item from Robert Pede, baker, at the Maid in the parish of St Mary Colechurch	6s. 8d.
Item from John Elsy at the George in Fenchurch Street in the parish of St Dionis	6s. 8d.

[*Scored*: [*Latin*]: Memorandum that it was allowed to Thomas Water, brewer of London, not to pay for his entry nor his quarterage, as appears]

Sum £6 8s. 4d.

There remains as profit to the Masters, written below, 55s., that is, William atte Wode and his fellows.

[4] [f. 2r]
Received from legacies to the said mistery devised by last testaments

First received from John Turmyn	6s. 8d.

Received for the hire of the Hall belonging to the said mistery

First received from the mistery of Glovers of London	18d.
Item received from the fraternity of the Master Clerks[5] of London	2s.
Item received from the mistery of Coopers of London	2s.
Item received from the mistery of Masons of London	3s. 4d.
Item received from the mistery of Point-makers of London	12d.

Received for Rent

First received from a tenant for rent for the tenement situated against the gate of the said Hall, that is for a whole year, from the feast of Christmas in the sixth year of the reign of the King [1418] until the following Christmas in the seventh year of the reign of the same King [1419]   26s. 8d.

---

5   It is not clear what is meant by 'Maistre Clerkes'; probably the fraternity of Parish Clerks.

Received for Quarterage payments from diverse brothers and sisters of the said fraternity, that is for one year

First received from Alexander Mylis [*scored*: for himself and his wife] 12*d.*

Item from David Soys	12*d.*
Item from Denise Barthorppe	12*d.*

Item from Agnes Bugge 12*d.*
Item from Adam Coppendale 12*d.*
Item from Alice Hore 12*d.*
Item from Agnes Stratton 12*d.*
Item from Alan Bret for himself and his wife 2*s.*

Item from Ellis Hardell 12*d.*
Item from Emma Canonne 12*d.*

Item from Constance Hosard for an old debt and for this year 2*s.* 6*d.*
[*scored*: [*Latin*] This Constance, it is said, was accustomed to pay 2*s.* for her quarterage, that is double quarterage]

[5] [f. 2v]

Item from Henry Lymber for himself and his wife 2*s.*
Item from Hugh Neell 12*d.*
Item from Henry Trebolans 12*d.*
Item from Henry Bedell 12*d.*
Item from Hugh Glene for himself and his wife –[6]
Item from Henry Serle 12*d.*

Item from John Thetford for himself and his wife 2*s.*
Item from John Philippe for himself and his wife 2*s.*
Item from John Ketyng 12*d.*
Item from John Riche for himself and his wife 2*s.*
Item from John Masonne for himself and his wife 2*s.*
Item from John Reyner for himself and his wife 2*s.*
Item from John More [*scored*: at Ludgate] 12*d.*
Item from John Stanntone for himself and his wife 2*s.*
Item from John Kenaky 12*d.*
Item from John Chapman 12*d.*
Item from John Tregolowe for himself and his wife 12*d.*

from John William for himself and his wife 12*d.*
from John More [*added*: at Aldersgate] for himself and his wife 2*s.*
from John Russell for himself and his wife 2*s.*
from John Refawe for himself and his wife 2*s.*
from John Turvey 12*d.*
from John Lucas 12*d.*
from John Humbre 12*d.*
from John Quyntyn for himself and his wife 2*s.*
from John Stone 12*d.*
from John Cole 12*d.*
[clerk's note: £3 6*d.*]
from Ideyne Hatton 12*d.*
from John Sondere 12*d.*
from Johanna Witleseye 12*d.*
from John Randolff for himself and his wife 2*s.*
from Johanna Carleton 12*d.*
from Julyan Hethersete, widow 2*s.*
from John Nasyng 2*s.*
from Johanna, the wife of John Horold, woolmonger, 12*d.*
from the wife formerly of Master William Cook 12*d.*

[6]   Masters and their wives did not pay quarterage during their year in office. It is not clear why Glene and his wife did not pay quarterage here.

Item from John Salter 12d.

Item from John Erle [*added*: who did not pay quarterage but was made a brother of the fraternity this year and paid 6s. 8d. for his entry]

from John Pykeyne for himself and his wife 2s.

from John Brook 12d.

from John Caryen for himself and his wife 2s.

from John Spenser 12d.

from John Eylond 12d.

from John Baily 12d.

from John Brewster for himself and his wife 2s.

from Johanna Oustarde, the wife of Piers Morle 12d.

from John Snell 12d.

from John Beenger for himself and his wife 2s.

from John Bray 12d.

from John Simman for himself and his wife 2s.

from John Sere for himself and his wife 12d.

from John Hardy 12d.

from John Turnour 12d.

from John Ryngesson for himself and his wife 2s.

from John Gedney 12d.

from John Assh 12d.

from John Southmede 12d.

from John Wodelonde 12d.

from John Lynne 12d.

from John Merston 12d.

from John Retford 12d.

from John Rothyng for himself and his wife 2s.

[6] [f. 3r]

Item from John Moyle 12d.

Item from Jacob Lenegro for himself and his wife 2s.

Item from John Waghorne 12d.

[*margin*: not paid] Item from John Riche, tailor, nil

Item from John William of Southwark 12d.

Item from John Penferne for himself and his wife 2s.

Item from John Ballard for himself and his wife 12d.

Item from John Samine 12d.

Item from John Fykays for himself and his wife 2s.

[*scored*: Item from Milicent Burgh for past times and for this year]
[*margin*: written in another place]

Item from Katherine Roche 12d.

Item from Michael Eve for himself and his wife 2s.

Item from Margaret Sydingbourne 12d.

Item from Michael Trerys for himself and his wife 12d.

Item from Milicent Burgh for past times and for this year 2s.

Item from Nicholas Kene for himself and his wife 2s.

Item from Nicholas Aleyn 12d.

Item from Nicholas Fuller 12d.

Item from Peter Haiford for himself and his wife 2s.

Item from Peter Carpenter 12d.

Item from Philip James 12d.

Item from Peter Roos 12d.

[*Above the line*: clerk's note: £3]

[7] [f. 3v]

Item from Richard Rowdon for himself and his wife	2s.
Item from Robert Smyth	12d.
Item from Robert Hilton for himself and his wife	2s.
Item from Robert Maihewe	12d.
Item from Robert Carpenter	12d.
Item from Robert Lynford for himself and his wife	15d.
[*added*: [*Latin*] paid the day after the Masters' account]	
Item from Richard Wythmour for himself and his wife	12d.
Item from Richard Aleyn for himself and his wife	2s.
Item from Richard Shirwode for himself and his wife	2s.
Item from Richard Neweman for himself and his wife	2s.
Item from Robert Nykke for himself and his wife	12d.
Item from Robert Gyles for himself and his wife	2s.
Item from Richard Frepurs for himself and his wife, for past times and for this year	2s.
Item from Richard Terill for himself and his wife, for last year and this year	2s.
Item from Richard Bryntone	12d.
Item from Richard Welde	12d.
Item from Robert Tanner	12d.
Item from Richard Harlowe for himself and his wife	2s.
Item from Robert Jewell	12d.
Item from Roger Baronne	12d.
Item from Richard Storm for himself and his wife for the last year	2s.
Item from Richard Rose in Southwark	12d.
[*added*: [*Latin*] paid the day after the Masters' account]	

Item from Simon Potkyn	12d.
Item from Stephen Roo, for last year and for this year	12d.
Item from Thomas Emond for himself and his wife	2s.
Item from Thomas Atcher for himself and his wife	12d.
Item from Thomas Yole for himself and his wife	12d.
Item from Thomas Godyng	12d.
Item from Thomas Webbe for himself and his wife	12d.
Item from Thomas Aleyn for himself and his wife	12d.
Item from Thomas Penson for the last year past	12d.
Item from Thomas Gratley	12d.
Item from Thomas Smalsho	12d.
Item from Thomas Jakes for last year past	12d.
Item from Thomas Kente for last year past and for this year	12d.
Item from Thomas Martyn for last year past and for this year	12d.
Item from Thomas Dewy	12d.
Item from Thomas Osbarne for himself and his wife	2s.
Item from Thomas Bristowe	12d.

43

[8] [f. 4r]

Item from Walter Riche for himself and his wife	2s.
Item from William atte Welle for himself and his wife	2s.
Item from William atte Wode for himself and his wife for the last year past	2s.
Item from William Ferrour for himself and his wife	12d.
Item from William Edrich for himself and his wife [added: £3 15s.]	2s.
Item from William Cophode for himself and his wife for last year past	2s.
Item from William Gedney	12d.
Item from William Geffray for himself and his wife	2s.
Item from William Petevyle	12d.
Item from William Harry	12d.
Item from William Bracy for himself and his wife	2s.
Item from William Wheleman	12d.
Item from William Cardell for last year past	12d.
Item from Walter Colshull for last year past	12d.
Item from William Bernard,	12d.
Item from William Robert	2s.
Item from William Claisonne for himself and his wife	2s.
Item from William Smalsho for himself and his wife	2s.
Item from William Canonne for last year	12d.
Item from William [partially erased: Baily] John	12d.
Item from William Bolton,	12d.
Item from William Bodevyle	12d.
Item from William Belle for last year	12d.
Item from William Baconne	12d.
Item from William Crane	12d.

Item from William Weston for the last year and the present year	12d.
	27s.

Sum of quarterage this year
£10 8s. 9d.[7]

[9]

[*Latin*] And from before this time, quarterage for this fraternity of the craft of Brewers was paid in various ways, so that the sum collected, that is, in one particular year was 100s., and in another year £6, and another £8 11s. and no more. So that it will be possible to show how things are at the present time in the Masters' account, deliberations were held about how the said quarterage could be increased in other years, for the profit of the company. By an oath to observe the wise profit and constitution of the company it was agreed to inspect the great table of the fraternity which specifies our brothers and sisters of that same fraternity, for evidence.[8] It was found that there were 120 and more persons of London, men whose quarterage had not been received nor paid, nor satisfaction given. For this reason, the names of those who have paid quarterage are recorded on this paper, as a matter of urgency, and the sums paid will be written and the persons named, so that it will be possible to identify who has and who has not paid. Thus from year to year and in subsequent years, it will be possible to see the quarterage paid and the identities of those who have paid, easily, written down for the profit of our mistery and craft.

---

[7] This total is 3s. too high, as is the subtotal on the previous folio [6].

[8] A board at Brewers' Hall, inscribed with the names of fraternity members, probably hanging on the wall.

[10] [f. 4v]

[*French*] Let it be remembered that the said Masters in that said year [1418–19] who were Masters of the said mistery of Brewers bought from various persons fine green cloth and coarse cloth, at various prices, for the livery of the said mistery of Brewers, which is plainly declared, that is:

First the Masters bought from William Weston, draper [*scored*: citizen] of London, 2 entire cloths of green fine cloth, each containing 32 yards length and 2 yards width, price of each 5*s*. the yard,   £16

Item the Masters bought from John Ryngsone, tailor and citizen of London, 1 piece of green cloth [*scored*: fine] 6 yards long and 2 yards wide, price each yard 5*s*.,   30*s*.

Item they bought from William Ferrour, one of the Masters of the aforesaid Brewers, a piece of green cloth containing 30 yards in length and 2 yards in width, price 5*s*. the yard,   £7 10*s*.

Item they bought from Robert Tatersale, draper [*scored*: citizen] of London, 1 piece of green cloth [*scored*: fine] 24 yards in length and 2 yards in width, price each yard 4*s*.,   £4 16*s*.

Sum total 124 yards.
Which amounts in money to the sum total of £29 16*s*.

Item the Masters bought from the said William Weston 5 other cloths of green cloth containing in length 16 yards, the second cloth 25 yards, the third cloth 27 yards, the fourth cloth 29 yards and the fifth cloth 30 yards and a half, and in width each cloth 2 yards wide, price the yard 3*s*. 8*d*.   £23 7*s*. 6*d*.

Item the Masters bought from the said John Ryngsone, 1 other piece of green cloth [*scored*: called coarse cloth] containing in length 21 yards and in width 2 yards wide, price the yard 3*s*. 8*d*.   £3 17*s*.

Item they bought from the said Robert Tatersale 2 pieces of green cloth [*scored*: called coarse cloth] one containing in length 21 yards, the second 15 yards, and in width each of these 2 yards wide, at 3*s*. 8*d*. the yard.   £6 15*s*. 8*d*.

Sum [*scored*: total of yards of coarse cloth] **184 yards which amounts in money to £29 16*s*.**

Sum total £34 0*s*. 2*d*.[9]

Sum total of coloured cloth 308 yards and a half

Money £63 16*s*. 2*d*.

---

9   There were many deletions on this page, some of which have been omitted, in order to present the clerk's final version.

[*scored*: [*Latin*] Which coloured cloth together with rays was delivered to various persons to a greater and lesser extent, according to the discretion and advice of the Masters for this year.]

[11] [f. 5r]
[*French*]
Rays
Item the Masters bought from John Griffith, draper of Salisbury, 16 cloths of ray cloth, each cloth containing 25 yards, price the yard 2*s*. each.
Each cloth cost 50*s*.

Sum total £40.

Of these, two were each half a yard short and for this default, the Masters were allowed 6*s*. 8*d*.

Sum total clear £39 13*s*. 4*d*.

Sum total clear of the said coloured cloth, fine cloth, coarse cloth and rays amounts to £103 9*s*. 6*d*.

[*scored*: these are the names of the men having livery of the aforesaid cloths, as appears in the following parcels]
Which livery cloth was delivered by the said Masters in the parcels below to various persons of the said mistery and fraternity as follows

Hoods

First Alexander Miles 8 rays with coloured cloth	8*s*.¹⁰
Agnes Bugge three quarters and a half of coloured cloth	6*s*.
a Alan John 7 rays with coloured cloth	6*s*.
b Adam Copendale 8 rays with coloured cloth	7*s*.

Gowns

b Davy Brownyng 28 rays with coarse coloured cloth	19*s*.

Hoods

Davy Soys 7 rays with coloured cloth	6*s*.

Gowns

Ellis Hardell 20 rays with coarse coloured cloth	15*s*.

Sum Rays 78

Money 67*s*.

---

¹⁰ The clerk used symbols resembling the letter 'a' or two pen strokes, and 'b' to the left of some names. Their significance is unclear but is perhaps connected with payment. Individual amounts of rays taken were listed here, but individual amounts of coloured cloth were listed only rarely. The sums of money recorded here are presumably for both kinds of cloth and probably include charges for tailoring, too.

[12] [f. 5v]

Gowns

Henry Lymber 32 rays with best coloured cloth	25s.
Henry Fereby 26 rays with coarse coloured cloth	18s.
b Hugh Neell 32 rays with coarse coloured cloth	22s.
b Henry Trebolannce 1 yard of ray and 1 ray more with 4 yards and a half of green of the cloth called coarse cloth	23s.

Hoods

b Henry Bedell 7 rays with coloured cloth	8s.
b Hugh Glene 8 rays with coloured cloth	7s.
a Henry Serle 7 rays with coloured cloth	6s.

Gowns

John Thetford 34 rays with best coloured cloth	27s.
b John Philippe 32 rays with best coloured cloth	25s.
b John Ketyng 32 rays with best coloured cloth	26s. 6d.
b John Riche 5 yards of coloured cloth with 1 yard of ray of best cloth	31s.
b John Mason 32 rays with best coloured cloth	26s.
b John More at Ludgate 35 rays with best coloured cloth	27s. 6d.
b John Stannton 32 rays with best coloured cloth	25s.
b John Kenaky 36 rays with coarse coloured cloth	24s. 8d.
b John Tregelowe 28 rays with coarse coloured cloth	19s.
b John Salter 32 rays with coarse coloured cloth	22s.
b John Neweman 33 rays with coarse coloured cloth	23s.
b John Erle, called Lumbard, 26 rays with best coloured cloth	20s.
a John Serle 28 rays with best coloured cloth	22s.
b John Pekeyn 33 rays with coarse coloured cloth	23s.
b John Broke 30 rays with coarse coloured cloth	19s. 8d.

Sum 572 rays

Money £23 10s. 4d.

[13] [f. 6r]

b John Caryen 34 rays with coarse coloured cloth	24s.
b John Spenser 24 rays with coarse coloured cloth	17s. 2d.
b John Eylond 26 rays with coarse coloured cloth	18s.
a John Laurence 28 rays with coarse coloured cloth	19s.
a John Bailly 24 rays with coarse coloured cloth	17s.
b John Brewester 28 rays with coarse coloured cloth	18s. 10d.
b John William 34 rays with best coloured cloth	27s.
b John More at Aldersgate 30 rays with best coloured cloth	24s.
b John Russell 32 rays with best coloured cloth	25s.
b John Basset 26 rays with cloth of best colour	21s.
b John Reefawe 28 rays with coarse coloured cloth	19s.
a John Turvey 28 rays with coarse coloured cloth	20s.
a John Lucas 30 rays with coarse coloured cloth	20s.
b John Humbre 26 rays with coarse coloured cloth	18s.

a John Quyntyn 4 yards & a half of coloured cloth with 1 yard of coarse ray cloth   23*s*.
b John Stone 30 rays with coarse coloured cloth   20*s*. 6*d*.
b John Aleyn at the Crutched Friars 30 rays with coarse coloured cloth   21*s*.
b John Chapman 20 rays with coarse coloured cloth   15*s*.
John Reyner 36 rays with best coloured cloth   —[II]
Item for three quarters and a half more of best coloured cloth for his wife   —

Hoods

b John Snell 7 rays with coloured cloth   6*s*.
a John Benge 8 rays with coloured cloth   7*s*.
a John Bray, butcher, 8 rays with coloured cloth   7*s*.
a John Simnian 6 rays with coloured cloth   5*s*. 6*d*.
a John Sere 6 rays with coloured cloth   5*s*. 6*d*.
a John Hardy 7 rays with coloured cloth   —
a John Aleyn 5 rays with coloured cloth   5*s*.
a John Turnour 7 rays with coloured cloth   7*s*.
a John Ryngeston 7 rays with coloured cloth   —
a John Wake 7 rays with coloured cloth   6*s*.
a John Gedeney 7 rays with coloured cloth   6*s*.

Sum Rays 597

Money £21 2s. 6d.

[14] [f. 6v]

a John Assh 7 rays with coloured cloth   6*s*.
a John Southmede 8 rays with coloured cloth   7*s*.
John Wodelonde 6 rays with coloured cloth   5*s*. 6*d*.
b John Lynne 6 rays with coloured cloth   5*s*. 6*d*.
b John Merstone 6 rays with coloured cloth   5*s*. 4*d*.
a John Dunche 6 rays with coloured cloth   6*s*.
b John Tooke 6 rays with coloured cloth   5*s*. 6*d*.
John Retford 8 rays with coloured cloth   7*s*.
John Rothyng 8 rays with coloured cloth   7*s*.
John Moyle 8 rays with coloured cloth   7*s*.
b Jacob Lenegro 7 rays with coloured cloth   6*s*.
a John Waghorn 5 rays with coloured cloth   5*s*.
a John Riche, tailor of Fleet Street, 7 rays with coloured cloth   6*s*.
a John Riche, brewer at the Angel, 7 rays with coloured cloth   6*s*.
a John William at the Lamb in Southwark 7 rays with coloured cloth   6*s*.
John Penferne 8 rays with coloured cloth   7*s*.
John Grace 8 rays with coloured cloth   7*s*.
John Aleyn, baker, 5 rays with coloured cloth   4*s*. 6*d*.
a John Ballard 7 rays with coloured cloth   6*s*.

[II]   Reyner, one of the masters of the fraternity 1418–19, was not charged for livery cloth for himself and his wife, whilst John Hardy was the cook at Brewers' Hall and Ryngesson, tailor, had supplied some of the livery cloth to the Brewers, which may explain why these men were not charged.

b John Elsy 6 rays with coloured cloth	5*s*. 6*d*.
John Awdree 4 rays with coloured cloth	3*s*. 4*d*.
John Haverill 7 rays with coloured cloth	6*s*.
John Samme 7 rays with coloured cloth	6*s*.
a John Fykays 6 rays with cloth of colour	5*s*.
b John Bechapme 6 rays with cloth of colour	6*s*.

Gowns

b Michael Eve 30 rays with 2 yards and a half of best coloured cloth	25*s*.

Sum Rays: 196

Money £8 12*s*. 2*d*.

[15] [f. 7r]
Hoods

Michael Trerys 8 rays with coloured cloth	7*s*.
b Morys Tranaill 7 rays with coloured cloth	6*s*.
b Michael Tregononne 9 rays with coloured cloth	8*s*.

Gowns

b Nicholas Muryell 26 rays with coloured cloth	18*s*.
a Nicholas Kene 34 rays with best coloured cloth	27*s*.
b Nicholas Aleyn 30 rays with coarse coloured cloth	20*s*.

Hoods

b Nicholas Agomnaylok 7 rays with coloured cloth	6*s*.
b Nicholas Fuller 7 rays with coloured cloth	6*s*.
Nicholas Yonge 6 rays with coloured cloth	5*s*. 6*d*.

Gowns

b Peter Hayford 5 yards of coloured cloth with 1 yard of ray of best cloth	31*s*.
b Peter Carpenter 28 rays with best coloured cloth	22*s*.

Hoods

a Philip James 7 rays with coloured cloth	6*s*.
a Peter Sevyer 5 rays with coloured cloth	4*s*.
a Peter Roos 8 rays with coloured cloth	6*s*. 8*d*.

Sum Rays 190

Money £8 13*s*. 2*d*.

[16] [f. 7v]
Gowns

b Richard Rowdon 4 yards and a half of best coloured cloth with 1 yard [*scored*: of best] ray cloth	29*s*.
b Robert Smyth 34 rays with best coloured cloth	27*s*.
b Robert Hilton 36 rays with best coloured cloth	27*s*. 8*d*.
b Robert Mayhewe 30 rays with best coloured cloth	24*s*.

49

b Robert Carpenter 30 rays with best coloured cloth	24*s*.
b Roger Blissot 30 rays with coarse coloured cloth	22*s*.
a Robert Lynford 20 rays with coarse coloured cloth	15*s*.
Richard Withmour 26 rays with coarse coloured cloth	18*s*.
b Richard Aleyn 34 rays with best coloured cloth	27*s*.
b Richard Shirwode 34 rays with best coloured cloth	26*s*. 8*d*.
Richard Neweman 30 rays with coarse coloured cloth	20*s*.
b Robert Nykke 31 rays with coarse coloured cloth	21*s*.
b Robert Gyles 28 rays with coarse coloured cloth	19*s*.
b Robert Elkyn 24 rays with coarse coloured cloth	18*s*.
b Roger Swannyffelde 32 rays with coarse coloured cloth	23*s*.
[*Added*: Sir Robert, chaplain, called Steynton, 4 yards of coloured cloth	17*s*.]

Hoods

a Robert Pede, baker, 7 rays with coloured cloth	6*s*.
b Robert Tannere 8 rays with coloured cloth	7*s*.
+ [*scored*: Richard Bygbury 7 rays with cloth of colour,	6*s*]
[*Margin* [*Latin*]: He did not have this. Dederyk Claysson has this said hood]	
a Richard Harlowe 7 rays with coloured cloth	6*s*.
a Richard Crosse 7 rays with coloured cloth	6*s*.
Robert Jewell, grocer, 1 yard of best green cloth	6*s*. 8*d*.
Richard Rose in Southwark 7 rays with coloured cloth	6*s*.
a Roger Baronne 7 rays with coloured cloth	6*s*.
b Robert Walram 8 rays with coloured cloth	6*s*. 8*d*.
Richard Storme 6 rays with coloured cloth	5*s*. 6*d*.

Gowns

b Symkyn Potkyn 24 rays with coarse coloured cloth	17*s*.

Sum Rays 515

Money £21 17s. 2d.

[17] [f. 8r]

Simon atte Welle 8 rays with coloured cloth [*scored*: 4*s*.]	7*s*.
Simon Petsyn 8 rays with coloured cloth	7*s*.

Gowns

b Thomas Emond 34 rays with best coloured cloth	25*s*. 4*d*.
b Thomas Hatcher 34 rays with best coloured cloth	25*s*. [*scored*: 8*d*.]
b Thomas Yole 26 rays with coarse coloured cloth	18*s*.
b Thomas Godyng 26 rays with coarse coloured cloth	18*s*.
Thomas Webbe 32 rays with coarse coloured cloth	22*s*.
a Thomas Grene 34 rays with coarse coloured cloth	22*s*. 8*d*.
a Thomas Aleyn 30 rays with coarse coloured cloth	21*s*.

Hoods

a Thomas Penson 7 rays with coloured cloth	6*s*.
b Thomas Hancook 8 rays with coloured cloth	6*s*. 8*d*.
Thomas Ludvyngton 6 rays with coloured cloth	5*s*. 6*d*.

50

a Thomas Gratley 7 rays with coloured cloth	6s.
b Thomas Smalsho 6 rays with coloured cloth	5s. 6d.
a Thomas Botelere 8 rays with coloured cloth	7s.
Thomas Donyngton 7 rays with coloured cloth	5s.
[*scored*: Thomas Wyngfelde 7 rays with coloured cloth	6s.]
[[*Latin*] He did not have this. Reyner has this hood]	
b Thomas Ayle 7 rays with coloured cloth	6s.
a Thomas Jakes 7 rays with coloured cloth	6s. 8d.

Gowns

Walter Riche 30 rays with best coloured cloth	24s.
b William atte Welle 30 rays with best coloured cloth	24s.
b William atte Wode 34 rays with best coloured cloth	—[12]
& 1 yard of green cloth for his wife. Item 6 rays for 1 hood	
b William Ferrour 36 rays with best coloured cloth	—
Item three quarters & a half of best green cloth for his wife	

Sum Cloth 438

Money £13 14s. 4d.

[18] [f. 8v]

b William Edriche 34 rays with best coloured cloth	—
Item three quarters and half of best green cloth for his wife	—
b William Porlond, clerk, 4 yards of best coloured cloth & three quarters of best green cloth	—
b William Cophode 32 rays of best cloth,	26s. 6d.
Item 1 yard of best green cloth for his wife,	5s. 6d.
+ William Gedney 24 rays with coarse cloth of colour	17s.
[*Added*: [*Latin*]: He did not pay money for cloth which he had and returned]	
b William Greffray 26 rays with coarse coloured cloth	17s. 6d.
b William Petevyle 24 rays with coarse coloured cloth	17s.
b William Harry 30 rays with coarse coloured cloth	20s.
b William Bracy 34 rays with best coloured cloth	25s. 8d.
William Wheleman 24 rays with coarse coloured cloth	17s.
b William Cardell 30 rays with coarse coloured cloth	20s.
b Walter Colshull 32 rays with coarse coloured cloth	22s.
b William Bernard 29 rays with coarse coloured cloth	18s. 4d.
William Robert 32 rays with coarse coloured cloth	22s.
b William Claysson 34 rays with coarse coloured cloth	24s.
b William Smalsho 32 rays with coarse coloured cloth	22s.
b William Canonne 28 rays with coarse coloured cloth	19s.
b William Payn 30 rays with coarse coloured cloth	20s.

Hoods

b William Bailly of Smithfield 7 rays with coloured cloth	6s.

---

12   William atte Wode and Ferrour and Edriche were masters 1418–19 and did not pay for
     livery for themselves and their wives. Porlond, the clerk, did not pay for his livery.

a William Devenyssh 7 rays with coloured cloth	5*s*.
b William John 6 rays with coloured cloth	5*s*. 6*d*.
a Walter Glyn 7 rays with coloured cloth	6*s*.
a William Pethin 7 rays with coloured cloth	5*s*.
b William Bolton 7 rays with coloured cloth	7*s*.
b William Boteler 7 rays with coloured cloth	6*s*.
a William Bodevyle 9 rays with coloured cloth	8*s*.
b William Belle 7 rays with coloured cloth	6*s*.
a William Bakone 7 rays with coloured cloth	6*s*.
b William Crane 7 rays with coloured cloth	6*s*.
b William Termeday 7 rays with coloured cloth	6*s*.
b William Illyng 7 rays with coloured cloth	6*s*.
Walter Copsye 7 rays with coloured cloth	6*s*.
William Hert 8 rays with coloured cloth	7*s*.
a William Mulshowe 8 rays with coloured cloth	7*s*.

Sum: Rays 590

Money £20 12*s*.

[f. 9r]
Sum total: Rays 3,176 and distributed among the said Masters and the tailors [*page damaged*]
Sum total of money £121 8*s*. 8*d*.

Sum total of drapery in money is: £185 4*s*. 10*d*.

[*There is a blank space here, with an asterisk at its top left and lower right, and remnants of letters on the left. A supplementary piece of paper, now lost, was once affixed here.*]

[19]
These are the names of those who had clothing without payment in this year
[1418–19]

First William atte Wode 34 rays with best green coloured cloth
Item the same William had 6 rays with coloured cloth for a hood
the same William had 1 yard of best green cloth for his wife
William Ferrour had 36 rays with best coloured cloth
Item three quarters & a half of best coloured cloth for his wife
John Reyner 36 rays with best coloured cloth
Item three quarters & a half of best coloured cloth for his wife
William Edrich 34 rays with best coloured cloth
Item three quarters & a half of best coloured cloth for his wife
William Porlond 4 yards & three quarters of best coloured cloth
John Hardy 7 rays with coarse coloured cloth for a hood
John Ryngesson 7 rays with coarse coloured cloth for a hood
+ [*scored*: William Devenyssh 7 rays with coarse coloured cloth for a hood]
[*scored*: Item given by the fraternity from the common box to the same
W. Devenyssh previously at the start of the year for his hood [*page damaged*].]

52

Rewards

Paid to John Ryngesson, tailor, for departing[13] and cutting of our livery, that
is, for gowns and hoods this year,   6s. 8d.

Item to the same Ryngesson for Nicholas, his apprentice, for his work in
carrying the gowns and hoods   2s.

[*Margin note* [*scored*: Reward] [*Latin*] because in another place] Item to
the said William Devenyssh for his allocation for making ready the hall this
same year   6s. 8d.

[20] [f. 9v]

**These are the names of those brothers and sisters of our Fraternity who have
paid their quarterage but did not have our livery cloth for this year**

Alice Hore	12d.
Agnes Stratton	12d.
a Alan Brette for himself and his wife	2s.
Constance Hosard	2s. 6d.
Denise Barthorpe	12d.
Emmote Canon	12d.
Katherine Roche	12d.
Johanna Cole	12d.
Idonea[14] Hatton	12d.
a John Sonder	12d.
Johanna Wuleseye	12d.
a John Randolf with his wife	2s.
Johanna Carleton	12d.
Julianna Hedersete, widow	2s.
a John Nasyng	2s.
Johanna the wife of John Horolde, woolmonger,	12d.
The widow of Master William Cook	12d.
Johanna the widow of Piers Morle	12d.
Margaret Sydyngbourne	12d.
Milicent Burgh	2s.
a Richard Frepurs for himself and his wife	2s.
a Richard Terell for himself and his wife	2s.
a Richard Brynton	12d.
Richard Welde	12d.
a Stephen Roo	12d.

---

13   Dividing.
14   The scribe wrote 'Ideme' or 'Idenne' here for 'Idonea'.

[21] [f. 10r]

a Thomas Kent	12*d.*
a Thomas Martyn	12*d.*
a Thomas Dewy	12*d.*
a Thomas Osbarne	2*s.*
a Thomas Bristowe	12*d.*
William Weston	12*d.*

[22]

These are the names of those who were admitted and are entered in the table of our fraternity in this year and have hoods of our livery and have not paid their entry fees nor their quarterage.

Alan John at the Basket in Fenchurch Street in the parish of All Hallows Staining
Thomas Botiler at the Bell in Red Cross Street in the parish of St Giles

[*Latin*] The said Alan John, lately, as above, paid his entry fee, quarterage etc and everything was settled in the time of Thomas Grene, John Peken, Robert Hilton and Robert Carpenter, Masters of the craft of Brewers. [1419–21]
The said Thomas Boteler paid his quarterage and as for his entry, the same Thomas was fined 5*s.* for a certain transgression against the craft and was excused payment for admission to the craft of Brewers, in the time of Robert Smyth, William Crane, John Philippe and Hugo Neel, Masters [1421–3] as above.

[23] [f. 10v]

[*French*] **These are the names of those persons who are brothers and sisters of our Fraternity, with their names inscribed upon our table, and yet who have not paid their quarterage in this year, nor in other years before these times**

aa[15] Alice, the widow of James Knyght
Cristiane, the wife of John Ballard
Elyne, the wife of William Crane
Emmotte Wykes
aa Henry Semere
aa Henry Anketill & Alice his wife
Hugh Sharp
Hugh Glene & Margaret his wife
John Wightmour & Johanna his wife
aa John Hatfelde
aa John Marybone & Johanna his wife
a John Philippe, glover, & Johanna his wife
aa Isabel Morby

Anneys the wife of Alexander Milys
Anya the wife of Robert Smyth
aa Anneys the wife of Richard Wightmour
Alice the wife of Robert Nikke
aa Alice the wife of Thomas Yole
aa Anneys the wife of William Herry
Alice the widow of Richard Kirkeby
Adam Preston

aa John Rotherby, formerly the parson of All Hallows London Wall[16]
aa John Chapman, maltman
aa John Awdre, sheather

[15] The symbols may denote the number of years of payment owed.
[16] His name is not found in Hennessy, *London Clergy*.

aa John Symond & Anneys his wife
aa John Dowble
aa John Bargon and Anneys his wife
aa John Berston & Julyane, his wife
aa John Sell, maltman, & Maude his wife
John Grace
John Perye
aa Margaret, the wife of Thomas Hatcher
Michael Tregononne

a Laurence Davy & Johanna his wife

Nicholas Muryell
aa Nicholas Yonge & Agnes his wife
aa Nicholas Kebbel & Margaret his wife

aa Philip Carpenter
Piers Morley
Richard Crosse
aa Roger Menyan & Johanna his wife
a Richard Biggebury & Katherine his wife

aa Johanna the wife of John Tregelowe
aa Thomas Newchapman & Anneys his wife
aa Thomas Crowser
aa Thomas Sylke & Isabel his wife
William Payne
Vincent Syward & Isabel his wife
aa William Repon & Margery his wife
aa William Hert & Alice his wife
William Overton, woodmonger
aa William Devenyssh

aa John Wake at Gisors Hall[17]
aa John Serle & Johanna his wife
aa John Cok
aa John Fitz Robert & Johanna his wife

aa Jonette the wife of Adam Copendale
aa Juliane the wife of John Chapman
aa Johanna the wife of John Salter
Johanna the wife of John William in Thames Street

aa Isabel the wife of John William in Southwark
aa Johanna formerly the wife of Michael Trerys
aa Johanna the wife of Thomas Aleyn

aa Thomas Sebarn, maltman
aa Thomas Lodyngton
aa Thomas Honchon & Anneys his wife
Thomas Grene

[24]
The names written in this part of this leaf list those who had livery but have not paid their quarterage in this year [1418–19] that is

Hugh Glene had 1 hood and owes quarterage for himself and his wife
William Hert had 1 hood and owes quarterage for himself and his wife
John Serle had 1 gown and owes quarterage for himself and his wife

John Wike had 1 hood and owes quarterage for himself
[*scored*: John Grace had 1 hood and owes quarterage for himself]
[*added*: paid for this year and the following year as appears]

17   Or Gerard's Hall Inn, Basing Lane. Harben, *Dictionary*, 257.

Richard Crosse had 1 hood and owes quarterage for himself
[*scored*: William Payne had 1 gown and owes quarterage for himself]
[*added*: he paid for quarterage in the time of Thomas Grene and his associates in the following year, the 8th year of the reign of King Henry V] [1420–1]
William Devenyssh had 1 hood and owes quarterage for himself
John Awdre had 1 hood and owes quarterage for himself

Thomas Grene had 1 gown and owes quarterage for himself

[25] [f. 11r]
These are the names of those who are entered in the book of our fraternity in this year but their names are not recorded as brothers of the fraternity and whose names have not been written upon the table with the names of our fraternity

Davy Brownyng

Henry Fereby

John Newman
John Aleyn
John Dunche
John Riche, tailor
John Riche, brewer
John Bechamp, maltman

Peter Sevyer

Robert Elkyn
Roger Swannyfeld

Simon Petsyn
Simon atte Welle

Thomas Ayle
Thomas Ayle[18]

William Pethin
William Mulshowe

[26] [f. 11v]

[*Latin*] **The entry of the names of various crafts exercised in the city of London, used since ancient times and still continuing to this ninth year of King Henry V [1421–2] and here specified so that in effect it may in any way profit the Hall and commonalty of Brewers.[19]**

[18] The scribe entered Thomas Ayle twice: presumably there were two men with this name.
[19] See Figure 6. This list of 112 crafts is written in a more ornate hand, which may not be Porlond's own. It is unclear whether the order of the crafts, listed in three columns, is significant.

[*English and Latin: NB The names are transcribed here rather than translated*]

Mercers	Tanners	Ropers
Grocers	Curriours[20]	Lanternmakers
Pannarii[21]	Pouchemakers	Heymongers
Piscenarii[22]	Bowyers	Bokebynders
Aurifabri[23]	Fletchers	Scriptores Texti[24]
Vinetarii[25]	Horners	Stacioners
Pelliparii[26]	Spuriers[27]	Pulters
Cissores[28]	Heurers[29]	Clokmakers
Sellarii[30]	Wodmongers	Chapemakers[31]
Ferrones[32]	Scriptores litterae curialis[33]	Sheders[34]
Zonarii[35]	Lymnours[36]	Male makers[37]
Allutarii[38]	Lechis[39]	Tablemakers
Haberdasshers[40]	Ferrours[41]	Lokyers[42]
Cultelarii[43]	Copersmytes	Fourbours[44]
Armurarii	Upholders[45]	Burlesters[46]
	Galochemakers	
[27]	Hatters	Latoners[47]
Telarii Lanarum[48]	Coffrers[49]	Setters[50]

20   One who dressed and coloured leather after tanning.
21   Drapers.
22   Fishmongers.
23   Goldsmiths.
24   Writers of text hand.
25   Vintners.
26   Skinners.
27   Makers of spurs.
28   Taylors.
29   Hurers: makers of, or dealers in, woollen hats and caps.
30   Saddlers.
31   Makers of buckle pieces. See *CPMR, 1413–37*, 93, n. 3.
32   Smiths or ironmongers.
33   Writers of Court hand [Scriveners].
34   Sheath-maker?
35   Girdlers.
36   Illuminators of text.
37   Makers of travelling bags.
38   Cordwainers or leather dresser, tawyer.
39   Leeches: informal healers.
40   Dealer in various articles, including hats and caps.
41   Workers in iron, smiths, or possibly farriers.
42   Locksmiths.
43   Cutlers.
44   Polishers of metal, especially armour.
45   Dealers in second-hand clothing.
46   Retailer of victuals from door to door. See *Cal. Letter-Book, G*, 123, n. 6.
47   Worker in or maker of latten, a mixed metal resembling brass.
48   Wool weavers.
49   Cofferers: makers of coffers.
50   One who sets or lays stone.

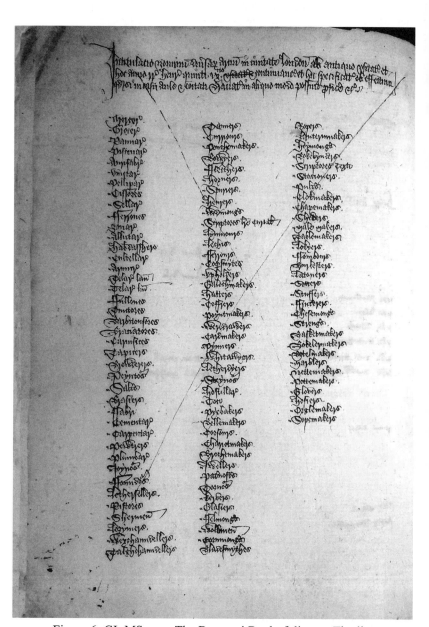

Figure 6. GL MS 5440 The Brewers' Book, folio 11v. The list
of Crafts in London c.1421–22. © The Brewers' Company.

Telarii Linearum[51]   Poyntmakers[52]   Stuffers[53]
Fullones[54]   Weredrawers[55]   Fruterers
Tinctores[56]   Cardmakers   Chesemongers
Barbitonsores[57]   Pynners   Strengers[58]
Braciatores[59]   Whitawyers[60]   Basketmakers
Carnifices[61]   Letherdyers   Bokelermakers[62]
Tapicers[63]   Steynours[64]   Botelmakers
Browderers[65]   Hostilarii[66]   Marblers[67]
Peyntours[68]   Coci[69]   Nettemakers
Salters   Pyebakers   Pottemakers
Brasiers[70]   Bellemakers   Glovers
Fabri[71]   Corsours[72]   Hosiers
Cementarii[73]   Chariotmakers   Orglemakers[74]
Carpentarii   Brochemakers[75]   Sopemakers.
Pewtrers[76]   Jwellers
Plumbarii[77]   Paternosters
Joynours[78]   Tornours
Foundours[79]   Kervers[80]
Lethersellers   Glasiers
Pistores[81]

[51] Linen weavers.
[52] Maker of points (laces).
[53] One who stuffs cushions?
[54] Cloth-fullers.
[55] Wire-drawers: draw metal into wire.
[56] Dyers.
[57] Barbers.
[58] Makers of strings for bows or instruments.
[59] Brewers.
[60] Maker of white leather, or leather for saddles and harness.
[61] Butchers.
[62] Bucklers: makers of buckles.
[63] Tapestry weavers.
[64] Stainers, usually of leather.
[65] Embroiderers.
[66] Innkeepers.
[67] Workers in marble: makers of tombs.
[68] Painters.
[69] Cooks.
[70] Workers in brass.
[71] Smiths.
[72] Couriers or horse dealers.
[73] Masons or plasterers.
[74] Organ makers.
[75] Makers of skewers and spits.
[76] Pewterers.
[77] Plumbers.
[78] Joiners.
[79] Founders. Those who found or cast metal to make objects.
[80] Carvers in wood.
[81] Bakers.

Shermenne[82]	Felmongers[83]
Lorymers[84]	Wollmen
Wexchanndellers	Cornmongers
Tallghchandellers[85]	Bladesmythes

[28] [f. 12r]

[*French*] **The costs of a dinner made by the aforesaid Masters** [William atte Wode, William Ederiche, John Reyner, William Ferrour the Elder] [*scored*: these are parcels of a dinner made on] **on 5th September in the 7th year of the reign of King Henry V** [1419] **and other persons who were Masters** [*scored*: in the year before or lately of our said] **of the mistery and aforesaid fraternity in times past, and others of the same fraternity.**

First 2 necks of mutton, 3 breasts, 12 marrow bones, and portage of a quarter of coals,	2s. 5d.
Item for 6 swans	15s.
Item for 12 conies[86]	3s.
Item for 200 eggs	18d.
Item for 2 gallons of frumenty[87]	4d.
Item for 2 gallons of cream	8d.
Item for 4 gallons of milk	4d.
Item for white bread	2s.
Item for trencher bread[88]	3d.
Item for mayn cakes[89]	6d.
Item for half a bushel of flour	7d.
Item for 1 kilderkin of good ale	2s. 4d.
Item for the hire of 2 dozen earthen pots	4d.
Item for 2 dozen white cups	6d.
Item for various spices	2s. 4d.
Item for portage of water, to the water bearers	4d.
Item for 1 pottle of fresh grease[90]	8d.
Item for 4 dozen pigeons	4s. 4d.
Item for 100 pears	7d.
Item for 11 gallons of red wine	9s. 2d.
Item given to the Minstrels	16d.
Item given to John Hardy, Cook, for himself and for his servants	3s. 4d.
Item given to William Devenyssh, panter	6d.
Item for 1 quart vinegar	1d.

---

82   Shearers of woollen cloth.
83   Those dealing in animal skins.
84   Maker of metal bits and mountings for horse bridles.
85   Tallowchandlers.
86   Rabbits.
87   Hulled wheat boiled in milk, flavoured with cinnamon and sugar.
88   Loaves made of coarse flour. The slices were used as disposable plates.
89   Fine quality wheaten bread, pandemain.
90   Liquid melted fat or lard. Pottle: Jug or tankard containing half a gallon.

Item for pack thread[91]	1*d.*
Item for the hire of 2 dozen pewter vessels	14*d.*
Item for 1 quart of honey with a new pot	4*d.*
Item for salt	1*d.*
Item for carrying out dung	½*d.*
Item for the laundry of napery	4*d.*

Sum total: 55*s.* 3½*d.*

[*scored*: without faggots and coals]

[29] [f. 12v]
The Ordinance for our Feast in this Year [1419]

The First Course
Brawn with mustard
Cabbages in pottage
Swan Standard[92]
Capons Roasted
Grand Custards

The Second Course
Venison in broth with white mortrewes[93]
Cony standard
Partridges with cocks, roasted
Leche Lumbard[94]
Dowcettes[95] with little pastries

The Third Course
Pears in syrup
Large birds mixed with small
Fritters[96]
Payn puff[97] with a cold bake-meat[98]

---

91 Strong thread for tying bundles.
92 Perhaps served in an upright position.
93 Thick stew or pottage with meat or fish.
94 Sliced meat with eggs, fruits, spices in jelly, or spiced, boiled pudding with dried fruits and eggs in wine and almond and milk sauce, Constance Hieatt and S. Butler, eds, *Curye on Inglysch: English Culinary Manuscripts of the Fourteenth Century (Including the Forme of Cury)* (London and New York, 1985), 197.
95 Sweet custard or sweetened meat pie.
96 Fried batter, with apples and herbs.
97 Round pastry as a coffin or pie, Hieatt, *Curye*, 204.
98 Pastry, a pie.

[30] [f. 13r]
The expenses for the same Feast

First, the Saturday [2 September 1419] next before the Feast for oysters and
mussels 5d.
Item for herbs 1d.
Item for baked herring with fresh herring 15d.
Item for salmon 21d.
Item for 1 codling head 8d.
Item for 5 pikes 6s. 8d.
Item for lampreys 13d.
Item for turbot 3s. 4d.
Item for porpoise 10d.
Item for eels 2s. 4d.

Sum 18s. 5d.

For the Pantry
First for chete bread[99] 11s. 7½d.
Item for white bread 7s.
Item for mayn cakes 2s. **Sum 26s. 5½d.**
Item for trencher bread 16d.
Item for 2 bushels of coarse flour 2s. 6d.
Item for 1 bushel of fine flour 2s.

For the Buttery
First for 1 hogshead of red wine 53s. 4d.
Item paid to 4 porters for portage of the wine 18d.
Item paid for 4 barrels of best beer at 2d. the gallon, sum 18s. 8d.
Item for 1 barrel of beer at 1½d. the gallon, sum 3s. 8d.
Item for 1 kilderkin of penny ale 12d. **Sum £4 5s. 6d.**
Item for 8 dozen white cups, price the dozen 8d., sum 5s. 4d.
Item for the hire of earthenware pots 23d.
Item for taps 1d.

For the Kitchen
First for cabbages and wortes[100] 9d.
Item for sanders[101] 1d.
Item for an oven for the baking of 200 custards and
wardens[102] 2s. 6d.
Item for wardens at other times 3s.
Item for 12 gallons of cream 4s. **Sum 22s. 8d.**
Item for 8 gallons of milk 8d.
Item for 100 faggots, 7 and a half quarters of coals 8s.
Item for 8 ells of linen for aprons for the cooks, price
the ell 5½d., sum 3s. 8d.

[99] Manchet, fine quality wheaten bread.
[100] Greens and leafy herbs.
[101] Red sandalwood or saunders.
[102] Old variety of baking pear.

[31] [f. 13v]
Poultry

First for 21 swans, price the piece 3s. 4d., sum	£3 10s.
Item given in reward for scalding the said swans	1d.
Item for 2 geese, price the piece 8d., sum	16d.
Item for 40 capons, price the piece 5d., sum	16s. 8d.
Item for portage of the same capons	2d.
Item for 43 conies, price the piece 3d., sum	10s. 9d.
Item for 37 partridges, price the piece 4d., sum	12s. 4d.
Item for 12 woodcocks, price the piece 4d., sum	4s.
Item for 11 dozen and a half [*dozen*] large birds, price each dozen 6d., sum	5s. 9d.
Item for 3 dozen plovers, price the dozen 3s., sum	9s.
Item for 18 dozen larks, price the dozen 4d., sum	6s.
Item for 6 dozen small birds, price the dozen 1½d., sum	9d.
Item for 900 eggs at 14d. the hundred,	10s. 6d.

Sum £7 7s. 4d.

Butchery

First for 60 marrow bones with crushed marrow	5s.
Item for carriage of the said marrow bones	4d.
Item for costs encountered during the purveyance of the same marrow bones	3d.
Item for 2 rounds of beef with fillets of pork	10d.
Item for 5 pieces of suet of Cheap, that is, neats tallow and tharnes[103]	17d.
Item for 3 gallons and a half of fresh grease, price the gallon 16d., sum	4s. 8d.
Item for 1 boar bought from John Bray, butcher,	10s.

Sum 22s. 6d.

Spicery

First for 1 lb and a half of powder of pepper	3s.
Item for half a quarteron of saffron	2s. 8d.
Item for 1 lb *canell*[104]	20d.
Item for 1 lb ginger	20d.
Item for 1 quarteron of cloves	9d.
Item for 1 quarteron of mace	9d.
Item for 16 lbs almonds called *Valens*,[105] price the pound 2d., sum	2s. 8d.
Item for 11 lbs dates, price the pound 3d., sum	2s. 9d.
Item for 4 lbs raisins of Corinth[106]	12d.
Item for 3 lbs rice flour	9d.

Sum £2 2s.

---

[103] Neats: cattle. Tallow: hard fat from around kidneys of animals. Tharnes: entrails. See f. 257v for the description 'tharnes called guts'.
[104] Cinnamon, perhaps including the similar but inferior Cassia bark.
[105] Of Valencia.
[106] Raisins of Corauntz or Corinth, now called currants.

Item for half lb of sanders	6*d.*
Item for 1 lb aniseed powder	4*d.*
Item for 4 lbs damask prunes	12*d.*
Item for 2 lbs white sugar	3*s.*
Item for 1 lb aniseed in comfit	16*s.*
Item for 3 gallons of fine honey	3*s.* 6*d.*

[32] [f. 14r]
Grocery

First for 1 peck *Berflete* salt[107]	4¾*d.*	
Item for 1 peck onions	2½*d.*	
Item for garlic	½*d.*	
Item for 1 gallon, 1 pottle and 1 pint of honey	23*d.*	
Item for 1 quarter of galantine[108]	1½*d.*	
Item for 1 pottle ginger	3*d.*	**Sum 4*s.* 9¾*d.***
Item for 1 gallon of mustard	6*d.*	
Item for 1 gallon & 1 quart of vinegar	5*d.*	
Item for 1 quart of verjuice[109]	1*d.*	
Item for pack thread	2*d.*	
Item for 5 lbs of cotton candle	7½*d.*	
Item for oatmeal	1*d.*	

[33]
Rewards made and given as appears
[*scored*: expenses made to diverse officers written]

First to the players of 2 harps as appears [*scored*: one was a Welshman] and to other minstrels, Kyngeston Surveour, and to Thomas Wakefelde, porter,	10*s.* 10*d.*	
Item to John Hardy, Cook, for himself and for his servants	22*s.*	
Item to the *turnbrochers*[110]	18*d.*	
Item to John Hardy for carriage of diverse things and vessels in a cart, for the kitchen, that is, pots, pans, spits, racks, fat trays,	8*d.*	**Sum 58*s.* 5*d.***
Item to William Devenyssh, panter,	6*s.* 8*d.*	
Item to a servant of the pantry	8*d.*	
Item to William atte Lee, pewterer, for the hire of 18 dozen pewter vessels,	10*s.*	
Item for portage of the same vessels	1*d.*	
Item to William Cophode for venison	6*s.*	

---

[107] Salt from a special place, perhaps Benfleet, Essex, which has a saltmarsh area.
[108] Sauce served with fish or poultry, made from the jellied juices, spiced and thickened with breadcrumbs.
[109] Sour juice of unripe grapes or crab apples.
[110] Turnspits.

Expenses for Necessaries

First for hooks, clowes & trashes[III]	3d.	
Item for 8 burdens of rushes, with carriage	2s. 4d.	
Item to [*above the line*: another painter for] the amendment of the [*scored*: garlands] chaplets[112] of the Masters	12d.	**Sum 4s. 4d.**
Item for the laundry of the board cloths	6d.	
Item for carriage of dung	3d.	

Item for the Monday next following after the feast, for 17 hens	4s. 5d.	**Sum 7s. 3d.**
Item for 1 dozen conies	2s. 10d.	

[*scored*: Item given in reward for venison to William Cophode 6s.]

Sum for the aforesaid Feast on the Sunday with the previous Saturday and the Monday after, £21 5s. ¼d.

[34] [f. 14v]

[*Latin*] **These are the names of the brothers and sisters of the craft of Brewers who were in the present year at our Hall on the day of our Feast and who paid, as appears hereafter**

[*French*] Adam Copendale for himself	12d.	John Assh for himself and his wife	2s.
Agnes Stratton for herself	12d.	John Soughtmede for himself	16d.
		John Lynne for himself	16d.
Dederyk Claysson, Dutchman, for himself	16d.	John Merston for himself	16d.
		John Moyle for himself	16d.
		John Riche, tailor,	16d.
Henry Lymber for himself	12d.	Michael Eve for himself and his	
Henry Fereby for himself	16d.	wife	2s.
Henry Trebolans for himself	16d.	Michael Tregononne for himself	16d.
Hugh Glene for himself	16d.		
		Nicholas Muryell for himself	16d.
John Thetford for himself	12d.	Nicholas Kene for himself	12d.
John Philippe for himself	16d.	Nicholas Aleyn for himself	12d.
John Ketyng for himself and his wife	2s.	Peter Carpenter for himself and	
John Riche of Wood Street for himself	12d.	his wife	2s.
		Peter Roos for himself	16d.
John More at Ludgate for himself and his wife	2s.	Richard Rowdon for himself and	
John Stannton for himself and his wife	2s.	his wife	2s.
		Robert Smyth for himself	2s.

III Hooks, clowes (balls of twine) and trash-nails, perhaps used for fixing scenery and decoration.

112 Wreath for the head, usually a garland of flowers.

John Kenaky for himself	16d.	Robert Hiltone for himself	12d.
John Erle for himself	12d.	Robert Carpenter for himself and	
John Pykeyne for himself	16d.	his wife	2s.
John Brook for himself and his wife	2s.	Roger Blissot for himself	16d.
John Caryen for himself and his		Richard Aleyn for himself and	
wife	2s.	his wife	2s.
John Eylond for himself	16d.	Richard Neweman for himself	
John Laurence for himself	16d.	and his wife	2s.
John Brewester for himself and		Robert Nykke for himself and his	
his wife	2s.	wife	2s.
John Basset for himself	12d.	Robert Elkyn for himself	16d.
John Refawe for himself	16d.	Robert Tanner for himself	16d.
John Turvey for himself and his		Richard Rose of Southwark for	
wife	2s.	himself	12d.
John Humbre for himself	16d.		
John Stone for himself	16d.		
John Sere for himself	16d.		
John Turnour for himself	16d.		
John Gedeney for himself	16d.		

[35] [f. 15r]

Simon Potkyn for himself	16d.	**[36]**	
Stephen Roo for himself	16d.	[*Latin*] **These are the names of the**	
		brothers and sisters who did not come	
Thomas Emond for himself	12d.	**to our Hall on the day of our Feast**	
Thomas Hatcher for himself	12d.	**and who paid the following amounts**	
Thomas Grene for himself and			
his wife	2s.	Agnes Bugge	12d.
Thomas Aleyn for himself	16d.	John Aleyn, baker	7d.
Thomas Hankcok for himself	16d.	Robert Jewell, grocer	16d.
Thomas Gratley for himself	16d.	William Petevyle	12d.
Thomas Ayle for himself and his		William Canon	12d.
wife	2s.		
Thomas Osbarne for himself	16d.	**Sum received for our Feast**	
		£6 11d.	
William atte Welle for himself			
and his wife	2s.	**These are the persons who were**	
William Gedney for himself	16d.	**present on the day of our Feast in our**	
William Bracy for himself and		**hall, who were served with full service**	
his wife	2s.	**without payment received or sought**	
William Cardell for himself and		**for their dinner**	
his wife	2s.		
Walter Colshull for himself	16d.	Sir Robert Steynton, chaplain	
William Bernard for himself	16d.	Henry Anketyll, shearman	
William Robert for himself and		John Ryngesson, tailor	
his wife	2s.	John Fykays	
William Smalsho for himself and		Thomas Webbe	
his wife	2s.	William Cophode, maltman	
William Payn for himself	16d.	Johanna, the wife of William Koke who	
William John for himself	16d.	was once a Master, pauper	

Walter Glyn for himself	16*d.*
William Bodevyle for himself	16*d.*
William Bacon for himself	16*d.*
William Crane for himself	12*d.*
William Termeday for himself	16*d.*
Walter Copseye for himself	16*d.*

The 4 Masters and their 4 wives

**These are the names of those not of
our fraternity but present at the Feast
on our principal day**

The Rector of All Hallows London Wall
Hegge, attorney in the Guildhall
Heywode, beadle
William Petham, aletaker
A certain chaplain
John Steven
A stranger with Cophode
A stranger with Rowdon
Three strangers, two men and a woman

[37]
**These are the names of the persons who were clothed of the livery of the
Brewers but not of our fraternity of Brewers who were with us at our hall and
paid well and faithfully as is shown above**
John Riche, tailor
Robert Elkyn
Thomas Ayle for his wife.

[f. 15v]

[*Latin*] [*scored*: Names entered in the book of the four Masters]

[38]
**Here are noted the expenses made for a Breakfast after the day of account of
the said Masters, to wit William atte Wode and his fellows, on the 13th day of
February in the 7th year of the reign of King Henry V** [1420]

[*Scored*: And on the same day the Masters at that time, to wit Thomas Grene, Robert
Hyltone, Robert Carpenter and John Pyken,[113] with the counsel and unanimous
consent of all the Masters of the Brewers' craft, licensed and granted to William
Porlond, common clerk of the aforesaid craft, to his wife, children and servants, free
and quiet dwelling in the hall of the company commonly called Brewers' Hall, with
the use of the chamber and of other utensils and necessaries belonging to the said
hall].

[*French*]
The First Course

Gruel made as pottage
Parcels of pork in green sauce

---

[113] Masters 1419–21: atte Wode was one of the masters 1418–19, and then a searcher or
warden **[97]**.

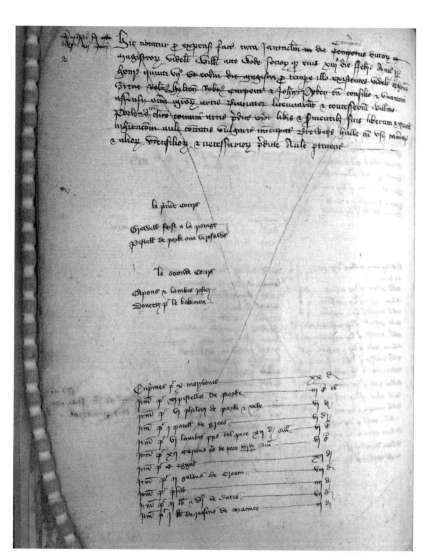

Figure 7. GL MS 5440 The Brewers' Book, folio 15v.
Entries in Latin and French. © The Brewers' Company.

The Second Course

Roast capons and lamb
Doucettes for the bake-meat

First 10 marrow bones	20*d.*
Item for 11 parcels of pork	3*s.* ½*d.*
Item for 6 fillets of pork and veal	6*d.*
Item for 1 pottle of grease	6*d.*
Item for 6 lambs, price each	12*d.*, sum 6*s.*
Item for 12 capons, price 6*d.* each, sum	6*s.*
Item for 100 eggs	12*d.*
Item for 2 gallons of cream	8*d.*
Item for parsley	4*d.*
Item for 2 lbs and a half of dates	7*d.*
Item for 2 lbs of raisins of Corinth	3*d.*

[f. 16r]

Item for saffron	2*d.*
Item for diverse sauces at the chandler[114]	8*d.*
Item for white bread	20*d.*
Item for trencher bread	4*d.*
Item for coarse flour	3*d.*
Item for 1 kilderkin of ale	2*s.* 4*d.*
Item paid to water bearers for portage of water	3*d.*
Item paid to John Hardy, Cook, for himself and his servants for their work	3*s.* 4*d.*
Item for 3 gallons of red wine	2*s.*
Item for laundry of board cloths	2*d.*
Item for carrying out dung	4½*d.*
Item for 2 earthenware pots	1*d.*
Item for the hire of pewter vessels	6*d.*

Sum 32s. 8d.

Sum total for this dinner with our feast, and another dinner made on the 5th day of September [1419] as has been written before £25 12s. 11¾d.

[39]

[*Latin*] In this year William Payne, living at that time at the Swan beside the Hospital of St Antony in the parish of St Benet Fink, became rebellious and acted against the Masters of the craft of Brewers at the time, because in that year, it was ordered by the mayor and aldermen of London that ale should be sent to our Lord King, then being over the sea. The mayor ordered the Masters of the craft of Brewers and certain other Masters of their crafts to contribute one or two barrels of ale. And at that time the aforesaid William Payne withdrew his ale from the mayor and the Masters, that is John Thetford, Thomas Emond, Walter Riche and Henry

---

114   A supplier of candles, or a retailer in provisions and groceries.

Lymber and did not wish to give ale to the King.[115] Because of this, the said mayor
sent him to Newgate prison and he spent one or two days there. His friends pleaded
with the mayor that he might be delivered from prison and went to the mayor to
seek pardon and to plead for him, and thus it was granted to him, on condition that
he sought mercy from the aforesaid Masters for his misdemeanour, and that he
behaved well, especially towards the aforesaid Masters, and upon condition that he
paid 3s. 4d. for a swan. Thus it was granted to him afterwards. Soon the Masters
held a breakfast at Brewers' Hall and the aforesaid William Payne was present and
had his share of the swan. Afterwards however, the aforesaid Masters sought 3s. 4d.
from him for the swan, as he had promised. He responded that they should have the
money, many times, but he did not pay.

[40] [f. 16v]

And he did not pay what he owed to them that year. On account of which, he was
dismissed from his office.[116] The next Masters, that is to say, William atte Wode,
William Ederich, William Ferrour and John Reyner, certified that the aforesaid
William Payne did not pay 3s. 4d. for his swan that he had promised to them for
his new debt. Then the aforesaid William atte Wode and his associates sent for the
aforesaid William Payne at various times to come to Brewers' Hall, but he did not
come. When however, he finally came, the same Masters were badly aggrieved
that he had not come to meet them. They wished him to make amends for his old
debt, and for his new debt. He replied that he wished to. And then the said Masters
ordered that he should pay 3s. 4d. for his new debt, that is to say for a swan, and
that he should come to the eating of his swan, and that he would have his share and
there he could pay 6s. 8d. for his old and new debts, and seek mercy for his ill will.
Afterwards, truly and within a short time, the aforesaid Masters sent livery clothes
of the Brewers to the said William Payne, but he did not wish to receive them and
protested strongly and was imprisoned. He said that he was not able to choose
and that it was against his will, and that he was in debt, and wished to buy better
clothing for his household. He did not wish to be levied for this in the present year,
nor in the following two years.

And afterwards, the aforesaid Masters, hearing his words, sent for him by the
clerk of their craft, to [be sent to] John Hyll, then chamberlain of the Guildhall
of London. Payne did not wish to come at their precept. They certified to the
chamberlain that Payne was rebellious and [acted] contrary to their advice. The
aforesaid John Hyll sent for him by a sergeant, under penalty of being close
confined. The said William came to the Guildhall and there met the Masters and
spoke before them. Then the Masters said that they had certified to the chamberlain
that he was rebellious, and that he would lose 10s. and be thrown into prison for
ten days. Then Payne became very much afraid and sought mercy and pardon and
promised to amend his debt.

And thus with the consent of those Masters and of William Payne, two men, that is
to say Robert Smyth and Thomas Grene, were elected to make the amendment to his
debt. They ordained that he should seek pardon from the Masters and ordained that

---

[115] Masters 1416–18, succeeded by atte Wode, Ederich, Ferrour and Reyner, 1418–19.
[116] It is unclear what office Payne held. He was not listed as a master at this time. The
searchers and wardens were not listed in the *City of London Letter-Book* for this year.

he should ride with the mayor in his entire livery and be present at a breakfast in Brewers' Hall for the Masters and the said Robert & Thomas.

This breakfast was held at the house of John Hardy, Cook, for which the aforesaid William Payne paid 4s. 3½d., and he was thus excused. Afterwards he governed himself well and honestly, towards these and the other subsequent Masters.

[41] [f. 17r]
This present writing declares and notifies that the aforesaid Masters, that is, William atte Wode and his fellows, have completely and wholly given their account for the foregoing year [1418–19] on the day and year rendered above. Also they have rendered to the commonalty of the fraternity aforesaid for every freeman admitted in that year to the freedom [*scored*: London] in the craft of the Brewers [*above the line*: London] 6s. 8d., and for each brother admitted to the fraternity 3s. 4d., according to an ancient custom ordained and approved by the unanimous assent of the brothers, as appears in an ancient paper [*above the line*: with a red calf-skin binding] in the fourth quire and first folio, and as an example and for the information of future successors, to be regarded and observed.

[42]
The account of William atte Wode, William Ederich, William Ferrour, John Reyner, Masters of the fraternity of All Hallows beside London Wall, of all receipts for the use and profit of the aforesaid fraternity at the Feast of All Hallows [1 November 1418] in the 6ᵗʰ year of the reign of King Henry V until the same feast of All Hallows in this next year [1419] that is, for a whole year.

Received for the preceding year
First they account for £11 7s., received from the delivery and surplus rendered from John Thetford, Thomas Emond, Walter Riche and Henry Lymber [1416–18], last Masters of the said fraternity.
And there remains in the company box from the preceding year

Sum £11 7s.

Rent received for the year
The same account for 26s. 8d. by them received for rent from the tenement beside the gate of the Hall, that is, for the year during the time of this account.

Sum 26s. 8d.

[43] [f. 17v]
Received for Hire of the Hall
They account for 9s. 10d. received by them for the hire of the hall, that is, 18d. from the company of Weavers; from the Master Clerks 2s.; from the Coopers 2s.; from the Latteners 3s. 4d.; and from the Point-makers for one quarter 12d.

Sum 9s. 10d.

Received for admission to the freedom
The Masters deliver £5 13s. 4d. from seventeen men admitted to the freedom during the time of this account, that is

71

William Hyllyng
Thomas Webbe
Roger Blissote
Henry Grene
John Froste
Gilbert Botonne
William Knott
William Gros
Morias Tranayll
William Rykherst
John Ferman
John Beauchamp
John Cheseman
Stephen Clean
Robert Staple
John Yver
Dederic Claysson
That is, from each of them, 6*s.* 8*d.*

Sum £5 13*s.* 4*d.*

Those admitted to the freedom without payment, that is
Henry Forteyn admitted at the instance of the mayor[117]
John Laurence at the instance of John Stantonne

[44]
Entry to the Fraternity
The same delivered for the entries for twenty-four brothers received during the time
of this account, that is
John Lumbard
Michael Tregononne
John Basset
William Gros
Morias Tranaill
Sir Robert Steynton
William Porlond
Walter Glyn
John Laurence
Roger Blissote
Nicholas Agomnailok
Thomas Hancok
John Aleyn, baker
William Yllyng
William Termeday
William Baylly
John Toke
William Botiler

---

[117]   William Sevenoke, mayor 1418–19.

Robert Walram
Robert Pede
Dederick Clayssone
John Elsy
Thomas Webbe
Walter Copeseye
That is from each of them 3s. 4d.

Sum £4.

Quarterage received from the brothers and sisters
The same deliver £10 6s. 9d. received from the brothers and sisters of the abovesaid fraternity according to the said account for the year, as appears in a certain schedule of the names and sums recorded in this particular account.

Sum £10 6s. 9d.

[45] [f. 18r]
Testamentary Legacies
The same rendered 6s. 8d. from the legacy of John Turmyn

Sum 6s. 8d.

Sum total of receipts £33 10s. 3d.
Expenses by the said Masters for the profit and use of the said fraternity during the time of this account

Wax in the Chapel
First for wax used in the chapel 20 lbs new wax, price the lb 5½d.
Item for making old wax 6 lbs, price the lb ½d. Sum 9s. 5½d.

Sum 9s. 5½d.

Stipends
Item paid to Sir Edmund, chaplain,[118] for one quarter and 8 weeks, 53s. 4d.
Item paid to Sir Robert [Steynton], chaplain, for half a year £3 6s. 8d.
Item to William [Porlond], the clerk, for three quarters of a year and a half 33s. 4d.[119]

Sum £7 13s. 4d.

Bread and Wine for the Chapel
Item paid for bread and wine for use in the chapel bought within the time of this account 12d.

Sum 12d.

[118] Sir Edmund was probably Robert Steynton's predecessor as fraternity chaplain.
[119] Porlond's salary was 40s. yearly, so this payment for three and a half quarters is 1s. 8d. short. Later in the book he referred to 'advantages' or bonuses, and 'casualties' or incidental charges in his payments, which may explain this [330].

Alms given

Item in alms given as appears to a certain Johanna Cole in alms for a year, 30s. 4d.
Also to a certain poor woman, the widow of William Cook for a year, 30s. 4d.

Sum £3 8d.

[46] [f. 18v]
Customary payments

Item to the Rector of Aldermanbury[120] for his oblations for the year 3s. 4d.
Item to the parish clerk there for the year, by custom 12d.
Item for holy bread there, 4d.
Item in one wreath called a rose garland rendered for rent for our Hall 1d.[121]
Item payment to the parish clerk of All Hallows London Wall[122] abovesaid, for the year during the time of this account, 12d.

Sum 5s. 9d.

[47]
Repairs Made

Item paid in repairs to the Hall, that is for timber boards for repairs to the latrine 2s. 8d.
Item paid to a certain carpenter for two days 16d.
Item for keys & *nonsshyns*[123] 2½d.
Item for nails, clickets,[124] staples and for mending a lock
[*above the line*: 16d. and for one bucket with mending]
Item for mending the iron fountain there 20d.
Item for one labourer for mending the gutter and other things 13½d.
Item for carriage of two loads of robux[125] 8d.
Item given to the tenant there 3d.
Item for one labourer for mending a gutter in the middle of the Hall there 2d.
Item for inscribing the names of the brothers and sisters upon the table 4d.

Sum 9s. 9d.

Trentals

Item paid for trentals[126] during the time of this account, for the soul of
John Turmyn

---

[120] St Mary Aldermanbury was the Brewers' parish church and became their fraternity church in 1438, see ff. 290v, 305r.
[121] Payment for a rose garland for rent of the Hall was recorded annually. The former Brewers' archivist, Jerome Farrell, traced this to a deed of enfeoffment of 1291–2 from Walter of Fychingefeld, citizen, goldsmith and alderman of London, which required the annual rose garland quit rent to be paid at the feast of the Nativity of John the Baptist (24 June), CLC/L/BF/G/143/MS05503 [sub number 1]. See Introduction, 16–19.
[122] All Hallows London Wall was the Brewers' fraternity church until 1438, ff. 290v, 305r.
[123] A drink or snack taken in the afternoon.
[124] Clicket: latch of a door or gate.
[125] Refuse, debris.
[126] A set of thirty requiem masses.

Richard Hetersete
Roger Stoktonne
Walter Riche
Richard Storme, that is, paid for each of these, 2s. 6d.

Sum 12s. 6d.

Rewards given
Item for 4 hoods for the use of fraternity given to various men, 20s., that is
Sir Robert, fraternity chaplain
William Petham[127]
Thomas Donyngton
& William Devenyssh

Sum 20s.

Fees Paid
Item to the aforesaid Thomas Donyngton for his fee for the whole year during the
time of this account, 6s. 8d.

Sum 6s. 8d.

[f. 19r]
Parchment, paper and ink
Item for parchment, paper and ink during the time of this account for the said year 2s.

Sum 2s.

Sum total of expenses £14 13½d.

[*scored*: And thus there remains in the common box for the use and profit of the
aforesaid fraternity in the clear £19 9s. ½d.]

[48]
[*English*]
This is a process[128] that was made because of the toll of malt, as it shows, with all
the working that was done before, as you may find afterwards, kept by diverse bills
[*above the line*: written], one long and the other [*in*] short form. And in the same
bills mention is made of the said toll, with the rewards, and the salary, for each
brewersman, what he shall take for the year for his said salary, as the bills make
mention of the same matter, and also the said two bills make mention of foreign beer
brewers who retail their beer, to great harm of the Brewers' craft of London.[129]

---

127   Pethin was the aletaker [36]. Donyngton was a sergeant at the chamber of the Guildhall,
     sometimes employed by the Brewers [186]. Devenyssh was listed as a panter, panterer
     and once as a tailor, and may have been the Brewers' steward in charge of the pantry
     [28].
128   This section, dated 1424–5, has been added later, on a formerly blank page.
129   This is the first mention of beer rather than ale, and of foreign beer brewers, seen here
     as a threat to the Brewers' craft.

Be it remembered that in the time of John Michell, mayor of London [1424–5], John Seman and John atte Water, being sheriffs at the same time, that is to wit in the 3rd year of the reign of King Henry the Sixth after the Conquest [1424–5], the said John Seman and John at the Water, sheriffs, did enhance and *heyne*[130] the tolls at the gates of London by [*up to*] £10 higher than it had been before that time, as men said. Whereupon Thomas Goodyng, brewer and citizen of London, a franchised [*above the line:* man] had malt and other things coming in at Bishopsgate, upon foreign horse, whereupon the toll collector at that place, being constrained for the toll of the malts, [*charged for*] a quarter of malt with an halter, and upon that, the same Thomas Goodyng went and complained to the Masters of the craft, whereupon the Masters went to the mayor and complained in this wise and said that no freeman of London should pay any toll, according to old records that had been granted in olden times. And thereupon the mayor said that no freeman should pay any toll for his merchandise carried upon his own horse or cart, but that for those that were led by a foreigner,[131] the foreigner should pay. Whereupon the aforesaid Masters said that by their aforesaid grant of kings, who had been [*kings*] before, that [*whether*] by ships, boats, horse and carts, no freeman of London should pay any toll, neither by water nor by land.

And upon this the said mayor commanded John Carpenter, the common clerk of the Guildhall, to look [*scored:* the record] out the record, the record in the hall, [*to see*] if there were any such ordinance. And thereupon, he did so and came again to the mayor and said there was none in the book of record, but in a little quire beside, which stood for no record, and thereupon the mayor bade them go home until he sent for them.

It was said and told by various persons that there was a pannier with apples, which was sent for a present and therefore [*yet*] he [*the collector*] took for the toll an halfpenny.[132] Examined.

[49] [f. 19v]

[*Latin*]

Ordinances needful for the whole commons of the city of London, required of the mayor and aldermen of that city, by the Brewers, because they would not pay any toll for their malt and other victuals coming to the said city.

[*Copy of the minutes of two Courts of Common Council:*]

On Monday, the 7th day of September in the 3rd year of the reign of King Henry IV after the conquest of England [1402].

Those present were

John Shadworth, mayor [1401–2], Matthew Suthworthe, recorder, John Hadlee, William Stannden, Richard Whytyngton, Drew Barentyn, Thomas Knolle, John Fraunceys, John Walcote, William Parker, John Warner, William Venour, sheriff, John Wakeler, Geoffrey Broke, & Thomas Polle, aldermen, as well as others in the Court of Common Council at that time.

---

130   Raise.

131   One from another district, outside the city's jurisdiction, and not a member of a particular guild.

132   This anecdote about a heavy toll on apples, which were a gift and not for sale, has been added to illustrate the unfairness of the increased tolls.

Supplication was made to the said mayor and aldermen by the aforesaid Common Council that since all citizens of the said city by virtue of its charters, conceded by various kings of England and confirmed by our present King, should be quit of every toll and custom by the whole power of the King for carriage hither and thither from sea to sea and through the ports on this side of the sea or beyond, it was conceded unanimously by the said mayor, recorder, sheriffs and aldermen that no minister of the said city should henceforth take any tolls and customs from the said citizens of the said city for merchandise, victuals and necessary goods brought to the said city by ships, boats, horses or carts, in whatever way brought into the city or taken away from it.

[50]
On Tuesday, the 12ᵗʰ day of May in the year abovesaid [1403][133] in the presence of the said mayor, William Venour, William Fremelyngham, sheriffs, John Hadlee, John Hende, William Stanndon, Richard Whytyngton, Thomas Knolles, John Fraunceys, John Walcote, John Wodecok, William Parker, William Brampton, William Askeham, John Warner, Thomas Wilford, John Wakelee, William Walderne, Thomas Polle & Thomas Falconer, aldermen also of the Common Council and others of the Common Council were summoned by the clerks of the wards.
It was agreed unanimously and affirmed that no citizen of London should pay any toll and custom for their goods, merchandise or victuals entering the gates of the city, nor for goods, merchandise and victuals brought there on horses, ships, boats and carts.
And neither by horse, ships, boats or carts in this way [*for*] goods, merchandise, or victuals should pay tolls, at whichever gate of the said city they are.

[51]
[*English*] This is a bill made to the mayor and to the aldermen of London about the toll of malt and other things and for wages and salaries that Brewers' men should take and also for foreign beer brewers about retailing their beer, as it shows in the bills afterwards.

To the right worshipful and discreet mayor and aldermen of the city of London, we, your servants all the Brewers, citizens of the same city, beseech meekly and charitably for the common profit, for as much as during about the first and second year of King Henry IV [1399–1401], progenitor of our Liege Lord now, was unduly used[134] by diverse servants, officers of the said city, to take toll and custom for the goods, merchandise and victuals belonging to citizens of the same city, carried and brought on ships, carts, horse, at all the ports of the said city, against the liberty of the same city.
There in the 3ʳᵈ year of the reign of the [*scored*: king] said King Henry IV [1401–2], a supplication was presented to John Shadworth, then mayor, and to the worthy aldermen of the said city at that time, comprehending that all the citizens of the same city from that time forward, might be quit of all manner of toll and custom, by all Kings' power, as well on this side of the sea as on the other side, after the form and effect of the Kings' charters, granted and conceded to them from ancient time.

---

133   May 1402, in the third year, or perhaps May 1403, in the fourth year of King Henry IV.
134   Accustomed.

Wherefore on the 12th day of May in the said 3rd year of the reign of King Henry IV [1401–2] abovesaid, in the Guildhall of the same city, by the said mayor, Mayken Suthworth, recorder, William Fremlingham [*continued at* [23] *on f. 20r*]

[f. 20r]

[*Latin*] **The Oath of Freemen admitted
to the Freedom of the City of London**

[52]

[*French*] You vow that you will serve the King, Henry, King of England, and his heirs royal loyally.

And will be obedient to the mayor & masters who guard the city according to the franchise and customs of the said city, maintaining, by your power and that of the city government, vested in you, guarding and taking, without damage, in all things touching the city, contributions and ancient tolls and other charges like other freemen of the said city.

You vow not to take the goods of foreigners, which the king may take, by custom.

You will not take any apprentice less than 7 years old, and you will enrol their fee in the first year of your covenant, and at the end of their term, if they are good and have behaved well and loyally, to enrol them.

And if you know of foreign merchants of the craft in the city, [*you are*] to warn the chamberlain or the sergeants of the chamber.

You vow not to plead [*against*] any man who is of the franchise of the said city, outside the same city, if you are able to have the right given by the ministers of the said city,

And if certain congregations assemble to act against the peace, you will warn the mayor of the time, and you will take no apprentice if he may not become a freeman, newly named.

[*margin* [*Latin*]: in L[ibro] H]

Treating the points abovesaid, you will guard them well and loyally, if God and his saints aid you. Examined.

[53]

[*English*] [*continued from folio 19v*] William Venour, sheriffs, John Hadley, John Hende, William Standonne, Richard Whitingtonne, Thomas Knolles, John Franceys, John Walcote, John Wodecok, William Parker, William Braunton, William Askham, John Warner, Thomas Wilford, John Wakelee, William Walderne, Thomas Polle and Thomas [*scored*: Faconer] Fawconer, then aldermen, and by that time a notable number of worthy commons of the same city, were chosen from all the wards and thereto summoned.

It was recorded, granted and fully affirmed and to be entered in the books of record in the said Guildhall, and so soon afterwards [*entered*] in a book of record, that no manner of citizen of the said city from that time forward, should pay any toll or custom at ports of the said city for their proper[135] goods, merchandise or victuals, even if the said goods, merchandise or victuals were brought to the same city or

---

135   Own.

carried there upon horse, ships, boats or carts belonging to strangers,[136] and that the same strangers should be quit of all manner of toll and custom at any port of the same city for their horse, ships, boats and carts, so carrying such said goods, merchandise or victuals of the said citizens, and moreover your said beseechers meekly beseech you to consider that aliens[137] dwelling near the city walls brew beer and sell it at retail within the said city

[54] [f. 20v]

freely as any of the said citizens who are at lotte[138] and all other charges of the said city do for their ale and other victuals, against the liberty of the said city [*scored*: as freely] and [*to the*] derogation of the common profit to the chamber of the said city, as it seems to them. Also your said beseechers grievously complain of the great grievance of their servants, sometimes servants by the year and sometimes by the day. The chief servant of the Brewers at that time took but 40s. for the year, with meat, drink and his clothing. And the second servant of the Brewers 33s. 4d., with meat, drink and clothing. Whereas now the said servants of the Brewers have made a confederacy and gathered themselves together and have made amongst them a brotherhood, against the law and good rule of the said city, and so have made an ordinance amongst them that they should not serve except by the week, the chief Brewers taking 2s. for the week with meat, drink & [*scored*: clothing] his advantages[139] and the second servant 16d. and 12d., with meat, drink and his advantages. Which is to your said beseechers a great hindering and undoing. Wherefore would you, according to your noble and wise discretion, put and ordain all such servants of the Brewers to serve by the year, taking yearly a salary by an ordinance made after your wise discretion, and that the pain[140] thereupon may run upon them, after the petitions which your said beseechers have put in before you, before this time, as it is of record. Wherefore may it please your high, pure bred and noble discretion to rule, govern and ordain such comenable[141] and sufficient remedy upon these matters aforesaid, for the ease and common profit, that the said beseechers thereby may also be eased & remedied, for God's love and in way of charity.

[55]

[*Latin*] In the 7th year of the reign of King Henry V [1419–20] on the morrow after St Martin,[142] in the month of November, the aforesaid Brewers of London, by their custom, held their feast in the hall of the commonalty of the craft of Brewers. And at that time the Masters were William atte Wode, William Ederych, William Ferrour, and John Reyner. And on that day Thomas Grene, Robert Hylton, Robert Carpenter and John Peken were elected as Masters, Richard Whytyngton, mercer, then being mayor of the city of London [1419–20], Robert Whetyngham, draper, and John Boteler, mercer, then being sheriffs of the same city.

---

[136] One not resident in a town.
[137] Non-English resident in the city of London.
[138] Paying scot and lot charges.
[139] 'Avanntages' and 'nanntages' both mean advantages or benefits.
[140] Penalty.
[141] Convenient, appropriate.
[142] 12 November, the morning after St Martin's Day, 11 November 1419.

And on the next Monday, at around the first hour of the day, on the day when the mayor came to office, he came with his household to the home of William Herry, beside the Stocks in the parish of St Mary Woolchurch, called Long Entry, and there a proclamation was made that he must sell all the ale at his house, namely 12 or 16 large vessels full of ale, for 1 penny a gallon.

Also on that day he came and gave the same advice in the same way, at the Unicorn in Lombard Street, at the Swan in Cornhill, at the Swan at St Anthony's and at the Cock in Fynkys Lane. Then the mayor used such a warning as he had made previously: if the ale was deficient in measure, the brewer was to be punished. It was commonly said

[56] [f. 21r]

that they had had fat swans at their feast for 30 or 40 years and more, whilst he said that he was paying for other causes. He sent by John Thetford for the former Masters, William atte Wode, William Ederych, William Ferrour and John Reyner, so that they should have a meeting with him in council before the judiciary court of the said King and faithfully deliver through his office.

He swore to observe his office faithfully and to punish the Masters and the newly elected Masters and others of the craft by his year, who were greatly troubled.

No money, raised by the commonalty, amongst the council, [*prevailed*] against the statute against the craft, in this book, and it would not lessen the anger of the mayor. The gallons must be pleasing to the prescription of the mayor. When they came into his presence in the hall of the mayor, he read out at length in a harsh voice, their misdeeds against him, and said that he would impose ruin upon them for their unlicensed fat swans and other delicacies that they ate and drank, to such a degree, and for the precious vestments and furs in the style of their said superiors, [*that they had*] and gold and silver and other goods in the commonalty, so that he asserted that by his authority they would pay for this and other, greater dishonesty. The Brewers were greatly troubled by these causes for the whole year, and not well disposed to approach his presence.

[57]

[*French*] Notwithstanding all the good ordinances and decisions made and established in these last hours, it is not possible to restrain the bad government that the Brewers of the city have made and observed. They sell their ale at excessive price, above the assize, without just measure, in their large and small vessels, that is to say barrels and kilderkins, gallons, pottles and quarts, which should all be seen and are liable to the ordinance made during the time of William Staunden, former mayor [1407–8] in the ninth year of King Henry IV [1407–8], when the ordinance was made, with grievous penalties, that all the Brewers of the city should, as agreed in friendship, have all their barrels, kilderkins & other vessels sealed and marked with a sign on the outside, by a deputy of the chamberlain, according to this ordinance, so that it can be known how much clear ale is contained within each vessel. The said Brewers paid little or no regard to this ordinance made before the ordinance that the vessels should be marked and sealed. Without the aforesaid mark, the common people can be deceived.

Richard Whityngtonne, the mayor, and the aldermen, with the assent of the commons, wished to procure due remedy against the said company. It was ordained and established by the authority of the said common council that the former ordinance in all points and articles, made in friendship for all days, was to be firmly guarded and held, together with this amendment. Similarly

[58] [f. 21v]
any brewer defaulting, having sold ale to any person, of whatsoever estate or condition he might be, by barrels, kilderkins or other vessels, unless they are marked with the seal according to the former ordinance, and contained in barrels, kilderkins or other vessels marked with a seal which shows what measure the mark or seal bears, according to the past ordinance, which thereupon treats the said vessels with a mark and those not marked with a mark, in the infallible & discernible manner abovesaid & for which the ale contained within them, or the same value, if the ale cannot be had, will be forfeited by the work of the commonalty upon the brewer who owes ale in this manner, barrels, kilderkins or other vessels, in which forfeitures the person who is the cause of the forfeiture of ale will have the half, after first declaring and disclosing to the mayor or chamberlain of the said city of London at that time.
Item the said mayor, aldermen and commons, by the authority of the present common council, ordain that [*according to*] the regulations ordained before by the mayor and chamberlain of the said city to mark or seal such vessels, those marked fraudulently or with evil intent or by making or having no mark upon certain vessels, or if it is not right and only according to the terms of the past ordinance, that he will be imprisoned in body and spend a day in the pillory, at the discretion of the mayor and aldermen. And so that the Brewers of the city do not excuse themselves, by ignorance or too rigorous haste in this part, it was ordained by the authority of the said present common council, that the forfeiture in such cases will not begin to take force until the Feast of the Purification of our Lady[143] next coming, during which time the Brewers may present themselves well and honestly without harm, fulfilling the effect of the said ordinance, if they wish.

Item that by an ordinance established in the whole city, it is forbidden for any brewer, hosteler, huckster, cook or pie baker to sell a gallon of best ale inside their house more dearly than for 2*d.* the measure, sealed and full of clear ale, and outside their houses for more than 1½*d.*, and this for a sealed measure full of clear ale, the same clear ale that they sell inside their houses.
Notwithstanding the said ordinance, the said brewers, hostelers, hucksters, cooks and pie bakers sell from one to another a gallon of best ale for 3*d.*, 4*d.*, and 5*d.*, and this by hanaps[144] and not by gallon, pottle, nor quart, in full measure and sealed.
And moreover, the said Brewers openly make and sell outside their houses, other weaker ale of less strength, for 1½*d.*, which they sell inside their houses for 2*d.*, expressly against the abovesaid good ordinance. Upon this it was ordained by Richard Whytyngton with the mayor, aldermen and commons in this present council assembled, that no brewer, hosteler, huckster, cook nor pie baker, as stated before, may sell to anyone, of whatever estate or condition he might be, a gallon of best ale in their homes more dearly than at 2*d.* the measure, and if the measure is not

---

143   2 February.
144   *Cal. Letter-Book, I*, 98, fn.14. Drinking vessel of no fixed measure, to be supplied by brewers and hostelers for drinking purposes, whilst ale was to be sold in sealed measures, according to ordinances of 1382, 1388, and 1392, *Cal. Letter-Book, H*, 201, 337, 373.

properly sealed in a gallon, pottle, quart or pint, full of clear ale, [*the seller*] will forfeit the vessel and the value of all the ale that may be in the vessels which he sells otherwise, and meanwhile his body will be held in prison at the wish of the mayor and aldermen at the time.

Item if any brewer having made or sold ale out of his house before, to any person of whatever estate or condition, at 1½*d*. the gallon, of less value or weaker, feebler ale than the best ale

[59] [f. 22r]

which he sells at his own house, price 2*d*. the gallon, he can be reasonably convinced that he will forfeit, by the work of the commonalty, all the ale or the value of the ale being sold contrary to the said ordinance, and that the person by whom the said forfeiture is first declared & disclosed to the mayor or chamberlain will receive half. And if any person of the said city, of whatever estate or condition he might be, buys ale from a brewer contrary to the abovesaid ordinance, he will forfeit the said ale, or the value placed upon it, as much for the buyer as the vendor. And if any brewer of bad courage and purpose, because of this ordinance, which so affects the craft, stirs up other brewers or makes weaker ale, he will forfeit all such weaker ale made and will have his body imprisoned, according to the judgement made, according to the right of the commons and the custom of the city in such cases.

[60]

[*Latin*] In this present year, the 8th of the reign of King Henry V [1420–1], Simon Potken, citizen and brewer of London, at that time dwelling at the Key at Aldgate in the parish of St Botolph without Aldgate, became rebellious towards Thomas Grene, Robert Hilton, Robert Carpenter and John Peken, the Masters of the craft of Brewers of London at that time, because that year Richard Whityngton, mayor of the same city, ordered by the common council that the said craft of Brewers were to declare by words that they were not observing the ordinance of the council, and he badly vexed and troubled the said craft. Certain persons of the craft conceded and gave various sums of silver towards having the statutes modified by the common council, and the Masters tried to obtain modification of the said ordinances. Simon Potken, by the advice and order of the very worthy men of the craft of Brewers, paid 20*d*. After payment of the sum the Searchers of the aforesaid craft came to the house of the said Simon Potken & took from him the bad measure that he was selling of one quart full of best ale for a halfpenny, and they presented his name to the chamberlain of the Guildhall, as they did for others, because of which they lost 22½*d*. for a kilderkin.

He maliciously and ignorantly stood against the Masters of the said craft and said to the chamberlain that he had paid the money to the said craft in order to sell his beer without a price, at his own will and in whatever way he wished.

The chamberlain declared and told the aforesaid mayor of London that all the Masters, Wardens and Searchers and most worthy men of the said craft there were to meet and they returned to him the money previously received from him for seeking modifications for the said craft, with great anger.

The said Simon Potken was investigated. All the Masters of the craft of Brewers stood unanimously against him. He sought pardon from them for his grave transgression made because of his ignorance and he humbled himself before the Wardens and affirmed that he would amend his debt for his default and disobedience

82

and that he wished to be governed and ruled by them and never fail again. Then the Masters pardoned him, for which he paid 3*s*. 4*d*. to them, with goodwill, for a swan to be eaten by the Masters, but he came and had his share.

[61] [f. 22v]

[*English*] This is a bill of less matter and shorter, that I[145] made about the toll, written before, about remedy for the outrageous wages and salary that the servants[146] of Brewers' craft demand for the week and by *Bretherne*[147] and also by the day, as it shows by this bill written and rehearsed afterwards, and also of beer brewers retailing their beer in the city of London, against the franchise:

To the right worshipful and discreet mayor and aldermen of London, your servants all the Brewers of London beseech you that for as much as in the third year of King Henry IV [1401–2] a supplication was put to John Shaldworth, at that time mayor of the said city, beseeching him that all the citizens of [*the*] said city might be quit of all manner of toll and custom by all the king's power, as well on this side [*of*] the sea as on the other side, after the form of the king's charter thereof to them granted. Wherefore it was granted and accorded by [*the*] said mayor, the recorder, sheriffs and all the aldermen, that no servant of the said city, from that time forwards, should take any toll or customs from any citizens of the said city for any of their merchandise, victuals or other necessaries [*brought*] by ships, boats, horse or carts unto the said city, to be brought [*into*] or to be carried from the same city, and also on the 12th day of May[148] the same year, in the presence of the said mayor and aldermen and all the common council thereto summoned, it was accorded and fully affirmed that no citizen of the aforesaid city from that time forwards [*scored*: should pay no toll] should pay any toll or custom at the ports of the said city for their goods, merchandise or victuals falling upon the said [*above the line*: merchandise] goods or victuals [*that*] were brought to the said city or carried from the same upon horse, ships, boats or carts of strangers, and that the same strangers should be quit of toll and custom at any port of the said city for their horse, ships, boats and carts so carrying the said goods, merchandise or victuals of the said citizens, and [*more*] over that you [*may*] like to consider that aliens dwelling within the city brew beer and sell it to retail as freely as any of the said citizens, and also notwithstanding various ordinances made in times before, that no servant of Brewers' craft shall serve by the week nor by day, but by the year, taking salary after the form of the said ordinances, that is to say: the chief Brewer 4 marks[149] by year with meat, drink, clothing and his advantages and the second Brewer 40*s*. by year with meat, drink, clothing and his advantages, upon pain of imprisonment and forfeit [*of*] 6*s*. 8*d*. and their outrageous salary so taken against the ordinances. And now by confederacy made amongst them, that they will not serve but[150] by week or by day, without that[151] they have too outrageous a salary, to great hindering of the said beseechers, if they do not have your help and succour in this matter. May it please your high discretions so to ordain

---

145   Porlond apparently wrote this passage himself, and the draft petition that follows.
146   Perhaps apprentices, or former apprentices no longer living with a master.
147   It is not clear what the clerk meant by 'Bretherne'. Burden, perhaps?
148   The same date, and year, perhaps, as in [49] and [50].
149   A mark was 13*s*. 4*d*.
150   Except.
151   Unless.

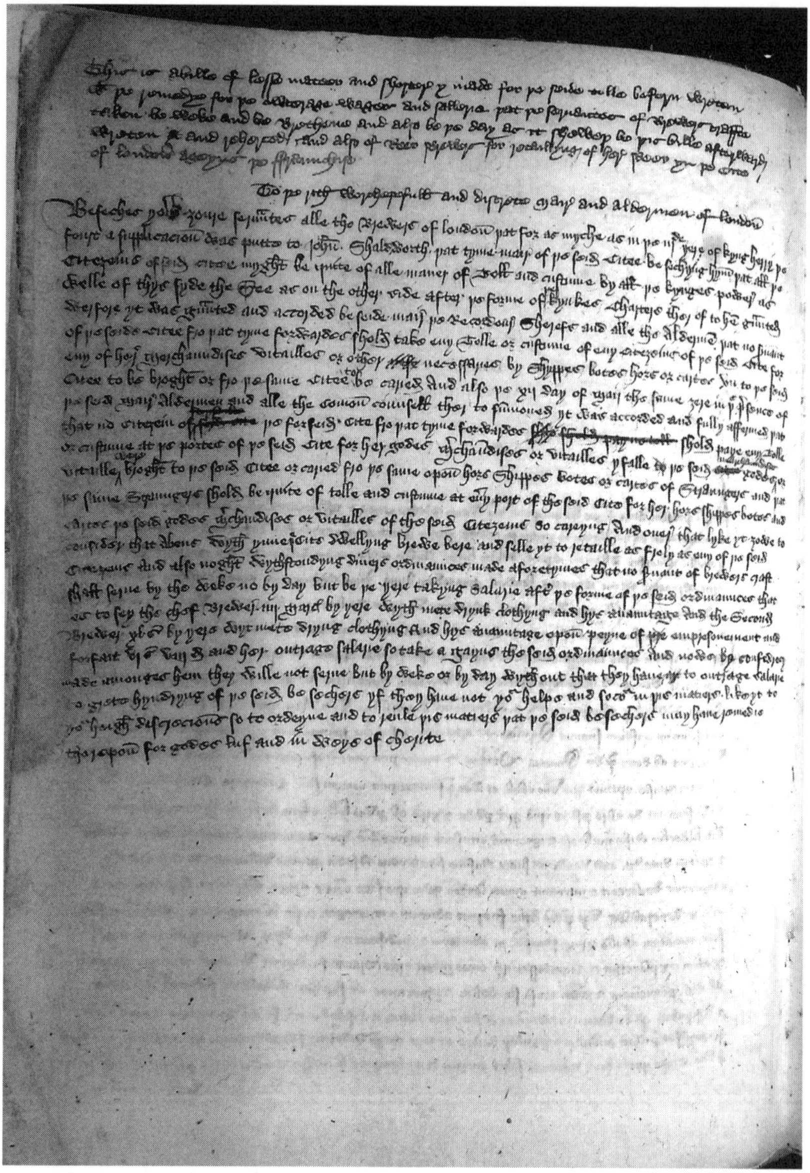

Figure 8. GL MS 5440 The Brewers' Book, folio 22v. The top line has 'a bill … y made' probably written by William Porlond. © The Brewers' Company.

and to rule these matters that [*your*] said beseechers may have remedy thereupon, for God's love and in way of charity.

[62] [f. 23r]
[*Latin*]
There follows a reformation & modification by Richard Whetyngton, mayor and alderman of the city of London, of certain grievous statutes set forth in the time of the said mayor, against the craft of Brewers.

[*French*] To the honourable Lords, the mayor and aldermen of the city of London, the poor humble freemen of the mistery of Brewers of the same city beseech you to consider the feebleness of the world and how all in the commonalty of the realm have had great misfortune in their occupation, and excessive costs and expenses other than those normally imposed which had to be paid.
Of your gracious discretion, the humble men of this simple mistery, which is a poor member, supporting in our degree all the charges in the said city established by the good ordinance made when John Wodecok was mayor, [1405–6][152] whom God assoil, ask you to moderate and modify the last ordinance made in common council upon the aforesaid mistery, in the manner contained in a schedule attached. Of your charity, very wise lords, consider that our intention is only to guard proper measure and sell at a reasonable price, as we have promised, capably and under our supervision.

[*Latin*: [?] I came to ... London]

First for guarding loyally and observing just measure for large vessels, that is, barrels and kilderkins, that all the Coopers of the said city are charged and summoned before you now to visit and search all barrels and kilderkins of all customers, Brewers and others. Those who are found false, disloyally making any relaxations to anyone, and those who are found loyal, signing with their proper mark, will be entered and enrolled on record before you.
And the said Coopers are charged not to mark any barrel in future with a measure of less than 30 gallons, nor any kilderkin with less than 15 gallons, under certain grievous penalty ordained by you.

[63] [f. 23v]
Item the said Brewers pray that they may sell their ale at retail in large and small measures, that is gallons, pottles and quarts, inside as well as outside their houses, for 2*d.* a gallon.

Item, to guard loyally and observe just measures for the small vessels, that is gallons, pottles and quarts and to ensure that the small vessels are sold to the people full of clear ale, and to be assured that the ale is good, agreeable and sold at a suitable price in accordance with that endorsed by the mayor annually. The Masters & Wardens of the same mistery are annually brought before you, with their diligent

---

[152] Mayor 1405–6. C. Rawcliffe, 'Woodcock, John (d. 1409)', *History of Parliament. Cal. Letter-Book, I*, 50–1.

searches about these things and others and any complaint from anyone. In cases where the Masters and Wardens find ale at any house in the city that is not according to the price given by the mayor, they must put a suitable price upon it, according to the said council. If the Masters and Wardens find ale in false measures, or people selling measures that are not full of clear ale, or sold otherwise and contrary to the price that the mayor, the Masters and Wardens have given, in the form and manner abovesaid, then they will be presented and their names will be given to the chamberlain, without any concession to anyone. If the Masters and Wardens do not remedy each complaint, and are found negligent or remiss in these matters abovesaid, then they, too, will be punished according to your gracious discretion and wishes.

On the 17th day of January in the 7th year of the reign of King Henry V after the Conquest [1420] all the persons using the mistery of Brewers in the city of London and in the suburbs of the same city came and presented a supplication and schedule to Richard Whittington, then mayor, and to the aldermen of the same city, the terms of which appertained to 2 articles attached.[153] The supplication and schedules aforesaid concerned the ordinance made in the time of the late mayor, John Wodecok, whom God assoil, as was prayed in the same petition.

It was agreed that the said ordinance was not being maintained and your servants the Brewers were allowed until the next Easter before the effect and content of the same ordinance would be established, as seemed reasonable to the mayor and aldermen.[154]

Item touching the first article of the said schedule, that is to say, observing just measure of large vessels, barrels and kilderkins, which, it is prayed by the said Brewers, and to the mayor and aldermen, must be marked by the Coopers of the city and the suburbs:
And under certain penalty, ordained as is contained in the said schedule, moreover, it was plainly agreed that the said article would be confirmed upon condition that the said Brewers would enter the same promise that the Coopers made, that they must not serve to the people any barrels or kilderkins not given a mark in the manner abovesaid, or unsealed, and they must have two gallons in each barrel and one gallon in each kilderkin & moreover they must pay in money

[f. 24r]
and in the same manner and under the same penalty contained in the ordinance of William Standen[155] made in the 9th year of King Henry IV [1407–8] and confirmed by the past common council.

153 No attached articles have survived, but this refers to the two articles above, about just measure and asking to sell ale inside and out at 2d. a gallon, a request which was refused. See *Cal. Letter-Book, I*, 232–7. Although the clerk here referred to the price of 1d. the gallon for ale served outside, the price had been set at 1½d. when served outside.

154 See *Cal. Letter-Book, I*, 236.

155 Mayor 1407–8. C. Rawcliffe, 'Standon, William (d. 1410) of Wimpole, Cambs and London', *History of Parliament*.

[64]

Item touching the second article of the said concession, by which the said Brewers pray that they may sell at small retail, that is to say only by gallon, pottle & quart, at 2*d.* a gallon of their best ale, inside their houses and outside: because of certain causes in the court, it was not agreed that they could sell their best ale at retail outside their houses for 2*d.* the gallon, because that would be expressly against the good agreement of the common council before upon this said matter.[156]

Every time, unless the strict penalty made in the said common council upon the said matter is modified and moderated in the manner following, that is with the said penalty of imprisonment for each default and [*the offender*] is to lose, each time, all the vessels and the value of the ale contained in those that are being sold more dearly than at 1*d.* the gallon.

Moreover, it was agreed that no brewer, hosteler, huckster, cook nor pie baker should sell any of their best ale at retail outside their houses more dearly than at 1*d.* each gallon, upon pain of being arrested according to the discretion of the mayor & aldermen in the same manner as was made before these hours. This modification is made and granted, upon this condition, that the said brewers, hostelers, hucksters, cooks and pie bakers do not sell their ale by hanaps, but in full measure, sealed, in a gallon, pottle or quart, and this with clear best ale, so that each time no one has anything but the best ale, and by the operation of this ordinance, they take no more than 1*d.* for each gallon.[157] This should be the best ale and the same ale that they sell inside their homes for 2*d.* the gallon. This aforesaid penalty was ordained by the previous common council.

Item concerning the thirtieth article, that is, regarding the just measure of the aforesaid small vessels, and ensuring that they are sold to the common people full of clear ale, and the ale should be according to the price endorsed by the mayor, according to their discretion about this, and to present all defaulters to the chamberlain, it is ordered by the mayor & aldermen, if the commons seem agreeable, that the said Brewers have the right to survey, search and assay all the things said before, in the manner contained in the said article, for all the time that it shall be profitable to the commons and that they should make [*above the line*: as before] all their ale good and fine quality and at a suitable price.

[65]

And that there should be the space of a day and a night since the last [*brewing*] at the brewhouse, to allow for cleansing, before ale may be taken to the house of anyone, as is contained in the ordinance of William Stanndonne. Moreover that they will put their loyal work and diligence from one day to another towards searching and presenting all the defaulters, without concealment, in the manner contained in their said petition.

And if the said Brewers do not make good ale, according to the price put upon it, or do not sell just measure, or if the Masters & Wardens of the same mistery at the time do not make due survey, search and redress to each who complains, or do not set a reasonable, just price, the true value of all the ale that is not at the price set by

---

[156]   This was refused by the mayor and aldermen. *Cal. Letter-Book, I,* 236.
[157]   See *Cal. Letter-Book, I,* 237.

the mayor in the manner below, they will be found negligent and remiss in the things said above, or some of them, and for these, faithfully committed or attended, the Masters and Wardens of the said mistery at the time, for each such commission or occasion will be punished by imprisonment of their body, according to the discretion of the mayor & aldermen, and furthermore, the mistery will lose £20 for each commission, to be levied upon all the people using the said mistery of Brewers in the franchise of the city of London.

And otherwise, it is ordained and agreed by the said mayor & aldermen that the ale of no

[f. 24v]
foreign person may be sold by any foreigner outside the franchise of the said city, on pain of forfeiture, according to the work of the commonalty, of the value of all the ale sold in the abovesaid form. For each forfeiture, the Masters and Wardens of the said Mistery at the time are to have a quarter part each [*above the line*: time] that they present to the chamber the cause of such a forfeiture.

[66]
[*Latin*] In the 7th year of the reign of King Henry V [1419–20],[158] Richard Whytyngton being mayor at that time, Thomas Grene, John Pyken, Robert Hylton, and Robert Carpenter at that time being Masters of the craft of Brewers in the city of London, by the unanimous assent and consent of the said Masters and Wardens and others of the commonalty of the aforesaid craft, it was agreed that they and their successors should meet every Monday during the year, except for three, that is, during the week of the Nativity of Our Lord, Easter, and Pentecost, and also if a double festival of the year should fall on a Monday, it should be held on another day of that week at the discretion of the Masters.
The Masters and their successors should meet at their hall, called Brewers' Hall, there to consider whatsoever necessaries of the same craft were to be inquired of, scrutinised and executed by the aforesaid Masters, as should seem most expedient for the honour and prosperity of the aforesaid craft in all things.

[67] [f. 25r]
[*Latin*] **Voluntary Taxation**
Here are the names of those who have paid for procuring dominion[159] for the modifications and declarations of the common council against the Brewers, promulgated during the time of Richard Whetyngtonne being mayor [1419–20] as more plainly appears in the second folio.

Alice Herty	5s.	Gilbert Botonne	20d.
Alan John	2s.		
Alexander Myles	4s.	Hugh Glene	3s. 4d.
Agnes Carletonne	5s.	Henry Feriby	20d.
Alexander Marcowe	3s. 4d.	Peter Schort	6s. 8d.

---

[158] This passage has not been crossed through, so it is probably a later addition.
[159] The power to control.

Adam Copendale	3s. 4d.	Hugh Neell	3s. 4d.
Austyn Hanwell	20d.	Henry Trobolans	20d.
Cristiana Bekeswelle	6s. 8d.	John Riche de Wood Street	13s. 4d.
		John Tregolow	6s. 8d.
David Soys	20d.	John Stone	3s. 4d.
David Bronnyng	4s.	John Broke	13s. 4d.
		John Carien	6s. 8d.
Elias Hardell	6s. 8d.	John Kenagy	2s. 8d.
		John Eylonde	2s. 8d.
Sum 53s. 4d.		John Philippe	6s. 8d.
		John Spenser	5s.
		John Bedford	12d.
		John Chapman	5s.
		John Aleyn	20d.
		John Rothyng	3s. 4d.

Sum £4 9s.

[68] [f. 25v]

John Humber	3s. 4d.	John Reyner	6s. 8d.
John Brewstere	20d.	John William	6s. 8d.
John Castonne	3s. 4d.	John Jurdan	3s.
John Amwelle	3s. 4d.	John Merstonne	20d.
John More at Aldersgate	6s. 8d.	John Bassett	2s.
John Lutonne	20d.	John Riche, tailor	2s.
John Serle	3s. 4d.	John Thetford	13s. 4d.
John Bayly	20d.		
John Toke	20d.	Katherine Pynchebeke	2s.
John Ballard	6s. 8d.		
John Luke	3s. 4d.	Luce Stoetman	20d.
John Ketyng	10s.		
John Ratforde	3s. 4d.	Michael Tregonon	2s.
John Freke	2s.	Michael Eve	2s.
John Norman	2s.	Margaret Setingbourne	2s.
John Hardyng	20d.		
John Stokes	3s. 4d.	Nicholas Aleyn	2s.
John Elsy	5s.	Nicholas Fuller	2s.
John Refhawe	5s.	Nicholas Kene	6s. 8d.
John Canonne	5s.		
Juliane Hetersete	20d.	Phillip Porcell	6s. 8d.
John More at Ludgate	6s. 8d.	Peter Hayforde	3s. 4d.
John Lumbard	3s.	Peter Carpenter	5s.
John Thomas, tailor	12d.	Philip Godfrey at *Osbern at Dawe*	20d.
John Lynne	2s.	Peter Shorte	6s. 8d.[160]

---

[160]   The entry for Peter Shorte was added in a different hand, and his payment has not been included in the total. Earlier in this list 6s. 8d. was recorded for Petrus (Peter) Schorte **[67]**.

John Randolfe	3s. 4d.	Robert Smyth	13s. 4d.
John Golderyng	3s. 4d.	Richard Harlow	3s. 4d.
John Newman	6s. 8d.	Richard Bryntonne	3s.
John Parys	3s. 4d.		
John Russell	13s. 4d.	**Sum £4 12s.**	
John Bate	10s.		
John Hosier	20d.		
John Waghorne	20d.		
John Nassyng	2s.		
John Moyle	3s. 4d.		
John Stantonne	13s. 4d.		
John Mason	6s. 8d.		
John Assh	2s.		

Sum £7 19s.

[69] [f. 26r]

Richard Lucas	2s.	Thomas Grene	6s. 8d.
Richard Frepurs	3s. 4d.		
Richard Flete	3s. 4d.	William Crane	6s. 8d.
Richard Cros	20d.	Walter Colshull	6s. 8d.
Richard Aleyn	6s. 8d.	Walter Glyn	2s.
Roger Swannyffelde	6s. 8d.	William Petevyle	3s. 4d.
Roger Ware	2s.	William Belle	3s. 4d.
Reynold Broke	12d.	William Baily	3s. 4d.
Roger Blissote	2s.	William Stile	3s. 4d.
Reynold Beauchamp	3s. 4d.	William Gefferey	2s.
Robert Maylond	3s. 4d.	William John	2s. 4d.
Robert Elkyn	3s. 4d.	William Canonne	3s. 4d.
Robert Pede	3s. 4d.	William Mark	2s.
Robert Coventre	2s.	William Barte	3s. 4d.
Richard Newman	3s. 4d.	William Englyssh	20d.
Robert Gyles	3s. 4d.	William Bacon	3s. 4d.
Robert Hylton	6s. 8d.	Walter Copseye	20d.
Robert Carpenter	6s. 8d.	William Bernard	2s.
Robert Tannere	20d.	William atte Well	5s.
		Walter Bronn	2s.
Robert Walram	3s. 4d.	Walter Boteler	2s.
		William Edrych	13s. 4d.
Stephen Roo	20d.	Walter Coke at *Mangerad*	3s. 4d.
Simon Petesyn	3s. 4d.	William Myemys	10s.
Stephen Bugge	20s.	William Bolton	2s.
		William Bussh	2s.
Thomas Osbarne	2s.	William Hyll	2s.
Thomas Boteler	2s.	William Frank	2s.
Thomas Wermyngton	3s. 4d.	William atte Wode	6s. 8d.
Thomas Nonnzeglys	20d.	William Payn	5s.
Thomas Hancok	3s.	William Illyng	12d.
Thomas Godyng	3s. 4d.	William Smalsho	3s. 4d.
Thomas Emond	8s.	William Bracy	6s. 8d.

Thomas Grateley   3s. 4d.   William Herry   6s. 8d.

William Robert   3s. 4d.

Sum £6 8d.

Sum £6 13s. 4d.

Sum total of money collected to obtain dominion as above £31 17s. 4d.

[70] [f. 26v]
[*Latin*] Money collected to obtain dominion and the parcels[161] distributed in the following manner

First to Robert Whetyngham, sheriff of London, by the hands of Thomas
Grene and Robert Smyth   £20

Item for 2 pipes[162] of red wine given by the hands of John Thetford to the
butler of Richard Whetyngton   £7 3s. 4d.

Item by the hand of Thomas Grene given to John Carpenter, the mayor's
clerk, for his advice and diverse labour   20s.

Item according to the precept of Thomas Grene, Master of the Brewers that
year, for 2 butts of Malmsey wine given by the hand of William Porlond,
clerk of the aforesaid craft, to Thomas Fakoner, alderman, and the other to
the recorder of London at the time   32s.

Item for portage of the same butts   8d.

Item for writing of the same bills to the mayor and aldermen   6d.

Item for so much money lost between the collectors   6d.

Sum of money collected and spent as aforesaid £29 17s.

And there remains for the common use and profit 40s. 4d.

[71] [f. 27r]
**This is the account of William Ederich of money received by him from the
Treasurer of England for ale delivered by various Brewers of the city of London
to the household of the Lady Katherine the Queen, after the passage of King
Henry V last made into the parts of France, to wit in the 9ᵗʰ year of his reign
[1421–2] as appears below**

The same William discharges himself in money received from John Ward,
Thomas Gare, John Tyndale, all citizens of York, by a certain obligation
given,   £55 4s. 7d.

---

161 'Percelles'.
162 Two hogsheads or sixty-three wine gallons.

And the same discharges himself of the money received from diverse merchants by another obligation £38 19s. 9½d.

And the same discharges himself of confirmation of delivery of money by him received as above £11 5s.

Sum total received £105 9s. 4½d.

And the said William discharges himself in money repaid to the said Treasurer by the hands of John Stanntone for certain reasons, 14s. 2½d.

And to the attorney in the court of the said King for a writ together with other expenses 16s. 8d.

And paid to a certain maltman called Dolphyn for helping in the aforesaid matter 20d.

And to the lord Nicholas Dikson, a baron of the Exchequer of our King, in the price of 6 capons, 4s.

Sum of expenses 36s. 6½d.

And there remains declared in our hands £103 12s. 10d.

Which shall be distributed among the creditors as below. And first

[72] [f. 27v]

Sums owed to various Brewers of the city of London for ale delivered to the inn[163] of the Lady Queen, after the passage of the lord King into parts of France, to wit in the ninth year of his reign [1421–2] as appears below.

	Sums owed.	Received at one time on 7th December in the 9th year of the reign of King Henry V [1421]	Item received at another time, that is, on the 22nd May in the 10th year of King Henry V [1422]	Owed to the same	Deducted for necessary expenses	And thus is owed net
John Caryonne	£17 6s. 6½d.	100s.	£10	46s. 6½d.	3s. 11d.	42s. 7½d.
William Ederich	£11 0s. 6½d.	45s.	£6 19s. 9½d.	35s. 9½d.	2s. 6d.	33s. 3½d.
John Thetford	62s. 8½d.	20s.	40s.	2s. 8½d.	8d.	2s. 0½d.
John Stannton	£25 13s. 9d.	£8	£15	53s. 9d.	5s. 10d.	47s. 11d.
John More	£12 8s. 5d.	£4	£6	48s. 5d.	2s. 9½d.	45s. 7½d.
John Russell	£9 12s. 9½d.	50s.	£5	32s. 9½d.	2s. 2d.	30s. 7½d.
John Refawe	£15 8s. 7d.	100s.	£8	48s. 7d.	3s. 6d.	45s. 1d.
Roger Swannefeld	£10 22d.	60s.	£6	21s. 10d.	2s. 3½d.	19s. 6½d.

Sum total of money to be owed £104 15s. 2d.[164]
Sum received at one time £31 5s.
Sum received at another time £58 19s. 9½d.
Sum to be repaid £14 10s. 5d.
Deducted 23s. 8d.
Net amount due £13 6s. 9d.
These were all paid by William the clerk.

163 Accommodation for the Queen's retinue and store for provisions, possibly Northumberland House, (Aldersgate), known as the Queen's Wardrobe. Mary D. Lobel, *The City of London from Prehistoric Times to c. 1520* (Oxford, 1989), 81.

164 This figure seems to be ½d. short.

[73] [f. 28r]
[Latin with English place names]
The names of those who did not observe the correct measures in the selling of ale, received in the year when the Masters were: Thomas Grene, Robert Hylton, Robert Carpenter, John Peken and their 11 associates as Wardens: William atte Wode, William Ferrour, Thomas Hatcher, John Salter, Thomas Emond, John Mason, William Crane, William atte Well, John Chapman, John Lombard & William John.
And in the year when Richard Whetyngton was mayor of London [1419–20] **some lost a barrel, some half a barrel, by order of John Hyll, chamberlain of the Guildhall, as appears** [*scored*: in the names written below]

Item, first William Harry, brewer, at Long Entry beside le Stocks	1 barrel
Item Thomas Hunte, the beadle, beside the fountain of the church of St Nicholas Shambles	
John Bronne at Paternoster Row	
Item a huckster beside the Stocks	
John, water bailiff de Billingsgate	
Rose beside le Dolphin at the church of St Magnus	
Margaret Greneway	
Thomas Matthyng, the beadle in Cheap	
Alicia Bradmore at *Bradwey le Horne* in Gracechurch Street	
Item le Tabard in Gracechurch Street	1 barrel
Simon Corduwayner at Leadenhall	
The wife of David in Honey Lane	1 barrel
The tapster at le cellar at the end of Bread Street	1 kilderkin.

[74] [f. 28v]

A tapster at le Crosse in Cheap at the Basket	1 barrel
John Maystone beside the cross in Holborn	1 barrel of 8 gallons
Agnes Syon beside the cross in Holborn	
Agnes Poule at Paul's Wharf above Baynard's Castle	1 barrel
William Raulyn at the Cock in Wood Street	1 barrel
A huckster in the parish of St Benet	1 kilderkin
Agnes Syon	1 kilderkin
Cryour at Newgate	1 kilderkin not delivered
Huckster at the Goat opposite the church of St Helen	1 kilderkin
Cristiana Zork, huckster beside	–
Cecilia Bedewell in the parish of All Hallows London Wall,	1 kilderkin
Matilda Maryett there	
Petronilla at the Cow Head in Cheap	1 barrel
Baldok in New Alley in Cornhill	1 kilderkin
Johanna, huckster at Fleet Bridge beside the Rose	1 kilderkin
The wife at the George in Fleet Street	1 barrel
William, ostler at the Castle there	1 kilderkin
John Kyrke, ostler at the Falcon	1 kilderkin
The cook beside the said John there	1 kilderkin
John, ostler at the Saracen's Head in Fleet Street	1 barrel

A wife at the George. The ostler in the parish of St Dunstan there[165]   1 kilderkin
John Brewster, brewer at the Snipe in East Cheap   1 kilderkin
Huckster at the Dagger in Cheap   1 barrel

[75] [f. 29r]
Huckster at *Ormnpe*   1 barrel
Isabelle in Bell Alley in Cheap   1 kilderkin
William Fox at the market at the church of St Nicholas [*Shambles*]   1 barrel
The wife of John, bladesmith, in the Bailey   1 kilderkin
Skynner at Paul's Head in the parish of St Mildred in Bread Street   1 kilderkin
Thomas Kent, brewer, dwelling at the Basket at Billingsgate   1 kilderkin
John Grymmesby, brewer, beside the drain at Billing[*sgate*]   1 barrel
Agnes, huckster, dwelling at the Ship there   1 kilderkin
Huckster dwelling at le Bole there   1 kilderkin
Widow Brewster dwelling at le Cock beside St Magnus   1 barrel
John Lannder dwelling in Old Jewry   1 kilderkin
Hosteler at the Horn in Gracechurch Street   1 barrel
Hosteler dwelling at the Tabard in Gracechurch Street   1 kilderkin
Agnes Aleyn beside le Star in Thames Street   1 kilderkin
John Cateryk in la Ropery   1 kilderkin
Walter Trewman at Dowgate   1 kilderkin
Thomas Gerard, pie baker, dwelling in la Vintry   1 barrel
John Kebyll, brewer at the Key in the parish of St Mary Somerset   1 kilderkin
Agnes Huckster dwelling beside Thomas Gerard, pie baker in the Vintry   1 kilderkin
Another huckster dwelling opposite the aforesaid pie baker   1 kilderkin
William Ferrour   1 barrel
Agnes Myllere dwelling in la Vintry beside le Crane   1 barrel
Huckster dwelling outside the inn of the church of St James Garlickhithe   1 kilderkin

[76] [f. 29v]
The wife of Mekerby dwelling at le Queenhithe   1 kilderkin
Katrina Walwyngham dwelling there   1 kilderkin
The water bailiff of Queenhithe   1 kilderkin
Another huckster dwelling beside the water bailiff   1 kilderkin
John Clerk dwelling there   1 kilderkin
Isabella Ratcheforth   1 kilderkin
Margery Warewyke in the parish of St Mary Somerset beside le Key   1 kilderkin
William Wodeherste at Old Fish Street end   1 kilderkin
Parnell at Cow Head in Cheap   1 kilderkin
The huckster at the Cardinal's Hat at Billingsgate beside the Christopher   1 b.
Johanna Rooche, [*scored*: another] young huckster next to the Cardinal's
Hat there   1 barrel
Katherine, huckster, dwelling beside the aforesaid Johanna Rooche there   1 kilderkin
William Boteler at the Cock at Lime Street end   1 k.
George Spenall at the Pewter Pot opposite the church of St Andrew Cornhill   1 k.
John Feyrman, another freeman, dwelling at Billiter Lane end   1 barrel
Issenda Wake dwelling there   1 kilderkin

[165] The entries for the wife and the ostler are both on one line, separated by a full stop.

Henry Serle at the Hartshorn in the parish of St Katherine Christ Church	1 barrel
John Essex, cordwainer, below Aldgate	1 kilderkin
John Robert, the pattenmaker, without Aldgate	1 kilderkin
Simon Potkyn at the Key without Aldgate	1 kilderkin
John Dunche at the Axe there	1 kilderkin
Agnes Goldstone dwelling between Bishopsgate and Aldgate	1 kilderkin
John Cheseman, brewer, dwelling at the Garland outside Bishopsgate	1 k.
Peter Roos, brewer, at the Hart's Head outside Bishopsgate	1 k.

[77] [f. 30r]

Sibille at the Crown there	1 kilderkin
Richard Lewias at the Nun outside Aldgate, brewer,	1 barrel
The brewer at the Bell and Dolphin outside Bishopsgate	1 kilderkin
Gavin Tyler dwelling at the Castle in Bishopsgate Street	1 kilderkin
Elena, huckster, dwelling in Abchurch Lane beside the corner at Lombard Street end	1 k.
Clement Grene dwelling in Sithebourne Lane	1 kilderkin
Alice Erdard dwelling in St Swithin's Lane	1 barrel
Margaret Bullok dwelling there	1 kilderkin
Agnes Mone dwelling in le Poultry	2 pottles
William Denton, cordwainer, beside the Castle at St Mary Somerset	1 k.
Margery Blakmor dwelling there	1 kilderkin
Alice Hylton at Paul's Wharf	1 kilderkin
William Mark, brewer, dwelling at the Three Kings outside Aldgate	1 barrel
Elena Sely beside le Squirrel in Fenchurch Street	1 k.
Margaret Everard dwelling in St Clement's Lane	1 kilderkin
Simon Wyryng staying at the Fountain with Two Buckets in the parish of St Martin	1 kilderkin
Isabella Ware staying at Tower Hill	1 k.
John Aleyn at Crutched Friars	1 kilderkin
Alice, huckster, staying at Tower Hill	1 kilderkin
Sibilla Carpenter staying at the Crutched Friars	1 k.
The wife of Henry Andreau in Tower Street, beside the cross of the brewhouse	1 k.
Jonette, huckster, in Tower Street of the parish of [*All Hallows*] Barking	1 k.
Richard Russell in Tower Street in the aforesaid parish	1 k.
Katherine Harlyng staying in Tower Street	1 kilderkin

[78] [f. 30v]

The wife of the beadle dwelling in Tower Street outside the Standard	1 k.
Godelefe dwelling in Smithys Lane	1 k.
William Okyng dwelling in the parish of St Andrew in Love Lane[166]	1 k.
The huckster at the Wharf beside le Bull at Queenhithe	1 k.
Richard Shyrwode, brewer, at the Cock in Fynkes Lane beside St Antony's	1 barrel
Alice Gyldesburgh at the Three Nuns in Sithebourne Lane	1 k.
The wife of Swyfft, weaver, beside the Thames at Dowgate	1 k.
Johanna Stacy, huckster, beside Thomas Emond, brewer,	1 kilderkin
The wife of Thomas Ely opposite the church of St Alban in Wood Street	1 k.

---

[166]   St Andrew Hubbard.

Alice Skydmour in Wood Street beside the Rose at Cripplegate	1 k.
The wife of Thomas Trayles at London Wall	1 kilderkin
Nicholas Adam, a bargeman at Queenhithe for forfeited ale that he had in his custody to sell,	1 kilderkin
Thomas Botelmaker at the Cock below Ludgate forfeited because of selling beer against the price ordained by the Masters,	1 barrel and 1 kilderkin
Katherine Gerard in Secoll Lane in the rent of St Paul's there	1 kilderkin
Johanna Tyler there	1 kilderkin
Alison, hosteler, at the corner beside the church of St Sepulchre	1 k.
Simon Covert, corsour, in the rent of the Swan in the Bailey	1 k.
John Thebawde at the Swan in the parish of St Ethelburga in Bishopsgate Street	1 barrel
William Mynikan at the Dolphin in the parish of St Mary Magdalen, Old Fish Street	1 k.
William Maskall, brewer, at the Swan in the parish of St Andrew Holborn	1 barrel

[79] [f. 31r]

John Holdernesse, brewer, at the White Bear in the parish of St Andrew Holborn	1 k.
John Grymmsby at the Bell in the parish of St Andrew Holborn	1 k.
John Sturmyn dwelling at the Swan in Pissing Lane	1 barrel
A huckster dwelling outside the conduit in Cornhill in the south part	1 kilderkin
A huckster dwelling in the corner at the west end of the church of St Michael Cornhill	1 k.
Alice Trayles, huckster, dwelling outside the old latrine at London Wall beside [*scored*: Bishopsgate] the fountain there	1 k.
Helena, huckster, dwelling opposite the lane in St Martin O[rgar], Candlewick Street, beside the shearman there	1 kilderkin
Margaret Mawnde, huckster, dwelling at London Wall beside Bishopsgate	1 kilderkin
A certain huckster dwelling in Abchurch Lane in a certain cellar at the corner of the aforesaid Abchurch Lane beside Lombard Street	1 kilderkin
Margaret Chenerell in Abchurch Lane	1 k.
An huckster outside the Rose in Jewry	1 kilderkin
Simond Inglonde dwelling opposite Quentin the brewer in the parish of St Michael le Querne	1 k.
William Fox, brewer, dwelling at the Ship at the market of St Nicholas [*Shambles*]	1 k.
A huckster dwelling at the Ball at the aforesaid market, that is St Nicholas,	1 k.
A widow, formerly the wife of John Penferne, dwelling at the Swan at Newgate	1 k.
Simon Kyng dwelling at the Pannier in the parish of St Giles without Cripplegate in White Cross Street	1 k.
Agnes de London, huckster, dwelling there beside the Bars	1 k.
John Lovell staying at the Fleur de Lys in Golding Lane, brought by the gate keeper of the Counter of John Boteler, sheriff of London[167]	1 k.
A certain huckster, the wife of Henry Fletcher, dwelling at the end of Grub Street in the parish of St Giles without Cripplegate	1 k.

[167]   The Counter in Bread Street, the sheriff's prison.

[80] [f. 31v]

Le brewer dwelling at the Castle in Fleet Street	1 k.
Michael Eve, brewer, at the White Leg in the aforesaid Fleet Street	1 k.
John Rowlond, brewer, dwelling at the Key beside Dowgate	1 k.
John Broghton, dwelling at the George at the end of Showe Lane	1 k.
Roger Baronne, brewer, dwelling at the Swan outside Aldgate	1 k.
John Oseye, brewer, dwelling at the Cock outside Bishopsgate	1 k.
Henry Basset dwelling at the Cock & le Belle beside Holborn Cross	1 k.
A certain huckster dwelling in a certain cellar beside Holborn Bridge beside the parchment maker	[?]
John Riche, brewer, dwelling at the Ram in the parish of St Dunstan in Fleet Street	1 k.
John Thomas, brewer, dwelling at the Hartshorn in the parish of St Bride in Fleet Street	1 k.
Thomas Botelmaker, brewer, dwelling at the Cock below Ludgate	1 k.
Beatrix Tye dwelling at the Cup in Crooked Lane	1 barrel
The wife of Roger Baronne dwelling in la Vintry	1 k.
John Clerk dwelling at the Pie in la Riole	1 k.
Richard Kilsole dwelling at the Cock in the parish of St John Zachary	1 k.
The wife of William, clerk at the church of St Margaret in Friday Street	1 k.

[81] [f. 32r]

[*Latin*] **In the present year, the 8ᵗʰ of the reign of King Henry V [1420–1] in the month of July, Richard Whetyington, then being mayor of the city of London ordered that all sellers of ale called in English 'hucksters' in that city should come to the Guildhall, and they came according to his precept.**

And there the same mayor made them swear upon the sacred Gospels of God and declare from which particular Brewers they procured the ale that they sold in their houses and also at what price they bought it. And certain persons among the hucksters responded, according to the sacred oath made to the mayor, that they bought ale for 4s. 8d. a barrel, some for 4s. 6d., some for 4s. 4d., and some for 3s. 6d. And all the names of the aforesaid hucksters and Brewers were written in the book of the chamberlain from the information of the said hucksters.
And soon the mayor commanded by various among the said Brewers of London to appear at the Guildhall on the 22ⁿᵈ day of August following, that is, those Brewers whose names were written in the book of the chamberlain from the information from the said hucksters. And the same Brewers came and soon they were called to come into the chamber to the council, to be present at the court of the mayor and aldermen, that is, Thomas Grene, John Thetford, Robert Smyth and others.
There, the same mayor made them swear upon the book¹⁶⁸ that they told the truth about how they sold their ale to the said hucksters. The said Brewers replied to the mayor that some were selling at 4s. 8d. and others at a greater or lesser sum, as is declared above.
Then the mayor reprehended them, saying that they were false and would not be able to sell their goods, because of their iniquity and falsehood and he swore that he would have a sum of money from them for their transgressions. Similarly, he said

---

¹⁶⁸ Presumably the Gospels or the entire Bible.

that the said craft of Brewers were obliged by a certain recognizance at that time to forfeit a penalty of £20 from the craft.

The Brewers responded to the mayor saying that they had not transgressed, because the Searchers of the craft guarded the ale and other things pertaining to the said craft, and that they faithfully made and completed all duties incumbent upon their craft. And the mayor said that they had transgressed and lied under penalty of their obligation about how they sold their ale to the hucksters in large flagons for 1½d.

[82]

Then one brewer, whose name was Thomas Dryffeld responded to the mayor and aldermen saying that in this way the truth was shown between the accounts rendered by the hucksters and the goods of the Brewers. It was best to agree to pay a sum called in English 'a common fine' so that they could sell their best ale to our hucksters.

He said to all the aldermen present that this was a false thing, and he ventured to place his life in doubt over this fight with them.

Then the mayor said with a scornful countenance that they were false transgressors. 'I say to you that by the power vested in me by all men, that all the trade of the Brewers of London will be suspended, because it is recorded in this court that you were bound by an obligation and you must respond to me on this matter on Tuesday, that is the 28th day of August.'

Then on the Monday before the said Tuesday, the greater part of all the Brewers using the craft of Brewers of the city of London were gathered on that day at Brewers' Hall to ordain persons of the livery to reply to the mayor about various matters for which the mayor proposed to admonish them and their craft.

On the last day before the Tuesday, various persons were nominated and ordained by the said craft of Brewers, whose names were: Thomas Grene, Robert Hylton, John Pyken, Robert Smyth, Thomas Dryffeld, John Mason, John Riche, Thomas Emond, Roger Swanneffeld, John Ketyng, Adam Copendale, William Ferrour, John Caston, Thomas

[f. 32v]

Hatcher, John Moyle, [*and who*] appeared at the court of the mayor at the Guildhall on the said day to hear what the mayor and aldermen intended or wished to impose upon the said craft of Brewers. And when they came before the council, the mayor & aldermen said 'You, the craft of Brewers are bound by an obligation given to you by which the craft is bound, that is, by a recognizance. All this time you have neglected to pay the £20.'

[83]

The said persons of Brewers' craft elected for this responded and said that they had never conceded to such an obligation. Others said that they were ignorant of such an obligation.

And then the mayor responded as above in an evil way and said: 'You are false.' The mayor & aldermen said that the Brewers would be advised to appear again in 8 days and that they had a copy of their obligation. The aforesaid Brewers contradicted this and said to him that they had never had such a copy, or if they had, that it was lost, therefore they asked the mayor and aldermen for a new copy of the bond. The mayor & aldermen responded that they did not have another copy of the bond at that court. The mayor said to the Brewers standing there, 'I believe that you propose to destroy this court, but this does not stand in your power.'

And then certain aldermen spoke to the Brewers and gave them advice to submit to the mayor's authority. The said Brewers said that they would not submit to the mayor's domination but would please him with goods given. The mayor and aldermen did not promise that the Brewers could have a copy of the said obligations and modifications. The Brewers supplicated to the mayor that they might hear the said ordinance read before them and John Carpenter, common clerk to the mayor at the time, read the said obligation and ordinance in the court of the mayor, to the aldermen and the said Brewers. Then the said Brewers denied that they had ever had the ordinance and obligation. The mayor immediately arose in the court and in these words said that during his time of office he would soon punish the craft of Brewers of London.

On the 26th day of the month of September of the said year, the mayor ordered the common council [*to act*] against the Brewers. In that council it was ordered that the Brewers of London should submit themselves to the power and government of the mayor and remain in all things licensed and honest according to his will, otherwise he would destroy the freedom of the Brewers.

And they would not be designated amongst the other crafts of the city of London.

After this, on the first day of the month of October, the mayor commanded the most discreet and worthiest of the craft of Brewers, to come to his court at the Guildhall, accompanied by 3 sergeants of the chamber.

[84]

They came and stood in the court of the mayor. Various aldermen advised the Brewers to submit to the power of the mayor. The said mayor and aldermen said to the Brewers that in this case if they conceded to the will and proposals of the mayor, the same mayor and aldermen would order an honest and suitable agreement with the said Brewers in such a form as the said Brewers and the craft would find reasonable, and by such flattering words, the Brewers were induced to agree.

Upon this, the said Brewers responded to the mayor saying that we, the freemen of our craft, without the assent of other freemen of other crafts and those who use our craft, and those who are not free in our craft, do not wish to consent to other impositions upon our craft.

Then the mayor told the Masters of the craft of Brewers that they should appoint [*representatives*] on behalf of all those who used the Brewers' craft in the city of London, from whatever craft, and that they [*should*] be freemen and that they should come to the hall of Brewers by the precept of the mayor on the day assigned by the Masters of the craft of Brewers.

The Masters and freemen of the craft came to Brewers' Hall and there were assigned by the Masters of the craft of Brewers to deliberate and to respond to the mayor as above. Others of the said craft were obedient to the said mayor and aldermen. The names of those who did not come were recorded and the mayor punished them by a fine and rebuked them. Then the Masters sent to all those persons who used the Brewers' craft of the city of London, to meet at Brewers' Hall on the Thursday, in 10 days following, that is

[f. 33r]

the 3rd day of October, the month and year aforesaid [1420] and more than 200 Brewers were admitted there on the aforesaid day. Their names were called, and those who had not come were to be punished and noted for this deficiency.

[85]

They debated between themselves in what way to reply to the mayor on the Sabbath day next following, the 5th day in the present month of October. Amongst themselves certain of them said that the mayor proposed to have £20 from the Brewers of London, because the said Brewers sold flagons of their best ale for 2d., from [*outside*] their homes and tenements, against the ordinance of the mayor. The mayor at that time wished the Brewers to concede to be governed in the form in which the Masters and other good men of the craft of Brewers proposed for governing the aforesaid matter, and they must consider how to pay the said sum of money which he had ordered by his discretion, so that they should continue to be able to sell from their houses.

By the counsel of the said Brewers amongst themselves, the said ordinance was confirmed by the craft of Brewers and persons of the craft were to meet on the next Sabbath day following, the 5th day of the month of October, to come to the Guildhall in the presence of the mayor and aldermen. The mayor and aldermen at once sought a response from those Brewers, that is, for the obligation of £20, in which they were bound and obliged, and whether they wished to obey the court or not.

And one brewer by the name of Thomas Grene said there are 16 of our craft, Masters and Searchers of our craft and we wish to pay towards the works at the Guildhall, each paying 20s., that is the sum of £16, and that no others of our craft should pay towards the said sum except we 16. Then the mayor said that they must be governed by that court. Nothing would please him at that time except for them to submit themselves to the mayor and aldermen. After this the mayor licensed the said Brewers to leave the court as directed. Then the mayor and aldermen deliberated and ordained that the said Brewers of London must pay £20 towards the works on the Guildhall. Then they sent for the Masters of the craft of Brewers on the Sabbath day, that is, the 12th day of the month of October. On that day the said Brewers did not come to the Guildhall except for one, named Thomas Grene. The mayor and aldermen were not well pleased or contented by this. Thomas Grene said by excuse that none of his associates had been summoned, except for him.

[86]

The same mayor assigned to them a new day to come to his court, that is Tuesday, the 15th day of the same month of October, on which day it was ordered that the aforesaid Brewers should be sent to the mayor at the Guildhall, with each person under a penalty of £20.

And on the aforesaid day, Thomas Grene, Robert Hylton, Robert Smyth and others of the craft came to the Guildhall and appeared at the court of the aforesaid mayor and aldermen. The mayor said 'You, the Brewers, know that you were ordered by a bond in the presence of this court to pay £20 towards the work of the Guildhall, as quickly as possible, and that unless it is paid by the Sabbath day, the 26th day of this month, your craft will have to pay £100 towards the same works.'¹⁶⁹

---

¹⁶⁹ Saturday, 26 October 1420, rather than Sunday.

However, that day and for some other days, they had no response. Concerning this, Thomas Grene, Robert Carpenter, John Pyken, John Mason, John Riche, William Ferrour, Roger Swannefeld and others, by advice, ordered and accounted amongst themselves how the Brewers of London should pay towards the said sum, as appears, by a certain tax amongst them, noted and written down. And after the ordinance was made for levying the aforesaid sum, the four Masters, that is, Thomas Grene and his associates, came to the Guildhall on the said 26ᵗʰ day of October, and there Richard Osbarn, clerk of the chamber, coming to the same Masters, sought from them the said £20, at the request of the mayor.[170]

They responded to him saying that they did not carry the sum and petitioned the mayor for a later day. And the mayor sent back the appointed Richard Osbarn to reiterate that unless they paid the aforesaid

[87] [f. 33v]

sum on the assigned day, the Brewers would have to pay a £40 fine and he promised this faithfully. According to the mayor's precept, they were to go to the Guildhall on the Monday next, that is on the day of the Apostles Simon and Jude.[171] On that day the Brewers of London did not come, because they were advised not to appear. And on that said day, the day before the mayor retired from the office of mayor, he sent for John Bitterden, then chamberlain of the Guildhall, and commanded him to receive the £20 from the Masters of the craft of Brewers, or else the Brewers must shut down and fasten up their doors, that is, on the 30ᵗʰ day of the month of October. However notwithstanding this, it was still not paid 6 days later. And on the 6ᵗʰ day of November, John Bitterden, chamberlain of the Guildhall, sent to the four Masters of the aforesaid craft, under penalty of closing their doors, that they must pay the aforesaid sum of £20.

[88]

And on that day the said Masters came and sought the mayor, that is William Cambrigge,[172] and supplicated him to grant to them a new day to pay the said sum, that is £20. The same mayor ordered them to pay £10 to the chamber in part payment and this they did without contradiction. In the above matter, the mayor said to them that they might pay the remainder when they could conveniently collect it without grievance to the Brewers of the said city of London.

In this matter the Masters of the said craft soon commanded various Brewers of the city of London to come to their Hall and make payments for the sum imposed upon them by the said Masters and Searchers of the same craft. And certain of them did not come, so the Masters of the said craft at the time complained to John Bitterden, chamberlain, about those who did not come.

The said chamberlain dealt with one obstinate by the name of John Sturmyn, dwelling at the Swan in Pissing Lane in the parish of St Pancras, who did not wish to come with his associates to the Hall nor to obey the Masters of their craft of Brewers.

[170] See R. A. Wood, 'Richard Osbarn, Guildhall Chamber Clerk, 1400–37', *Trans LAMAS* 69 (2018), 181–95 (181).
[171] 28 October.
[172] Whittington was the mayor 1419–20 and he was succeeded by William Cambrigge, mayor 1420–1.

The same aforesaid John, chamberlain, sent for him by a sergeant of the chamber, and ordered him to make an agreement with the said Masters of the craft of Brewers and to stand with them in the court of the mayor and aldermen, with the said Masters of the craft of Brewers, to hear his indictment for his disobedience. The same John Sturmyn promised to come to the chamber and that he would come to the Masters and submit to them. However, he did not come and instead sent his wife to Brewers' Hall, who paid 6s. 8d. towards the aforesaid sum of £20.

Afterwards some Brewers did not wish to come to Brewers' Hall and delayed paying the said sum. Then the aforesaid Masters of the Brewers' craft elected 8 willing and discreet men of the said craft to receive money for the said sum by 4 districts of the city of London. Rolls were delivered to them with the names of Brewers and the sums paid by each were written upon them.

The names of the collectors of the said sums were: John Riche, William Petervile, Robert Smyth, John Rothyng, John Ketyng, Hugh Neel, John Broke and Peter Carpenter.

[89]

The Masters supplicated and asked the 8 discreet and elected men to record the names of those who spoke against this and would not pay, and to put down and inscribe them in those rolls for the Masters of the said craft of Brewers, so that those named could be castigated, as above, by the mayor and aldermen, also by the chamberlain of the city of London, and all [*others*] paid their sum, notwithstanding, according to the records.

After this the said collectors went into the quarters of the city of London which were occupied by the said craft, that is, of Brewers, and collected from them various sums of money, specified and named in the rolls. They collected between them £16 3s., with difficulty, before the feast of the Nativity in the same year.

Before the collection of that sum, John Bitterden, then chamberlain, by the motion of Richard Whytyngton, former mayor of London, sent to the 4 Masters, under penalty of closure of their doors, that they should bring to the chamberlain the said £10 not then paid and owed since the 16th day of the month of October in the 8th year of the reign of King Henry V [1420–1].

Afterwards the Masters came willingly to the said Guildhall and presented that same sum to the said chamberlain, John Bitterden.

[90] [f. 34r]

At that time, the chamberlain repaid 64s. 4d. to the said Masters, for a quarter part of the fines of £12 17s. 4d., received by John Hill, the former chamberlain of the Guildhall in the time of Richard Whetyngton being mayor of London.[173] That sum was received from certain persons who sold ale without the proper measure, unsealed, whether from brewers or hucksters who sold barrels and kilderkins not sealed with the cooper's mark according to the order of the mayor, or with defective malt falsely taken to the common market in Gracechurch. Notwithstanding the said fine taken by the said John Bitterden, chamberlain, they paid the former chamberlain, John Hill, 20s. 3d., in consideration of the money already paid first by them, before receiving the said sum. A copy of all the sums forfeited in various ways, as aforesaid, was made, so that it could be entered on this present paper, that

[173] John Hyll was chamberlain 1416–20, and he was succeeded by John Beterden, 1420–34.

is according to the principle [*established*] during the mayoralty of the said Richard Whytyngton and still continuing today.

And a quarter of the levy of the said £20 was granted to the works of the said Guildhall, as was prescribed by a certain taxation by the Masters of the Brewers, made amongst the Brewers and those using the said craft in the city of London. Some paid generously and fully towards this taxation, others lessened their sum, some because of poverty and others, for various causes, paid nothing. Nevertheless, the said common taxation of £34 6s. 6d., was levied by the Brewers in various ways and spent on the same works.

[*scored*: A certain roll of parchment attached to this paper, as evidence, can be seen]
[*added*: The evidence can now be seen in this present folio now following.]

[91]

[*English*] **This is a copy of an ordinance made by John Welles, late mayor of London, for the governance of Brewers' craft when the said John Welles was mayor of the said city** [1431–2].[174]

For as much as it is given to the mayor and aldermen to understand that the Brewers, hostelers, cooks, pie bakers and hucksters and other persons selling ale by retail within the franchise and liberty of London, sell their ale by pots, cups, tankards and other unofficial measures, to the great deceit and harm of the common people, so the aforesaid mayor and aldermen, by the advice and assent of the commons in their full common council have made and ordained various establishments[175] for the common profit, to be proclaimed and observed through the city, which are shown hereafter and are such:

the first that if any person asks for a gallon, pottle, quart or pint of ale from any brewer, hosteler, cook, pie baker, huckster or any other person, whatsoever he is, who has ale to sell, then that brewer, hosteler, cook, pie baker, huckster, be it within his house or outside, should bring and take him such measure as the said buyer requires and asks for, and none other, and that it should be a measure according to the assize, and sealed with the seal of the Guildhall, and full of clear ale, and that none should resell ale for retail by other measures, nor in any other manner, upon pain of imprisonment, at the first time for 6 days and to pay 40d. to the chamber, and at the second time he is attainted of this, have imprisonment for 24 days and pay 6 marks, and so increasing the default, he shall increase the payment according to various *cyon*[176] of the mayor and aldermen.

Item that no brewer sell ale in great outside his house to any lord, gentle, or commons, by barrel, kilderkin or other great vessel more dearly than 1½d. for the gallon of the best [*ale*].

---

[174]   John Welles was the mayor 1431–2, so this passage, in English, and uncrossed, which continues overleaf, is a much later addition, written in a formerly blank space.
[175]   Arrangements.
[176]   Scion, branch or shoot? Here it seems to mean rules.

[92] [f. 34v]
Item that from henceforth within every ward, there shall not be but oo[177] number,
that is to say a certain [*number*] of hucksters of ale, which after the discretion
of the alderman of the same ward shall be suitable and competent to serve the
common people, and that none be of that number unless they are of good fame and
condition and a free man or woman of the city, and they should find good surety
to the chamber of 100*s*., or 5 marks, at the discretion of the chamberlain, to keep
the ordinance written hereafter. That is to say that they do not hold a bordel,[178]
bawdiness or any other losengerie[179] within their houses.
And that they should not buy any ale in retail from any brewer except by barrels,
kilderkins [*scored*: gallon] and other vessels justly marked outside with their good
and true holding within, no more dearly than at 1½*d*. the gallon, abating[180] in every
barrel 2 gallons, and in every kilderkin 1 gallon and every other vessel should be
according to the assurance and quantity for the draughts.
And that they should not sell more dearly when retailing within their houses than
at 2*d*. the gallon, 1*d*. the pottle, ½*d*. the quart and a pint for a farthing, and so by
measure sealed and full of clear ale, upon pain of paying 20*d*. for the first offence,
40*d*. for the second, 6*s*. 8*d*. for the third time, when confession will be good *preeff*,[181]
or other good, reasonable manner, at the discretion of the mayor and aldermen or the
chamberlain of the time if convicted or attainted of the contrary.
If he again contravenes the ordinance a fourth time, he and his pledges will [*be*]
forfeit and instead of the penalty [*he will pay*] 100*s*. or 5 marks or be committed to
prison at the discretion of the mayor and aldermen and be sequestered and forbidden
from the occupation and haunting[182] of huckster for evermore, at the discretion of the
mayor and aldermen.

This ordinance will begin at the Feast of the Purification[183] next coming, to this
end, that in the meantime, men must find their surety. If any after the fourth time
still holds such a huckster's house, then he will not be admitted nor find surety as
aforesaid, and he will forfeit the value of what he has sold and put out by hucksters,
and nonetheless [*will suffer*] imprisonment of his body at the will and discretion of
the mayor and aldermen.

So that it can be known how many hucksters in certain houses should be admitted
within each ward, let their names be presented amongst others at the great court of
the mayor, to be held on the Monday after Epiphany.[184]
[*A folio has been cut out here*]

---

[177]   The scribe wrote oo, not an actual number.
[178]   Brothel.
[179]   Loose behaviour.
[180]   Perhaps the sense of 'ending in' was intended.
[181]   Practice, proof?
[182]   Habit, practice.
[183]   2 February (1432?).
[184]   6 January (1432?).

[93] [f. 35r]
[Latin]
Here are written the names of those bringing malt to the common market of London and because it was found by the Masters and Wardens to be defective, the same was forfeited and sent to John Hyll, chamberlain at the Guildhall in the year as above [1420].[185]

[Latin with names in English]

First from John Hogge 3 quarters of malt	forfeited
Item from Thomas Howe 1 quarter of malt	forfeited
Item from John Sharpe 1 quarter of malt	forfeited
Grene staying at Barnet 1 quarter of malt	forfeited
A certain John Hentewode, formerly the servant of Tyler, maltman, 1 quarter	forfeited
John Valentyn, maltman, 2 quarters of malt	forfeited
John Woodeleff of Ware 1 quarter of malt	forfeited
Simon West of Edlesborough in the county of Buckingham, 1 quarter	forfeited
Fulke, maltman of Barnet, 1 quarter of malt	forfeited
William Herte of Ware 1 quarter of malt	forfeited
Hamond of Westmill 2 quarters of malt	forfeited
Grene of Barnet 1 quarter of malt	forfeited[186]
John Belton of Barnet 1 quarter of malt	forfeited
From a stranger, unknown, 1 quarter of malt	forfeited
From a man in the county of Cambridge 1 quarter of malt	forfeited
John Dolphyn was loader of the said malt	–
William Caphode 1 quarter of malt	forfeited

Thomas Dowhete of Hoddesdon in the county of Hertford 1 quarter forfeited, 21st day of June 58s.

William Crowche, maltman of the county of Hertford 3 quarters forfeited, 7th August By Mason and Wode

A certain maltman in the county of Cambridge forfeited 6 quarters, which were found at the house of Roger Swannefelde, dwelling at the Two Staples in the parish of St Benet at Paul's Wharf.

[94] [f. 35v]
[Latin] **Ordinances made by the mayor and aldermen against those who bring grain and malt to the city and do not sell them in the common market, but elsewhere, in contravention of the said ordinances written below.**

[French] That any stranger who sells grain and barley[187] should sell it only in the open market and nowhere besides, nor by samples, upon pain of forfeiture of their said grain and malt, and that the said grain and malt will be taken to sell entirely in the market, and not placed in a hiding place, under the same penalty.

---

[185]   See **[90]**.
[186]   Perhaps Grene of Barnet offended twice, or there were two men called Grene.
[187]   *Cal. Letter-Book, I*, 46, fn.2, 'bredz crew' was translated as 'broken barley'.

Item that no manner of grain be sold at Billingsgate nor at la Ryve la Reine,[188] nor at Gracechurch nor Newgate before the Masters who are ordained by them [*ensure that they are not*] persons under forfeiture of grain otherwise sold.

That no foreign merchant going towards the city by land or by water should sell his grain beforehand by sample, but should take it to the open market, to the places abovesaid, upon pain of forfeiture.

[*Latin*] Memorandum that by virtue of the ordinances written above, the seizures and presentations of malt, as appear in the following, were taken to the use of the sheriffs of the city.

[95] [f. 36r]
The names of those selling malt by samples and taking it to private places, and thus defaulting against the statutes of London, and by the Masters and Wardens of Brewers' craft certified to the accountant of Robert Whetygham, sheriff of London, for which transgression they submitted to the said sheriff and made a fine to him.

[*Latin with English place names*]
First 4 quarters of malt found in the home of Michael Tregononne, brewer   –
Item John Hogge 2 quarters   –
Item 4 quarters in the house formerly of Walter Riche, brewer,
                seized by Hylton and Mason
Item 6 quarters from Gurney, maltman, which were found in the
house of Walter Glyn in Aldersgate Street,   seized by Ferrour and Carpenter
Item 6 quarters which were found in the house of Thome Wegge at
the Swan with the Ship in Red Cross Street,   seized by Grene and Hylton
Item 4 quarters which were found in the market at Gracechurch in a
tavern,   seized by Hylton, Wode, Mason & Chapman
Item 8 quarters which were found in the house of John Farman
outside Bishopsgate,   seized by Pyken & Carpenter
Item on the Wednesday, that is the vigil of the Supper of the Lord,[189]
4 quarters of malt found in the house of Mymmys fishmonger,
        seized by Weste, Sergeant on the order of William atte Wode
4 quarters which were in the house at the Cup in Crooked Lane,
        seized by Valentyn Traynell, sergeant, on the order of the Masters
Item in Easter week, 8 quarters which were found in the house of
John More at Ludgate,   seized by William atte Wode
Item 6 quarters in the same week which were found
in the lodging house of the Abbot of Ramsey,
        seized by the porter of the accountant of Robert Whetyngham
Item 3 quarters in the house of Robert Lynford at the Horse Head in
la Poultry,   seized by Crane

---

188   Queenhithe.
189   3 April 1420, the eve of Cena Domini, the Last Supper of Our Lord, commemorated on Maundy Thursday.

[96] [f. 36v]

Item 4 quarters which were found in the house of Robert
Sqwyer at the Cock in Cornhill in the parish of St Christopher,
seized by a sergeant by order of the Masters.
Item 9 quarters which were found in a house at the Cock outside
Leadenhall, seized by Robert Carpentyer
Item 7 quarters which were found in the house of Thomas atte Wode
at the Fleur de Lys beside Queenhithe, seized by William Crane
Item 7 quarters which were found in the house of John Lucas at the
Glene [*Wheatsheaf*] beside Queenhithe, seized by William Crane
Item 10 quarters which were found in a tavern at the home of a
certain widow called Margaret Leonard at the Cock beside the
Augustinian Friars, seized by William Crane
Item 6 quarters from John Wodeleff which were found in the house
of Richard Frepurs at the Cock, seized by –
Item 2 quarters which were found in the house of Robert Lynforde at
the Horse Head in the Poultry in the parish of St Mary Colechurch,
seized by William atte Wode
Item 4 quarters found in the house of John Lwcas at the *Glene* beside
Queenhithe, seized by William atte Wode
Item 16 quarters or more, which were found in 2 taverns at the
house of Margaret Stockett at the Star and the Moon in the parish of
St Mary [*Aldermary*] called Aldermary church, seized by Salter & Hylton
Item 6 quarters from Matthew Stepyng which were found in the
house of a widow at the Pannier beside Queenhithe, seized by West, Sergeant
Item 3 quarters from Thomas Payn of the county of Cambridge,
which were found in the house of John Canonne at the Lion in the
parish of St Botolph beside Billingsgate, seized by Wode, Mason & Ferrour
Item 8 quarters which were found in the house of Jacob Lenegro at
the Pie beside Queenhithe, seized by Salter
Item 5 quarters from Typpynge otherwise Kyppynge, maltman, which
were found in the house of John Bayley at the Swan in Silver Street,
seized by Hylton & Wode
Item 5 quarters which were found in the house of John Thomas,
tailor, at the Hartshorn in Fleet Street in the parish of St Bride
[*St Brigide*] seized by Hylton
Item 6 quarters which were found in the house of Henry Grene at the
Chequer in East Cheap, seized by Crane and West, Sergeant
Item 4 quarters which were found in the house of William Payn at
the Swan beside St Anthony's, seized by Crane
Item 6 quarters found in the house of Robert Sqwyer at the Cock in
Cornhill in the parish of St Christopher, seized by Salter.

[97] [f. 37r]

[*Latin*] **Memorandum that the said Masters and Wardens, that is,
Thomas Grene, Robert Hylton, Robert Carpenter, William atte Wode,
John Peken and their associates received, on 30th day of May in the 8th
year of the reign of King Henry V [1420–1], for transgressions abovesaid,
for their part, that is, a quarter part of the fines, by the hand of Richard
Tewkesle, on behalf of Robert Whetyngham, sheriff of London,** 18s. 1d.

[*English*] This is the answer to the said John Welles, mayor [1431–2],[190] and to the aldermen of the city of London, made by the advice of the craft of Brewers of London, as it shows, with 6 articles following, after the bill, as you may read and find it written.

Full meekly and in the most humble wise shown, all the enfranchised men of the craft of Brewers of the city beseech that it would please your full noble and rich wise discretion tenderly to consider the full grievance and importable costs and charges with which your said beseechers continually from day to day stand charged, within the said city, as in diverse articles written underneath, more openly rehearsed, and thereupon that it would please your noblesse, by your full wise discretion, graciously to ordain for the good rule and governance of the said craft, to the worship of God, the profit and commodity of our most sovereign lord and of all his full worthy lords spiritual and temporal, and for the wealth of all the common people, to grant and assent that the article or articles ensuing, by the common assent of all the people of the said craft, made here and compiled with little knowledge, as they must so be,[191] by your full wise discretion, may be accepted, ratified, confirmed and put in perpetual record.

First that whereas the said good folk of Brewers' craft in time past were accustomed to buy 9 bushels of clean malt for the quarter, now, because of diverse ordinances and statutes, made before this time, [*they*] may not buy past[192] 7 bushels for the quart of clean malt [?]*vanned*, to great harm and hindering of all the buyers of any such malt within the said craft.
Examined.
[*continued at* **[101]** *on f. 38r*]

[98] [f. 37v]
[*Latin with English*]
The names of freemen of the city of London made in the craft of Brewers of London during the time of Thomas Grene and his associates being Masters of the same craft, with the sums of money paid, as appears below, in the 8ᵗʰ and 9ᵗʰ years of the reign of King Henry V [1420–2].

William Ferrour at the Bell in St Margaret Pattens Lane	13*s.* 4*d.*
Henry Basset at the Cock and the Bell beside Holborn Cross	26*s.* 8*d.*
William Rawlyn at the Mill in St John Street	26*s.* 8*d.*
John Thomas at the Eagle in the malt market	16*s.* 8*d.*
John Bedeford at the Seven Stars in Smithfield	20*s.*
Nicholas Grenewode at the Elms in St John Street	26*s.* 8*d.* deceased.
John Fekenham at the Harp in St Clement's Lane	13*s.* 4*d.*
Henry Rowe at the Dragon outside Bishopsgate	20*s.*
Thomas Sore formerly at the Bell outside Bishopsgate	13*s.* 4*d.*
William Antrou formerly at the Swan beside Billingsgate	13*s.* 4*d.*
Richard Mayhew at the Lamp outside Bishopsgate	13*s.* 4*d.*

---

190 Mayor 1431–2. This passage is a later insertion, not crossed through. The subsequent similar passages in English are uncrossed, up to **[117]**.
191 'sewen mawen'.
192 More than.

William Totewell at the Hartshorn in Southwark	23s. 4d.
Simon Henry at the Bear in St Clement's Lane	16s. 8d.
Robert Ketyng beside Aldgate	16s. 8d.
John Newman, servant at the Red Lion outside St Martin the Grand	16s. 8d.
William Riche at the Vernacle in the parish of St Bartholomew the Less	13s. 4d.
William Eyre at the Pie in Smithfield	13s. 4d.
John Brownyng at the Moon outside Bishopsgate	20s.
John Parker at the Angel in the parish of St Michael Queenhithe	16s. 8d.
Edmund Disse at the Ship outside Cripplegate	10s.
Richard West at the Pewter Pot in the parish of St Andrew in Cornhill	13s. 4d.

[99]
These are those who have paid the Masters for their freedom but have not been entered by the chamberlain of the Guildhall

Richard Carowe at the Key in Holborn	13s. 4d.
John More at the Rose in White Cross Street	13s. 4d.

Here are written below those who have paid the Masters in part for their freedom

John Davy formerly at the Pie in Holborn in part payment of 16s.,	8s. 8d.

Sum £19 18s. 8d., of which £8 is for the common profit and there remains
£11 18s. 8d.

[100] [f. 38r]
The names of brothers entering the fraternity this year, with sums of money paid, as appears below.

Baldewyne Hoper at the Purse outside Cripplegate	3s. 4d.
William Boune at the Pie in the Moor	3s. 4d. deceased
Robert Elken at the George in Fenchurch Street	3s. 4d.
John Goldryng at the Katherine Wheel in Thames Street	3s. 4d.
John Jacob at the Red Lion outside St Martin the Grand	3s. 4d.
Stephen Clean at the Bell beside Aldersgate	3s. 4d.
John Hardyng at the Cock in Holborn	3s. 4d.
Alan John at the Swan beside Billingsgate	3s. 4d.
Henry Basset at the Cock & Bell beside Holborn Cross	3s. 4d.
John Riche at the Angel in Fleet Street	4s.
Robert Dellowe at the White Cross outside Cripplegate	4s.
Phillip Godfrey formerly at the Mill in Thames Street	5s.
John Holbek at the Lamb in Distaff Lane	5s.

Sum 48s. of which for the common profit 43s. 4d., there remains 4s. 8d.

[101]

[*English*] [*continued from* **[97]** *on f. 37r*] Also that your said beseechers were accustomed in time past to brew and make their ale with well water through the said city. Now the said persons, enfranchised Brewers, buy all their water from bouges[193] and carters, and brew and make their ale with it, to the great charge and cost of all the said craft, in as much as whatever brewer of the said city that so buys his water and occupies the feat of brewing in the said city, pays yearly the cost of buying his said water, some at 12 marks, sometimes 10 marks, and at the least 4 marks or more.

Also whereas every brewer enfranchised within the said city, occupying the said craft of Brewers in time past might have had his chief brewer for 40s. a year, with meat and drink, and his second brewer for 30s. a year with meat and drink, and his third brewer for 20s. by the year with meat and drink, now no enfranchised brewer and householder within the said city may have nor hire a servant chief brewer to serve by the year, but only by the week, and taking no less than 2s. or 20d. the week, after £5 or 6 marks a year with meat and drink, and the second brewer 4 marks and more and meat and drink, to the great charge, cost and hindering ... Examined.

[102] [f. 38v]

Also for as much as the said persons, Brewers enfranchised and householders within the said city readily most occupy and hold their brewhouses which are of great rent and charge, wherefore your said beseechers, because of holding their said houses of great rent from day to day, are more grievously taxed, with all manner of charges to bear in the said city, as in taxes, tallage,[194] loans, gifts and such other to their importable cost and charge.

Please it to your full wise discretion that all these promises by your full worthy noblesse, tenderly considered, to ordain and grant unto your said beseechers, the Brewers enfranchised within the said city, that they from henceforth may sell and retail their ale within their houses and without, by just measure, sealed, that is to say in gallons, pottles and quarts, like and in all wise according to the good ordinances thereof made and ordained in the time of Richard Whityngton, late mayor of the said city.

All of which articles, in summary before declared, after the said great and importable charges, by your wise discretion plainly considered, of your full worthy noblesse, may it please you graciously to reform, ordain and establish according to your full wise discretion, to please God and for the common ease of the people, in the way of charity.

[103]

This is a bill made and ordained for the governance of servants as for their salary, and what they should take by year, which bill with all the articles following, was granted in the time of John Gedeneye being mayor of London [1427–8], and was to have been put on permanent record and enrolled in the Guildhall, but Robert Carpenter, Hugh Glene and Alexander Myles and Peter Carpenter were the cause

---

[193] Bouge: wallet or bag, made of hide.
[194] Toll or customs duty.

of it not being enrolled at that time, and yet it cost the craft 20 marks and more money.[195]

To the right worshipful lords and wise mayor and aldermen of the city of London, all the enfranchised folk of the craft of Brewers of the same city show how in time past many and diverse ordinances have been made and ordained within the franchise of the aforesaid city, by you and your noble predecessors, governors of the same city, for the good rule and governance of the said craft. May it please your wise discretion to grant and assent that those articles following, by common assent of all the good folk of the said craft, made and compiled from their little knowledge as they so may be, by your right wise discretion, may be accepted, ratified, conceded, and put on perpetual record.

[104] [f. 39r]
First that no servant of the said craft that is chief brewer take more by year for his salary from any master brewer that is a householder of the said craft than 53s. 4d. sterling, [*with*] meat, drink and clothing and his advantages.

Also that no second brewer's servant of the said craft should take any more by the year for his salary than 40s., with meat, drink and clothing and his advantages.

Also that no master brewer who is a householder of the said craft should give more salary to his servant than allowed, before specified and expressed, and if any master brewer who is householder of the said craft gives more to his servant yearly than specified before, then he should pay to the chamber of the Guildhall of London 40s., of which the half part is to be delivered to the Wardens of the said craft, to the use of the commonalty of the said craft of Brewers. And if any servant brewer of the same craft takes more salary yearly than is expressed before, in the manner abovesaid, then he is to pay to the said chamber for a fine 6s. 8d. and the excess that he takes over the salary, limited as before, in the manner written before, of which half should go to the use of the commonalty of the said craft of Brewers, and the body of the said servant is to be punished by imprisonment, by the advice and discretion of the mayor of the said city at the time, as the quantity of the forfeit against the ordinance asks. And so as often as any person or persons, servant or servants of the same craft be found or shall be found defective in this said ordinance and thereof be duly committed, by examination or in any other wise, and thereupon is not to be delivered out of prison until such servants have found sufficient surety to observe, keep and fulfil the ordinances written above.

[105]
Also that no servant of the said craft being single and having no wife hold nor occupy any chamber, except in his master's house, upon pain of paying a fine to the chamber and being imprisoned at the discretion of the mayor at the time, and the said fine is to be made to the value of the rent that the householder pays yearly for his said chamber.

---

[195] Masters 1426–8. This passage, which starts at **[97]** and is continued at **[101]**–**[102]** is a later insertion.

Also that no servant of the same craft should stand, nor be in any place within the city to be hired by the day, if he be required by any person who is a householder of the same craft to serve by the year, after the form of the ordinance written before. And if any such will not serve by the year, then he is to be punished by way of imprisonment until he finds sufficient surety to serve according to the ordinance abovesaid, and so to be punished as often as any such servant of the same craft will not serve by the year if he be required.

Also if any servant of the said craft of Brewers voids, or is absent or else refuses the said occupation of brewer and puts himself into any other occupation of labour within the same city, because of the aforesaid ordinances, while they may be withheld in service in the same craft, then they will be punished by way of imprisonment and will make a fine, at the discretion of the mayor of the said city and be restored to serve a householder of the same craft, according to the ordinances abovesaid, and such covenants made so become void and nought. Examined.

[106] [f. 39v]
To the right worshipful lords and wise mayor and aldermen of the city of London: All the enfranchised folk of the craft of Brewers in the same city show very meekly that they have, in times past, had many and diverse ordinances that have been made and ordained within the franchise of the aforesaid city by you and your noble predecessors of the said city, for the good rule and governance of the said craft. May it please your wise discretion to grant and assent that these articles following, made by the common assent of all the good folk of the said craft, made with their little knowledge, compiled as they must be,[196] by your right wise discretion, be accepted, ratified, confirmed and put in perpetual record.

[107]
First that no servant of the said craft that is chief brewer, having the ability to rule and govern diligently, who belongs to the aforesaid [*craft of*] brewing, of whatever manner or condition he be, should take more by the year from any householder occupying or using the said craft, for his salary than 53s. 4d., with meat, drink, clothing and his advantages.

Also that no second brewer's servant of the said craft should take more than 40s., with meat, drink, clothing and his advantages.

Also that no householder abovesaid of the said craft should give more salary to his servant than is allowed, as it is expressed and specified before. If any householder abovesaid of the said craft should give more to his servant yearly than has been specified before, then he shall pay 40s. to the chamber of the Guildhall of London, of which the half part shall be delivered to the Wardens of the said craft for the use of the commonalty of the craft of Brewers.

And if any servant brewer of the said craft, takes more salary yearly than is expressed in the manner abovesaid, then he shall pay 6s. 8d., of which half shall return to the chamber, and the other half, with the excess that he has taken above

196 'sewen mawen'.

113

the salary as limited above, shall come to the use of the commonalty of the craft of Brewers, in the manner written before. And the body of the said servant is to be punished by imprisonment, according to the advice and discretion of the mayor at the time, as the quantity of the forfeit against the ordinance asks.

And as often as any person or persons, servant or servants of the same craft be found or shall be found defective in these said ordinances, and duly convicted thereof, by examination or in any other way, and thereupon is not to be delivered from prison until such servants have found sufficient surety to observe, keep and fulfil the ordinance written above. [*continued at* [110] *on f. 41r*]

[108] [f. 40r]
[*Latin with English surnames and place names*]
The names of those selling malt by samples and taking it to private places, and thus defaulting against the statutes of London, and certified by the Masters and Wardens of the craft of Brewers to the accountant of John Botelere, sheriff of London, for which transgression they humbled themselves before the said sheriff and made a fine to him.

First Thomas Howe 3 quarters   –
Item 4 quarters found in the house of William Harry called
Long Entry,   seized by Ferrour, Peken, & Hatcher
Item 4 quarts from William Preest in the house of Henry Bedell,
brewer,   seized by Robert Carpenter
Item 4 quarters found at Broken Wharf,   seized by Carpenter
Item 3 quarters found in the house of John Bragour in Smithfield
Item 7 quarters which were found in the house of Richard Bragour, ostler, at the Ram in Smithfield
Item 9 quarters from Matthew Stepyng which were found
in the house of Peter Carpenter in Bower Rowe at Ludgate
                          seized by Grene, Hylton, Wode & Chapman, Mason:

Item 2 quarters which were found at the house of Hugh Glene opposite the Friars Minor
Item 5 quarters which were found at the house of Roger Ware at the Salt Wharf beside le Queenhithe
Item 5 quarters from William Bodevyle which were found at the
house of Sturmyn in Pissing Lane at the Swan in the parish of
St Pancras   seized by Hylton, Wode, Mason, Chapman:
Item on the Easter Vigil 8 quarters found in the house at the Cock at
the end of Ivy Lane,   seized by Horsle, Sergeant, on the orders of the Masters
Item in that same week 5 quarters found in the home of John Bedford
at the Seven Stars in Smithfield at the Bars,   seized by William atte Wod.

[109] [f. 40v]
Item 4 quarters from John Bechamp which were found in the lodging
house of William Claysson, beerman,   seized by William atte Wode
Item 6 quarters from the said John, which were found in the lodging
house of David Soys, brewer,   seized by Ferrour and Salter

Item 1 quarter, no more, which was found in the house of John Chapman in Grub Street,	seized by Wode
Item 6 quarters which were found at the house of John Cherman, cooper, at the Lamb in Grub Street,	seized by Chapman
Item 4 quarters which were found in the house of Peter Hayforde at the Vine in the Riole,	seized by William atte Wode
Item 5 quarters which were found in the house of John Laurence at the Horse in Aldersgate Street,	seized by Salter
Item 8 quarters which were found in the house of Michael Eve at the White Leg beside Fleet Bridge,	seized by Wode
Item 10 quarters which were found in the house of John Mayne at Paul's Wharf,	seized by Wode

Memorandum that the aforesaid Masters and Wardens, that is, Thomas Grene, Robert Hylton, Robert Carpenter, John Peken, [*above the line*: William atte Wode] & their associates received on the 20th day of June in the 8th year of the reign of King Henry V [1420], from the transgressions above said, for their part, that is, a quarter part, by the hands of John Selby, on behalf of John Botelere, sheriff of London, 19s. 5d.

[110] [f. 41r]
[*English*] [*continued from* [107] *f. 39v*]
Also that any servant of the said craft who is single and has no wife should not occupy a chamber except in his Master's house, upon pain of a fine to be paid to the chamber of the Guildhall, to the value of the rent that he should pay for his chamber, and also to be imprisoned, by the discretion of the mayor at the time.
Also that no servant of the said craft should stand nor be in any place within the city to be hired by the day, if he is required by any person who is a householder of the same craft to serve by the year, after the form of the ordinances written before, and if any such will not serve for a year then he is to be punished by way of imprisonment, until he finds sufficient surety to serve according to the ordinances written before [*scored*: and if any such will not serve by the year] abovesaid and so to be punished as often as any servant of the said craft of Brewers will not serve by the year, if he is required.

[111]
Also if any servant of the said craft of Brewers should void, be absent, or else refuse the said occupation of brewer and put himself into any other occupation of labour within the same city, because of the aforesaid ordinances, while they may be withheld in service in the same craft, then they are to be punished by way of imprisonment and pay a fine at the discretion of the mayor of the said city, and be restored to serve a householder of the same craft, according to the ordinances abovesaid, and such covenants made so become void and nought.
Also if any enfranchised brewers in the city or brewersmen bear out of any house from others, customers, a barrel or kilderkin that is void and empty and is not his, nor is marked with his mark, and keeps it still for his own, that [*they*] may be duly punished (upon him) and he will be convicted, through which deceit much harm falls

to the loser of the vessel. Therefore he who thus keeps the vessel must pay a fine of one noble[197] to the use of the chamber.

And if any brewersman bears out such a vessel, outwitting[198] himself that it is not his Master's, that he should make a fine at each time that he is so convicted, to pay to the chamber 3s. 4d.

And if it is so that any Brewer enfranchised erases away another man's mark and sets thereon his own mark, or else keeps within his house that vessel so erased and the rightful mark done away, he will be convicted of this and make a fine to the chamber of 6s. 8d., the fourth part of which will return to the said enfranchised Brewers for their travail. Examined. By Coket.[199] [*continued at* [**117**] *on f. 42v*]

[**112**] [f. 41v]

[*French*] **The ordinance of a dinner, with the costs thereon, made on the day of the Conversion of St Paul[200] in the month of January in the first year of King Henry VI** [1422–3] **in the time of William Walderne, mayor of London,**[1422–3] **Robert Smyth, William Crane, John Philippe, Hugh Neel at that time being Masters of the same mistery of Brewers, which parcels following ought to have been written in the 31st folio hereafter.[201]**

The first course:	The second course:
stewed wood doves	lambs
roast capons	partridge or cock with
	6 large birds in one dish.

Costs for the Dinner

First for 3 quarters of charcoal	2s. 9d.	Item paid to Repon, butler,	4d.
Item for 20 faggots	10d.	Item for the exchange of 2	
Item for 5 dozen earthenware		platters of pewter	5d.
pots at 4d.,	20d.	Item to the players	2s. 8d.
Item to a woman for washing the		Item for 1 harper	8d.
pots and portage of them	6d.	Item to Johanna in the buttery	
Item for white bread for trencher		and pantry	4d.
bread	5s. 6d.	Item to Robert Smyth for wine in	
		various places	4d.
[**113**]		Item to Hugh Neel for wine at	
Spicery		the Horn on Milk Street	9d.
Item to Robert Jewell for half a			
quarteron of cloves & maces	5d.		

---

[197]   6s. 8d.

[198]   Deceiving.

[199]   This passage is a much later insertion, uncrossed. Robert Coket was Porlond's assistant and successor, who otherwise first appeared in this book on f. 241r (c.1433–4).

[200]   25 January 1423.

[201]   The scribe acknowledged that the chronology of the book was incorrect here and again at [**226**]. The subsequent account of the funeral of King Henry V disrupted record keeping.

& for 1 quarteron of powder of
pepper 6*d.*
& for 1 quarteron of ginger &
1 quarteron of canell 10*d.*
& for sandalwood 2*d.* & for 1 lb
of raisins of Corinth 11*d.*
& for 1 quarteron of sugar 3*d.* &
for 2 lbs dates 8*d.* & for saffron 5*d.*

Sum 4*s.* 1*d.*

Item to William Bacon for 11
lambs at 11*d.* apiece, 10*s.* 1*d.*
Item for 3 quarts of grease 12*d.*
Item for portage 1*d.*
Item to John Bray for 4 lambs at
10*d.* 3*s.* 4*d.*
Item for portage 1*d.*
Item to the said John for beef, 6*d.*
Item for the allowance²⁰² of 4
dozen pewter vessels 2*s.*
Item for 1 lb of cotton candle 1½*d.*
Item for carriage of fime²⁰³ 1*d.*
Item for bread for browes²⁰⁴ 1*d.*
Item paid to John Hardy 7*s.*
Item to Devenyssh, panter, 12*d.*

Item to William Crane for
portage of 3 barrels ferrers²⁰⁵ full
of red wine 3*d.*
Item to the said William for 1 lb
of ginger for Tuesday at dinner 1*d.*
Item for 36 capons at 6*d.* apiece, 18*s.*
Item for 6 dozen stock doves at
2*s.* the dozen, 12*s.*
Item for 16 partridges at 4*d.*
apiece, 5*s.* 4*d.*
Item for 16 woodcocks at 3*d.*
apiece, 4*s.*
Item for 16 dozen birds at 4*d.* the
dozen, 5*s.* 4*d.*
Item for 100 eggs 11*d.*
Item for 30 Jeroboams²⁰⁶ & 1 pint
of red wine at 8*d.* a gallon, 20*s.* 1*d.*
Item for the washing of board
cloths and towels, 1 for the high
table 2*d.*
2 sanapes²⁰⁷ for the same table 2*d.*
2 cloths for tables dormant 4*d.*²⁰⁸
2 board cloths for the middle table 2*d.*
1 cloth for the dressing board and
for cleaning the vessels and for
2 hand towels before eating and
afterwards for the commons of
the mistery 2*d.*, 12*d.*

Sauces
Item for half a peck of salt 1½*d.*
1 pint of honey 2*d.*
for 1 pint of mustard ½*d.*
for 1 pint of verjuice ½*d.*
for 1 pint of vinegar ½*d.*
for 1 quarteron of white ginger
2*d.*, & for pack thread ½*d.*, 7½*d.*

Sum 113*s.* 11*d.*

²⁰² Hire.
²⁰³ Dung.
²⁰⁴ Broth, liquid in which beef and vegetables have been boiled, sometimes thickened with bread.
²⁰⁵ Iron-hooped.
²⁰⁶ 1 gallon wine containers.
²⁰⁷ Strip of cloth placed over the outer part of the tablecloth to keep it clean.
²⁰⁸ A permanent table, as opposed to one laid upon trestles and taken away after the feast.

[114] [f. 42r]
[Latin with English]
The names of those invited to the company breakfast written below, who came and were each taxed and paid 6d.

John Spencer	John Eylond	John Masonne	John Salter
Michael Tregononne	John Laurence	William Bailly	John Bedford
John Frost	Robert Hyltonne	William Bacon	John Assh
William Belle	Nicholas Agonmaylok	John Riche	John Broke
William Boteler	William Ederiche	Baldewyne Hoper	William Grosse
Thomas Aleyn	William Payn	John Wyghtmour	Roger Blissote
Thomas Driffeld	Thomas Aylle	John Yver	Robert Smyth
Hugh Neel	Robert Jewell	Roger Swanneffeld	John Riche of
Henry Bedell	William atte Wode	Thomas Pensonne	Fleet Street
Thomas Yole	Deric Johnson	Peter Hayforde	John Brewster
William Ferrour at	Peter Roos	Thomas Goding	John Lumbard
the Cony	Richard Harlowe	William Ferrour Junior	Simon Petesyn
Robert Elken	Robert Carpenter	Randolph Mark	Richard Aleyn
William Reponne	Hugh Glene	William Andreu	Stephen Clean
William Rawlyn	William Termeday	Sir Robert Steyntonne	John Jacob
William Crane	Thomas Grene	Peter Carpenter	Robert Nikke
John Fekenham	John Reyner	John Stone	John Holbek
Roger Ware	Walter Colshull	Henry Trebolans	Thomas Emond
John Caryonne	John Pyken	Nicholas Fuller	Thomas Grateley
William Dowdale	William Canonne	John Syre	Stephen Roo
Robert Pede	Michael Eve	William Smalsho	Thomas de Kent
John Humber	John Castonne	John Philippe	Robert Delowe
John Riche, tailor		John Retford	John Reeffawe
Robert Mayhewe			Henry Lymber

[115]

The names of those invited to the said breakfast who did not accept yet came

William Mascall	John Bailly	Alexander Marcow	William Pompe
William Claissonne	Grene, maltman	John Chapman	William atte Welle
Nicholas Aleyn	William Petevyle	John with his	The wife of
John Donche	Simon atte Welle	wife, formerly the	William Bolton
John Turnour	John William	wife of William	Robert Gyles
		Bolton[209]	
		Thomas Hatcher	
		Spore, ferrour	

The names of those who came to the aforesaid Breakfast but were not invited and did not pay

Gilbert Aletaker
A certain chaplain
Thomas Donyngton[210]
The Lord of the Fee with his [*damaged*: [?] servant]

---

[209] See 'the wife of William Bolton' in the next column. Without a surname for John, it is difficult to identify him.
[210] Sergeant of the chamber **[194]**.

[116] [f. 42v]
**The names of those who were invited to the abovesaid breakfast and accepted
but did not come and did not pay**

John Toke	Robert Tannere	William Lacy
John Gedeney	Robert Walram	John Qwyntyn
Adam Copendale	Henry Grene	Thomas Merssh
William Copwode	Henry Noble	

Sum total of the breakfast written below 113s. 11d.

And which was collected by the taxation at 6d., 49s. 6d.

**And thus the Masters of the said craft paid clearly for the said breakfast
64s. 5d.**

**And lastly, the said sum was paid by each of the said 4 Masters for a
kilderkin of ale of their own account**

Each kilderkin at 2s. 4d.

[117]
[*English*] [*continued from f. 41r*][211] Unto the wise and discreet person the Speaker of
the Parliament and the worthy commons of the realm, the victuallers, the Brewers
of the city of London, meekly beseech that for as much as the said victuallers serve
our sovereign lord King as well as other lords both spiritual and temporal, with
other of the King's lieges, with all the said city as of ale, the which victuallers buy
their chief stuff, that is to say malt, at great disavayle[212] in so much as the sellers of
malt diversely deceive the said victuallers, that is to say in selling of bellied malt,[213]
that is to say stiff malt that will never come [*to ripeness*], of *wynel* eaten malt,[214]
that is to say with worms of dusty malt with drawk,[215] darnel, *kerloksode*. Also of
edgrewcorne[216] that never had the full growing, of unclean malt, that is to say with
small stones, congealed earth and gravel. And the said brewers now have only
8 bushel strike[217] of malt for the quarter, with filth and other. Where they were ever
used to having 9 bushels, because of the filth, so the said brewers now only have
but 7 bushels for the quarter of clean malt, whereby it yields less ale to the seller
and the buyer, as may be openly proved, and for as much all these defaults were
openly proved before this time, the said victuallers had 9 bushels for a quarter by
the Great Charter[218] and the custom of the city used[219] and approved, [*may it*] please
you by your wise discretion to consider the aforesaid deceits and aforesaid defaults
in the malt and to ordain due remedy, whereby the said victuallers may have clean

---

211 The remainder of this entry, in English, is not crossed through and is a later addition.
212 Disadvantage.
213 Already swollen, whereas germination of grain was part of the brewing process.
214 Worm-eaten?
215 Wild grass growing as weed amongst corn.
216 Hedgerow corn?
217 A bundle or handful of corn stalks.
218 Magna Carta, 1215.
219 Accustomed.

chaffure[220] and full measure, as the sellers should have good money, for the common profit of all the King's people, for the love of God and in the way of charity. Examined.

[118] [f. 43r]
[Latin]

A statute was decreed by Richard Whetyington, mayor, and the aldermen of the city of London, that all barrels and kilderkins should be sealed, in the 8th year of the reign of Henry V [1420–1] before the feast of Easter, as is more manifestly declared in the statute, and because the persons written in the following by no means fulfilled the statute, they humbled themselves to the mayor, and made a fine to John Hille, chamberlain of the Guildhall of the said city.

[Latin with English] First John Smalhobbes dwelling at the Horseshoe outside Aldgate, foreigner, had 2 kilderkins not sealed in the house of the huckster called Clemens in Sithebourne Lane
And the aforesaid John had 1 kilderkin not sealed in the house of Marioire, huckster, in the same lane

Item Nicholas Zonge, brewer, at the Lamb in Abchurch Lane had 1 kilderkin not sealed in the house of Clement, huckster, in Sithebourne Lane.
Item the wife of a certain Robert Gyldesborogh at the Three Nuns above the corner of Sithebourne had 1 kilderkin not sealed in the house of Isabel the wife of William Oenewes, goldsmith in the same lane [*added*: whom God loves][221]
Item John Sander, brewer, foreigner, dwelling outside Aldgate at the Hand, had 1 kilderkin not sealed in the house of John Ware, dwelling at the Tower on the hill, between the tawyers
The same John had 1 kilderkin not sealed in the house at the Tabard in Gracechurch Street
Item Roger Baronne at the Swan at Aldgate had 1 unsealed kilderkin not sealed at the same house
And the said Roger had 1 unsealed kilderkin in the house at the Tabard in Gracechurch Street
The widow who was the wife of Leonard Pyle, brewer, [*added*: whom God loves ...] at the Cock beside the Augustinian Friars had 1 barrel not sealed at the Saracen's Head beside the gate of the Guildhall
The wife of Matthew Barbour in St John's Street had 2 kilderkins not sealed in the house of William, clerk at the church of St Margaret in Friday Street
Henry Bedell, brewer, at the Welshman outside Ludgate had 1 kilderkin not sealed in the house of the said William, clerk of Friday Street, and a servant put the said kilderkin into a flagon for 1d.
John Clerk, weaver and a brewer, in the Pie in la Riole had 1 kilderkin not sealed at the house of Katherine Robert in the parish of St Mildred in Bread Street

---

[220] Trade.
[221] Perhaps the goldsmith, or his wife, and Pyle (see four entries below) had died.

[119] [f. 43v]

Michael Tregononne in the parish of St Botolph [*scored*: Aldgate] outside Aldersgate Street at the George had 1 kilderkin not sealed in the house of William Botle, hosier, dwelling outside Newgate in the parish of St Sepulchre

John Turvey, skinner, who lives in the parish of St Dunstan in the West in Fleet Street at the Fleur de Lys has 1 kilderkin not sealed in the house of a glazier dwelling by the [*scored*: church] tower of the said church, that is, St Dunstan

Katrina Norlond, foreigner, dwelling at the Lamb in St John Street outside the Liberty, has 1 kilderkin not sealed at the house of Emmote Qwyntyn, huckster, dwelling in the parish of St Nicholas Shambles beside the tavern of le Rose on the Hope [*added*: it was marked however]

John Westezerde at the Crane in le Flesh Shambles, that is, St Nicholas, had 1 kilderkin not sealed in the house of a shepster[222] by the Saracen's Head at Paul's Chain

William Cardell dwelling in the house where John Hore used to dwell, in the parish of St Alphage at Cripplegate, has 2 kilderkins not sealed which were found openly in the street

Walter Honspell, brewer & draper, at the Horse Head in the parish of St Andrew in Holborn, has 1 kilderkin not sealed in the house of a huckster, the wife of John Abron, grocer, in the lane of St Swithin, opposite the skinner

John Grymmysby who dwells at the Bell in Holborn in the parish of St Andrew, has 1 kilderkin not sealed which was found openly in the street, that is, Cheap

John Nasyng at the Saracen's Head and One Maid outside Cripplegate had 1 kilderkin not sealed in the house of a huckster who dwells in Wood Street outside the Old Counter

Margareta Stockett at the Star & Moon in the parish called Aldermary's church [*St Mary Aldermary*]: all the barrels and kilderkins of the said Margaret were not sealed

Thomas Wegge at the Swan and Ship in Red Cross Street had 1 kilderkin not sealed in the house of a huckster called Margaret Clerk in Milk Street, Cheap, who was once the wife of the clerk at the church of St Mary Magdalene, off Milk Street

Item the aforesaid Thomas had 1 kilderkin not sealed in the house of a huckster in Ironmonger Lane, who is the wife of Robert, formerly chief clerk at the church of St Mary Magdalen in Milk Street

John Rowlonde at *le Glene* [*Wheatsheaf*] in Coleman Street had 1 barrel not sealed in the house of Mariory Sergeant, huckster, who dwells above the corner opposite the sepulchre of the church of St Michael Bassishaw, by the Swan on le Hoop.

[120] [f. 44r]

John Stokynton, brewer, at the Key in Bassishaw had 1 kilderkin not sealed in the aforesaid house of Mariory Sergeannt, huckster

John Westezerde at the Crane at St Nicholas Shambles had 1 kilderkin not sealed in the house of Agnes Brewer, huckster, dwelling beside Newgate

Margaret Sokett[223] dwelling at the Star & le Moon in the parish called Aldermary church had 1 kilderkin not sealed in the house of Alice Brampton, dwelling at the

---

222   Female cutter-out of material, dressmaker.

223   Stockett, in the parish of St Mary Aldermary.

Mill at the end of Coleman Street and the aforesaid kilderkin was seized and the prohibited money in the hands of the said Alice[224]

John Brokford at the Dragon in Coleman Street had 1 kilderkin unsealed in the aforesaid house and it was seized and the prohibited money in the hands of the said Alice

William Cardell beside Cripplegate in the former home of John Hore had 1 kilderkin unsealed in the said house, and it was seized and the prohibited money in the hands of the said Alice Brampton

William Mawncyple of Grays Inn, foreigner, dwelling outside the Liberty in Holborn, had 1 kilderkin sealed with the sign of the coopers, in the house of Alice Tawnton, huckster, dwelling in Staining Lane in the rent formerly of Drugo Barentyn, and the aforesaid kilderkin was seized and the prohibited money in the hands of the aforesaid Alice.[225]

John at the Cock, foreigner, dwelling outside the Liberty in Holborn had 1 kilderkin without ale, not sealed in the said house, that is, of Alice Tawnton. And the said kilderkin was seized with money paid to the said John with the arrest made.[226]

[121]

A certain armourer [*above the line*: Clemens Bischopp] brewer, dwelling in Southwark had 1 kilderkin not sealed in the house of Cristiane Bronnfelde dwelling at Studys Crane,[227] and the aforesaid kilderkin was seized and the prohibited money in the hands of the same Cristiane

Nicholas Aleyn dwelling at the Ewe & Lamb in Thames Street, had 1 kilderkin not sealed at the house of Katherine, huckster, dwelling in the parish of All Hallows the Less opposite the Hart's Head[228] there

Gilbert Boton dwelling at the Christopher in Golding Lane in the parish of St Giles Cripplegate had 1 kilderkin of his ale unsealed in the house of Cristiane Henbrigge, huckster, dwelling beside the Bars in the rent of John Westezerde in Aldersgate Street. And the aforesaid kilderkin was seized and placed in the custody of John Eston at the Lion in the abovesaid street.

Adam dwelling at the Bell, foreigner, in the neighbourhood of St John had 2 kilderkins unsealed at the home of Agnes London, dwelling opposite the lodging house of the Abbot of Ramsey in White Cross Street and the said 2 kilderkins were seized and the prohibited money in the hands of the aforesaid Alice.[229]

Thomas Wyngefelde dwelling outside the Liberty in the parish of Whitechapel had 1 kilderkin not sealed and it was placed in the custody of David Soys, dwelling at the Eagle in Gracechurch Street.

---

[224]   For those who had made or sold ale contrary to the regulations, or received it, it seems that the barrels or kilderkins were confiscated, along with the money made from the sale of such ale.

[225]   The kilderkin was sealed and marked with a cooper's mark, but Mawncyple had infringed the regulations concerning 'foreigners'. Barentyn was the mayor 1398–9 and 1408–9.

[226]   The Latin word for prohibited is not found in this clause and John received some payment for the seizure of his empty kilderkin.

[227]   Study's Lane or Three Cranes Lane?

[228]   Hertis*horne*lane, rather than Hertishede, was near the church of All Hallows the Less.

[229]   Perhaps this is a mistake for Agnes London, or refers to Alice Tawnton, huckster, mentioned above.

[122] [f. 44v]

John Benge at the Cup in the parish of St Nicholas at the market has 1 barrel not sealed in the house of Katherine Ely, who dwells opposite the inn of the church of St Alban in Wood Street

Reginald Broke dwelling at the Bell called Savage's Inn in Fleet Street: all his barrels and kilderkins were not sealed

Alice Gyldysburgh dwelling at the Three Nuns in the parish of St Mary Woolnoth had 2 kilderkins not sealed in a certain cellar of Isabel Goldsmyght, huckster, beside the aforesaid Three Nuns in Sithebourne Lane

Richard Terrell of the parish of St Giles, dwelling at the Greyhound in Beech Lane, had 1 kilderkin not sealed in the house of John Eston at the Lion in Aldersgate Street next to John Tregalow, brewer. And the aforesaid kilderkin was seized and the prohibited money in the hands of the aforesaid John.

[123]

Thomas Aleyn, smith, dwelling at the Star in Golding Lane in the aforesaid parish of St Giles had 1 kilderkin not sealed in the house of John Spencer dwelling at the Vernacle in la Barbican, and the said kilderkin was seized and the prohibited money in the hands of the said John Spencer

And the same Thomas had 1 kilderkin not sealed in the house of Margaret Bulle, huckster, in la Barbican and the said kilderkin was seized and the prohibited money in the hands of the said Margaret

Henry Wykeston, fishmonger, at Shoreditch, had 1 kilderkin not sealed in the house of Margaret Broke, huckster, dwelling in Grub Street beside Henry Osbern, fletcher, at the end of the said Grub Street in the parish of St Giles. And the aforesaid kilderkin was seized and the prohibited money in the hands of the said Margaret

John Catour at the Moon outside Bishopsgate had 2 unsealed kilderkins in the house of Isabelle Rodelond, huckster, dwelling in a certain cellar opposite the inn of St Martin Outwich. And the said kilderkin was seized [*blank*] in the hands of the said Isabell

Robert dwelling at the Peacock outside Aldgate, foreigner, had 1 kilderkin not sealed at the house of Alice Trayles, huckster, dwelling in the parish of All Hallows London Wall, and the said kilderkin was seized and the prohibited money in the hands of the said Alice

And the same Robert had 3 sealed kilderkins at the house of Johanna Carpenter, woman, beside a certain cobbler in the parish of St Katherine Christchurch in the wall of the said Christchurch[230]

Someone dwelling at the Hartshorn in the neighbourhood of St John outside the Liberty, had 1 kilderkin not sealed in the house of Katherine, huckster, dwelling at the Cardinal's Hat beside the hospital of St Mary[231] outside Bishopsgate, and the said kilderkin was seized and the prohibited money in the hands of the same Katherine[232]

[124] [f. 45r]

Henry Wykeston, fishmonger, dwelling at the Cup in the parish of Shoreditch had 1 kilderkin not sealed at the house of Isabel Rodian and Morys, another huckster,

---

[230] Perhaps the sealed kilderkins were also recorded to mitigate Robert's offence?

[231] The priory and hospital of St Mary Bethlehem or the priory and hospital of St Mary without Bishopsgate.

[232] This entry was added in a different hand.

dwelling opposite the hospital of St Mary outside Bishopsgate. And the said kilderkin was seized and the prohibited money in the hands of the same Isabel, huckster

Thomas Cope, foreigner, dwelling at the Lion outside Bishopsgate beside the Bars there had 1 kilderkin not sealed at the home of Isabel Rodyan, huckster, dwelling opposite the hospital of St Mary there

Also the said Thomas had 1 kilderkin not sealed at the house of Johanna Cole, huckster, dwelling in the parish of St Benet Fink beside the Augustinian Friars

John Holbek dwelling at the Pie in Smithfield in the parish of St Sepulchre had 1 kilderkin not sealed and the aforesaid kilderkin was found in the common street

Margaret Nyghtyngale dwelling at the Lamb in Mart Lane in the parish of All Hallows Staining had 1 kilderkin not sealed in the house of Ade Walssh, bouge-man, at Tower Hill.[233]

[125]

John Broker, dwelling at the Mill in Thames Street in the parish of St Laurence Pountney, had 1 kilderkin not sealed and 1 barrel, similarly not sealed, in a certain cellar in Candlewick Street opposite a barber of the parish of St Mary Bothaw

George Spenall dwelling at the Pewter Pot in the parish of St Andrew Cornhill had 2 kilderkins not sealed at the house of Margaret Chenerell in Abchurch Lane

Item the said George had 1 kilderkin not sealed at the house of Henry Fandenat, Dutchman and broiderer, dwelling in New Alley in the parish of St Bartholomew the Less[234]

The brewer dwelling at the Key in White Cross Street in the house formerly of Walter Riche had 3 kilderkins not sealed which were found in a cart, full of ale in the common street, that is, beside Holborn Bridge

Henry Brewer, foreigner, dwelling at the Ship outside Temple Bar has 1 kilderkin not sealed at the home of Stephen atte Welle dwelling beside Temple Bar opposite the gate of the Temple. And the said kilderkin was seized and the prohibited money in the hands of the same Stephen

Reginald Becham at the Three Legs in the parish of St Dunstan in Fleet Street had 1 kilderkin unsealed in the home of John Martyn dwelling at the end of Showe Lane beside the George there

John Stokes dwelling at the Star in Fenchurch Street had 1 kilderkin not sealed which was found full of ale in the common street, upon the shoulders of his servants

[126] [f. 45v]

John Oseye, brewer, dwelling at the Cock outside Bishopsgate had 1 kilderkin not sealed which was found in the common street outside Aldgate

John Frost, brewer, dwelling at the Hartshorn outside Newgate had 2 unsealed kilderkins in the home of John Salusbury, salter, dwelling outside the church of St Sepulchre

[Margin note: He was not amerced [*fined*] by the chamber because he did not have such kilderkins without a seal]

---

[233] Bouges were bags made of hide containing water. A bougeman was perhaps a water carrier.

[234] New or Longhorns Alley is near St Bartholomew the Less.

Thomas Boteler dwelling at the Bell in Red Cross Street in the parish of St Giles without Cripplegate had 1 unsealed kilderkin at the house of Agnes Gray, the wife of William Gray, draper, dwelling in Watling Street, in a certain cellar, in the parish called Aldermary church [*St Mary Aldermary*] by a certain barber there.

Memorandum of 20s. 3d. received from John Hill, chamberlain at the Guildhall, that is, for a quarter part of the money forfeited for malt and unsealed kilderkins and also for ale sold without the proper measure during the time of Richard Whityngton being mayor.
And of 6s. 6d. received from Robert Whetyngham and John Boteler, sheriffs of the city of London that year, for malt confiscated which did not come to the common market.

Sum 26s. 9d.

Which was divided amongst 8 people, that is: Thomas Grene, Robert Hylton, John Pyken, Robert Carpenter, William atte Wode, Thomas Hatcher, William Ferrour and John Salter, that is 3s. 4d. each; to William Purlond, clerk, 6d.; and for 1 other, 8d., and for another 3d.

Sum as above.

And of 64s. 4d. confirmed received from John Beterden, chamberlain on account of and for various forfeitures during the time of Richard Whityngton's mayoralty
And of 31s. confirmed received from the sheriffs abovesaid

Sum £4 15s. 4d.

[127]
which was divided amongst
7 persons, that is: Thomas Grene, Robert Hylton, John Pyken, Robert Carpenter, William atte Wode, William Ferrour & John Salter who each had 8s. 4d.
4 persons, that is: William Crane, John Masonne, Thomas Hatcher and John Chapman, who each had 5s.
And William Porlond, clerk, 2s.
And given to the common profit 6s. 8d.
And in provision of 2 breakfasts given by Thomas Grene, Master, 8s. 4d.

Sum as above

And a memorandum that William atte Welle, Thomas Emond and William John at Aldgate were, as always, enraged at the fines prescribed and did the least and have received nothing.

[128] [f. 46r]
The Account of William atte Wode of moneys by him received at the Receipt of the Exchequer as for a sum due to various Brewers of London written below for ale for our Lord King Henry V, from the time when he came from the parts of France and for the Coronation of the Lady Katherine, the Queen, that is in the same 8th year of his reign [1420–1] as appears below.

First the same discharges himself of money by him received from John Bolton and his associates in the county of Yorkshire for an obligation of	£101 2s. 11d.
And of money agreed received from William Bronne of Kilworth and his associates in the county of Leicester for an obligation of	71s. 3d.
And of money confirmed received from William Spencer and his associates in the county of Northampton for an obligation of	£12 9s. 7d.
And of money received at the said Receipt of the Exchequer in cash counted into his hands	108s. 8½d.

Sum £122 12s. 5½d.

The same discharges himself for money in payment of his fellows on account of expenses made for various amounts concerning acquiring the money 50s. 4½d.

Sum as appears[235]

Sum total received £125 2s. 10d.

And the same discharges himself in money paid written below, by his associates in payment of money owed to him

£122 12s. 5½d.

Sum as appears

[129]
And the same accounts for money paid to the 2 ale takers for the hiring of a horse between Canterbury and London 4s.
Item paid to London scriveners for writing 2 rolls with the names written below, 8d.
Item for portage of a letter missive to diverse merchants in the county of Yorkshire 2d.
Item for a breakfast made for certain men who made payment of a bond of £101 2s. 11d., 12d.
Item for prosecution of a writ upon that bond, that is to one named John and his fellows, 6s. 8d.
Item paid to John Cannterbury, cooper, for money not allowed nor paid by the King's Book[236] 10s. 10d.

---

[235] Here there are nine figures of the letter S in two lines.
[236] Royal records.

Item in the price of a golden girdle which nobody wishes to receive because
of the weakness of the money bag, so it remains in the hands of William
Porlond, clerk, 3s. 4d.
Item in various expenses upon the execution of a bond upon a writ
containing 71s. 3d. in the name of William Bronne of Kilworth 6s. 8d.
Item paid for the execution of a writ upon a bond during the time of
Henry V, late King of England, which was taken during the time of King
Henry VI, 9s. 6d., upon the obligation of £12 9s. 7d., in the name of William
Spencer and his fellows of the county of Northampton, now received from
the attorney at the Exchequer 6s. 8d. for the following said bond, in total 16s. 2d.

Sum 49s. 6d.
Sum of payments and expenses £125 23½d. And still owed: 10½d.

[130] [f. 46v]

**Parcels owed by the lord our King Henry V to the Brewers of London written
below, being when he came from parts of France and for the coronation of the
lady Katherine the Queen, that is in the eighth year of his reign [1420–1][237]**

	Owed by the King	Of whom received	There is owed to them	Necessary expenses	And thus there is owed net
First John Stanntonne	£19 8s. 2d.	£18 16s. 8d.	11s. 6d.	8s. ½d.	3s. 5½d.
William atte Wode	£24 7s. 1d.	£19 15s. 8d.	£4 11s. 5d.	10s. 1½d.	£4 15½d.
John Reffawe	£9 10s. 4d.	£7 18s. 8d.	31s. 8d.	3s. 11½d.	27s. 8½d.
John Caryonne	£7 8s.	£6 2s. 6d.	25s. 6d.	3s. ½d.	22s. 5½d.
John Russell	£9 5s. 8½d.	£7 14s. 8d.	31s. ½d.	3s. 10d.	27s. 2½d.
John Thetford	76s. 6½d.	60s. 9d.	15s. 9½d.	18½d.	14s. 3d.
John Ballard	46s. 1½d.	38s. 5d.	7s. 8½d.	11d.	6s. 9½d.
Richard Newman	46s. 1½d.	38s. 5d.	7s. 8½d.	11d.	6s. 9½d.
Thomas Emond	46s. 1½d.	35s. 1d.	11s. ½d.	11d.	10s. 1½d.
John More at Ludgate	£6 18s. 5d.	£6 15s. 4d.	3s. 1d.	2s. 10d.	3d.
William Cardell	27s. 3d.	22s. 8d.	4s. 7d.	6½d.	4s. ½d.
William Ederich	102s. 6d.	£4 5s. 5d.	17s. 1d.	2s. 1½d.	14s. 11½d.
Robert Smyth	£4 4d.	67s.	13s. 4d.	20d.	11s. 8d.
Roger Swanneffeld	113s. 5d.	£4 14s. 6d.	18s. 11d.	2s. 4d.	16s. 7d.
John Riche	26s. 9½d.	22s. 2d.	4s. 7½d.	6d.	4s. 1½d.
John Newman	29s.	24s. 2d.	4s. 10d.	7d.	4s. 3d.
William Ferrour	29s. 3d.	24s. 3d.	5s.	7d.	4s. 5d.
Thomas Grene	27s. 3d.	22s. 9d.	4s. 6d.	6½d.	3s. 11½d.
John Luke	47s. 0½d.	39s. 2d.	7s. 10½d.	11½d.	6s. 11d.
Richard Rowdonne	26s. 9½d.	22s. 5d.	4s. 4½d.	6½d.	3s. 10d.
John de Lynne	27s. 3d.	22s. 8d.	4s. 7d.	6½d.	4s. ½d.
Peter Short	27s. 3d.	22s. 4d.	4s. 11d.	6½d.	4s. 4½d.
Peter Hayford	£4 2s. 2d.	68s. 6d.	13s. 8d.	20½d.	11s. 11½d.
John Moyle	53s. 6½d.	45s. 5d.	8s. 1½d.	13d.	7s. ½d.

---

[237]   The coronation of Queen Katherine was on 23 February 1421, in Westminster Abbey.

Sum total of money owed £122 12s. 5½d.
Less received thence previously £104 19s. 7d.
There remains owed for this £17 12s. 10½d.
Deduction 50s. 4½d.
Net amount owing £15 2s. 6d.
And paid by William the clerk.

[131] [f. 47r]
The names of the brothers and sisters of the craft and fraternity of Brewers
paying quarterage in the time of Richard Whityngtonne mayor of London,
Thomas Grene, Robert Hylton, John Pyken, and Robert Carpenter being
Masters of the said craft, as appears in the following, that is the eighth year of
the reign of King Henry the fifth after the conquest [1420–1].

Alice Hore, widow,	12d.	[Ff]	
Agnes Bugge	12d.		
Adam Copendale	12d.	[G]	
Agnes the widow of Nicholas Stratton	12d.	Henry Serle	12d.
Alan Bret and Isabella his wife	2s.	Hugh Neel	12d.
Alexander Miles	12d.	Hugh Glene and Margery his wife	2s.
Alan John	12d.	Henry Lymber and Felicia his wife	2s.
Agnes the widow of Walter Riche	12d.	Henry Bedell	12d.
		Henry Trebolans	12d.
Constance the widow of Robert Hosard [*bracketed with*] Alice Savage	18d.	Hugh Sharppe	2s.
		John Stanntonne and Matilda his wife	2s.
Dionysia the widow of John Barthorppe	12d.	John Russell and Alice his wife	2s.
		John Tregilyowe	12d.
Dederik Clayssonne and Weveyn his wife	2s.	John Rothyng and Johanna his wife	2s.
David Soys	8d.	John Wodelond	12d.
		John Lynne	12d.
		John Nasyng and Alice his wife	2s.
Ellis Hardell	12d.	John Spenser	12d.
Emma Canonne	12d.	John Philippe and Matilda his wife	2s.
Emmota the widow of William Robard	12d.	John Samine	12d.

[132] [f. 47v]

John Wightmour and Johanna his wife	2s.	John Humber and Margaret his wife	2s.
		John Laurence	12d.
John Thetford and Margery his wife	2s.	John More and Cristiana his wife at Aldersgate	2s.
John Riche & Margaret his wife	2s.	John Basset	12d.
John Ballard & Cristiane his wife	2s.	John Ser, glover,	12d.
John Benge & Alice his wife	2s.	John Baily	12d.
Johanna the wife of John Horold	12d.		

John Fekays, maltman of *Hornimede*,[238] and Agnes his wife,	2s.	John Southmede	12d.
John Salter	12d.	John Waghorn	12d.
John Eylond	12d.	John William in Southwark	12d.
John Ryngesson	12d.	John de Dene paid quarterage for	
John Mason and Felicia his wife	2s.	last year but not this	12d.
Johanna Carleton	12d.	Johanna the widow of Richard	
John Chapman	12d.	Storm	12d.
John Ketyng	12d.	Juliana Etersete	12d.
John Simman and Elizabeth his wife	2s.	John Peken and Alice his wife	2s.
Idonia Hatton, the wife of Roger		John Perye, maltman	2s.
Swanneffeld	12d.	John Selle, maltman	12d.
John William and Johanna his		Johanna Cole	12d.
wife in Thames Street	2s.	Johanna Awmbele	12d.
John Randolf and Juliana his wife	2s.	John Aleyn, baker	12d.
John Carion & Alice his wife	2s.	John Turveye	12d.
John Reyner and Agatha his wife	2s.	John Grace, armiger,[239]	2s.
John Refhawe & Juliana his wife	2s.		
John Merston	12d.	Katherine Roche	12d.
John Gedney de Westminster	12d.		
John Rotford, glover	12d.		
John Penverne	12d.		
John Qwyntyn and Agnes his wife	2s.		
John Broke	12d.		
John Lucas	12d.		
John Brewster and Johanna his wife	2s.		
John Sander	12d.		
John Hardy, Cook,	12d.		
John Bray	12d.		
Jacob Levegro and his wife Alice	2s.		
John Moyle	12d.		
John Stone	12d.		
John Assh	12d.		
John Kenaky	12d.		
John More at Ludgate	12d.		
John Elsy	12d.		
John Erle at Lumbard	12d.		
John Toke & Alice his wife	2s.		
John Turnour, shearman	12d.		
John Snell	12d.		

238 Hormead, Hertfordshire?
239 Esquire.

[133] [f. 48r]

Margaret Sydingbourne	12d.	Roger Baron	12d.
Milicent the widow of Adam Burgh	12d.	Richard Shirwod and Alice his wife	2s.
Michael Eve & Elizabeth his wife	2s.	Richard Harlowe and Johanna his wife	2s.
Michael Tregononne	12d.	Richard Rowdonne & Johanna his wife	2s.
Morys Tranaill	12d.		
		Richard Newman and Alice his wife	2s.
Nicholas Kene and Katherine his wife	2s.	Richard Frepurs and Johanna his wife	2s.
Nicholas Fuller	12d.	Richard Wightmour	12d.
Nicholas Muryell	2s.	Robert Nikke and Alice his wife	2s.
Nicholas Agomnaylok and Johanna his wife	2s.	Richard Tirell and Isabella his wife	2s.
Nicholas Aleyn	12d.	Richard Brynton	12d.
		Robert Tanner	12d.
Peter Hayforde & Matilda his wife	2s.	Richard Aleyn and Johanna his wife	2s.
Peter Roos	12d.	Robert Gyles and Johanna his wife	2s.
Philip James	12d.	Robert Smyth and Anna his wife	2s.
Peter Carpenter	12d.	Robert Mayhewe in Shoreditch	12d.
		Roger Blissote	12d.
		Robert Pede	12d.
		Robert Walram and Alice his wife	2s.
		Richard Welde	12d.
		Robert Hilton and Margaret his wife	2s.
		Robert Carpenter	12d.
		Robert Steynton, chaplain	12d.
		Robert Lynford & Margaret his wife 3s. for last year and for this	
		Richard Crosse	12d.
		Robert Jewell, grocer	12d.
		Richard Rose of Southwark for last year and he has not paid for this	12d.

[134] [f. 48v]

Stephen Roo	12d.	William Claysson and Isabella his wife	2s.
Simon Potkyn	12d.	William atte Welle & Alice his wife	2s.
Thomas Bristowe	12d.	William Smalsho and Margaret his wife	2s.
Thomas Emond and Sibilla his wife	2s.	William Bernard	12d.
Thomas Aleyn	12d.	William Geffrey and Anna his wife	2s.
Thomas Osbarn and Isabell his wife	2s.	William Bray and Alice his wife	2s.
Thomas Hawcher	12d.	William Canonne	12d.
Thomas Yole	12d.	William Ederich and Alice his wife	2s.
Thomas Kent	12d.	William Crane and Elena his wife	2s.
Thomas Grateley	12d.	William Cophode, maltman, and Isabell his wife	2s.
Thomas Goding	12d.		
Thomas Penson	12d.		

Thomas Martyn	12d.	William Petvyle	12d.
Thomas Jakes, maltman of Barnet,	12d.	William John	12d.
Thomas Smalsho	12d.	William Herry	12d.
Thomas Boteler	12d.	William Ferrour and Agnes his wife	2s.
Thomas Dewy	12d.	William atte Wode and Katherine	
Thomas Hancok	12d.	his wife	2s.
Thomas Grene	12d.	William Belle	12d.
Thomas Howe, maltman,	12d.	William Porlond & Dionysia his	
		wife	2s.
		William Cardell	12d.
		Walter Colshull	12d.
		William Boltonne	12d.
		William Wheleman	12d.
		William Payn	2s.
		William Bayly	12d.
		Walter Glyn	12d.
		William Boteler	12d.
		William Illying	12d.
		Walter Copseye	12d.
		William Termeday	12d.
		William Bakon, butcher,	12d.
		William Bodevyle	12d.
		William Gros	12d.

**Sum total of quarterage this
year £12 12s. 2d.**

The increase of the said sum over and
above the preceding year consists of
various persons entering the fraternity
in this year and other persons paying
arrears of their quarterage
[*Scored*: and also whose names appear
separately and fully in the following]
[*Added*: whose names are separately
written for the said year]

[135] [f. 49r]
[*Latin*] **The names of brothers and sisters written below & received into the
fraternity in the preceding year and paying their first quarterage in this year,
that is, the 8th year of the reign of King Henry V [1420–1].**

[*Latin with English surnames and place
names*]
Alan John
Dederick Claysson and Weveyn his wife
Emma the wife of Hugh Neel
John Elcy
John Lumbard
John Toke and Alice his wife
Margaret the wife of John Humber

[136]
**The names following have arrears and
paid for this year and the last**

Richard Rose of Southwark paid for last
year and not for this
Robert Lynford
William Payn
John Grace

John Laurence
John Basset
Maurice Travaill
Nicholas Agomnaylok and Johanna his wife
Margaret the wife of Robert Lynford
Roger Blissote
Robert Pede
Robert Walram and Alice his wife
Thomas Boteler
Thomas Hancok
Agnes the wife of William Ferrour
Walter Glyn
William Bailly
William Boteler
William Illying
William Copseye
William Termeday
William Gros
Robert Steyntonne
Thomas Grene
Thomas Howe
William Porlond & Dionysia his wife
John Aleyn, baker

Hugh Sharpe
John Perie
Nicholas Muriell
John de Dene paid for last year and not for this at this time

The names of those who are in the fraternity table and paying quarterage in this year but not in various other elapsed years.

Hugo Glene and Margaret his wife
John Wyghtmour and Johanna his wife
Cristina the wife of John Ballard
Johanna the wife of John William in Thames Street
Alice the wife of Robert Nikke
Anna the wife of Robert Smyth
Elena the wife of William Crane
Richard Crosse

The names of those who entered the fraternity in the preceding year and have paid their quarterage this year, but owe for their fraternity entry

Thomas Grene
Thomas Howe maltman

The names following paid their quarterage in this year and have died

David Soys
John Samine
John Penverne
Alice Walram
Ellis Hardell
William Englissh
Richard Newman

The following names are those who have died this year and had not paid their quarterage

Michael Treryes
Richard Storm
William Robert
Walter Riche
The wife of John Ryngessonne

[137] [f. 49v]

The names following of those who abandoned the fraternity in this year, from whom quarterage was received last year

Johanna the widow of Peter Morle
Richard Rose of Southwark
William Westonne, draper

The names of those who paid quarterage in the preceding year but not this year because of annulment

Thomas Webbe[240] formerly at the George in Thames Street in the parish of St Dunstan
William Gedeney at the Ship in Tower Street

Names being in the fraternity table but not paying their quarterage in this year nor in many years elapsed

Alice the widow of James Knyght
Johanna the wife of Richard Wightmore
Alice the wife of Thomas Yole
Agnes the wife of William Herry
Henry Somers
Henry Anketill and Alice his wife
John Hatfeld
John Marybone and Johanna his wife
Isabella Morby
John Symond and Agnes his wife
Johanna Double
John Bargonne and Agnes his wife
John Berstonne and Julianne his wife
John Sell, maltman, and Matilda his wife
John Rotherby formerly the Rector of All Hallows London Wall
John Chapman, maltman
John Awdre, sheather
John Wake de Gisor's Hall
John Serle and Johanna his wife
John Cok
John FitzRobert and Johanna his wife
Isabella the widow of Vincent Syward
Juliana the wife of John Chapman
Johanna the wife of John Salter
Isabella the wife of John William in Southwark
Johanna the widow of Michael Trerys
Letitia the wife of Thomas Aleyn
Margery the wife of Thomas Hatcher
Nicholas Yonge and Agnes his wife
Nicholas Aleyn

Philip Carpenter
Roger Menyan and Johanna his wife
Johanna the wife of John Tregelowe
Thomas Newchapman and Agnes his wife
Thomas Crowser
Thomas Silke & Isabell his wife
Thomas Sebarn, maltman
Thomas Honchon and Agnes his wife
William Repon and Margery his wife
William Herty and Alice his wife
William Devenyssh
William Gedeneye
Thomas Webbe and Margery his wife

---

240   His death was noted at the foot of the same page.

[138]
Those who have rendered and paid during the time of William Cambrigge
[1420–1], **Robert Chichele** [1421–2] **and William Walderne** [1422–3].

Of which are dead

John Selle, maltman
John Cok, poulter
Thomas Crowser
Thomas Webbe

Johanna the widow of Richard
Wyghtmore
Alice the wife of Thomas Yole
John Bargonne, tallow chandler
John Sell, maltman
John Serle
Isabella the widow of Vincent Syward
Johanna the wife of John Salter
Letitia the wife of Thomas Aleyn
Margery the wife of Thomas Hatcher
Johanna the wife of John Tregelowe
William Repon and Margery his wife
William Devenyssh
William Gedeneye

[139] [f. 50r]
[Latin] **The time of the mayoralty of William Cambrigge: William Cambrigge:**
the beginning

The aforesaid Richard Whityngdon, mayor of the city of London [1419–20] during
the eighth year of the reign of King Henry V [1420–1] above noted, imposed
penalties and payments, and in other unaccustomed ways aggrieved the Brewers
of the same city in his time, as is written before, so that the same Brewers denied
themselves feasts, also company breakfasts and livery of the fraternity, with the
assent of the Masters and all of the said craft, during his aforesaid time.
His successor, William Cambrigge, mayor in the same city [1420–1], that is, in the
ninth year of the said King [1421–2] behaved wisely and discreetly towards them
in all the freedoms, customs and other things incumbent upon the said craft, and
also after many meetings with the aforesaid Brewers, asked that they behave well
honestly and faithfully towards the commons of the city of London and that the
Wardens and Searchers of the said Brewers and others in the governing of their
said craft, should make diligent watch and make arrests and presentations, so that
full notice of their acts of governance and diligence in all things could appear. And
thereupon the said Brewers, by the benevolence and discretion of the wise mayor,
conceded to him in all things. And the worthiest of the said craft ordered Thomas
Grene, Robert Hylton, John Pyken, and Robert Carpenter, then Masters, that they
should continue and thus they stood for two whole years, which was ordered for
their successors to implement also. And in that year they took livery, made a feast
and elected new Masters and did other things as agreed amongst the most noble of
the craft. It was agreed to implement what they had said every second year as should
seem most expedient to them.

[140]
Names of diverse [*persons*] selling ale not by the measure they ought to this year, and upon this they were presented to John Beterdene, chamberlain of the Guildhall

[*Latin and English*]

First William Richeman, master of the King's ship, dwelling at the Lion in the parish of All Hallows Barking, for defective measure,	1 barrel
Matthew Barbour dwelling opposite the said William Richeman, for defective measure,	1 kilderkin
John Bardolf, shipman, dwelling at the Leaden Porch there	1 kilderkin
Matilda the wife of Goryng, shipman, dwelling beside *Stowels Keye*²⁴¹ opposite John Barbour,	1 kilderkin
Claris the wife of Henry Cordewaner, Dutchman, dwelling opposite *Grayeskeye*²⁴² in Thames Street beside le Moon	1 k.
Nicholas Aleyn, brewer, dwelling at the Ewe and le Lamb in Thames Street in the parish of St Martin Orgar	1 barrel
John Trevelers dwelling beside the water bailiff at Billingsgate,	1 kilderkin
The wife of Nicholas Bargeman dwelling at the Chough with 2 store houses at Billingsgate beside the sign of Christopher,	1 kilderkin
Alice Dyers, the wife of Richard, custodian of the wharf of Billingsgate, dwelling beside the said Nicholas	1 k.
The widow of John Tebawde dwelling at the Swan opposite St Helen's	1 k.
John Humbere dwelling at the Lamp beside Bishopsgate	1 k.
Peter Roos dwelling at the Swan outside Bishopsgate	1 barrel
William Grokere dwelling at the Crown outside Bishopsgate	1 kilderkin
Johanna Osey dwelling at the Cock, the widow of John Roper,	1 k.
Richard Flete, capper, dwelling at the Hind in the parish of All Hallows Staining, beside the parish church of Fenchurch	1 k.
Cristiana Soys, the widow of David Soys, dwelling at the Eagle and le Garland in the parish of St Benet Gracechurch,	1 kilderkin
Robert Strace, ostler, dwelling at the Hart opposite the inn of the church of Gracechurch,	1 barrel
The wife of Roger, clerk at St Martin Ludgate dwelling in the Bailey opposite the Cross	1 kilderkin

[141] [f. 50v]

Alice Draper dwelling at the Horse Head in the parish of St Sepulchre for defective measure,	1 kilderkin
A wife dwelling at the Harp beside Holborn Bridge	1 k.
Richard Spray, barber and brewer dwelling at le Lion beside Secoll Lane	1 k.
Thomas Norton, drover & brewer at the Elms in Smithfield	1 k.
The huckster in Smithfield dwelling opposite the door of Ade atte Welle	1 k.
Cecilia Cotes, huckster, dwelling beside the corner in the flat field, opposite the White Bull there,	1 k.
Cristiana Martyn, huckster, dwelling beside Holborn Bridge	1 k.

²⁴¹ Stew Key, All Hallows Barking?
²⁴² Graves' Wharf?

Beatrix Freke dwelling at le Christopher at Baynard's Castle	1 k.
Thomas Pothill, turner and brewer, dwelling at the Swan below Newgate	1 barrel
John Amwell, skinner and brewer, dwelling at the Cock in the parish of St Nicholas Shambles	1 barrel
Alice Hunte, huckster and chandler, dwelling opposite le Poultry Hill there	1 k.
John Westzerd dwelling at the Crane in the parish of St Nicholas Shambles	1 k.
The wife of William Cowle dwelling at the Ball in The Old Change	1 k.
The brewer dwelling at the Pannier in Paternoster Row	1 k.
The huckster dwelling opposite Qwyntyn Brewer, beside the pie baker in the parish of St Michael le Querne	1 k.
John Broke dwelling at the Seven Stars in la Poultry	1 barrel
William Andrew dwelling at the Horse Head in the parish of St Sepulchre	1 kilderkin
Le Trump in Cheap	1 k.
Le Dagger in Cheap	1 k.
Robert Merdyk, pie baker in Bread Street beside the door of Shadworth[243]	1 k.
Le tapster dwelling at le George in Smithfield	1 k.
Katherine, huckster, dwelling at the cellar beside *Renderersgate*[244] at the Horse Pool in Smithfield	1 k.
The ostler dwelling beside Fleet Bridge at le White *Colver* [*dove or pigeon*]	1 k.
Le huckster dwelling at the cellar in Paternoster Row before the gate, formerly of William Storteford, canon of the church of St Paul,	1 k.
John Broughton dwelling at the George in Fleet Street sold 1 kilderkin of ale, price 22*d.*, for 2*s.* 5½*d.*, to the Abbot of Walden	
Item 1 kilderkin of ale price 2*s.* 4*d.*, for 3*s.* 1½*d.*	
Alice Clerk opposite the fountain between the Crutched Friars and Aldgate	1 k.
A woman dwelling beside the Cross in Thames Street	1 k.
Thomas Kent dwelling at the Basket beside Billingsgate	1 k.
Katherine Baker, huckster, dwelling beside the corner opposite Dowgate	1 k.
Agnes Paule dwelling beside Paul's Wharf	1 k.
The wife of John Walissh, cordwainer, dwelling beside Ludgate	1 k.
Le brewer dwelling at the Key in Coleman Street	1 barrel
A certain huckster dwelling between le Swan on the Hoop and Ivy Lane in the parish of St Nicholas Shambles	1 barrel
William Fox dwelling at the Ship in the same parish	1 kilderkin

[142] [f. 51r]

John Westzerd dwelling at the Crane in the parish of St Nicholas at the market [*Shambles*]	1 barrel
Robert Maylond dwelling at the Castle in Wood Street	1 barrel
Richard Kilsole dwelling at the Cock at the end of Gutter Lane	1 barrel
A certain huckster dwelling at the corner cellar of Bread Street	1 barrel
Le brewer at the Ship, formerly of Michael Trerys	1 barrel
Richard, ostler, dwelling at the Falcon beside John Stannton, brewer,	1 kilderkin

[243] Perhaps John Shadworth, mayor 1401–2, d. 1430, buried at St Mildred Bread Street. See C. Rawcliffe, 'Shadworth, John (d. 1430) of London', *History of Parliament.*
[244] Renner Street?

6 quarters of malt were forfeited from a certain maltman in the home of Roger Swanneffeld

Item John Woodleff of Ware and others had 4 quarters which were forfeited in the common market at Gracechurch

[*Scored*: Memorandum that John Beterden, chamberlain received from the barrels and kilderkins written before, and also for forfeited malt, 60s. 5½d. from which a quarter part was refunded to the said craft of Brewers, by custom, and commonly owed, by the hands of William,[245] 15s.]

[143]

In this year during the time of William Cambrigge being mayor [1420–1] that is, on the 20th day of the month of May, [1421] Thomas Grene and his associates held a breakfast for the noblest members of the aforesaid craft as appears in the following

[*French*] The First Course:	The Second Course:
broth in pottage	jusell[246] in pottage
chickens	capons
knuckles of veal	*doucettes*
geese	

The expenses made for the same Dinner on the day and year aforesaid.

First for bread	3s.	Item for herbs and cream	10½d.
Item for French bread	4d.	Item for 6 knuckles of veal	18d.
Item for trencher bread	3d.	Item for 26 chickens with portage	3s. 2d.
Item for 1 peck and a half of flour	9d.	Item for 19 marrowbones	2s. 5½d.
Item for red wine	7s.	Item for 12 capons with portage	13s. 7d.
Item for 1 kilderkin of ale the gallon at 2d.,	2s. 4d.	Item for 13 geese	7s. 11d.
		Item for 1 quart of grease	4d.
Item for 1 kilderkin of ale the gallon at 1½d.,	22d.	Item for 200 eggs	15d.
Item for white hanaps	15d.	Item for 1 lb of almonds, 1 pykerell[247] and 1 lamprey	2s. 6d.
Item for spices 4s.	1½d.	Item to the Cook and his servants	5s. 4d.
Item for pewter vessels	2s.	Item to a water bearer for water	3d.
Item to a butler for making the trenchers	2d.	Item for laundering of diverse napery	3d.
Item for wood and coals	15½d.	Item for carriage of fime	2d.
Item for honey, verjuice, Galantine, ginger and salt	8d.		

Sum total of expenses: 64s. 7d.

---

245 Porlond.
246 Broth with herbs. Constance B. Hieatt, *Cocatrice & Lamprey Hey: Late Fifteenth-century Recipes from Corpus Christi College, Oxford* (Totnes, 2012), 81.
247 Small pike.

[144] [f. 51v]
[Latin]
The names of various Brewers who came to the Breakfast written below

John Ketyng	John Mason	John Chapman
John Salter	John Spenser	John Reeffawe
William Petevile	Robert Smyght	William Bray
Adam Copendale	John Reyner	William Crane
William Ederich	William Smalsho	William atte Well
John Broke	John Philippe	William atte Wode
William Ferrour	John Riche	Thomas Hatcher
Peter Carpenter	Hugh Nell	John Stannton
Henry Trobolanz	Peter Hayford	Thomas Emond
Thomas Driffeld	Robert Hylton	Robert Carpenter
Thomas Grene	William Rawlyn	William Totwell
John Pyken	Sir Robert, chaplain	
Alan Brett	Symkyn Potekyn	
Roger Swanneffeld		

[145]
The names of various persons who were summoned to the Breakfast and did not come

Richard Shirwod	John Tregelowe	John More
John Ballard	Nicholas Kene	John Russell
John Thetford	Henry Lymber	Richard Rowden
Nicholas Grenweye	John Wightmore	William Ferrour at the Bell

The names of those coming to the said Breakfast without invitation
William Repon,
John Spor, ferrour

Acquisition made in the presence of the Masters and others

A Memorandum that during the time of the mayoralty of the said William
Cambrigge, Robert Tanner, brewer, dwelling at St Katherine's Wheel in the parish
of St Lawrence Pountney in Thames Street remitted and released all demands and
complaints to John Morys, John Zork and Hugh White, servants in the Brewers'
craft, on 17 March in the 8th year of the reign of King Henry V [1421] in the presence
of Thomas Grene, John Pyken, Robert Carpenter, Masters of the said craft.[248]
William atte Wode, Hugh Neel, John Broke were also present there in the parlour of
the hall called Brewers' Hall.

---

[248]   The fourth master, Robert Hylton, was not listed.

[146] [f. 52r]
[Mostly Latin]
Malt from diverse maltmen, confiscated during the time of William Cambrigge being mayor of London, and presented to John Wells, grocer, and John Boteller, draper, sheriffs of the same city at that time.

First 5 quarters of malt which were found in the house of Katherine Pynchebek of a certain man called Burgeys, maltman, and seized by W. atte Wode.
Item 5 quarters of malt which were found in the house of Robert Walram of certain men and seized by W. atte Wode
Item 3 quarters of malt of John Beauchamp de Barnet which were found in the house formerly of David Soys, dwelling at the Eagle and le Garland, in the malt market at Gracechurch
Item 6 quarters of malt which were found in the house of Walter Colshill, seized by W. Crane
Item 4 quarters of malt which were found in the house of John Thomas, tailor of Fleet Street
Item 3 quarters which were found at le Swan outside Bishopsgate and seized by W. atte Wode
Item 4 quarters that were found at the Crown in the parish of St Dionis and seized by the same W.
Item 4 quarters of malt that were found in the house of William Riche dwelling at the Vernacle in the parish of St Bartholomew the Less and seized by W. Crane
Item 6 quarters were seized in the house of Thomas atte Wode and by Thomas Grene
Item 6 quarters were seized in the house of John Elsy and by the same Thomas.

[147]
And a memorandum that of the money levied upon malt confiscated as above during the time of William Cambrigge as mayor, John Wellys and John Boteler as sheriffs, none of the money came into the hands of the Masters and Wardens that year, whereas in preceding years, it had been accustomed for them to receive a quarter part, confiscated in this way, as above.

During the time of William Cambrigge, former mayor of London [1420–1], William Porlond, clerk to the craft and fraternity of Brewers, received from John Beterden, chamberlain at the Guildhall, from various forfeits, 15s., as appears in the folio immediately preceding.[249] However, on account of the weakness of the money, the said sum was not worth more than 12s. 4d. in the exchange.
This sum was in fact divided between 6 persons, that is: Thomas Grene, John Pyken, William atte Wode, William Ferrour, William Crane and John Salter, who each had 20d., and the said William Porlond, clerk, 2s. 4d.
Robert Hylton and Robert Carpenter received nothing because they refused to be employed in this business.

---

[249] See **[142]**.

[148] [f. 52v]
[French]
The following parcels were paid by Thomas Grene, Robert Hylton, John Pyken and Robert Carpenter, that is, for a Dinner, made on 21ˢᵗ April in the 10ᵗʰ year of the reign of King Henry V [1422] for diverse people, written afterwards, who were present for the reading of the accounts, on the day abovesaid, as appear afterwards

The ordinance of this Dinner that is for 8 messes[250]

The First Course
Bread in broth
Chicken
Veal
Roast capon

The Second Course
Jussel
Roast pigeon
Dowcettes

Costs of the Dinner

First for white bread	15*d.*	Item for 1 dish of butter	3*d.*
Item for trencher bread	3*d.*	Item for 9 tankards of water	3*d.*
Item for French bread	2*d.*	Item for carriage of dung	1*d.*
Item for 1 peck of flour	5*d.*	Item for 1 labourer for his work	4*d.*
Item for 1 kilderkin of good ale	2*s.* 4*d.*	Item for laundry of the board	
Item for 1 pottle of penny ale	4*d.*	cloths and towels	2*d.*
Item for 1 round of beef	4*d.*	Item to John Hardy, Cook, for	
Item for 5 legs and 3 fillets of		himself and his servants	3*s.* 5*d.*
veal	2*s.* 5*d.*	Item for cream	6*d.*
Item for 12 marrow bones	20*d.*	Item for honey, salt and verjuice	3*d.*
Item for 8 capons 4*s.*	4*d.*	Item paid for 9 gallons and a	
Item in payment for the meat of		pottle of red wine	6*s.* 4*d.*
the capons	2*d.*	Item for the allowance of 1 dozen	
Item for 16 chickens	2*s.* 2*d.*	plates with earthenware pots for	
Item for 3 dozen pigeons	2*s.* 9*d.*	ale and wine	2*d.*
Item for saffron	4*d.*		
Item 1 lb dates	2*d.*		
Item for herbs: hyssop, sage,			
parsley and sorrel	4*d.*		
Item for 200 eggs	14*d.*		

Sum 32*s.* 4*d.*

[250] People.

[149]
The names of persons who were at the Dinner for the Garniture of William the clerk.

John Turvey	William atte Wode	Peter Carpenter	John Reyner
Robert Smyth	Thomas Hatcher	William Crane	William Ferrour
Peter Hayforde	Hugh Neel	John Ketyng	Thomas Emond
William Edrych	William Smalsho	John Riche	John Phillipe
Richard Welde	Robert Hilton	Robert Carpenter	John Pyken
Sir Robert Steynton	Robert Lynford	John Masonne	John Salter

And the names of those who came to the Dinner abovesaid without the garniture of the craft

Henry Trebolans, Richard Lucas

And the names of persons who were garnished but did not come to the abovesaid Dinner

William Rawlyn	William atte Well	Richard Shirwode	William Bracy
William Cophode	Robert Nikke	John Wyghtmore	Thomas Osbarn
John Beauchamp, maltman	Alan Bret	Henry Lymber	Thomas Grene

Memorandum that William Porlond collected in the Hall at the said Breakfast from the brothers abovesaid, 20*d.*, of which 12*d.* was paid to a certain harper minstrel. And 8*d.* was paid to William Devenyssh.

[150] [f. 53r]
[*Latin*]
First for various drapery during the time of William Cambrigge, mayor of the city of London in the 9th year of the reign of King Henry V [1421–2] that is, rays and cloth of blood colour, called coarse cloth, for the livery of the brothers and sisters of the fraternity of [*scored*: the Holy Trinity] [*above the line*: All Hallows]²⁵¹ of the craft of Brewers in the same city, Thomas Grene, Robert Hylton, Robert Carpenter, and John Pyken then being Masters of the same craft.

Rays First John Griffith, draper of Salisbury for 16 cloths called rays, each containing 25 yards, and each yard containing 8 rays, in total 3,200 rays bought from him, cloth at 50*s.*, in total £40, from which 66*s.* 8*d.* was deducted from the same John on account of the weakness and unsuitability found in the said rays, thus £36 13*s.* 4*d.*

Coloured Cloth John Glyn, draper of London, for 1 cloth of blood colour containing 20 yards at 3*s.* 8*d.*, 73*s.* 4*d.*
To the same for 1 remaining cloth of the same colour, 5 yards and 1 quarter at 4*s.*, 21*s.*

²⁵¹ 'Holy Trinity' was deleted and 'All Hallows' was written above in a different hand.

And to the same for 1 cloth of the same colour containing 21 yards and a half at 4*s*., as above, £4 6*s*.,

from which 28*s* was deducted for 7 yards of the said cloth that were unsuitable through cockling[252] and other said defects, in total 58*s*.

To John Ryngesson of London for 1 cloth of blood colour containing 29 yards at 4*s*. 6*d*., £6 10*s*. 6*d*.

To the same for 1 remaining cloth of the same colour containing 3 yards at 4*s*., 12*s*.

To the same for 1 other remaining of the said colour containing 5 yards as above, 20*s*.

To the same for 1 cloth of colour containing 39 yards at 3*s*. 6*d*., £6 16*s*. 6*d*.

To the same for each other cloth of colour containing 28 yards, as above, £4 18*s*.

And to the same for 1 other cloth of the said colour containing 17 yards at 3*s*. 2*d*., 53*s*. 10*d*.

To Thomas Grene for 1 cloth of blood colour containing 30 yards at 3*s*. 6*d*., 105*s*.

To the same Thomas for 1 other cloth of the same colour containing 30 yards as above, 105*s*.

And to the same for a certain other cloth in the same colour containing 28 yards half at 2*s*. 8*d*., 76*s*.

John Brokle, citizen and draper of London, for 1 cloth of blood colour containing 24 yards half at 3*s*. 6*d*., £4 5*s*. 9*d*.

To the same for 1 other cloth of the same colour containing 12 yards half at 3*s*. 4*d*., 41*s*. 8*d*.

And to the same for a certain remnant in the same colour containing 7 yards half at 3*s*. 5*d*., 25*s*. 7½*d*.

To John Ketyng for a certain cloth of blood colour containing 39 yards at 4*s*. 8*d*., £6 15*s*. 4*d*.

John Leon of Bocking in the county of Essex for 1 cloth of blood colour containing 29 yards at 3*s*. minus 20*d*. by recommendation, in total £4 5*s*. 4*d*.

Sum of cloth of colour 351 yards 3 quarters
Money £53 2*s*. 10½*d*.

Sum total of drapery
Rays 3,200
Coloured cloth 351 yards 3 quarters
Money £99 16*s*. 2½*d*.

---

252   Puckering, wrinkling, creasing.

[151] [f. 53v]
Issue of the same drapery at the same time and in the same year, as appears in the following

A 77 rays, 6 yards half & half quarter, money 59s.[253]

[*Mostly French*] **Gowns**
n Alexander Marcow 32 rays with 2 yards 3 quarters blue cloth   23s. 8d.[254]
n Alexander Miles 30 rays with 2 yards half best blue cloth   24s.

Hoods
n Adam Copendale 8 rays with 3 quarters blue cloth   6s.
Alan John 7 rays with half yard & half quarter blue cloth   5s. 4d.

B 8 rays, half yard half quarter cloth of colour, money: 5s. 8d.
Item Hood
n Baldewyne Hoper 8 rays half yard half quarter blue cloth   5s. 8d.

Gowns
D 34 rays, 7 yards half quarter c[*olour*] m[*oney*] 35s. 3d.
Gowns
[*scored*: Sir Robert Steynton, chaplain, 4 yards 1 quarter blue cloth of Essex   12s. 9d.]
[*Added* [*Latin*]: who had no rays][255]
n David Bronnyng 27 rays with 2 yards 1 quarter blue cloth   17s.
Hood
Dederick Johnsonne 7 rays with half yard half quarter blue cloth   5s. 6d.

E 8 rays, half yard half quarter 1 nail, m[*oney*] 6s.
Item Hood
Edmund Disse 8 rays with half yard half quarter 1 nail blue cloth   6s.

G 7 rays, half yard c[*olour*], m[*oney*] 4s. 8d.
Item Hood
Gilbert Boton 7 rays with half yard blue cloth   4s. 8d.

H 142 r[*ays*], 18 yards 3 quarters c[*olour*] £6 12s. 8d. m[*oney*]

[152]
Gowns
Hugh Glene 7 rays with 4 yards 1 quarter blue cloth   23s. 4d.
Henry Bedell 32 rays with 2 yards 3 quarters blue cloth   24s.
Henry Lymber 34 rays with 2 yards 3 quarters & half blue cloth   22s. 4d.
Hugo Nell 32 rays with 2 yards half & half quarter blue cloth   23s.
Henry Trobolans 7 rays with 3 yards half blue cloth   17s.

253   The clerk seems to have used capital letters to indicate specific pieces of cloth.
254   The scribe annotated the list with some 'n' figures, which have been included. They could indicate payments made or still due.
255   The priest had the colour but not the rays, as a member of the fraternity but not of the craft. Cloth of Essex could refer to the purchase from John Leon of Essex.

Hoods

n Henry Rowe 8 rays with 3 quarters blue cloth		6s.
n Henry Basset 8 rays with 3 quarters blue cloth		6s.
n Henry Grene 7 rays with half yard half quarter blue cloth		5s. 6d.
Henry Serle 7 rays with half yard half quarter blue cloth		5s. 6d.

[153]
Gowns

n John Jacobb 32 rays with 2 yards half blue cloth	21s. 10d.
n John Farman 31 rays with 2 yards half blue cloth	22s. 8d.
n John Masonne 7 rays with 4 yards half blue cloth	23s.
n John Dunche 24 rays with 2 yards blue cloth	17s. 8d.
n John Salter 32 rays with 2 yards half blue cloth	23s. 4d.
n John Laurence 28 rays with 2 yards half blue cloth	21s.

[f. 54r]

n John Philippe 6 rays with 4 yards half of blue cloth	24s.
n John More of Aldersgate 7 rays with 4 yards of blue cloth	22s.
n John Tregolowe 28 rays with 2 yards 1 quarter of blue cloth	20s.
n John Basset 28 rays with 2 yards 1 quarter of blue cloth	20s.
n John Reyner 30 rays with 2 yards half of blue cloth	22s.
n John Newman 30 rays with 2 yards half of blue cloth	22s.
n John Davy of Fleet Street 30 rays with 2 yards half of blue cloth	21s. 4d.
n John Pyken 32 rays with 5 yards of blue cloth	25s. 6d.
n John Hardyng 28 rays with 2 yards 1 quarter of blue cloth	20s. 4d.
n John Caryen 28 rays with 2 yards half of blue cloth	22s. 8d.
n John Chapmanne 30 rays with 2 yards 3 quarters of blue cloth	23s. 4d.
n John Toke 24 rays with 2 yards 1 quarter of blue cloth	20s. 4d.
[*scored*: John] Jacob Lenegro 24 rays with 2 yards of blue cloth	18s.
n John Stone 31 rays with 2 yards of blue cloth	19s. 4d.
n John Kenaky 30 rays with 2 yards half of blue cloth	22s.
n John Brewster 28 rays with 2 yards half of blue cloth	21s.
n John Broke 32 rays with 2 yards half of blue cloth	22s. 8d.
n John Spenser 28 rays with 2 yards half of blue cloth	22s.
n John Humber 13 rays with 5 yards of blue cloth	28s.
n John More at Ludgate 8 rays with 4 yards 3 quarters of blue cloth	27s. 4d.
John Lynne 30 rays with 2 yards half of best blue cloth	26s. 8d.
John William 31 rays with 2 yards half of best blue cloth	27s.
John Stannton 8 rays with 4 yards half of best blue cloth	30s.
John Riche 7 rays with 5 yards of blue cloth	28s.
John Russell 32 rays with 2 yards half of blue cloth	25s. 8d.
John Ketyng 8 rays with 8 yards 3 quarters and half of best blue cloth	55s. 11d.
John Aleyn 28 rays with 2 yards half of blue cloth	19s.
John Ryngesson 34 rays with half yard half quarter of blue cloth	10s. 10d.
John Reffawe 28 rays with 2 yards half of blue cloth	19s.
John Sharpe, maltman, 28 rays with 2 yards half of inferior blue cloth	17s.
John Beauchamp 24 rays with 2 yards 1 quarter of inferior blue cloth	15s.

[154]
Hoods

n John Norman 6 rays with half yard of blue cloth	5*s*.
n John Bronnyng 8 rays with 3 quarters of blue cloth	6*s*. 8*d*.
n John Goldyng 7 rays with half yard half quarter of blue cloth	5*s*.
n John Snell 7 rays with half yard half quarter of blue cloth	5*s*. 6*d*.
n John Blostmere 6 rays with half yard of blue cloth	4*s*.
n John Holbek 7 rays with half yard half quarter of blue cloth	5*s*. 4*d*.
n John Frost 7 rays with half yard half quarter of blue cloth	6*s*.
n John Lumbard 7 rays with half yard half quarter of blue cloth	5*s*. 6*d*.
n John Grymmesby 7 rays with half yard of blue cloth	5*s*.
n John Bray, butcher, 7 rays with half yard of blue cloth	5*s*.
n John Merston 7 rays with half yard of blue cloth	5*s*.
n John Baily 6 rays with half yard of blue cloth	5*s*.

[155] [f. 54v]

n John Eylond 7 rays with half yard half quarter of blue cloth	6*s*.
n John Waghorn 6 rays with half yard of blue cloth	4*s*. 4*d*.
John Turveye 8 rays with half yard half quarter of blue cloth	6*s*.
John Sere, glover, 6 rays with half yard of blue cloth	5*s*.
n John Hardy 7 rays with half yard half quarter of blue cloth	5*s*.
n John Tornour 8 rays with 3 quarters of blue cloth	6*s*. 8*d*.
n John Benge 8 rays with half yard half quarter of blue cloth	6*s*.
n John Wake 8 rays with 3 quarters of blue cloth	6*s*.
n John Riche of Fleet Street 6 rays with half yard of blue cloth	5*s*.
n John Thomas 7 rays with half yard half quarter of blue cloth	5*s*. 6*d*.
n John Aleyn of the parish of St Giles 7 rays with half yard half quarter of blue cloth	5*s*. 6*d*.
n John Cherchisseye 8 rays with 3 quarters of blue cloth	6*s*. 8*d*.
n John Bedeford 7 rays with half yard half quarter of blue cloth	5*s*. 6*d*.
John Yver 7 rays with half yard half quarter of blue cloth	5*s*. 6*d*.
John Sonder 7 rays with half yard half quarter of blue cloth	5*s*. 8*d*.
John Luke 7 rays with half yard half quarter of blue cloth	5*s*. 6*d*.
John Assh 7 rays with half yard half quarter of blue cloth	5*s*. 6*d*.
John Serle 5 rays with half yard of blue cloth	4*s*.
John Bargon 7 rays with half yard half quarter of blue cloth	5*s*.
John Fekenham 12 rays with 1 yard 1 nail of lesser blue cloth	8*s*.

[156]
I [*or J*] 1,150 R[*ays*] 133 yards 1 quarter 1 nail C[*olour*] £51 19*s*. 5*d*. M[*oney*]

n John Parker 7 rays with half yard half quarter of blue cloth	5*s*. 6*d*.
n John Southmede 8 rays with 3 quarters of blue cloth	6*s*. 8*d*.
n John de Dene 6 rays with half yard of blue cloth	4*s*. 6*d*.

Gowns
M 90 R[*ays*] 7 yards half C[*olour*] 64*s*. 8*d*. M[*oney*]

n Michael Tregononne 28 rays with 2 yards 1 quarter of blue cloth	20*s*. 8*d*.
n Michael Eve 32 rays with 2 yards 3 quarters of blue cloth	24*s*.
n Maurice Tranaill 30 rays with 2 yards half of blue cloth	20*s*.

Gowns

N [*damaged*] 93 Rays 6 yards 3 quarters C[*olour*] 64s. 8d. M[*oney*]

n Nicholas Agomnailok 26 rays with 2 yards 1 quarter of blue cloth	20s. 4d.
n Nicholas Muryell 24 rays with 2 yards of blue cloth	17s. 4d.
n Nicholas Aleyn 26 rays with 2 yards half quarter of blue cloth	22s.

Hoods

n Nicholas Fuller 7 rays with half yard of blue cloth	5s.

Gowns

P 93 R[*ays*] 11 yards half 1 nail C[*olour*] £4 11s. 6d. M[*oney*]

n Peter Carpenter 28 rays with 2 yards 1 quarter of blue cloth	20s. 8d.
n Philip Godfrey 31 rays with 2 yards half of blue cloth	25s.
n Peter Hayford 7 rays with 4 yards half of blue cloth	25s.

Hoods

n Philip James 6 rays with half yard of blue cloth	4s. 4d.
n Philip Porcell 7 rays with half yard half quarter of blue cloth	6s.
n Peter Roos 8 rays with half yard half quarter 1 nail of blue cloth	6s.
n Peter Sevyer 6 rays with half yard of blue cloth	4s. 6d.

[157] [f. 55r]

Gowns

Robert Steynton, chaplain, 4 yards and 1 quarter of blue cloth of Essex	12s. 9d.

R [*illegible*]

n Robert Mayhew 28 rays	9s. 4d.
n Richard Lucas 29 rays with 2 yards 1 quarter of blue cloth	20s. 5d.
n Robert Hylton 32 rays with 3 yards 3 quarters of blue cloth	20s. 11d.
n Robert Gyles 7 rays with 4 yards of blue cloth	20s. 4d.
n Richard Shirwod 30 rays with 2 yards half of blue cloth	22s.
n Robert Tanner 29 rays with 2 yards half of blue cloth	21s. 10d.
n Richard Rowdon 8 rays with 4 yards of best blue cloth	26s.
n Robert Smyth 32 rays with 2 yards half of best blue cloth	26s.
n Richard Aleyn 28 rays with 2 yards 1 quarter of best blue cloth	23s.
n Robert Elkyn 28 rays with 2 yards half quarter of best blue cloth	22s. 2d.
n Roger Swanneffeld 32 rays with 2 yards 3 quarters of best blue cloth	27s.
Robert Carpenter 34 rays with 3 yards 3 quarters blue cloth	21s. 5d.
n Randolph Palmer 28 rays with 2 yards half blue cloth	20s.
n Robert Squyere 24 rays with 2 yards half blue cloth	16s.

[158]

Hoods

n Robert Lynford 6 rays with half yard blue cloth	3s. 3d.
n Robert Dorwell 7 rays with half yard half quarter blue cloth	5s. 6d.
Roger Ware 8 rays with half yard half quarter blue cloth	6s.
Roger Blissote 7 rays with half yard blue cloth	4s. 8d.
Robert Walram 7 rays with half yard half quarter blue cloth	5s. 6d.
Richard Crosse 7 rays with half yard half quarter blue cloth	5s. 4d.
Richard Terrell 7 rays with half yard half quarter blue cloth	6s.

146

Richard Harlowe 7 rays with half yard half quarter blue cloth	5s.
Richard Brynton 7 rays with half yard half quarter blue cloth	5s. 8d.
Richard²⁵⁶ Baron 7 rays with half yard half quarter blue cloth	5s. 8d.
Robert Pede 8 rays with 3 quarters blue cloth	6s.
Richard Maihewe 7 rays with half yard half quarter blue cloth	5s. 6d.
Robert Nikke 8 rays with 3 quarters blue cloth	6s.
Robert Ketyng 6 rays with half yard blue cloth	5s.
Robert Bullard 7 rays with half yard half quarter blue cloth	5s. 6d.
Richard West at the Pewter Pot 7 rays with half yard half quarter blue cloth	5s.

Gowns

S [*illegible*]

n Simon Potekyn 28 rays with 2 yards half blue cloth	21s. 4d.

Hoods

n Simon Petesyn 7 rays with half yard half quarter blue cloth	5s. 6d.
n Stephen Clean 7 rays with half yard half quarter blue cloth	5s. 10d.
n Stephen Roo 7 rays with half yard half quarter blue cloth	5s.
n Simon Harry 7 rays with half yard half quarter blue cloth	5s. 6d.

Gowns

n Thomas Ayle 7 rays with 4 yards half blue cloth	24s.
n Thomas Godyng 26 rays with 2 yards 1 quarter blue cloth	20s.
n Thomas Emond 6 rays with 4 yards blue cloth	20s. 8d.
n Thomas Aleyn 32 rays with 2 yards 3 quarters blue cloth	24s. 4d.
n Thomas Hatcher 32 rays with 2 yards half best blue cloth	25s.
n Thomas Yole 26 rays with 2 yards blue cloth	16s. 8d.
n Thomas Grene 34 rays with 4 yards blue cloth	23s. 2d.
Thomas Howe 30 rays with 2 yards half blue cloth	18s.

[159] [f. 55v]

Hoods

n Thomas North 7 rays with half yard half quarter blue cloth	5s. 10d.
n Thomas Pothill 7 rays with half yard half quarter blue cloth	5s. 6d.
n Thomas Pensonne 8 rays with half yard half quarter 1 nail blue cloth	5s. 8d.
Thomas Hancok 8 rays with half yard half quarter 1 nail blue cloth	5s. 8d.
n Thomas de Kent 7 rays with half yard blue cloth	5s.
n Thomas Smalsho 7 rays with half yard half quarter blue cloth	5s. 6d.
n Thomas Hill, maltman, 6 rays with half yard blue cloth	4s.
n Thomas Boteler 8 rays with 3 quarters blue cloth	6s. 8d.

T 267 R[*ays*] 31 yards half 1 nail C[*olour*] £11 9s. 4d. M[*oney*]

n Thomas Gratley 8 rays without more	2s. 8d.
n Thomas Merssh 8 rays with half yard half quarter 1 nail blue cloth	6s.
n Thomas Donyngton for 1 yard 1 quarter half [*quarter*] blue cloth	5s.

---

²⁵⁶   A mistake for Roger.

147

Gowns

n William Baily 26 rays with 2 yards 1 quarter blue cloth	18s. 10d.
n William atte Well 28 rays with 2 yards 1 quarter blue cloth	21s. 8d.
n William Belle 26 rays with 2 yards 1 quarter blue cloth	19s. 4d.
n William Grosse 30 rays with 2 yards half blue cloth	22s.
n William Herry 30 rays with 2 yards half blue cloth	22s.
n Walter Colshill 28 rays with 2 yards half blue cloth	21s. 4d.
n William Boteler 26 rays with 2 yards blue cloth	18s. 8d.
n William Payn 30 rays with 2 yards half blue cloth	22s.
n William Bolton 24 rays with 2 yards 1 quarter blue cloth	19s.
n William EdeRiche 6 rays with 4 yards half blue cloth	23s. 4d.
n William Petevyle 8 rays with 4 yards half and half quarter blue cloth	26s. 8d.
n William Ferrour 32 rays with 2 yards half best blue cloth	26s.
n William atte Wode 8 rays with 5 yards best blue cloth	32s.
n William Cardell 32 rays with 2 yards half best blue cloth	26s. 8d.
n William Crane 26 rays with 2 yards 1 quarter best blue cloth	18s.
n William Geffray 28 rays with 2 yards half blue cloth	17s. 4d.
n William Canon 30 rays with 2 yards half blue cloth	22s.
n William Illyng 24 rays with 2 yards blue cloth	16s.
n William Claisson 28 rays with 2 yards half blue cloth	19s.
n William Bracy 30 rays with 2 yards half blue cloth	22s.
n William Porlond for 6 yards 1 quarter blue cloth of diverse sorts	22s. 8d.
n William Bodevyle 28 rays with 2 yards half blue cloth	17s.
n William Cophode 33 rays with 3 yards blue cloth	20s.

[160]
Hoods

n William Rawlyn 8 rays with 3 quarters blue cloth	6s.
n William Levill 8 rays with half yard half quarter blue cloth	5s. 10d.
n William Mark 7 rays with half yard half quarter blue cloth	5s. 4d.
n William Style 6 rays with half yard blue cloth	5s. 4d.
n William Borne 5 rays with half yard blue cloth	4s.
n William Bakon, butcher, 7 rays with half yard half quarter blue cloth	5s. 4d.
n William Termeday 8 rays with half yard half quarter blue cloth	5s. 8d.
n William Pethin 8 rays with half yard half quarter blue cloth	5s.
n William Devenyssh 7 rays with half yard half quarter blue cloth	5s.
n William Ferrour 8 rays with half yard half quarter blue cloth	5s. 8d.
n William Riche 7 rays with half yard half quarter blue cloth	5s. 6d.
n William Smalsho 8 rays with 3 quarters blue cloth	6s. 8d.
n William Mascall 8 rays with 3 quarters blue cloth	6s.
n William Bernard 6 rays with half yard blue cloth	5s.
n William Eyre 7 rays with half yard half quarter blue cloth	5s. 6d.

[161] [f. 56r]
W R[*ayes*] C[*olour*] M[*oney*] [*illegible*]

n William Antrou 7 rays with half yard half quarter blue cloth	5s.
n William Repon 8 rays with half yard half quarter 1 nail blue cloth	6s.
n William Totewell 7 rays with half yard half quarter blue cloth	5s. 6d.

[*Mostly Latin*] Which is:

n **Sum total** issued to the drapers:
Rays 3,200 with 12 rays in store etc.
Coloured cloth 354 yards 3 quarters half
Money £137 9s. 10d. Examined.

[Clerk's note: [*Latin*] qui est defensor anime][257]

Sum of rays received from the draper of
Salisbury 3,200

n For cloth of blood colour agreed
received from diverse 351 yards
3 quarters
n For which was divided for the said
gowns & hoods 354 yards 3 quarters
n And in increase for the said cloth for
parcels divided 3 yards half quarter

[162]
Which was delivered in the various gowns and hoods as clearly appears. And this
equals

Sum above noted, that is, £137 9s. 10d. From which deduct £99 6s. 2½d. Bought
from diverse drapers.
And 31s. 6d. for shearing to the same draper.
And £6 12s. 9d. in the price of vestments for the 4 Masters & others given livery,
that is Thomas Grene 23s. 2d., Robert Hiltonne 20s. 11d. John Piken 25s. 6d. Robert
Carpenter 21s. 5d. William Purlond 22s. 8d. John Ryngessonne for his labour about
stretching the cloth, for his allowance 10s. 10d. John Hardy 5s. Robert Lynford of
alms 3s. 3d.

And 36s. in money not levied & the same total aforesaid that is
Maurice Travaill 20s. Philip Godfrey 6s. 8d.
And John Ryngessonne for silver received from Robert Mayhewe 9s. 4d.
And 42s. 6d. in pardoning clothing to Alexander Marcowe [*scored*: Gilbert Boton]
and his associates written by name fully in the same roll of paper.

And £18 12s. 6½d. for expenses of the Masters for the feast called the Brewers' Feast
and 64s. 7d. for a certain breakfast for the noblest of the aforesaid craft.
And 32s. 4d. for a certain breakfast made by Thomas Grene and his associates on the
day of the accounts
And 19s. 10d. for diverse exchanges in washing, shearing and more.[258]
And from 11s. 6d. from which in money paid for ale at the house of John More
outside Cripplegate 2d.
And in the aforesaid money between Thomas Grene, John Piken and William
Purlond, clerk, towards alleviating the money in the common box 7s. 1½d.
And for halling by William Devenyssh, he took as payment at the time 3s. 4d.

257 The meaning in this context is unclear.
258 The Latin word looks like 'peior', meaning literally 'worse' or perhaps more troublesome,
harmful, or expensive.

And for one leaf of parchment for indentures between the Masters of the craft and John Griffith of Salisbury 8*d.* and for red wax for the same ½*d.*

For portage of a letter missive to the said John Griffith and in ale ½*d.*

And in coals 1½*d.*, with 2 faggots sent for the fire before the Masters and William atte Wode on the 9th day November in the 8ᵗʰ year [1420]

And 3*s.* 4*d.* for a certain breakfast made at le Greyhound in East Cheap at the time when William Ferrour Junior and Nicholas Grenewode were made freemen of the craft of Brewers

And 6*s.* 8*d.* paid for a certain breakfast made in East Cheap by Thomas Grene, Robert Carpenter, John Piken and his wife on the day of accounts amongst themselves.

And 5*d.* for wine at the accounts with Thomas Grene, Robert Carpenter and John Piken upon the day when John Griffith, draper, received in payment 10 marks.

Sum £137 10*s.* 2*d.*

[163] [f. 56v]

During the time of William Cambrigge being mayor, that is in the 9ᵗʰ year of the reign of King Henry V [1421–2] on the 13ᵗʰ day of February, [1421] that is on the Thursday during Quadragesima²⁵⁹ the same Lord King came from parts of France to visit the city of London. The mayor rode with all the commons of the city to meet the said King. It was ordained by the mayor that all the commons should be clothed in white gowns with red hoods. It was ordered by the Masters & Wardens of our craft of Brewers that they should ride and increase the honour paid and that all householders of the company and Brewers of 40*s.* or more a year should be clad in cloth of colour, as above, and ride, under penalty of a fine upon the whole commonalty of 20*s.*

William the clerk, however, for his diligence towards the Masters, was granted a white gown by them. And concerning this penalty of 20*s.* noted above, certain freemen of the said craft were excused for not riding, some for various urgent causes, for the least sum, others for nothing. Those brewersmen who failed in the aforesaid matter were not punished, by the advice of the council.

And the Queen came to the said city, as the King did, above, on the 21ˢᵗ day of the same month, that is on the Friday and the mayor and whole commons came to the lord King to increase the honour to the King. And not long after this the said King called together Parliament at Westminster, that is on the second day of March in that same year, [1422] in which Parliament, amongst other decrees, it was ordained by a special statute that all the weirs and kiddles²⁶⁰ in the river Thames between London and Staines²⁶¹ on the one part and between London, Gravesend and Queenborough²⁶² on the other part, should be destroyed. And concerning this the King and the mayor of the said city intended to destroy the said weirs and kiddles as was ordered to be implemented in a statute in the said Parliament. And for this the said mayor called the whole council of the city, in which it was agreed and ordained that 26 crafts should progress with the mayor on this business. Concerning this, our craft of Brewers was sent to him with 6 other crafts, that is the Girdlers, Fletchers, Salters,

---

²⁵⁹ Cambridge was mayor 1420–1, during Lent (Quadragesima) 1421.
²⁶⁰ Kiddle: Dam or weir with nets.
²⁶¹ To the west.
²⁶² East into Kent.

Barbers, Dyers and Tallow chandlers, to undertake to send in this way, by these orders, and to come in a certain barge.

[164]

But one of the six crafts called the Fletchers did not come and in the presence of the mayor they excused themselves in this fashion, that is that they were so occupied preparing artillery for the said King that it was not possible for them to work in this way. And concerning this, the said mayor conceded that if they did not come, themselves, they were allowed to find deputies, but by custom they had to make payment. And each of the 7 crafts found two suitable persons to travel with the said mayor to carry out this business. For our craft of Brewers, Thomas Grene and Roger Swanneffeld were chosen to travel towards Kingston and they spent 13s. 4d., and Robert Carpenter and John Mason to travel towards Gravesend and they spent 20s.,

[f. 57r]

each having a reward of 6s. 8d. And in this way our said craft of Brewers did not resist paying the chamber of the Guildhall for 3 labourers at 8d. the day for 28 days, for which they spent 56s.

And then for the money spent as above, by the precept and aforesaid ordinance of the said mayor, others in the said craft, meeting the Masters and Wardens of our craft, by sufficient agreement in the same, ordered a certain taxation to be levied upon our whole craft, which taxation some paid well and honestly.

[165]

Others paid the least possible. Others refused to pay the tax altogether. And others were not taxed on account of poverty and did not pay. [*scored*: Touching this singular matter certain rolls of parchment attached to this quarto fully declare those names]

[*Added*: And in subsequent folios are shown clearly]

And then in the abovesaid Parliament it was ordained by the Lord King, magnates and commons that gold at that time in the coinage, which by great inconvenience was worth less in the exchange value than its weight, during the feast of the Nativity of our Lord, would be renewed by an ordinance in Parliament. This statute was denied by the merchants of victuals, and craftsmen and others, so that in the city and even outside through the whole kingdom, the merchants of victuals and others in that city of London refused to receive gold for payment. Then there was a great shortage of silver, called white money, and great murmuring among the people as if the people would rise up suddenly. Concerning this, the Chancellor, the Treasurer and other lords and nobles of the council of the King, fully informed, sent to the mayor in the said city that he should come to them in council and he came.

Afterwards the mayor in the said city without delay sent for the Masters of the craft to come to his court at the Guildhall. At this meeting it was agreed by the mayor and the council of the King that until the feast of the Nativity of the Lord aforesaid, gold would continue to receive its value as formerly, unless it was of poor quality, or counterfeit, or worth less because horribly clipped.

And concerning this, it was declared to you for the easement of the aforesaid commonalty.

Which was completed during his whole time.

[166]
*[English]*²⁶³
Unto the right wise commons of the present Parliament,
the victuallers the Brewers of the city of London, meekly beseech that for as much
as the said victuallers serve our sovereign lord the King as well as the other lords
spiritual and temporal, with others of the King's lieges and all the said city, as in
ale, for which the victuallers buy their chief stuff, that is to say malt, at a great
disadvantage, in so much as the sellers of malt variously deceive the said victuallers,
that is to say in selling of bellied malt, that is to say stiff malt that will not come
[*to ripeness*], [*or*] wynnel eaten malt, that is to say with worms of dusty malt with
drawke, darnel and kerlowe seed. Also of hedgerow corn that has not had the full
growing, of unclean malt, that is to say with small stones, congealed earth, gravel,
and other various filth, and so when the said victuallers have made a quarter of malt
clean from the aforesaid filth, it will lack half a bushel, or a quarter, or 3 pecks, or
a bushel of the same [? fulsome] malt as can be proved openly. And for as much as
all these defaults were openly proved before this time, the said victuallers used to
have 9 bushels for a quarter, please unto your wise discretion to consider the deceits
aforesaid in the malt and to ordain due remedy, whereby the said victuallers may
have clean chaffure²⁶⁴ just as the sellers will have good money, for the King's avail
and for his liege people, for the love of God and in the way of charity.

[167] [f. 57v]
[Mostly French]
**The Ordinance of a Dinner called amongst us the Feast, held this year the 9ᵗʰ
year of the reign of King Henry V [1421–2].**

The First Course	**The Second Course**
Brawn with mustard	Venison in broth with
cabbage in pottage	white mortrewes
swan standard	cony standard
roast capons	roast venison
grand custards	partridges with cocks
	great birds with larks
	little perneaux²⁶⁵
	2 cold bakemeats

The Expenses of our said Feast in the same year

The Saturday

First on the Saturday next before the Feast, for oysters, mussels and onions	8*d.*
Item for 5 pikes at diverse prices	8*s.* 2*d.*
Item for 2 codlyng	3*s.* 8*d.*
Item for 3 quarters of red herring²⁶⁶ baked	14*d.*
Item for anguille and lamprons	2*s.*

Sum 15*s.* 8*d.*

---

²⁶³ This later insertion is another copy of the petition last written on f. 42v **[117]**.
²⁶⁴ Perhaps 'chaffer', meaning a good commodity or trade.
²⁶⁵ Sweet pies or pastries containing powdered ginger, currants and dates.
²⁶⁶ 'Sore' chopped herring, coloured red. Anguille: eels. Lamprons: river lamprey.

[168]
In the Pantry

First for chete bread	18s.
Item for pastry in the coffin[267] 2 bushels of coarse flour	3s.
Item for 1 bushel of fine flour	2s.
Item for maynbread 2s.	**Sum 25s.** Pardoned 11d.
Item for trencher bread	15d. Because of the present of the said baker.
Item for bread bought in East Cheap for the Monday	12d.
Item for oyster bread[268] and for the expenses on the Saturday before	4½d.

Sum 27s. 7½d. as accounted for above.

In the Buttery

First for 48 gallons and half red Gascony wine at 8d.,	32s. 4d.
Item for 6 barrels of good ale at 4s. 8d.,	28s.
Item 1 kilderkin of ale at 1½d. the gallon	22d.
Item for 1 other kilderkin of ale at 1d. the gallon	12d.
Item for 2 dozen new cups bought	16d.
Item for 4 dozen cups condual[269] at 4d.,	16d.
Item for taps and faucetts	1d.
Item for 8 dozen and a half terracotta pots and 1 large pot for wine conduit[270]	18d.
Item for 3 dozen and a half of broken terracotta pots at ½d.,	21d.

Sum 69s. 2d.

[169] [f. 58r]
Kitchen

First in caboches and other herbs for pottage	18d.
Item for 12 gallons & a half cream	4s. 2d.
Item for 2 lbs and half rice flour	8d.
Item for 100 faggots with carriage	4s. 4d.
Item for 6 quarters and 4 bushels coal at 9d., with le shetyng[271] and carriage at 1½d.,	5s.
Item for 7 ells and a half of old canvas at 4½d. for counters for the dresser and napery	3s.
Item for butter for basting etc.	9d.
Item 4 bushels of ledecole[272] to serve in the Hall and Chamber for chimneys	4d.

Sum 19s. 9d.

---

267 Pastry for the 'coffin' or pie shell, which was not eaten.
268 Barley bread eaten with oysters. 'The London Journal of Alessandro Magno 1562', ed. C. M. Barron, C. Coleman, C. Gobbi, *The London Journal*, 9:2 (1983), 136–52 (147–8). Magno observed that Londoners ate oysters in every possible way, 'but for preference they eat them raw before a meal with barley bread'. I am grateful to Martha Carlin for this reference.
269 Perhaps for a wine fountain.
270 Wine fountain?
271 Covering or loading?
272 Perhaps the best quality coal for the hall and chamber.

Poultry

First for 20 swans at 3s. 4d.,	66s. 8d.
Item for 58 capons at 4d.,	19s. 4d.
Item for 58 conies at 2½d.,	12s. 1d.
Item for 3 lambs at 6d.,	18d.
Item for 4 dozen and 1 woodcocks at 3d.,	12s. 3d.
Item for 26 partridges at 3d.,	6s. 6d.
Item for 5 plovers at 3d.,	15d.
Item for 15 dozen and 1 large birds at 6d.,	7s. 6d.
Item for 13 dozen and 1 of larks at 4d.,	4s. 4d.
Item for 8 dozen eggs at 10d.,	6s. 8d.
Item for the expenses of the said dinner in payment for the victuals of the poultry aforesaid,	9d.

Sum £6 18s. 10d.

[170]
Butchery

First for marrowbones	3s. 4d.
Item for 2 rounds of beef	6d.
Item for 1 leg of beef	1d.
Item for 6 fillets of pork	6d.
Item for 2 gallons of grease at 16d.,	2s. 8d.
Item for blood, neats and tallow	12d.
Item for 1 boar,	12s.
Item for 1 bushel [?]salt for cleaning the same boar	6d.
Item for portage and scalding of the boar	14d.

Sum 21s. 9d.

Spices

First for 1 lb pepper	20d.
Item for a half quarter saffron	22d.
Item for 1 lb ginger	18d.
Item for 1 lb canell for cinnamon	20d.
Item for 1 quarter cloves	9d.
Item for 1 quarter mace	9d.
Item for 2 lbs sugar price 16d.,	2s. 8d.
Item for a half quarter sanders	2d.
Item 8 lbs raisins of Corinth at 3½d.,	2s. 4d.
Item for 2 lbs prunes at 6d.,	12d.
[Clerk's note: verte].	

[171] [f. 58v]
[French & Latin]
Additional Spices

Item 2 lbs aniseed in powder	3d.
Item for half lb aniseed in red confit	7d.

Item for 12 lbs *anngdol* Jardyn[273] at 2½d.,	2s. 6d.
Item for 2 yards for strainers[274] at 3d.,	6d.
Item for 2 gallons honey at 14d.,	2s. 4d.
Item for a pot in which to put the said honey	1d.
Item for half lb aniseed in white confit	7d.
Item for 20 lbs [?]damsons at 1d.,	20d.

Sum 22s. 10d. and for the aforesaid in part payment 8d.

In Sauces

First for 1 peck of great salt	4d.
Item for a half bushel of *Beerfletesalt*	8d.
Item for 1 gallon and half mustard	6d.
Item for 1 gallon & 3 pints vinegar	6d.
Item for 1 quart verjuice	1d.
Item for 1 pint [?] ginger	1d.
Item for pack thread bought	1d.
Item for small salt for the pantry	1d.
Item for 1 pint of honey	2d.
Item for oatmeal	1d.
Item for onions	1d.

Sum 2s. 8d.

[172]

Diverse things and foreign expenses

First to John Hardy, Cook, for himself and his servants and for the carriage of vessels	21s. 8d.
to Kyngeston Sucrour	12d.
Item to the said John Hardy and his servants in reward for drink in Old Fish Street	2d.
Item to diverse *turnbrushes* in reward	11d.
Item to William Devenyssh, panter, for his reward	3s. 4d.
Item to John Dene, butler, for his reward	2s.
Item to Robert Barbour, porter, for his reward,	8d.
Item to 4 clerks, players, for their play	7s.
Item for hiring of 9 dozen pewter vessels, garnished, at 7d.,	5s. 3d.
Item for other hiring of 9 dozen pewter vessels, garnished, at 6d., 4s. 6d. In total	9s. 9d.
Item to 1 water bearer for water for the Masters	12d.
And for reward to Robert Carpenter 2d. (and for the Masters nil)	
Item for 3 wiping cloths for the pewter vessels	6d.
Item for portage of sousing ale 1d.	
Item for 1 *herrenbrush*[275] for cleaning the earthenware pots	1d.
Item for 3 loads of rushes with portage	12d.

---

273 Perhaps almonds, grown in the garden at Brewers' Hall, rather than almonds from Valencia.
274 Cloth for straining.
275 Bristle brush?

[*English*] Item for half x 100 pins to pin up the halling[276] in wet weather	2½d.
[*French*] Item for 3 lbs cotton candle at 1½d.,	4½d.
Item to 1 labourer for portage of the said tables, trestles, forms and other things on the Saturday	4d.
Item to another labourer for portage and making the house clean the following Wednesday and Tuesday	4d.
Item for location of 7 towels	10d.
Item in carriage of dung by 1 cart	4d.
Item in reward made to Thomas Grene for venison	6s. 8d.

Sum 57s. 2d.

[173] [f. 59r]
[*Latin*]
n And 2s. 10d. given in reward to one minstrel harper
Also 12d. given in reward to a minstrel lute player
They had nothing from the same money that was collected from certain of the fraternity sitting in the Hall at the Breakfast on the said Monday on the morning after the Feast. And nil.

Sum total for the Feast £18 15s. 5½d.

Deduct from this 2s. 11d. for the three causes noted above[277]

And thus is clearly left £18 12s. 6½d. Examined.

[174]
The names of brothers and sisters and others present at our said feast in the said 9ᵗʰ year [1421–2] appear in the following

n Alexander Marcowe with his wife	2s. 4d.	n John Stanntone for himself	12d.	n Robert Mayhewe for himself	16d.
n Adam Copendale with his wife	2s.	n John Riche for himself	12d.	n Richard Lucas with his wife	2s.
n Alan John with his wife	2s.	n John Ketyng with his wife	2s.	n Robert Smyth for himself	12d.
n Agnes Bugge 16d., paid	4d.	n John Reffawe for himself	16d.	n Richard Aleyn with his wife	2s.
		n John Sharpe, maltman, for himself	16d.	n Robert Elkyn with his wife	2s.
n Baldewyne Hoper for himself	16d.	n John Bronnyng for himself	16d.	n Roger Swannefeld for himself	16d. Paid 4d.
n Edmund Disse for himself 16d. Paid	1d.	n John Snell with his wife	2s.	n Roger Blissote for himself	16d.

---

276 Tapestry or painted cloth for decorating the hall.
277 Only the two payments to two musicians were noted above, sum 2s. 10d.

n Hugh Glene for
himself   16*d*.
n Henry Bedell
with his wife   2*s*.
n Henry Lymber
with his wife   2*s*.
n Hugh Nell for
himself   16*d*.
n Henry Trobolans
for himself   16*d*.
n Henry Rowe
with his wife   2*s*.
n Henry Basset for
himself   16*d*.
n Henry Serle with
his wife   2*s*. Nil.

n John Jacobb
with his wife   2*s*.
n John Farman for
himself   16*d*.
n John Masonne
with his wife   2*s*.
n John Dunche for
himself   16*d*.
n John Salter for
himself   16*d*.
n John Philippe for
himself   16*d*.
n John Davy de
Fleet Street for
himself   16*d*.
n John Caryen for
himself   16*d*.
n John Chapman
with his wife   2*s*.
n John Toke for
himself   16*d*.
n John Stone for
himself   16*d*.
n John Brewster
with his wife   2*s*.
n John Broke for
himself   16*d*.
n John Humber for
himself   16*d*.
n John More at
Ludgate with his
wife   2*s*.

n John Holbek for
himself   16*d*.
n John Lumbard
for himself   16*d*.
n John Merston for
himself   16*d*. Nil.
n John Eylond for
himself   16*d*.
n John Turvey
with his wife   2*s*.
John Tornour for
himself   16*d*.
n John Wake for
himself   16*d*. paid
                             4*d*.
n John Riche de
Fleet Street for
himself   16*d*.
n John Bedford for
himself   16*d*.
n John Yver for
himself   16*d*.
n John Assh with
his wife   2*s*.
n John Serle for
himself   12*d*.
n John Southmede
for himself   16*d*.
n Juliana Hetersete
for herself   12*d*.
n Michael
Tregononne with
his wife   2*s*.
n Michael Eve for
himself   16*d*.
n Moris Tranaill
with his wife   2*s*.
n Margery
Thetford for herself   12*d*.
n Nicholas
Agomnaylok for
himself   16*d*.
n Nicholas Aleyn
for himself   16*d*.
n Peter Carpenter
for himself   16*d*.

n Richard Harlowe
for himself   16*d*.
n Robert Ketyng
for himself   16*d*.
n Robert Jewell
for his wife   16*d*.
n Robert Delowe
for himself   16*d*.
n Simon Potekyn
for himself   16*d*., paid 4*d*.
n Stephen Roo for
himself   16*d*.
n Thomas Ayle
with his wife   2*s*.
n Thomas Godyng
with his wife   2*s*.
n Thomas Edmond
with his wife   2*s*. Paid 4*d*.
n Thomas Aleyn
for himself   16*d*.
n Thomas Hatcher
for himself   12*d*.
n Thomas Howe
for himself   16*d*.
n Thomas North
for himself   16*d*.
n Thomas Hancok
with his wife   2*s*.
n Thomas Smalsho
for himself   16*d*.
n William Grosse
with his wife   2*s*.
n William Herry
for himself   16*d*.
n Walter Colshill
with his wife   2*s*.
n William Cardell
for himself   16*d*.
n William Bolton   16*d*.
n William
Ederiche with his
wife   2*s*.
n William Ferrour
with his wife   2*s*.
n William atte
Wode with his wife   2*s*.

n Philip Godfrey
for himself 16*d.*
n Peter Hayford
with his wife 2*s.*

n Peter Roos for
himself 16*d.*
n Peter Seyver for
himself 16*d.* Paid 4*d.*

n William Crane
with his wife 2*s.*
n William Claisson
for himself 16*d.*
n William
Bodevyle for
himself 16*d.*
n William Rawlyn
for himself 16*d.*
n William Lovell
for himself 16*d.* Nil.
n William Mark
for himself 16*d.*
n William Style
for himself 16*d.*
n William Borne
for himself 16*d.*
n William
Termeday for
himself 16*d.* Paid 2*d.*
n William Smalsho
with his wife 2*s.*

Sum: Paid £7 7s. 9d.
Not paid 4s. 8d.
Pardoned 2s. 3d.

[175] [f. 59v]
The names of diverse persons who were at our said feast and did not pay nor was payment expected from them

The Rector of All Hallows
London Wall
William Cavendissh,
broiderer
One stranger by
Copendale
Isabell Walissh by
M[argery] Thetford
Janekyn Carpenter
Janekyn Stafford

The wife of Devenyssh,
panter
John Stephane
One stranger by Grene
Flexmer, bowyer
William at the Ram in
Southwark

Sir Robert Steynton,
chaplain
4 Masters and 3 wives
John Ryngsonne, tailor
John Burton by
W. Porlond

[176]
The names of diverse persons of the Brewers' livery and not of the fraternity
who were at the feast and well and faithfully paid all
[*Margin*: entered elsewhere]

Alexander Marcowe &	John Davy	Robert Ketyng
his wife	John Sharpe, maltman	William Mark
Thomas Ayle & his wife	Roger Swanneffeld	Peter Sevyer
The wife of Robert Jewell	John Wake	Edmund Disse
Richard Lucas & his wife	William Stile	
Thomas Howe, maltman		

Memorandum that in the due ordering of entitling of this guise, the expenses
of the Breakfast of Thomas Grene, John Pyken, Robert Hylton and Robert
Carpenter, former Masters of the aforesaid craft, that is, on the day of their
account, should have been entered hereafter in this leaf, but due to the
scantiness of paper, are not here: therefore seek this in the 8ᵗʰ leaf before and
there you will find it.[278]

Margin: [*scored*: Not in the Masters' paper].
By an entry of this clause made in the common book.[279]

After the said Breakfast, all persons there present with unanimous consent granted
to Robert Lynford and Stephen Lalleford alms of the fraternity and craft of Brewers,
that is, for their use 20 shillings yearly, at the four usual terms of the year during
their lives, and they received the first payment at the feast of the Nativity of St John
next following.[280]

[177] [f. 60r]
The Account of Thomas Grene, Robert Hylton, John Pyken, and Robert
Carpenter, Masters of the craft of Brewers and the fraternity of the Holy
Trinity in the church of All Hallows beside London Wall, of certain receipts and
expenses for the use and profit of the said craft and fraternity, from the feast of
All Hallows in the 7ᵗʰ year of King Henry V until the same in the 9ᵗʰ year of the
same king, that is, for two whole years [1419–21].

Remaining in the Common Box First the same accountants discharge themselves
of £19 9*s*. 1½*d*., out of the deliberations and surplus rendered to William atte Wode,
William Ederich, William Ferrour and John Reyner, last Masters of the said craft and
fraternity so that in money there remains in the common box

Sum as appears

---

278   Expenses for the breakfast on 20 May 1421 were entered, see **[153]**. Those attending or
     failing to attend were listed, see **[144]** and **[145]**.
279   Clearly other Brewers' company books were compiled. This phrase and the next
     paragraph have not been crossed through and may be later additions.
280   Probably 24 June 1422.

Rents Received And of 24s. 2d. of rent for a certain tenement next to the gate of the Hall below the said tenement. And otherwise the profit pertaining to the said tenement which is paid in rent each year is 26s. 8d. Nothing was paid and the sum is owed because of the loss of the tenant.

Sum as appears

[178]
Hire of the Hall
[*Latin with some French pronouns*]
And of 5s. 6d. received from the Point-makers occupying the said hall called Brewers' Hall for 3 quarter days and one day for the banquet called the Feast Day
And of 5s. 10d. received from the Girdlers occupying the said hall as above for 5 quarter days
And of 5s. 8d. received from the Parish Clerks of churches, occupying the said Hall for 4 quarter days & 1 feast day
And of 2s. 4d. received from the Barbers occupying as above for 3 quarter days
And of 3s. received from the Coopers occupying as above for 1 quarter day and 1 feast day
And of 4s. received from the Pinners occupying as above for 2 Feast Days
And of 20d. received from the fraternity of Roncesvalles[281] occupying as above for 1 quarter day
And of 4d. received from the Bellringers of St Laurence as for the least occupation
And of 8d. received from the brothers of the fraternity of St John at St Laurence for their occupation as above
And of 2s. received from the Haberdashers occupying as above for 1 feast day
And of 3s. 4d. received from the Armourers occupying as above for 1 feast day
And of 2s. received from the Glovers occupying as above for 1 feast day

Sum 39s. 8d.

[179]
Admission to the freedom
[*Latin*]
And for £8 received from 24 men for admission to the freedom during the time of this account, that is: William Ferrour, Henry Bassett, William Rawlyn, John Thomas, John Bedeford, Nicholas Grenewode, John Fekenham, Henry Rowe, Thomas Sere, William Antrou, Richard Mayhewe, William Tutteswelle of Southwark, Simon Herry, Robert Ketyng, John Newman, William Riche, William Eyre, Richard Carrowe, John Bronnyng, John Parker, Edmund Disse, Richard West, John Davy, John More.
That is, each of them paid 6s. 8d.

Sum as appears

---

[281]   The chapel and hospital of St Mary Roncesvalles were at Charing Cross.

160

[180] [f. 60v]
Fraternity Entry
And of 43s. 4d. received for entry of 13 brothers during the time of this account,
that is: Baldewyne Hoper, William Borne, Robert Elken, John Riche in Fleet Street,
Philip Godfray, John Goldryng, John Jacob, Stephen Clean, John Hardyng, John
Holbek, Alan John, Robert Dellowe & Henry Bassett
That is each paid 3s. 4d.

Sum as appears

Quarterage
And of £12 12s. 2d. received from the brothers and sisters of the said fraternity, that
is for the said 8th year [1420–1], during the time when Richard Whityngdonne was
mayor.

And of £11 4d. received from the brothers and sisters of the said fraternity, that is
for the said 9th year [1421–2] during the time when William Cammbrigge was mayor,
and no more that year.

Some brothers have weakened, some have died and some wickedly refuse to pay.
[*scored*: which names appear in certain quarterage rolls]

Sum £23 12s. 6d.

[181]
Testamentary Legacies
And of 43s. 8d. received as from
Henry Trobolans and his associates the executors of the testament of Cecilia Parker
15s.
from the wife of John Rothyng for the soul of the said John formerly her husband
6s. 8d.
from John Sedyngbourne for the soul of Margaret formerly his wife 2s.
And from the executors of the testament of John Soneman, whittawer, 20s.

Sum as appears

Fines for transgressions
3s. 4d. received from Simon Potekyn for a fine made by him for a certain rebellion[282]

Sum as appears

Given by the Masters
And of 6s. 8d., given by the Masters and Wardens to the whole commonalty, from
the money received from the chamber of the Guildhall, that is for a quarter part of
the forfeits during the time of this account

Sum as appears

---

[282] See **[60]**.

Receipt from Foreigners[283]
And of 4s. 8½d. received from John Beterdene, chamberlain at the Guildhall for recompense for various transgressions made by painters, carpenters and other workmen, in our hall
[*scored*: during the time of this account]
[*added*: by the work of various therefore, before the coming of the Lord King to England].

Sum as appears

Licence given
And of 10s. 8d. received from various persons excused for not riding at the coming of the King this year, that is:
Agnes Carleton 2s.
Thomas Boteler 20d.
John Fekenham 2s.
William Mark 2s.
John Norman 2s.
and Milicent Burgh 12d.

Sum as appears

[182]
Voluntary Taxation
And of 40s. 4d. remaining from a certain sum of £31 17s. 4d., received from the money agreed and levied by certain benevolent people of the said craft, who wished the said sum to be ordained and levied amongst them to be used in the best way for other causes and whose names here follow
[*scored*: are enrolled in a certain paper after this][284] [*added*: and will be written here]

Sum as appears

[183] [f. 61r]
General Taxation
And of 16s. 10d. remaining from the same sum of £34 6s. 6d. from money levied upon the whole commonalty of the craft of Brewers of the said city[285]
[*scored*: whose names appear in a certain roll of parchment with their sums and the cause of the said tax during the time of this account]
[*added*: during the time of Richard Whityngton mayor, as appears below and will be written upon the same roll]

Sum as appears

Sum total of the roll £62 15s.

[283] Those outside the craft, perhaps?
[284] See [67]–[69] for the list of contributors. This sum was collected to encourage Whittington to modify the ordinance regulating the brewing trade, but had no effect, because Whittington was not amenable to bribes.
[285] This second sum was collected to pay the £20 bond demanded by Whittington. See [81]–[89].

[184]
Alms
and the said Masters seek allowance for alms given to two poor women, that is, Johanna Cole and Johanna, formerly the wife of William Cook, each of them taking 30s. 4d. yearly, for 2 whole years within the time of this account, that is £6 16d.

Sum as appears

Bread and Wine for the celebration
And for bread and wine spent in the Chapel of the fraternity for consecrating the body of our Lord there, during the said time 4s.

Wax for the Chapel
And for 11 lbs new wax with the making at 6d., together with the making of 13 lbs old wax from torches, in great 6d. during the whole time of this account, 6s.

Sum as appears

Stipends
And for the stipend of Sir Robert Steynton, chaplain of the said fraternity taking £6 13s. 8d. yearly, that is for the said time of this account, £13 6s. 8d.
And in agreed customary stipend due to William Porlond, clerk of the said craft and fraternity, taking by the year 40s., that is for the said time of this account £4.[286]

Sum £17 6s. 8d.

Customary payments
And in money paid to the Rector of the church of Aldermanbury for his oblations, at 3s. 4d. yearly, that is for the time of this account, 6s. 8d.
And to the parish clerk of the same church, taking 12d. yearly, for the said time of this account, 2s.
And for Holy bread at 4d. yearly, that is for 2 years during the said time of this account, 8d.
And for the price of 2 rose garlands for the rent of the said Hall, twice during the time of this account, 5d.
And to the parish clerk of the church of All Hallows abovesaid at 12d. yearly, that is, for the time of this said account, 2s.

Sum 11s. 9d.

[185]
House Repairs
And for repairing one gutter under the hall and for lead and solder bought, with workmanship, at 25s.
And in the price of the aforesaid gown of white colour for William the clerk at the time of riding when he rode with the King, at 8s. 4d.

---

[286]   This was before Porlond's pay rise in 1424, which doubled his salary, see **[330]**.

163

The mending of rooms in the chambers of the Masters with free stone bought and workmanship of the same at 2s. 2½d.

Various small crests, timber, nails and hooks in the Hall, also 4 lattices in the chamber, chapel and other necessary places, with workmanship, 10s. 2d.

Various repairs in the tenement beside the gate, against the coming of John Stafford, at 14s.

Large timber bought for supporting the hall, with labour for the same at 8s. 11d., in total during the time of this account 68s. 7½d.

And in customary payments owed and expenses made in the said hall, for tiles, paving, loam, lime, sand, new and old tables, bought for the same repairs, for various workmen hired,[287] as plainly appears by a paper showing the parcels in total during the time of this account. Sum 47s. 9d.

Sum 116s. 4½d.

[186] [f. 61v]
Rewards Given
First 4 hoods given to 4 various persons, that is, Sir Robert, chaplain of the fraternity, William Pethin, Thomas Donyngton, & William Devenyssh during the aforesaid time of this account, 20s.

Sum as appears

Fees
And in fees to Thomas Donyngton, sergeant at the chamber of the Guildhall, taking 6s. 8d. yearly, that is, for 2 years, 13s. 4d.

Sum as appears

Parchment, paper and ink
and in the price of parchment, paper and ink spent by William the clerk of the said craft and fraternity during the time of the account abovesaid, 4s.

Sum as appears

Sum total of expenses £32 3s. 5½d. And there remains in the common box £30 11s. 6½d.
From which was received in the said box in the entry as above £19 9s. 1½d.
And from the said account was given to our box abovesaid £11 2s. 5d.
Which sum in true value was £7 3s. 6d., because 79s. 3d. was lost in the exchange for the coinage of the Lord King.

---

287   The English word 'werkmen' is amongst the Latin here.

[187]
[English]
Unto the right wise commons of this present parliament
The victuallers, the Brewers of the city of London, beseech meekly that, for as much
as the said victuallers serve as well our sovereign Lord the King and other lords both
spiritual and temporal, with other of the King's lieges, with all the said city, in ale,
the victuallers buy their chief [*ingredient*] that is to say, malt, at great disadvantage,
in so much as the sellers of malt [*sell it*] with drawk and darnel, [*deceive*] the said
victuallers, that is to say in selling of bellied malt, that is to say stiff malt that does
not come, of wynell eaten malt, that is to say with [*scored*: worms of dusty malt]
small stones, congealed earth, gravel and with other various filth, and so when the
said victuallers have made …²⁸⁸

[188] [f. 62r]
[Latin]
**Payments made for various repairs in the hall, chamber and the tenement next
to the gate, with various necessaries bought by William Porlond the clerk, to
the sum of 116s. 4½d., for the whole time when Thomas Grene, Robert Hylton,
John Pyken and Robert Carpenter were Masters of the craft and fraternity of
Brewers in the city of London, that is, the 8ᵗʰ and 9ᵗʰ years of the reign of King
Henry V [1420–2] as appears below.**

The Hall

First to a certain labourer for strengthening and remedying 3 round gutters under the hall,	2d.
Item for lead, sand, supplied by the weaver, newcast, for the said gutter with labour and putting it in place	25s.
Item for a table for guarding the said gutter with the work of a carpenter for saving the lead	17d.
Item for the price of one cart of loam bought for the said gutter	4d.
Item in reward to a dauber²⁸⁹ for daubing and remounting around our said gutter for 1 day with his *nonsheng*²⁹⁰	5½d.
Item in the price of an iron grate bought for the head of the same gutter	20d.
Item in reward to another dauber with his servant for daubing and mending defects in the floor of the said hall, and between the doors of one [*chamber?*] with mending the buttery floor, for 1 day with *nonsheng*	14d.
Item to a certain joiner for a crest for the dosser²⁹¹ of the said hall, together with placing the same	4s. 4d.
Item for 9 pieces of timber for costers for the said hall	8½d.
Item for large nails and small hooks for the hanging the halling	5d.
Item for 1 lb molten and 1 lb red lead for the said crest and colouring the timber	4d.

²⁸⁸ This incomplete fragment of a petition is uncrossed and was added later. See **[117]** and **[166]**.
²⁸⁹ Plasterer.
²⁹⁰ A drink or snack taken in the afternoon.
²⁹¹ Dossers and costers were ornamental cloths used as wall hangings.

Item in reward to a carpenter for fitting the said 9 pieces of timber and
putting in the said small hooks for the hanging coster and other necessaries
done, for 2 days   14*d.*
Item in the price of 200 large hooks for hanging the said halling, because the
said small hooks were unfit for bearing the same   16*d.*
Item in reward to 1 labourer for fitting the said 200 large hooks, for 1 day
with *nonsheng*   5½*d.*
Item in the price of 2 pieces of timber quartered for hanging the old stained
halling   6*d.*
Item for small hooks and nails for hanging the old stained halling   2*d.*
Item to the same carpenter for fitting the said timber and fitting the said
hooks and one bolt together with mending other necessaries for 1 day   6*d.*

[189]

Item for the price of 2 long pieces and 3 short pieces of timber bought for
setting under the hall in the southern part of the same   6*s.* [margin: ½*d.*]
Item for halving an estrich board²⁹² bought for mending the large table in the
hall, broken by the painter, and other work   2½*d.*
Item for glue for the same table   1*d.*
Item to the same carpenter for fitting the large timber under the hall and
mending the said broken table and forms, trestles and stools in the same hall
for 3 days at 8*d.*,   2*s.*
Item to the same labourer for sweeping the said hall after the work of the
painters and others together with portage of chalk and other stone from the
great cellar, in the price of portage of dung to carts and mending the roof of
the same hall, for 3 days at 5½*d.*, with *nonsheng*   16½*d.*
Item for carriage of dung twice by 6 carts at 3*d.*, from the said hall and other
places   18*d.*
Item for 4 loads of rushes for the said hall with carriage, at 3½*d.*, in total 14*d.*
Item for 7 latches and 7 catches bought for the doors of the hall and
windows in the pantry   20½*d.*
Item for 5 old tables for mending the wall in the buttery with nails for the same 7*d.*
Item in reward due to the same labourer for carpentry and daubing the same
wall with other defects there, for 1 day with *nonsheng*   5½*d.*
Item for the mending of a table for the parlour given by Robert Lynford,
with mending and darning²⁹³ of various napery   13*d.*
Item in the price of 2 loads and 1 sack of lime at various times and prices for
mending and tiling the said hall and other houses below the gate   2*s.* 2*d.*
Item for the said latches, latch nails and other nails for the work of the
carpenter, dauber and tiler on the hall stair   19½*d.*

[190] [f. 62v]
[Mostly Latin]
Item for 3 quarters of roof tiles bought for the same 6*d.*
Item for a cartful of gravel 5*d.*

---

²⁹²   Timber from the Baltic.
²⁹³   The word 'dernynge' was in English.

Item in reward due to a tiler and his servant for 1 day above the hall, cloister and other houses, with *nonsheng* 14d.

Item in payment to a mason and his servant to mend a certain wall in the cellar called the larder house, for 1 day with *nonsheng* 14d.

Item for the price of tables new and old for lining the wall in the said hall and walls in other houses below the guest chamber, for defence against water and other things 3s. 2d.

Item in reward due to a labourer to mend the same wall with loam and lime and other walls in the cloister for 2 days with *nonsheng* 11½d.

Item for an iron hammer for knocking on the door of the said hall, with mending of a clicket for the same door, various times 17½d.

[191]
Chamber

In 7 feet & half of free stone bought for the fireplace in the great chamber, at 3d.,	22½d.
Item in reward due to the same mason working above the same for half a day	4d.
Item in reward due to the same dauber for whitening the said great chamber with other chambers, for 2 days with *nonsheng*	11d.
Item for 1 lead cistern for the latrine in the said great chamber	8d.
Item to the same labourer for mending various defects in the same latrine outside the tenement	4d.
Item for 2 lattices in the great chamber, 1 lattice in the chamber above the parlour and 1 lattice in the chapel	3s.
Item in the price of 1 piece of timber called quartile[294] for staying supports in the said great chamber	2½d.
Item in the price of 2 small pieces of timber for railing for the counter in the said great chamber	2½d.
Item to the same carpenter for fitting lattices, working in the latrine and fixing the said timber in the great chamber, with other necessaries, for 1 day with *nonsheng*	8½d.
Item to another carpenter for making 2 pentices for the great chamber and 1 pentice above the window of Johanna Brigham, with *nonsheng*,	6½d.
Item for hooks and nails for hanging the costers in the said great chamber and for defects in the said latrine	2d.
Item to the same carpenter for mending tables, forms, stools and other necessaries in the said great chamber, in the hall and other various places ahead of the great feast	8d.

[192]

Item for new 2 locks bought for the counter in the said great chamber	6d.
Item for stiffening of one vestment with calico and mending of a little chest for the same calico	14d.

---

294 A quarter of a circle.

Item in mending a sleeved surplice[295] for placing in the chapel, an alb[296] and an amice ferialis,[297] one vestment and hanging the same on the wall at the side, in total | 3*d.*

Item for lining with 1 tape for mending the same amice, 1 fanon[298] with placing it with thread in a white vestment of gold and green cloth | 2*d.*

Item for the price of 1 cloth of linen bought for enlarging the sleeve of the said alb with the making of the same | 8*d.*

Item in reward made to the same tiler and his servant to mend defects in the great chamber and chapel with other adjacent rooms, for 2 days with *nonsheng* | 2*s.* 4*d.*

Item for 2 lbs solder for mending a gutter in the small chamber annexed to the great chamber with 1 gutter in the side of the kitchen, | 12*d.*

Item for mending a gutter in the room called Sir E[d]mond's chamber[299] in the price of 1 sack lime, 2*d.*, ½ x 100 tiles, 4½*d.*, with reward made to a tiler and his servant, 14*d.*, for 1 day with *nonsheng*, in total | 20½*d.*

Item for 1 lb solder bought for mending the said gutter, with 2 faggots of wood and for sand for heating the said irons, in total 7*d.*

[193]
Tenement by the Gate

For repairs to the tenement beside the gate against the coming of John Stafford, for 1 cart of loam with straw at ½*d.*, | 4*d.*

Item in latches bought for the same tenement | 4½*d.*

Item for sprig nails, transoms and other nails, great and small, for the same tenement | 18*d.*

Item for 1 load of lime for the same tenement | 12*d.*

Item for 1 cart of sand for the same tenement | 5*d.*

[f. 63r]

Item for 100 tiles for the same tenement | 8*d.*

Item to the same tiler with his servant for 1 day with *nonsheng* | 13*d.*

Item to the same dauber and his servant for making a cellar in the under tresance,[300] daubing and mending a certain wall of a latrine beside Harested, mercer, for 1 day with *nonsheng* | 13*d.*

Item for 1 lead cistern for the latrine for the same tenement with 1 earthenware pot for the same | 8½*d.*

Item 3 or 2 lbs solder for a gutter in the same tenement | 12*d.*

Item for an old door for the coalhouse, 2 hooks, 1 hasp, 2 staples, 1 quartile of timber for the said door | 7½*d.*

---

[295] These two words are in English.

[296] White vestment covering the body, worn by clergy and servers.

[297] Amice ferialis: rectangle of cloth worn by a priest around the neck as part of his mass vestments.

[298] Fanon, maniple: eucharistic vestment, strip of material suspended from left wrist.

[299] Edmund, chaplain, was paid for a quarter of a year, [45], before Robert Steynton became the fraternity chaplain.

[300] Passage, corridor.

Item for 10 small pieces of timber, quartelez,[301] for the tresance between the door and the entrance to the hall   3d.

Item for old tables, great and small, for mending rooms there and floors in other houses and other things 11d.

Item to the same labourer, working in mending doors, windows and floors in various rooms, with loam and mortar, for whitening the said hall and mending various floors with earth in various houses, for 4½ days with *nonsheng*, at 5½d., in total   2s. ½d.

Item in the price of 1 new lock and 2 old locks, with mending of 3 keys to the same lock, with repair of 1 key for one door in another place below the said tenement   8½d.

[194]
Diverse Necessaries

In mending the pavement beside the fountain and a gutter coming out of the tenement, with mending a gutter bar in the cloister beside the kitchen, in total   2s.

Item in gravel for amending the said defect   8d.

Item to the same carter for carriage of 6 carts of rubble from the Guildhall[302] for using in the said Hall to defend the walls from dripping water, at various prices   7d.

Item for 13 hoops, large and small, and 2 chyme[303] hoops used for cooperage, 2 vats and 2 tubs with a wagon, 1 *hogge* 1 *hened*,[304] in total   16d.

Item in money spent by William the clerk at the receiving of quarterage and from brothers entering the fraternity, and in ale   1½d.

Item to the Receiver 1 noble from John Rothyng[305] in the presence of the Masters for ale   2d.

Item in money given to the beadle of the Girdlers for procuring various crafts to the profit of the said hall   12d.[306]

Item for 1 acquisition of dues by Henry Trebolans & his associates, executors of the testament of Cecilia Parker   2d.

Item for writing the names of brothers and sisters of the fraternity upon the fraternity table, with illuminating the same   4d.

Item for 2 hurdles in the larder, with brushes of broom and birch   14½d.

Item in the price of a white gown for William the clerk for his riding at the coming of the King from France   8s. 4d.

Item in reward given to a sergeant sent by the Masters to the Coopers to bring the same to the court of the mayor, for various causes, that is, the marking of disallowed foreign barrels and kilderkins   8d.

Item in reward to a sergeant called Wode for continuing in various business in the absence of Thomas Donyngton   12d.

Sum 116s. 4½d.

301 The scribe used French 'quartelez' for quartiles of timber: a quarter of a circle.
302 Building work was taking place at the Guildhall. Rubble was brought into Brewers' Hall for building work there.
303 Chimney?
304 Hogshead?
305 Prayers for his soul were noted before, see [181].
306 See the list of crafts [26] and [27], compiled to profit the Brewers by the hire of their hall.

[195] [f. 63v]

[*Latin*] **The names of brothers and sisters of the fraternity of the craft of Brewers of London paying quarterage during the time of William Cambrigge being mayor of the city of London, [1420–1] Thomas Grene, Robert Hylton, John Pyken and Robert Carpenter being Masters of the said craft in the 9th year of the reign of King Henry V [1421–2] as appears in the following**

Agnes Carleton	12d.	John Pyken with Alice his wife	2s.
Alice Newman [*added*: otherwise Jacob]	12d.	John Caryen with Alice his wife	2s.
Alexander Miles	12d.	John Chapman	12d.
Adam Copendale with Emma his wife	22d.	John Toke with Alice his wife	2s.
		Jacob Levegro with Alice his wife	2s.
Alan John	12d.	John Stone	12d.
Alice Hore	12d.	John Kenaky	12d.
Agnes Bugge	12d.	John Brewster & Johanna his wife	2s.
Agnes Stratton	12d.	John Broke with [*above the line*: Cristiana] his wife	2s.
Agnes the wife of William Rendre	12d.	John Spenser	12d.
		John Humber with Margaret his wife	2s.
Cristiana the widow of John Ballard, with her husband, that is, the said John	2s.[307]	John More at Ludgate	12d.
		John Lynne	12d.
		John William with Johanna his wife	2s.
[*Scored*: Sir Robert Steynton	12d.]	John Stannton with Matilda his wife	2s.
Dionysia Barthorpe	12d.	John Riche with Margaret his wife	2s.
		John Russell with Alice his wife	2s.
Emma Canon	12d.	John Ketyng	12d.
Elizabeth Sonman with John her husband	2s.	John Ryngesson	12d.
		John Reeffawe with Juliane his wife	2s.
Hugh Glene with Margaret his wife	2s.	John Snelle	12d.
Henry Bedell	12d.	John Lumbard	12d.
Henry Lymber with Felicia his wife	2s.	John Bailly	12d.
Hugh Neel with Emma his wife	2s.	John Eylond	12d.
Henry Trebolans with Eleonor his wife	2s.	John Waghorn	12d.
		John William of Southwark	12d.
		John Ser, glover,	12d.
Johanna the widow of Richard Wightmour	12d.	John Turnour	12d.
Isabella the widow of Vincent Syward	3s.	John Benge with Alice his wife	2s.
		John Sonder	12d.
John Mason with Felicia his wife	2s.	John Luke	12d.
John Salter	12d.	John Assh	12d.
John Laurence	12d.	John Serle	12d.
John Philippe with Matilda his wife	2s.	John Southmede	12d.

[307] Perhaps John died after they had paid their quarterage.

John More of Aldersgate with
Cristiana his wife   2s.
John Basset   12d.
John Reyner with Agatha his wife   2s.

[196] [f. 64r]

John Dene	12d.	Richard Rowdon with Johanna	
John Turvey	12d.	his wife	2s.
Johanna Horold	12d.	Robert Smyth with Anna his wife	2s.
John Aleyn, baker,	12d.	Richard Aleyn	12d.
Idonea Hatton	12d.	Robert Carpenter	12d.
John Randolf with Juliana his wife	2s.	Robert Lynford	9d.
John Gedeney	12d.	Roger Blissote	12d.
John Retford	12d.	Robert Walram	12d.
		Richard Crosse	12d.
Johanna Cole	12d.	Richard Terrell with Isabella his	
Johanna Awmbele	12d.	wife	2s.
Juliana Hetersete	12d.	Richard Harlowe with Johanna	
Johanna the wife of John		his wife	2s.
Fekenham	12d.	Richard Brynton	12d.
Johanna Rothyng with John,		Roger Baronne	12d.
formerly her husband	2s.	Robert Pede	12d.
		Robert Nykke with Alice his wife	2s.
Katherine Roche	12d.	Richard Frepurs	12d.
		Robert Mayhewe	12d.
Michael Tregononne	12d.	Robert Jewell	12d.
Michael Eve with Elizabeth his			
wife	2s.	Simon Potekyn	12d.
Morris Tranaill with Margaret his		Stephen Roo	12d.
wife	2s.		
Margaret Thetford with John,		Thomas Godyng	12d.
formerly her husband	2s.	Thomas Emond with Sibilla his	
Millicent Burgh	12d.	wife	2s.
		Thomas Aleyn	12d.
Nicholas Agomnaylok with		Thomas Hatcher	12d.
Johanna his wife	2s.	Thomas Yole	12d.
Nicholas Muriell	12d.	Thomas Grene with Matilda his	
Nicholas Aleyn	12d.	wife	2s.
Nicholas Fuller with Alice his wife	2s.	Thomas Howe	12d.
Nicholas Kene with Katherine		Thomas Pensonne	12d.
his wife	2s.	Thomas Hancok with Dionysia	
		his wife	2s.
Peter Carpenter	12d.	Thomas de Kent	12d.
Peter Hayford with Matilda his wife	2s.	Thomas Smalshoo	12d.
Philip James	12d.	Thomas Boteler	12d.
Peter Roos	12d.	Thomas Grateley	12d.
		Thomas Bristowe	12d.
Robert Hilton with Margaret his		Thomas Martyn	12d.
wife	2s.	Thomas Dewy with Agnes his wife	2s.

171

Robert Gyles with Johanna his wife	2s.	William Bailly	12d.
Richard Shirwod with Alice his wife	2s.	William atte Welle with Alice his wife	2s.
Robert Tanner	12d.	William Belle	12d.
Robert Steynton, priest,	12d.[308]	William Grosse with Katherine his wife	2s.

[197] [f. 64v]

William Herry	12d.
Walter Colshull	12d.
William Boteler	12d.
William Payn	12d.
William Bolton	12d.
William Overton	2s.
William Petevyle	12d.
William Ferrour with Agnes his wife	2s.
William Cardell	12d.
William Crane with Helen his wife	2s.
William Geffrey with Anna his wife	2s.
William Canonne	12d.
William Illying	12d.
William Claisson with Isabell his wife	2s.
William Bracy with Alice his wife	2s.
William Ederich with Alice his wife	2s.
William Bodevyle	12d.
William Bacon, butcher	12d.
William Termeday	12d.
William Devenyssh	12d.
William Smalshoo with Margaret his wife	2s.
William Bernard	12d.
William Reponne with Margery his wife	2s.
William Porlond with Dionysia his wife	2s.
Walter Glyn	12d.
Weveyn Clayson with Dederik, her former husband	2s.
William John with Alice his wife	2s.

Sum total of Quarterage this year: £11 4d.

Those who are not paying because of poverty

Constance Hosard
Margaret Lynford

Those not paying because of weakness

Walter Copseye	John Ffykys and
John Merstonne	Agnes his wife

Those with a wicked mind who do not wish to pay

Alan Bret and	John Selle
Isabell his wife	John Perys
John Nasing and	Hugh Sharp
Alice his wife	
Johanna the wife	
of Richard Aleyn	
Thomas Osbarn &	
Isabell his wife	
Richard Rose of	
Southwark	

Those who did not pay before the Masters' accounts and paid afterwards

John Elcy	John Wyghtmour
William atte Wode	John Hardy, cook
Richard Welde	John Bray, butcher
John Tregelowe	John Qwyntyn
William Copwode	Thomas Jakes

Those who brought their wives into the fraternity this year, with William Devenyssh, and paid quarterage for the same year

Emma the wife of Adam Copendale

---

[308] Added in a later hand. See **[195]** for a deleted entry for Steynton under D for Dominus.

[198]

And no more this year, because some of the fraternity have died, some have not paid because of poverty and some for the third cause that they have weakened this year, struggle to pay wholly and by a certain evil mind do not wish to pay wholly.

And certain others, who did not wish to pay before the Masters' account, paid faithfully afterwards to the said account of the Masters, as will appear plainly in the future

Those who have died and thus are not paying

Henry Serle	John Grace
John Wodelond	Margaret
Agnes Qwyntyn	Setingbourne
John Moyle	Johanna Frepurs
	Richard
	Wightmour

Alianora the late wife of Henry Trebolans
Johanna formerly the wife of Richard Wyghtmour
Cristiana the wife of John Broke
Margaret the wife of Morris Travaill
Matilda the wife of Thomas Grene
Alice the wife of Nicholas Fuller
Dionysia the wife of Thomas Hancok
Agnes the wife of Thomas Dewy in Southwark
Katherine the wife of William Grosse
William Devenyssh, tailor
Alice formerly the wife of William John

Those paying quarterage for this year with arrears from preceding years

William Overton, woodmonger
Isabella formerly the wife of Vincent Syward at Lime Street
John de Dene paid 2s., of which Thomas Grene, by the assent of his associates reimbursed 12d. to him, for his own use

Those paying quarterage this year but refusing to pay their arrears

William Repon and Margaret his wife
John Serle

Those who are in the fraternity table but not paying since the time of the year of Richard Whityngton

[*blank*]

[199] [f. 65r]

[*Mostly Latin*]

In this year, Robert Smyth, Hugh Neel, John Philip and William Crane being Masters of the craft and fraternity of Brewers, Robert Chichely, a noble and wise man, stood in the office of mayor [1421–2] of the city of London in the 10th year of the reign of King Henry V [1422], who, in his whole time of power behaved well and honestly towards our craft of Brewers and was pleasantly disposed towards our said craft at his coming to the Guildhall, asking and exhorting us and our commonalty of our craft to bear the seal in such a way that no complaints about any pots belonging to us should come to his notice.

The said mayor ordered and prescribed that in our homes and when selling our ale it should be in pots made of pewter, marked with a seal and fitly [*scored*: in our houses, selling our ale by pots] And that those selling ale in this way should hold the pot in one hand, with a cup in the other hand. And that those who had unsealed pots should pay for a seal, as he had ordered and prescribed. But the said ordinance and command of the mayor had no effect in the said craft because no one was presented or punished in this way, and none wished to present defaulters.

However, when no one was punished, the said mayor imposed another ordinance upon barrels and kilderkins sent out from homes without the sign called the Cooper's mark, and unsealed, for a 40*s.* fine for barrels or kilderkins, as was ordered in the time of Richard Whittington. This penalty seemed insupportable to the said Brewers and for this reason they neglected to punish according to the said ordinance, which seemed onerous to them and they did not wish to present any defaulters to the court. And the said mayor, with his surprised supporters, seeing that no defaulters were presented by the said Brewers, nor amerced, made a new order that the said Brewers should pay 20*d.* for an unsealed barrel and 10*d.* for an unsealed kilderkin.

With this declaration, the Brewers presented many. The names and the amounts are written below, that is

[200]
[Latin and English]
John Reefawe dwelling at the Christopher in the parish of St Gregory had 1 unsealed kilderkin at the house of William Boltonne at Baynard's Castle
Thomas Pensonne dwelling at the Dragon in the parish of St Gregory had 1 unsealed kilderkin at the house of John Carpenter at Baynard's Castle
William Andreu staying at the Horse Head in the parish of St Sepulchre without Newgate had 2 unsealed kilderkins in the house of Thomas Warewyk dwelling in Thames Street at the Broken Wharf
Thomas Yole dwelling at the Garland in the parish of St Andrew [*Hubbard*] East Cheap had 1 unsealed barrel at the house of Richard Greneweye dwelling at Dowgate
Margaret Leonard dwelling at le Cock in the parish of St Peter, at the wall of the Augustinian Friars had 2 unsealed kilderkins at the house of Johanna Cole in the parish of St Benet Fink
Nicholas Yonge had 1 unsealed barrel at the house of Simon Brachell
Walter Colshull at the George in Coleman Street had 1 unsealed barrel at le Cow Head in Cheap
Michael Eve at le White Leg beside Fleet Bridge had 1 unsealed kilderkin at the house of Thomas Hueys at the Goat in the parish of St Bride
John Eylond at the Horn in Aldersgate Street had 1 unsealed kilderkin at the George beside Fleet Bridge
Reginald Broke at the Savage's Inn in Fleet Street had 1 unsealed kilderkin at the house of Johanna Bendale there
Thomas Boteler staying at the Helm in the parish of St Peter Cornhill had 1 unsealed kilderkin at the house of William Growte, tailor, in Candlewick Street
Thomas Emond at the White Lion in the parish of St Thomas the Apostle had 1 unsealed kilderkin in the house called Le *Trompe* in Cheap

Nicholas Fuller at the Bell in the parish of St Dionis [*Backchurch*] in Fenchurch
Street had 1 unsealed kilderkin in the house of a certain huckster in Philpot Lane
there.

[201] [f. 65v]
Thomas Martyn dwelling at the Peacock outside Aldgate had 1 unsealed kilderkin
and the same kilderkin was taken in the common street and placed in the house of
White Tyler outside Aldgate
Katherine Pynchebek at the Lion outside Aldersgate had 1 unsealed kilderkin at the
house of John Hardy, Cook, in Bread Street
Thomas de Kent at the Basket beside Billingsgate had 1 unsealed kilderkin and the
same kilderkin was found in the common street
The same Thomas had 1 unsealed kilderkin at the house of Grynder huckster beside
the Cock in East Cheap
William Bailly at the Snipe in East Cheap had 1 unsealed kilderkin at the house of
Robert Bailly there
Richard Lucas at the Two Nuns outside Aldgate had 1 unsealed kilderkin at the
house of William Ffysh, linen weaver
Robert Elken at the George in Fenchurch Street had 1 unsealed kilderkin at the house
of a certain huckster at the malt market in Gracechurch Street
Richard Harlowe, capmaker & brewer, at Copped Hall in the parish of St Dunstan
in the East below Tower Street had 1 unsealed kilderkin at the house of the porter of
St Katherine
Henry Wexen dwelling at the Cock opposite Leadenhall in the parish of St Peter
Cornhill had 1 unsealed kilderkin at the house of Lewys the tailor in Candlewick
Street
Felton, fuller and brewer dwelling at the Lamb in Mart Lane in the parish of All
Hallows Staining beside Fenchurch had 1 unsealed kilderkin at the house of the said
Lewys the tailor in Candlewick Street
John Randolf, capper and brewer, dwelling at the Cock in the parish of St Dionis in
Fenchurch Street had 1 unsealed kilderkin at the house of Baldok in New Alley in
Cornhill in the rent of the Prior of Canterbury

[202]
John Kendale at the Cock in Coleman Street had 1 unsealed kilderkin in Trump
Alley in Cheap
John Assh dwelling at the Christopher in the parish of St Michael le Querne had
1 unsealed kilderkin at the house of Alexander Child, draper, in Cornhill
Nicholas Yonge dwelling at the Lamb in Abchurch Lane had 1 unsealed kilderkin at
the house of Emma, fish wife in Sithebourne Lane
Richard Frepurs dwelling at the Cock in the parish of St Mildred in Poultry had
1 unsealed kilderkin at the house of Matthew Wayte, skinner, beside Lothbury Bridge
John Caston, tailor, at the Crown in the parish of St Giles without Cripplegate had
1 unsealed kilderkin which was found in the street, on the shoulders of his servant
Beatrix Tye dwelling at the Cup in the parish of St Michael Crooked Lane had
1 unsealed kilderkin at the house of a certain huckster dwelling in the same
Crooked Lane
John Frost at the Hartshorn in the parish of St Sepulchre without Newgate had
1 unsealed kilderkin at the house of Thomas Hull dwelling in the same parish

William Misterton at the Katherine Wheel in the parish of St Giles without
Cripplegate in Grub Street had 1 unsealed kilderkin below Trump Alley in Cheap
Thomas Ayle at the Eagle without Aldersgate had 1 unsealed kilderkin at the house
of Agnes Grene at the corner of Pissing Lane
William Ogle at the Angel and le Ball in the parish of St Andrew in Holborn had
1 unsealed kilderkin at the house of Edward Smyth in le Old Change
John Thomas at the Hartshorn in the parish of St Bride had 1 unsealed kilderkin at
le Goat in Fleet Street
Augustine Hawken at the Rose in the parish of St Bride had 1 unsealed kilderkin at
the house of a certain huckster beside the inn of St Augustine[309]
John Snell at St Andrew cross in Holborn had 1 unsealed kilderkin at the house of a
certain huckster opposite the Snipe, Flesh Alley[310]

[203] [f. 66r]
Noell Maragek at the Maid in Fleet Street had 1 unsealed kilderkin in the house of
Gilbert Cook
John Riche at the Angel in Fleet Street had 1 unsealed kilderkin in the house of the
same Gilbert Cook
Thomas Boteler dwelling at the Helm in the parish of St Peter Cornhill had
1 unsealed barrel and 1 unsealed kilderkin [*scored*: in the house of a huckster] which
were found on the shoulders of his servant in the open street by William Ferrour.
Roger Blissote dwelling at the Swan in the parish of St Nicholas Shambles had
1 unsealed kilderkin at the house of a huckster called John Robert in Gutter Lane
Simon atte Welle dwelling at the Golden Hart in the parish of St Giles without
Cripplegate had 1 unsealed kilderkin in the same house
John Elsy at the Popinjay in the parish of St Mary Fenchurch had 1 unsealed barrel
in the house of Thomas Matchyng, beadle, in Ironmonger Lane
John Parys, cordwainer, at the Key in the parish of St Mary Magdalene in [Old] Fish
Street had 3 unsealed kilderkins in the inn of the executors formerly of the Lord
Bishop of London
Thomas Whiting, butcher, at the Key in the parish of St Michael Bassishaw had
1 unsealed kilderkin at the house of Salmanne Poyntmaker in St Lawrence's Lane

[204]
**The names of those selling ale during the time of the aforesaid Robert Chichele
being mayor of London, not by the proper measures, in the year as above, and
for this they were presented to John Beterdene, chamberlain at the Guildhall
and amerced, as appears in the parcels written below.**

Simon Franke at the Key in the parish of St Mary Somerset for defective measure	1 kilderkin
Margaret Bury, huckster, dwelling at Queenhithe	1 kilderkin
The wife of William Hurre dwelling there, for defective measure	1 kilderkin
Alice, huckster, dwelling in the parish of St Antonin opposite the church	1 kilderkin

---

[309]   Hawken was in the parish of St Bride but the huckster was apparently near the inn of
St Augustine by St Paul's, or the hospital of St Augustine Papey.
[310]   The flesh market at Leadenhall, or the Shambles?

Richard Penson dwelling at the Swan in the parish of St Ethelburga beside
Bishopsgate for defective measure — 1 kilderkin
A certain ostler dwelling at the Angel there — 1 kilderkin
William Boteler at the Cock in the parish of St Andrew Cornhill — 1 kilderkin
John Cornyssh, huckster, dwelling beside the brothers of the Holy Cross[311] — 1 kilderkin
Nicholas Wynbawe dwelling in Thames Street beside Paul's Wharf for
defective measure — 1 kilderkin
Thomas atte Wode at the Fleur de Lys in the parish of St Mary Somerset
for defective measure — 1 barrel
Luna Clerk, huckster, at Queenhithe for defective measure — 1 kilderkin

[205]
The names of foreigners selling ale in the city to other foreigners within the city during the time of the said mayor, and the same forfeited the same ale, and were presented to the said John Beterden, chamberlain of the Guildhall as appears in the following

William Martyn, foreigner, dwelling in St Bride in the lane called Bride Lane had 1 kilderkin of foreign ale on account of which the money was prohibited and seized in the hands of the said William, to the profit of the Guildhall
Geoffrey Brewer, foreigner, dwelling in the aforesaid Bride Lane had 1 kilderkin of foreign ale, on account of which the money was prohibited and seized in the hands of the said Geoffrey, to the profit of the chamber of the Guildhall
Alice Tannton, foreigner, had 2 kilderkins of ale from John Thakworthe, foreigner, to sell, on account of which it was forfeited by the said Alice dwelling in Showe Lane
Someone called Smalhobbe, foreigner, dwelling at the Horseshoe outside Aldgate had 1 kilderkin of ale. And a certain Johanna, wife of a certain brewersman, foreigner, dwelling in the rent of Crowmer, opposite the fountain in le Poor Jewry beside the brothers of the Holy Cross, sold the said ale and forfeited the same

[206] [f. 66v]
[*Mostly Latin*]
The names of various persons bringing malt to the common market which was found defective by the Masters and Wardens. The same malt was forfeited and presented to John Beterden, the chamberlain, as appears in the following

Richard Tyler, maltman of Hoddesdon in the county of Hertford had 1 quarter of malt, forfeited
Bailly, maltman, had 1 quarter of malt, forfeited in the common market at Gracechurch
Edmund Veill of the county of Hertford in the town of Elstree had 2 quarters, forfeited
Thomas Howe de Enfield in the county of Hertford had 1 quarter, forfeited
John Sybbe de Barnet in the county of Hertford had 1 quarter, forfeited
A certain maltman of the county of Cambridge had 2 quarters of malt, forfeited in the house of Henry Serle and seized by Ferrour, Salter & Neell

---

311   Crutched Friars.

Roger Horne of the county of Bedford had 2 quarters of malt, forfeited on the vigil of the Nativity of Our Lord and seized by Hugh Neel

John Hogge of Enfield in the county of Middlesex had 1 quarter, forfeited, seized by John Philippe and his associates

William Heed called Cokkeshed, maltman, had 1 quarter of malt, forfeited, seized by Crane and others

John Bolton, maltman de Mimms in the county of Middlesex beside Barnet had 1 quarter of malt, forfeited, seized by Nell & others

Peter Bailly of Broxbourne in the county of Hertford had 1 quarter of malt, forfeited, seized by Crane, Ferrour & Philippe

A certain maltman called Rolff, had 2 quarters of malt, forfeited, seized by Ferrour and Salter

William Anncell of Streatley had 2 quarters, forfeited

Thomas Newechapman of Elstree in the county of Hertford had 1 quarter, forfeited

Langford, maltman of Edmonton had 1 quarter, forfeited

Michael Gent of Minden in the county of Hertford had 1 quarter, forfeited

John Hyntewode of Hoddesdon in the county of Hertford had 1 quarter forfeited

Thomas Porter of Aldenham in the county of Hertford had 1 quarter of malt, forfeited

John Dalygood of Ickleton in the county of Cambridge had 1 quarter, forfeited

[207]
Memorandum that fines made for barrels and kilderkins not sealed with the Cooper's mark and fines for selling ale without measure, also fines for foreigners selling ale and foreigners with malt forfeited in the common market, were accounted by the chamberlain of the Guildhall and amounted to £4 16s., from which 24s. was given to the Masters and Wardens of our craft of Brewers, that is a quarter part of the money from the aforesaid forfeitures.

Malt from various maltmen seized during the time of the said Robert Chichele being mayor, and presented to the sheriffs, William Weston, draper and Richard Gosselyn, fishmonger, at that time sheriffs of the same city

John Prest of the county of Buckinghamshire had 2 quarters of malt which were found in the house of William Bernard dwelling at le Peter & Paul in the parish of St Gregory and put in the account by Richard Gosselyn

Item 10 quarts of malt were seized by Ferrour, which were found in the house of Richard Flete, dwelling at the Hind at the corner of Mynchen Lane in Fenchurch Street

Item 4 quarts of malt of William Hede, maltman, seized in the house of the same Richard Flete in Fenchurch Street

[f. 67r]
Item 7 quarters of malt were seized which were found at the house of John Randolf dwelling at the Cock in the parish of St Dionis

Item 5 quarters of malt from John Prest of the Vale in the county of Buckinghamshire which were seized in the house of John Toke and placed in the accounts of Richard Gosselyn, and seized by Crane

Item 3 quarters of malt from John Newchapman of Edgeware in the county of Middlesex, which were arrested in the common market at Gracechurch by Ferrour and put in the accounts of Gosselyn by Robert Travas and John Hampton, servants to the sheriffs of London

Item 15 quarts of malt which were seized in the home of a certain hosteler called Drewe

And a memorandum that of the malt arrested as above, some devolved into the hands of the Masters and Wardens for their quarter part, by the precept of the said sheriffs, and the money was paid by Richard Tewkeslay, clerk to the accountant of the sheriffs, that is 5s. 9d.

[208]
Memorandum concerning Cornelius Gheen, Dutchman

Memorandum that a certain Cornelius Gheen, at the time when Drugo Barentyn was mayor of the city of London, [1408–9] was admitted to the freedom of the said city and was duly sworn into the mistery of his craft of Brewers of London and was with our Lord the King of England in various wars and business. Thus he was occupied as an esquire in the presence of the Lord King, and then because he desired to have the society of the said craft and fraternity, he was in arrears against the said craft and fraternity for the said time. At the behest of Robert Smyth, William Crane, Hugo Neel and John Philippe, Masters of the said craft and fraternity, and at the request and supplication of William Porlond, clerk to the company, it was agreed that on the Tuesday of the feast of St Katherine the Virgin in the year of Our Lord 1421[312] and the 9th year of the reign of King Henry V after the Conquest, the said Cornelius should pay 10s. to the company box of the said fraternity and craft and give satisfaction for the time elapsed and for his arrears, and for the next two years following after the said day of St Katherine, he should pay by his own hands, 2s. yearly.

And a memorandum that the aforesaid 24s. received from the chamber of the Guildhall and 5s. 9d. received from the sheriffs of the city of London, amounting to 29s. 9d., was distributed amongst 9 persons, that is: Robert Smyth, William Crane, John Philippe, Hugh Neel, Masters, William Ferrour, John Salter, Peter Carpenter and William Petevyle, Searchers, and also William Porlond company clerk, 3s. to each, and 8d. was given to the alms of the craft, and 2s. for carriage of the 24 quarters of malt forfeited in the common market at Gracechurch, to the use of the Guildhall, and 1d. for ale.
In total the sum is as above 29s. 9d.

[209] [f. 67v]
[*Latin*] **The names of the brothers and sisters of the craft and fraternity of Brewers of London paying their quarterage during the time of Robert Chichely being mayor of the city of London (1421–2) Robert Smyth, William Crane, Hugo Neel and John Philippe were the Masters of the Brewers' craft, that is in the 10th year of the reign of King Henry V and the first of King Henry VI [1422] as appears below.**

---

[312]   25 November 1421.

Agnes Carleton	12*d*.
Alexander Myles with his wife	
Isabel	2*s*.
Adam Copendale with Emma his wife	2*s*.
Alan John with Johanna his wife	2*s*.
Alice Hore	12*d*.
Agnes Bugge	12*d*.
Agnes Stratton	12*d*.
Agnes the wife of William Rendre	12*d*.
Alice formerly the wife of William John	12*d*.
Baldewyne Hoper with Johanna his wife	2*s*.
Cristiana the widow of John Ballard	12*d*.
Cornelius Gheen, Dutchman, for this year and for one year, for 10 following and for quarterage for various elapsed years	12*s*.
Sir Robert Steyntone	12*d*.
Dionysia Barthorpe	12*d*.
Dederic Johnson with Weveyn his wife	2*s*.
Emma Canonne	12*d*.
Elizabeth Sonman	12*d*.
Hugh Glene with Margaret his wife	2*s*.
Henry Bedell with Alice his wife	2*s*.
Henry Lymber with Felicia his wife	2*s*.
Hugh Neel with Emma his wife	2*s*.
Henry Trebolans with Elizabeth his wife	2*s*.
Henry Bassett at the Belle with Agnes his wife	2*s*.

[210] [f. 68r]

John Ser, glover,	12*d*.
John Hardy for this year and last	2*s*.
John Turner	12*d*.
John Benge with Alice his wife	2*s*.
John Sonder	12*d*.
John Luke	12*d*.
John Assh	12*d*.
John Serle	12*d*.
John Southmede	12*d*.

John Mason with Felicia his wife	2*s*.
John Salter with Johanna his wife	2*s*.
John Laurence	12*d*.
John Philippe with Matilda his wife	2*s*.
John More at Aldersgate with Cristiana his wife	2*s*.
John Tregelowe for this year and last	2*s*.
John Basset	12*d*.
John Reyner with Agatha his wife	2*s*.
John Pyken with Alice his wife	2*s*.
John Caryen with Alice his wife	2*s*.
John Chapman	12*d*.
John Toke with Alice his wife	2*s*.
Jacob Levegro	12*d*.
John Stone	12*d*.
John Kenaky	12*d*.
John Brewster with Johanna his wife	2*s*.
John Broke with Cristiana his wife	2*s*.
John Spenser	12*d*.
John Humber with Margaret his wife	2*s*.
John More at Ludgate and Mathia his wife	2*s*.
John Lynne	12*d*.
John William with Johanna his wife	2*s*.
John Stanton with Matilda his wife	2*s*.
John Riche with Margaret his wife	2*s*.
John Russell with Alice his wife	2*s*.
John Ketyng	12*d*.
John Ryngessonne	12*d*.
John Reeffawe with Juliana his wife	2*s*.
John Snell	15*d*.
John Lumbard	12*d*.
John Bray, butcher, for this year and last	2*s*.
John Bailly	12*d*.
John Eylond	12*d*.
Michael Tregononne	12*d*.
Michael Eve with Elizabeth his wife	2*s*.
Morris Tranaill with Margaret his wife	2*s*.
Margaret Thetford	12*d*.
Nicholas Agomnaylok with Johanna his wife	2*s*.

John Turvey with Margaret his wife	2s.	Nicholas Mueyell	12d.
John Wyghtmour with Johanna		Nicholas Aleyn	12d.
his wife for this year and last	4s.	Nicholas Fuller with Alice his wife	2s.
Johanna Horold, widow of John		Nicholas Kene and Katherine his	
Turmyn	12d.	wife	2s.
John Aleyn, baker,	12d.		
Idonea Hatton	12d.	Peter Carpenter	12d.
John Randolf with Julianna his wife	2s.	Peter Hayford with Matilda his wife	2s.
John Gedeney with Johanna his		Philip James	12d.
wife	2s.	Peter Roos	12d.
John Retford	12d.	Peter Short with Alice his wife	2s.
John Qwyntyn for this year and last	2s.		
Johanna Ambele	12d.	Robert Steynton, priest	12d.[313]
[Clerk's note: £3 4s. 3d.]		Robert Hylton with Margaret his	
Juliana Hetersete	12d.	wife	2s.
Johanna the wife of John		Robert Gyles with Johanna his wife	2s.
Fekenham	12d.	Richard Shirwode with Alice his	
Johanna Rothyng	12d.	wife	2s.
John Jacob with Alice his wife	2s.	Robert Tanner	12d.
John Holbek with Margaret his wife	2s.	Richard Rowdon with Johanna	
John Riche Junior de Fleet Street	12d.	his wife	2s.
John Goldryng with Johanna his		Robert Smyth with Anna his wife	2s.
wife	2s.	Richard Aleyn with Johanna his	
John Frost	12d.	wife	2s.
John Hardyng	12d.	Robert Carpenter and Margaret	
John Elcy for this year and last	2s.	his wife	2s.
John Bargon for this year and		Roger Blissote with Matilda his	
3 years elapsed	4s.	wife	2s.
John Waghorne	12d.	Robert Walram	12d.
John de Dene	12d.	Richard Crosse	12d.
		Richard Terrell with Isabel his wife	2s.

[211] [f. 68v]

Richard Harlowe with Johanna		William Gedeney for this year	
his wife	2s.	and 2 last years pertaining	3s.
Richard Bryntonne	12d.	William atte Wode with	
[Clerk's note: £3 4s.]		Katherine his wife	4s.
Roger Baronne	12d.	William Bourne	12d.
Robert Pede with Alice his wife	2s.	William Antrou of Fleet Street	12d.
Robert Nikke with Alice his wife	2s.	William Bailly	12d.
Richard Frepurs	12d.	William atte Welle with Alice his	
Robert Mayhew	12d.	wife	2s.
Richard Welde for this year and last	2s.	William Belle	12d.
Robert Jewell	12d.	William Gros with Katherine his	
Richard Lucas with Alice his wife	2s.	wife	2s.
Robert Delowe with Margaret his		William Herry	12d.
wife	2s.	Walter Colshull [*erased*: & Alice]	12d.

---

[313] This entry was added in another hand, without the customary priest's title Dominus.

Robert Elken with Cecilia his wife	2s.	William Boteler with Elizabeth	
Roger Ware with Alice his wife	2s.	his wife	2s.
		William Payne	12d.
Simon Potekyn	12d.	William Boltonne with Alice his	
Stephen Roo	12d.	wife	2s.
Stephen Clean	12d.	William Overtonne	12d.
		William Petevyle	12d.
Thomas Boteler	12d.	William Ferrour with Agnes his	
Thomas Jakes for this year and last	2s.	wife	2s.
Thomas Godyng	12d.	William Cardell	12d.
Thomas Emond with Sibilla his		William Crane with Helena his wife	2s.
wife	2s.	William Geffrey with Anna his wife	2s.
Thomas Aleyn with Letitia his wife	2s.	William Canonne with Elizabeth	
Thomas Hatcher with Margery		his wife	2s.
his wife	2s.	William Illying	12d.
Thomas Yole with Alice his wife	2s.	William Claissonne with Isabel	
Thomas Grene with Matilda his		his wife	2s.
wife	2s.	William Bracy with Alice his wife	2s.
Thomas Howe	12d.	William Ederych with Alice his	
Thomas Penson	12d.	wife	2s.
Thomas Hancok with Dionysia		William Bodevyle	12d.
his wife	2s.	William Bacon, butcher,	12d.
Thomas de Kent	12d.	William Termeday	12d.
Thomas Grateley with Margaret		William Devenyssh	6d.
his wife	2s.	William Smalshoo with Margaret	
Thomas Bristowe	12d.	his wife	2s.
Thomas Martyn	12d.	William Bernard	12d.
Thomas Dewy with Agnes his wife	2s.	William Reponne with Margery	
Thomas North	12d.	his wife	2s.
Thomas Ayle	12d.	William Porlond with Dionysia	
		his wife	2s.
		Walter Glyn	12d.
		William Copwod for this year	
		and last	4s.

Sum of Quarterage this year £14 13s. 9d. And for our cause this

[212] [f. 69r]
**sum accords as to those entering the fraternity in the preceding year, certain
other persons paying for their fraternity entry and quarterage this year, certain
others paying for the present year and the past year, certain other persons for
the said present year and subsequent years, and also for diverse years before
this said present year, and certain other persons for the present year and for
3 years preceding.**

Those who entered the fraternity during the preceding year
Baldewyne Hoper and Johanna his wife
Henry Basset and Agnes his wife
John Holbek and Margaret his wife
John Riche Junior of Fleet Street
John Goldryng and Johanna his wife
Robert Delowe and Margaret his wife
Robert Elkyn and Cecilia his wife
Stephen Clean
William Bourne
John Jacob
John Hardyng
Margaret the wife of John Turvey
Mathia the wife of John More
Margaret the wife of Robert Carpenter
Matilda the wife of Roger Blissote
Johanna the wife of Alan John
Alice the wife of Henry Bedell

[213]
Those who introduced their wives to the fraternity this year and paid quarterage for the same year
Isabel the wife of Alexander Miles
Elizabeth the wife of Henry Trebolans

[214]
Certain persons paying for entry and quarterage this year
Thomas North
Thomas Ayle
William Andrew of Fleet Street
Dederic Johnson, beerman
Richard Lucas and Alice his wife
John Frost
Roger Ware and Alice his wife
Peter Short and Alice his wife

Certain persons paying for this year and 2 past years
William Gedeney at Queenhithe

A certain person paying for this year and 3 preceding years
John Bargon, tallowchandler

Certain persons paying for this present year and subsequent years and also for diverse years before the said present year
Cornelius Gheen, Dutchman

Those who have died this year and who have paid their quarterage
Matilda the wife of John Philippe
Johanna the wife of John Gedeney

[215]
Those who have paid for the present year and past years
John Tregelowe
John Bray, butcher
John Qwyntyn
John Wyghtmore and Johanna his wife
William atte Wode and Katherine his wife
William Copwode
John Elsy
John Hardy, Cook
Richard Welde
Thomas Jakes

Various people refusing to continue in the fraternity this year
John William of Southwark
Katherine Roche beside the Augustinian Friars

Those paying quarterage in the past year and not this year, determined by various causes
John Ballard
Isabel Syward
Johanna Cole[314]
Katherine Roche
John Somnan
John Rothyng
John Thetford
William Overton

---

314 Johanna Cole became a Brewers' almswoman **[184]** and Robert Lynford received alms from the Brewers **[176]**.

Johanna the wife of John
Salter
Johanna the wife of John
Gedeney
Johanna the wife of
Richard Aleyn
Alice the wife of Robert
Pede
Letitia the wife of Thomas
Aleyn
Margaret the wife of
Thomas Gratley
Margery the wife of
Thomas Hatcher
Alice the wife of Thomas
Yole
Elizabeth the wife of
William Boteler
Elizabeth the wife of
William Canonne

Margaret the wife of
Robert Hylton
Richard Rowdon
William Bourne
William Bolton
Nicholas Kene

**Those who are in the
fraternity table, not
paying since the time of
Richard Whityngton**
[1419–20]
[*blank*]

Thomas
Smalsho
William
Devenyssh
William
John
Johanna
Wyghtmore

Robert
Lynford
John
William de
Southwark

[216] [f. 69v]
[*Latin*]
Whereas our mother tongue, that is, the English tongue, has nowadays begun to be honourably increased, enlarged and adorned, that which our most excellent lord King Henry V, both in his letters missive and in diverse affairs touching his own person, has more willingly chosen to declare the secrets of his will, and for the sake of the better understanding of his people, having set aside other common idioms, with a diligent mind, has procured the common idiom, to be commended by the exercise of writing. There are many of our Brewers' craft who have knowledge of reading and writing in the said English idiom, but in others, that is the Latin and French, which have often been used before these times, they have little knowledge or understanding. For these causes, with many other considerations, the greater part of the lords and faithful commons deem it worthy to begin to have their matters written in our mother tongue. Therefore we, in our said craft, following their steps in some manner, have decreed to commit to memory the things that concern us, as appears in the following pages.[315]

[217]
[*English*] [*On*] the Thursday, namely the 30th day of the month of July, in the 10th year of King Henry V [1422] in the time of Robert Chichele [*being*] mayor of London,[316] at a suggestion made by Richard Whityngton upon the Brewers of London, wherefore the said mayor sent for Robert Smyght, William Crane, Hugh Neel and John Philippe, Masters of the said craft of Brewers at that time [*above the line*: by a sergeant] and commanded them to bring with them 12 of the worthiest of the same craft to appear before the mayor at the Guildhall, [*on*] the day and the time abovesaid and when the aforesaid Brewers came before the mayor and aldermen,

315 See Figure 9.
316 1421–2.

Figure 9. GL MS 5440 The Brewers' Book, folio 69v.
The declaration in Latin of the clerk's intention to use
English in future. © The Brewers' Company.

John Fray, at that time being recorder of the said city³¹⁷ said to the Brewers in this wise 'Sirs, you have been accused here of selling dear ale and setting your ale at a greater price than you should do, without leave of this court, and moreover, you are bound in this court by a recognizance³¹⁸ of £20, [*by which*] at whatever manner of price malt is sold, you should sell your best ale out of your houses to your customers for 1½*d.*, that is, a barrel for 42*d.*, and no dearer.' And after this the mayor asked Robert Smyth how he sold a barrel of his best ale, and he answered 'For 5*s.*, and some barrels for 4*s.* 10*d.*' And on [*in*] this manner said the most part of the Brewers who were at that time there present. And the mayor showed them diverse examples of malt in the same court, to which malt the Brewers answered that they could make no good ale from such malt.

[218] [f. 70r]
For there was a sample of malt of Norfolk at 1 quarter for 4*s.*, which came from a ship at Billingsgate. The same malt was so (good) cheap that the mayor and Richard Whityngton and the aldermen, and the most part of the commons of the said city said that it was a false thing to sell their ale so dearly when they might have malt so (good) cheaply. But men said at that time that Brewers were the cause of the dearth of malt, with their riding into various countries³¹⁹ to buy malt, and also men said that the multitude of Brewers would have expensive malt, for the profit of the rich Brewers of London, and by a motion from Richard Whityngton, there being present, he said to the Brewers that they had ridden into the country and forestalled³²⁰ malt, wherefore it caused malt to be so dear. For 1 quarter of malt at that time was at 7*s.* 6*d.*, and within a little time before, 1 quarter of malt was sold in the market for 8*s.* 8*d.*, and some for 9*s.*
And after this the mayor commanded John Carpenter, clerk of the Guildhall, to read the same ordinance that was made in the time of Richard Whityngton [*being*] mayor of London. When it was fully read before the mayor, aldermen and before the Brewers, then the mayor and all the aldermen said that the Brewers were condemned in their bond of £20.

[219]
Therefore the recorder said these words and gave open judgement before the mayor and the aldermen, that the craft of Brewers should pay £20 towards the work of the Guildhall,³²¹ for they did not keep the ordinance that was ordained upon them. Therefore the mayor ordained and commanded that the aforesaid Masters of the Brewers' craft, that is to wit, Robert Smyth and his fellows, should be kept in the ward of the chamberlain of the Guildhall, in prison, until such time as the aforesaid Masters of Brewers' craft had found surety to pay the same £20, or else [*they were*] to pay it before they [*could*] go out of prison. And thus they did abide at the chamberlain's grace, still in the Guildhall, until the time when the mayor and aldermen had gone home to their meat.³²² And after this, the said Masters asked the

³¹⁷ John Fray, recorder of London, 1420–6.
³¹⁸ Bond, obligation.
³¹⁹ Counties.
³²⁰ Bought up all the malt before it came to market
³²¹ Building work taking place at the Guildhall was under the supervision of master mason John Croxton [**315**].
³²² Evening meals.

chamberlain and John Carpenter to wit what they should do. The said chamberlain and John Carpenter commanded them to go home to their houses, and so John Carpenter vowed to them at that time that they should have no more harm, neither through imprisonment of their bodies, nor the loss of £20, for they well understood and knew that all the aforesaid judgement of the mayor and aldermen was only done at that time to please Richard Whityngton, for he was the cause of all the aforesaid judgement.

[220] [f. 70v]
In this year, in the time of Robert Chichele [*being*] mayor [1421–2], our worshipful King Henry V passed out of this world, in the parts of France, on the last day of August, upon a Sunday on the eve of St Giles,[323] in the 10th year of his reign [1422], whose soul God assoil.
Whereupon, the said mayor and the aldermen, with a common council, ordained that the sheriffs who were chosen soon after that time, on the day of St Matthew,[324] that is to wit, William Estfeld [*above the line*: mercer] and Robert Tatersall [*above the line*: draper], should not ride upon horseback to Westminster to take their charge, but should only ride in barges with their crafts, and so the craft of Drapers was hooded in white and medley parted[325] and the sergeants of both sheriffs were gowned in the same suit, and the craft of Mercers went in their own clothing, with hoods of scarlet and in no other livery, as had been accustomed before this time.
And so they rode in barges to Westminster, as it was ordained before, and they took their charge as the manner is.

[221] [f. 71r]
[*English*]
And after this, William Walderne was chosen, on the day of St Edward next following[326] to be mayor of London for the next year ensuing. Upon this day it was ordained that the mayor and aldermen should wear black and ride by barge to Westminster, there for him to take his charge, with the crafts of London in diverse barges, in black clothing, without any minstrel or any other solemnity. For on the day of St Edward, it was ordained that every householder of every craft being of power[327] should ordain for himself a black gown with a hood of black, or else a russett gown with a black hood, for riding by barge with the aforesaid mayor to Westminster, and after that, in the same clothing of black or else russet, to be present at the interment of our said King Henry V, and in this manner it was ordained and done.

[222]
And after the aforesaid William Walderne was chosen as mayor, as he himself told William Ederych, brewer of the same city, he had 40 complaints against the Brewers' craft. He was sorely stirred by certain persons of diverse crafts to have dis-eased[328]

323 31 August. The feast of St Giles is on 1 September.
324 21 September.
325 Hoods parti-coloured in white and medley. Chambers and Daunt, *London English*, 257.
326 13 October 1422.
327 Being able.
328 'to have desesid'. Perhaps to deprive the craft of privileges, as suggested in Chambers and Daunt, *London English*, 257.

the craft of Brewers. [*scored*: and he said that with all the complaints he would have been right well advised what to do]

Whereupon he sent for the Masters of the craft of Brewers, that is: Robert Smyth, William Crane, Hugh Neel and John Philippe, soon after he had taken his charge at Westminster, and charged them to make good ale 'so that neither the lords nor the commons should have any cause to complain against you', and thus he charged them and prayed them to do well and truly. And so they answered the mayor that malt was of such price that year that they were busy to make a living[329] for the best malt was sold for 8*s.* 2*d.*, and some for 8*s.* 4*d.*, before the term of Easter in his time, and so because of the great price of malt, many brewers in that year left (up) their brewhouses and their brewing.

Considering the aforesaid mayor and knowing of this mischief and disease he licensed [*scored*: suffered] that other part of the Brewers to brew and live[330] so that they might hold their own. [*scored*: for the world was hard in taking money in that year for the craft of Brewers, for their customers did not pay them well and] [*above the line*: for as much as] the lords with the multitude of people were out of the realm at that time, to whom the Brewers were accustomed to sell and retail their ale [*above the line*: for their living].

[223]

And furthermore, it was ordained on the said day of St Edward that certain crafts should find torches to the number of 200 for the interment of the said King: some crafts 12, some crafts 8, some 6, some crafts 4 torches. And so our said craft of Brewers found 8 torches for the said interment of our aforesaid King, weighing in all 138 lbs, price of

[224] [f. 71v]

the lb, 4½*d*. Sum 51*s.* 9*d*. And so the chamberlain found for us, and for all other crafts, white gowns for the torchbearers, and the crafts paid the torchbearers their wages, so our craft of Brewers paid to each man who bore any of our torches 3*d.*, for his meat for a day, that is, to wit, 6*d.* for 2 days. The sum for 2 days paid to all the torchbearers, with their gowns, 4*s.*

And so the body, that is, to wit, the corpse of our said King came to London on the Thursday, the 5th day of the month of November in the first year of King Henry VI, son to the aforesaid King Henry V, at one of the clock, after noon on the same day, at which time and hour, the said William Walderne, mayor, with aldermen, and the sheriffs of the said city and certain crafts of London, clothed in black, met with the corpse of the King in Southwark at St George's Bar, all on foot. And our craft stood and stayed at St Margaret's church hawe[331] in Southwark. And when the corpse of the King had passed with all the lords, the mayor and the aldermen with the commonalty of the said city, followed forth to [St] Paul's. And the said torchbearers of London passed before the corpse of the King to Paul's and there they stood still whilst the Dirige was sung for the same King.

And so on the next day, that was Friday, a certain number of masses were sung by note[332] with the great solemnity of Bishops and other worthy lords spiritual and

---

[329] 'To leven'.
[330] 'leven' was changed to 'lyven'.
[331] Churchyard.
[332] Song, melody. Sung masses with music.

temporal. And so after noon on the Friday, when the lords had eaten, the corpse of the King was led forth to Westminster, with all the aforesaid lords, the mayor and aldermen, with the crafts of London and all the torches that the crafts had found for the same interment.

And so the same torches stood still in the town of Westminster until the corpse of the King had passed through and entered at the gate of the abbey of Westminster, with all the said lords aforesaid. Then the torch ends were brought home again to London, which weighed 112 lbs of wax, price 3*d.* the lb. Sum 28*s.* And then the said torch ends were sold for the use of the commonalty of our craft of Brewers.

And moreover, it was ordained ahead of the coming of the said corpse, that from the time that he entered over the bridge of London, each ward through which the corpse passed, within the franchise of the city, from St Magnus to the gate of

[225] [f. 72r]
Temple Bar, every householder dwelling along the same way that the corpse passed by, in the aforesaid streets and wards, should find a torch and in this manner [*have it*] burning with a servant holding the same torch at his door, and in this manner it was performed indeed. And on the Saturday, the 7th day of November, he was buried with great solemnity. For at the mass of Requiem 4 steeds, royally trapped, were offered up at the high altar of Westminster church, with a knight fully and wholly armed with the King's coat armour and a crown upon his head, sitting upon one of the steeds royally. And at the Dirige on the Friday and at the mass on the Saturday, 200 cloths of gold and more were offered in Westminster church upon the corpse of the said King, upon whose soul may Jesus have mercy and pity, and bring it to his bliss. **Amen.**

[226]
Here should be written the costs of a dinner made at the Conversion of St Paul in the month of January,333 for the multitude of Brewers of London, in the time of the said William Walderne being mayor of London [1422–3], in the first year of the reign of King Henry VI [1422–3], with Robert Smyth, William Crane, Hugh Neel and John Philippe being Masters of the aforesaid craft of Breweres at that time.

The which parcels, seek, and you shall find them written on the 31st leaf of this paper before this leaf.334

[227] [f. 72v]
[*Mostly Latin*]
In the second year of the reign of King Henry VI [1423–4], when William Walderne was mayor of the city of London [1422–3], he behaved well and honestly towards our craft of Brewers but nevertheless became unfriendly three weeks before the end of his occupation of the said office, when he reminded the Masters of our craft of Brewers of the many arguments and enquiries that had taken place by words. Concerning this, by the assent of the said Masters and certain of their associates, it was agreed that wishing to mitigate and to soften the sinister intentions of the said mayor, they would make a subtle and discreet present to him and his adherants. They ordered that 1 boar, price 20*s.*, and one ox, price 17*s.*, should be presented to him in

---

333 25 January.
334 Costs for this dinner were recorded some thirty-one pages before [**112**].

mitigation and thus they would pacify much of the discord with the aforesaid mayor until the end of the time of his aforesaid mayoralty.

[228]
The names of various brewers having unsealed barrels and kilderkins during the time of William Walderne being mayor of the city of London during the first year of the reign of King Henry VI [1422–3]. **And concerning this they were presented and amerced at le Guildhall.**

Margaret Leonard at the Cock beside the Augustinian Friars had 1 unsealed kilderkin at Blossoms Inn in the parish of St Lawrence in Jewry
Thomas Kirtot at the Red Lion in Wood Street in the parish of St Alphage had 1 unsealed kilderkin in Trump Alley
John Waghorn at the Cock in the parish of St Mary Woolchurch had 1 unsealed kilderkin at le Trump in Cheap
John Broke at the Seven Stars in the same parish had 1 unsealed kilderkin at the Counter in Cheap
Thomas Whiting at the Key in Bassishaw had 1 unsealed kilderkin in Cheap, opposite the same Counter there
John Newman at the Lamb in the parish of St Sepulchre without Newgate had 1 unsealed kilderkin in the house of Basill, corsour, at St Martin the Grand.
A certain huckster, foreigner, opposite the fountain at the market at St Nicholas [*Shambles*] had 1 kilderkin of foreign ale from a certain foreigner, brewer, on Turnmill Street
A certain huckster, foreigner, beside Hylton, corsour, in the said parish of St Sepulchre outside Newgate, had 1 kilderkin of foreign ale from a certain foreigner at the Cock in Turnmill Street

[229]
John Aleyn at the Mermaid outside Cripplegate had 1 kilderkin which was found upon a certain Slede in the Old Baily
The same John had 3 barrels and 6 kilderkins in a certain cart, found at Fleet Bridge
Augustin Hawkyn at the Rose beside Fleet Bridge had 1 unsealed kilderkin in the home of Johanna Kynle opposite the Black Horse there
John Hopkyn at the Horse outside Aldersgate had 1 unsealed kilderkin at the home of the huckster Skermer, in Gutter Lane
John Wightmore at the Unicorn in the parish of St Nicholas Olave had 1 unsealed kilderkin in that same house in Gutter Lane
John Ludlowe at the Chequer in the parish of All Hallows Staining, in Fenchurch Street had 1 unsealed kilderkin found in the common street upon the shoulders of his servant at St Margaret Pattens
Thomas Pensonne at the Dragon in the parish of St Gregory had 1 [*above the line:* not] sealed barrel found in the common street
Thomas Aleyn at the Harp in Thames Street beside Sevenoak[335] had 1 unsealed kilderkin in the house of a huckster opposite the cooper

---

[335] This may refer to William Sevenoke, mayor 1418–19, see P. Nightingale, 'Sevenoak [Sevenoke], William (d. in or after 1432), merchant and mayor of London', *ODNB*.

[230] [f. 73r]
The names of those with unsealed barrels and kilderkins are:

Robert Dorwell at the Lamb at Baynard's Castle had 1 unsealed kilderkin in the home of Allokston dwelling at the Saracen's Head outside Newgate
John Sheffeld at the Lamp opposite the Friars Minor had 1 unsealed kilderkin at the home of Ryngwode, bladesmith
Robert Smyth at the Swan in Thames Street had 1 unsealed kilderkin at the home of Gerard Pyebaker
A huckster, one Waller, foreigner, dwelling in the rent of Preston in le Barbican beside Aldersgate Street sold 2 kilderkins of ale from a certain foreigner dwelling at the Cock in Golding Lane and the same was presented to the chamber
A certain huckster, a foreigner, dwelling beside the Bars in Aldersgate Street sold 1 kilderkin of ale from a certain foreigner dwelling at the Swan in St John Street and the same was presented to the chamber of the Guildhall

[231]
And a memorandum that during the time of William Walderne being mayor, fines for the said unsealed barrels and kilderkins, together with foreign ale sold by foreigners, as appear above, by an assessment made in le Guildhall amounted to 33s. 3d., from which William Porlond, clerk to the craft of Brewers received there for the quarter part of the same money 8s. 4d., paid to the said craft. And the sum was divided amongst five persons, that is: William Crane 20d.; John Salter 20d.; Peter Carpenter 20d.; William Ferrour Senior 20d.; and the said William Porlond, clerk 20d.

And thus the sum is as above.

[232]
[English]
    This is the copy of the Charter of the Fishmongers of London, by which copy we have an example and informer to make the Charter of the Brewers' craft of London.[336]

[Latin]
In all things let it be known that by our special grace and by the advice and consent of our council, we and our heirs give licence and grant from us and our heirs to choose to bind the men of the Fishmongers of our city of London at this time, so that they and all the men of the mistery who are and shall be freemen of the said city at this time, may form one body in one name and one community in perpetuity. And that the same community each year may elect and make wardens for one year, to superintend, rule and govern the mistery and community in perpetuity and all the

---

336   This sentence in English was probably written by Porlond himself. It introduced the Latin text which continued overleaf. This copy of the charter was dated 8 February 11 Henry VI [1433] by the Brewers' clerk. The whole piece has not been crossed through, so it is a significantly later addition inserted into a previously blank space. The Charter of the Fishmongers was indeed dated 8 February 1433 and it is kept at Fishmongers' Hall amongst the Books of Ordinances and Transcripts, see P. Metcalf, *The Halls of the Fishmongers' Company: an architectural history of a riverside site* (London and Chichester, 1977), 13 and fn.20.

men and business of the same mistery and company in perpetuity and that the same
wardens and commonalty shall have successors and a common seal for the business
of the said mistery and company. They and their successors in perpetuity shall be
persons able and capable of reading and in land holding, to procure tenure of land,
tenements, rents and other possessions, for posterity. And those same Wardens, by
name Wardens of the mistery and company of Fishmongers of the city of London
will be able to litigate and appeal to the court.

Lastly, by our most abundant grace and with the assent and advice of our council,
we and our heirs grant and give licence to the wardens and commons of the said
mistery of Fishmongers to hold lands and rent in our demesne and reversion both
within our city of London and in the suburbs of the same within the borough of
Southwark, which are held of us in free burgage, to the value of 20 pounds a year, so
that they may acquire, have

[233] [f. 73v]

and hold for their successors for the aid and sustaining of the poor men and women
of the mistery and company aforesaid, in perpetuity, by statute, of lands and
tenements in mortmain, as well as those lands, tenements and rents thus acquired
and held from us in free burgage, as was promised notwithstanding however by
inquisition taken and returned to our chancellor by the account and by writ as
faithfully as possible without condemnation or punishment by us or our heirs.
And that certain ordinances and statutes by virtue of the present grant [*should*] not
be made that might lead to the prejudice or harm of us or our people, or the increase
[*in price*] of the sale of victuals, nor that the said wardens and their successors or
any one of them should uphold complaints unjustly, maintaining all in the same
manner.

In whose and etc T. R
Given at Westminster on the 8th day of February, in the year 11 King Henry VI
[1433].

[234] [f. 74r]

**First for diverse drapery during the time of William Walderne being mayor
of the city of London [1422–3] in the first year of the reign of King Henry VI
[1422–3], that is, rays and green coloured cloth called coarse cloth, for clothing
for the brothers and sisters of the fraternity of the Holy Trinity [*above the
line*: also of All Hallows] of the craft of Brewers of London, Robert Smyth,
William Crane, John Philippe and Hugh Neel being Masters of the same craft
of Brewers.**

Rays first to Robert Tatersall, draper of London, for 21 cloths and 3 yards of rays,
contained in diverse pieces of the same cloth, of which each cloth contains 24 yards
Sum 507 yards, of which account for 1 yard with another [sample or piece?] of
2 yards containing 17 rays.

Sum 4,309 rays
Sum in money   **£51 0s. 12½d.**

And to Robert Callow, shearman, for shearing the said 21 cloths and 3 yards
at 2s., in total   42s.

Coloured cloth

n to the said Robert Tatersall, draper, for 1 piece of coloured cloth containing
22 yards at 3*s*., in total   66*s*.

n to Robert Smyth for 1 piece of cloth of the same colour containing 32 yards
and a half at 3*s*. 9*d*.,   £6 22½*d*.

n to the same for 1 cloth of the same colour containing 32 yards green and
half as above at 3*s*. 9*d*.,   £6

n to the same for 1 cloth of the same colour containing 15 yards 1 quarter at
3*s*. 8*d*.,   55*s*. 11*d*.

n to the same for 1 cloth of the same colour containing 32 yards at 3*s*. 7*d*.,   114*s*. 8*d*.

b n to the same for 1 cloth of the same containing 31 yards at 3*s*. 3*d*.,   100*s*. 9*d*.

to the same for 1 cloth of the same colour containing 21 yards at 3*s*. 3*d*., as
above,   66*s*. 6*d*.

and to the same for 69 yards of cloth of the same colour, dyed and sheared
by him, as above, at 3*s*. 3*d*.,   £11 4*s*. 3*d*.

[235]

a John Ryngesson, tailor, for 16 yards of cloth of the same colour at 3*s*. 8*d*.,   58*s*. 8*d*.

n to the same for 7 yards and half of the same colour at 3*s*. 8*d*. as above   27*s*. 6*d*.

n to the same for 4 yards 3 quarters of the same colour as above at 3*s*. 8*d*.,   17*s*. 5*d*.

n to the same for 1 yard 3 quarters of the same colour for a hood for Adam
Copendale as above at 3*s*. 8*d*.,   6*s*. 5*d*.

n to the same for 1 yard and half for 2 hoods, for Roger Awdymer, vintner &
John Aston, of the same colour, at 3*s*. 8*d*., as above. Delivered by William
Crane with 24 rays,   5*s*. 6*d*.

n to the same for 1 yard 1 quarter of the same colour for 2 hoods for Thomas
Howe & Richard Tyler, maltmen, delivered by Hugh Neel at 3*s*. 8*d*., as
above,   4*s*. 7*d*.

n to the same for half a yard half quarter of the same colour for a hood for
Richard Frepurs as above at 3*s*. 8*d*.,   2*s*. 3½*d*.

n and to the same for 25 yards and half of the same colour at 3*s*. 4*d*.,   £4 5*s*.

n to the same for 5 yards of the same colour at 3*s*. 4*d*. as above,   16*s*. 8*d*.

a n and to the abovesaid Robert Smyth for 38 yards of the same colour at
3*s*. 6*d*.,   £6 13*s*.

Sum total of drapery   **Rays 4,309**
Coloured cloth 356 yards, half and
half quarter
Money £114 10*s*. 0½*d*.

[236] [f. 74v]
**Outgoings to the same draper at the said time and year as appears in the
following**

Gowns

n Alexander Myles 36 rays & 3 yards of green   26*s*. 8*d*.

n Alexander Marcowe 29 rays 2 yards 1 quarter of green   23*s*.

Hoods

n Adam Copendale 1 yard 3 quarters of green   10*s.*
n Sir Adam Dalton 1 yard of green   4*s.* 6*d.*[337]

Gowns

n Baldewyne Hoper 27 rays 2 yards of green   19*s.* 10*d.*

Gowns

[*scored*: *n* Sir Robert Steynton 4 yards half of green   16*s.* 10½*d.*]
[*margin*: who entered into the livery of B[rewers].]
n Dederic Johnson 42 rays 3 yards half quarter of green   29*s.* 4*d.*
n David Brownyng 36 rays 2 yards half of green   26*s.* 8*d.*

Hoods

n Emma Canonne 1 yard of green   5*s.* 6*d.*

Item Hoods

n Gilbert Botonne 8 rays half yard half quarter   6*s.*
n Gilbert Kyrton, formerly the aletaker, 9 rays half yard half quarter   6*s.*

Gowns

n Henry Trobolans 36 rays 3 yards of green   26*s.* 8*d.*
n Henry Nobill 31 rays 2 yards half of green   22*s.*
n Henry Grene 36 rays 3 yards of green   26*s.* 8*d.*
n Henry Bedell 28 rays 2 yards 1 quarter of green   22*s.*
n Hugh Neel with his wife 45 rays 4 yards of green   34*s.* 8*d.*

Hoods

n Henry Lymber 9 rays half yard half quarter of green   6*s.* 8*d.*
n Hugh Glene 9 rays half yard half quarter of green   6*s.* 8*d.*
n Henry Rowe 10 rays 3 quarters of green   8*s.*
n Henry Stapill 8 rays half yard half quarter of green   6*s.*
n Henry Fereby 8 rays half yard half quarter of green   6*s.*
n Henry Wykston, fishmonger, 9 rays half yard half quarter of green   6*s.* 8*d.*

Rays 416
Colour 41 yards 1 quarter half
Money £17 6*s.* 4½*d.*

[237] Gowns

n John Masonne 36 rays 3 yards of green   26*s.* 8*d.*
n John Salter 36 rays 2 yards half of green   24*s.* 2*d.*

---

337 Each name has the symbol *n* before it. Dots in the margin may indicate those entitled to a concession, or another category that the clerk wished to record. On this page there are dots to the left of: Sir Adam Dalton, Emma Canon, Gilbert Boton, Henry Nobill, Henry Grene, Henry Bedell, Henry Lymber, Henry Rowe, and Henry Fereby. Dalton was the priest at All Hallows London Wall, the Brewers' fraternity church, from 1417 until his death in 1430. Hennessy, *London Clergy*, 82.

n John Hopken 32 rays 2 yards 1 quarter of green	24*s*.
n John Chapman 32 rays 2 yards 1 quarter of green	24*s*.
n John Broke 36 rays 3 yards of green	26*s*. 8*d*.
n John Caryonne 36 rays 3 yards of green	26*s*. 8*d*.
n John Russell 34 rays 2 yards 3 quarters of green	26*s*.
n John Ketyng 36 rays 3 yards of green	26*s*. 8*d*.
n John Reyner 36 rays 3 yards of green	26*s*. 8*d*.

[238] [f. 75r]

n John Spenser 28 rays 2 yards of green[338]	22*s*.
n John Newman 34 rays 2 yards half of green	25*s*.
n John Stone 28 rays 1 yard 3 quarters of green	19*s*. 8*d*.
n John Tregelow 32 rays 2 yards 1 quarter of green	23*s*.
n John Brewster 32 rays 2 yards half of green	24*s*.
n John Riche 8 rays 5 yards of green	26*s*. 8*d*.
n John Elsy 35 rays 2 yards half of green	25*s*.
n John Bedford 29 rays 2 yards of green	22*s*. 4*d*.
n John Snell 30 rays 2 yards 1 quarter of green	23*s*.
n John Frost 32 rays 2 yards half of green	24*s*.
n John Faireman 36 rays 3 yards of green	26*s*. 8*d*.
n John Ryngesson 34 rays 2 yards 1 quarter	24*s*.
n John Holbek 34 rays 2 yards half and half quarter of green	24*s*. 8*d*.
n John Humber 38 rays 3 yards of green	27*s*. 4*d*.
n John Pyken 32 rays 2 yards half of green	24*s*.
n John Sharpe 32 rays 2 yards half of green	24*s*.
n Jacob Levegro 24 rays 2 yards of green	18*s*.
n John Bosvenon 34 rays 2 yards 3 quarters of green	25*s*. 4*d*.
n John Aleyn 32 rays 2 yards half of green	24*s*.
n John Basset 30 rays 2 yards and 1 quarter of green	22*s*.
n John Riche de Fleet Street 28 rays 2 yards 1 quarter of green	22*s*.
n John Reffawe 32 rays 2 yards 1 quarter of green	24*s*.
n John Laurence 32 rays 2 yards 1 quarter of green	24*s*.
n John Wyghtmore 30 rays 2 yards half of green	22*s*.
n John Kenaky 35 rays 2 yards half of green	25*s*.
n John Pekker, carpenter, 34 rays 2 yards 3 quarters green	25*s*.
n John Philippe with his wife 41 rays 4 yards green	33*s*. 4*d*.
n John Beauchampe, maltman, 28 rays 2 yards green	22*s*.

[239]
Hoods

n John Warsoppe 8 rays half yard half quarter of green	6*s*. 8*d*.
n John Mabile 10 rays 3 quarters of green	8*s*.
n John Sere 8 rays half yard half quarter of green	6*s*.
n John West 8 rays half yard half quarter of green	6*s*.
n John Hardy, Cook, 9 rays half yard half quarter of green	6*s*. 8*d*.

338   All names are preceded by a dot on this page.

n John de Dene 7 rays half yard of green	5s. 4d.
n John Swepston 14 rays 1 yard of green	10s.
n John Fekenham 16 rays 1 yard 1 quarter of green	10s.
n John Grymmesby 8 rays half yard half quarter of green	6s.
n John Barnewell at the Chequer in Fenchurch Street 10 rays 3 quarters of green	7s. 8d.
n John Barstone 8 rays half yard half quarter of green	6s.
n John de Van 8 rays half yard half quarter of green	6s.
n John Heylond 8 rays half yard half quarter of green	6s.
n John Bugby 8 rays half yard half quarter of green	6s.
n John More at Aldersgate 8 rays half yard half quarter of green	6s.
n John Toke for 9 rays half yard half quarter of green	6s. 8d.
n John Southmede 8 rays half yard half quarter of green	6s. 8d.
n John Hardyng of Holborn 8 rays half yard half quarter of green	6s.

[240] [f. 75v]

n John Turvey 9 rays half yard half quarter of green	6s. 8d.
n John Serle 6 rays half yard of green[339]	5s.
n John Parker 8 rays half yard half quarter of green	6s.
n John Luke 9 rays half yard half quarter of green	6s. 8d.
n John Lumbard 9 rays half yard half quarter of green	6s. 8d.
n Jacob Tolven 8 rays half yard half quarter of green	6s.
n John de Kent, cooper, 10 rays 3 quarters of green	8s.
n John Brownyng 9 rays half yard half quarter of green	6s. 8d.
n John Sonder 8 rays half yard half quarter of green	6s. 8d.
n John Thomas 8 rays half yard half quarter of green	6s.
n John Bayly 8 rays half yard half quarter of green	6s.
n John More in White Cross Street 8 rays half yard half quarter of green	6s.
n Jacob Itecombe 8 rays half yard half quarter of green	6s.
n John Pamplionne 9 rays half yard half quarter of green	6s. 8d.
John Aleyn beside the Augustinian Friars 9 rays half yard half quarter of green	6s. 8d.
John de Lynne 8 rays half yard half quarter of green	5s. 8d.
John Hanselappe 8 rays half yard half quarter of green	6s.
John Quintyn 9 rays half yard half quarter of green	6s. 8d.
John Jacob 8 rays half yard half quarter of green	6s.
John Davy 7 rays half yard half quarter of green	5s. 6d.
John Riche, tailor, 7 rays half yard half quarter of green	5s. 6d.
John Norman 7 rays half yard half quarter of green	5s. 6d.
John Waghorne 8 rays half yard half quarter of green	6s.
John Gedenay 9 rays half yard half quarter of green	6s.
Ivy Jacow 9 rays half yard half quarter of green	6s. 8d.
John Goldryng 9 rays half yard half quarter of green	6s. 8d.
John Aston 12 rays 3 quarters of green	10s.
John Gibbes 9 rays half yard half quarter of green	6s. 8d.
John Boys, chapman, 10 rays 3 quarters half of green	10s.

[339] All names are preceded by a dot except for Serle, Parker, Pamplione, Aleyne beside the Friars, Gibbs and Boys, on this page.

n John Kyllom 8 rays half yard half quarter of green   6*s.*
n John William 9 rays half yard half quarter of green   6*s.* 8*d.*

Hoods
n Katherine Wyrgeyne 1 yard of green   5*s.*

L & K. Rays 1,616
Colour 129 yards
Money £61 11s. 8d.

[241] Gowns
n Michael Eve 32 rays 2 yards half of green   24*s.*
n Michael Tregononne 32 rays 2 yards 1 quarter of green   24*s.*

Item Gowns
n Nicholas Muryell 28 rays 2 yards of green   20*s.*
n Nicholas Goonmailok 28 rays 2 yards 1 quarter of green   22*s.*
n Nicholas Fuller 36 rays 2 yards half of green   26*s.* 8*d.*

Hoods
n Nicholas Aleyn 8 rays half yard half quarter of green   6*s.*
n Nicholas Merton 12 rays 1 yard of green   9*s.*

Gowns
n Peter Carpenter 36 rays 3 yards of green   26*s.* 8*d.*
n Peter Heyford 8 rays 5 yards half green   28*s.*

Hoods
n Philip Godfrey 8 rays half yard half quarter of green   6*s.*
n Peter Roos 10 rays 3 quarters of green   8*s.*

L. Rays 238
Colour 23 yards
Money £10 0s. 4d.

[242] [f. 76r]
Gowns
n Robert Smyth with his wife 45 rays 4 yards of green   34*s.* 8*d.*
n Robert Hylton 36 rays 3 yards of green   26*s.* 8*d.*
n Richard Aleyn 36 rays 3 yards of green   26*s.* 8*d.*
n Robert Nikke 36 rays 3 yards of green   26*s.* 8*d.*
n Robert Elkyn 39 rays 3 yards of green   27*s.* 6*d.*
n Robert Carpenter 35 rays 2 yards half of green   25*s.*
n Randolf Mark 37 rays 2 yards half of green   26*s.* 6*d.*
n Robert Gilys 33 rays 2 yards half of green   24*s.* 4*d.*
n Roger Swannefelde 36 rays 3 yards of green   26*s.* 8*d.*
n Richard Lucas 36 rays 3 yards of green   26*s.* 8*d.*
n Randolph Palmer 36 rays 3 yards of green   24*s.*
n Richard Shirwood 28 rays 2 yards of green   22*s.*

[*English*: Robert Steinton, priest, 4 yards half of green   16s. 10½d.][340]

[243]
Hoods

n Robert Myles, maltman, 7 rays half yard of green	6s.
n Roger Blissott 10 rays 3 quarters of green	8s.
n Robert Bullard 11 rays 3 quarters of green	8s. 6d.
n Richard Osbarne 1 yard of green	5s.
n Richard Carrowe 9 rays half yard half quarter of green	6s. 8d.
n Robert Tanner 9 rays half yard half quarter of green	6s. 8d.
n Robert Walram 9 rays half yard half quarter of green	6s. 8d.
n Richard Harlowe 9 rays half yard half quarter of green	6s. 8d.
n Roger Baronne 9 rays half yard half quarter of green	6s. 8d.
n Richard West 8 rays half yard half quarter of green	6s.
n Robert Pede 8 rays half yard half quarter of green	6s.
n Robert Dellowe 8 rays half yard half quarter of green	6s.
n Richard Tyrell 8 rays half yard half quarter of green	6s.
n Richard Crosse 8 rays half yard half quarter of green	6s.
n Robert Lynford 6 rays half yard of green	5s.
n Robert Dorewell 8 rays half yard half quarter of green	6s.
n Roger Ware 9 rays half yard half quarter of green	6s. 8d.
n Richard Tyler, maltman, 9 rays half yard half quarter of green	6s. 8d.
n Robert Swyere 8 rays half yard half quarter of green	6s.
n Robert Ketyng 10 rays half yard half quarter of green	8s.
n Richard Waltham 1 yard half of green	7s.
n Rose, servant with William Porlond, 1 yard of green	5s.
n Richard Frepus 6 rays half yard of green	6s.
n Robert Charleton, sergeant, 1 yard 1 quarter of green	4s.
n Roger Awdymere 12 rays 3 quarters of green	10s.

[244]
Gowns

n Simon Potkyn 32 rays 2 yards 1 quarter of green	24s.
n Stephen Clean 32 rays 2 yards 1 quarter of green	24s.

Hoods

n Simon atte Well 6 rays half yard of green	5s.
n Stephen Roo 8 rays half yard half quarter of green	6s.
n Simon Petesyn 9 rays half yard half quarter of green	6s. 8d.
n Simon Herry 8 rays half yard half quarter of green	6s.

[R & S] Rays 709
Colour 60 yards and a quarter
Money £27 10s. 2d.

[340]   This entry was added in a different hand, without a dot before the sum of money. The same quantities and sum for Dominus [Sir] Robert Steynton were scored earlier **[236]**. Dots precede the names of: Myles, Ballard, Osbarn, Carrowe, Walram, Harlowe, Barron, West, Pede, Dellowe, Tyrell, Lynford, Dorewell, Tyler, Swyere, Frepurs, Charleton, Awdymere, atte Well, Roo, Petesyn and Herry.

[245] [f. 76v]
Gowns

n Thomas Hancok 36 rays 3 yards of green[341] 26s. 8d.
n Thomas Yole 27 rays 2 yards of green 21s.
n Thomas Haccher 36 rays 3 yards of green 26s. 8d.
n Thomas Grene 36 rays 3 yards of green 26s. 8d.
n Thomas Emond 32 rays 2 yards half of green 24s.
n Thomas Aleyn 36 rays 3 yards of green 26s. 8d.
n Thomas Godyng 26 rays 2 yards half quarter of green 20s.
n Thomas Ayle 28 rays 2 yards of green 20s. 8d.
n Thomas Kyrtot 34 rays 2 yards 3 quarters of green 25s.

Hoods

n Thomas Donyngton, sergeant, 10 rays 3 quarters of green 5s.
n Thomas Gratley 9 rays 3s. 4d.
n Thomas Merssh 8 rays half yard half quarter of green 6s. 8d.
n Thomas Smyth 8 rays half yard half quarter of green 6s.
n Thomas Molton de Aldgate Street 8 rays half yard half quarter of green 6s.
n Thomas North 8 rays half yard half quarter of green 6s.
n Thomas Bristowe 8 rays half yard half quarter of green 6s.
n Thomas Penson 9 rays half yard half quarter of green 6s. 8d.
n Thomas Howe, maltman, 9 rays half yard half quarter of green 6s. 8d.
n Thomas Melton de Yaxley in the county of Huntingdonshire 9 rays
half yard half quarter of green 6s. 8d.

Rays 377
Colour 29 yards half quarter
Money £13 16s. 4d.

[246]
Gowns

n William Crane 36 rays 3 yards of green 26s. 8d.
n William Porlond 6 yards of green 22s. 6d.
n William Petevile 32 rays 2 yards 1 quarter of green 24s.
n William Payn 36 rays 3 yards of green 26s. 8d.
n William Ferrour at the Maid 36 rays 3 yards of green 26s. 8d.
n William Bodevyle 33 rays 2 yards 1 quarter of green 25s.
n William Eyre 34 rays 2 yards 1 quarter of green 23s. 8d.
n William atte Wode 36 rays 3 yards of green 26s. 8d.
n William Claisson 36 rays 3 yards of green 26s. 8d.
n William Canonne 32 rays 2 yards 1 quarter of green 25s.
n William Bell 36 rays 3 yards of green 26s. 8d.
n William Copwod 32 rays 2 yards half quarter of green 24s.
n William Boteler 32 rays 2 yards 1 quarter of green 24s.
n William Bayly 28 rays 2 yards of green 21s.

341 On this page there were no preceding dots in the first list under Gowns. Dots precede
all but Thomas Smyth under Hoods; dots precede Eyre, Copwod, Boteler, Mascall
and William Robert under Gowns, and dots precede the names of Devenyssh, Geffray,
Baconne and Style under Hoods.

n William Ferrour Junior 34 rays 2 yards 3 quarters of green — 25*s*.
n William atte Well 32 rays 2 yards 1 quarter of green — 24*s*.
n William Grosse 32 rays 2 yards half of green — 24*s*.
n William Dowedale 36 rays 3 yards of green — 26*s*. 8*d*.
n William Mascall 25 rays 1 yard half & half quarter of green — 19*s*.
n William Robert 37 rays 2 yards half of green — 26*s*. 8*d*.

Hoods

n William Misterton 8 rays half yard half quarter of green — 6*s*. 8*d*.
n William Devenyssh 8 rays half yard of green — 6*s*.
n William Harry 8 rays half yard half quarter of green — 6*s*.
n William Rose 9 rays half yard half quarter of green — 6*s*. 8*d*.
n William Geffray 8 rays half yard half quarter of green — 6*s*.
n William Baconn 9 rays half yard half quarter of green — 6*s*. 8*d*.
n William Style 8 rays half yard half quarter of green — 6*s*.

[247] [f. 77r]
R. Smyth, W. Crane, H. Neel, J. Philippe.

n William Lacy 10 rays 3 quarters of green — 8*s*.
n William Reponne 10 rays half yard half quarter of green — 6*s*. 8*d*.
n William Andrew 7 rays half yard of green — 5*s*. 6*d*.
n William Termeday 9 rays half yard half quarter of green — 6*s*. 8*d*.
n William Robert 8 rays half yard half quarter of green — 6*s*.
n William Hyll 8 rays half yard half quarter of green — 6*s*.
n William Ryche 8 rays half yard half quarter of green — 6*s*.
n William Pompe 9 rays half yard half quarter of green — 6*s*. 8*d*.
n William Totewell 9 rays half yard half quarter of green — 6*s*. 8*d*.
n William Frank 8 rays half yard half quarter of green — 6*s*.
n William Illyng 9 rays half yard half quarter of green — 6*s*. 8*d*.
n William Pethin 9 rays half yard half quarter of green — 5*s*.
n Walter Colshull 9 rays half yard half quarter of green — 6*s*. 8*d*.
n William Bernard 8 rays half yard half quarter of green — 6*s*.
n William Watford 8 rays half yard half quarter of green — 6*s*.
n William Rawlyn 10 rays 3 quarters of green — 8*s*.
n William Myles, maltman, 9 rays half yard half quarter of green — 6*s*.
n William Smalsho 7 rays half yard half quarter green[342] — 5*s*. 6*d*.

W Rays 857
Colour 69 yards half & half quarter
Money £31 12s. 6d.

Sum total of outgoings to the draper   **Rays 4,212**
Colour 352 yards 1 quarter half
Money £161 17s. 4½d.

Examined.

---

[342]   In this section dots precede all names except for William Robert, William Pompe, Walter Colshull, William Bernard and William Watford.

Note that the sum of rays received from the draper of London was   4,309
Of which 4,212 were delivered to diverse persons for their gowns and hoods
And the remainder is   97 rays
The sum of green coloured cloth received from various people was
    356 yards half & half quarter
From which delivery was made to diverse people, as above,   352 yards 1 quarter & half
And the remainder is as above, 4 yards 1 quarter
And so as for the said 97 rays and 4 yards 1 quarter of green cloth that were not
delivered, as above, nor found in storage: it is believed and thought that they were
missing from their deliberations by negligent receipt and counting, or that these were
taken away by Guy Bribour. Therefore precautions are to be taken in future.

[248] [f. 77v]
[English]
   **Unto our most sovereign Lord the King and to his full noble, wise and
   discreet council** Examined.[343]

The victuallers the Brewers of the city of London, meekly beseech that for as much
as the said victuallers serve you, Sovereign Lord, as well as others of your lords,
both spiritual and temporal, with other of your liege's, dwelling and abiding within
the said city, the which victuallers buy their chief stuff, that is to say malt, at great
disadvantage, in so much as the sellers of malt diversely deceive the said victuallers
in selling of bellied malt, that is to say stiff malt, that never came [*to ripeness*],
also raw malt, that is to say malt that has not had its full drying, which does much
deceit in brewing and is the cause of making long[344] ale. Also of malt that is of
barley *mowe* burnt that is to say corn that is [*above the line*: wet] in the field and
shows coming[345] and is housed wet. Also they sell hedgerow corn that never had
the full making. Also they sell acre spired malt, that is to say malt that runs out of
both ends.[346] Also wynnel eaten malt, that is to say with worms of dusty malt, with
drawk, darnel, kerlok seed and cockle, of unclean malt, that is to say with small
stones, congealed earth and gravel. And the said Brewers now have only 8 rase[347]
otherwise called 8 bushel strikes of malt for the quarter [*with*] filth and other, where
they were ever used to have 9 bushels [*above the line*: to the quarter], because of
the filth. So that the said Brewers have now only 7 bushels for the quarter of clean
malt, because they must cleanse it, to the great harm and prejudice of all such buyers
of any such malt, as is openly shown, and for as much as all these defaults were
openly proved before this time, the said victuallers had 9 bushels for the quarter,
which 9 bushels after the cleansing contain only 8 rase of clean malt, that is to say
8 bushels. And whereas the aforesaid beseechers, finding themselves sorely hurt and
grieved in the buying of such malt, put up various bills to the commons of this realm
in this last Parliament, praying them to make a supplication to you, our sovereign

---

343   This copy of a petition about the selling of malt is probably a later insertion. It is similar
      in content and handwriting to earlier drafts, see **[106]**, **[107]**, **[110]**, **[111]** and **[187]**, and
      to the copy of the Charter of Fishmongers, which was dated c. 1433. See **[232–3]**.
344   Weak?
345   Shows ripeness and is taken for storage when still wet.
346   Malt grains that have not swollen.
347   Levelled as opposed to heaped measure.

Lord and to the other lords spiritual and temporal assembled in the said Parliament, showing the said grievous hurt and great deceit, praying for a remedy of the said mischiefs, whereas now, right Sovereign Lord, your said beseechers cannot but feel that their supplications have been rejected,

[249] [f. 78r]

befiled[348] and laid aside by certain persons, who for their singular advantage [*scored*: that they daily take and have in selling of their own malt] would suffer no remedy to be had for the great advantage that they take daily and have in selling their own malt, and thus your said beseechers are put off without any remedy [*above the line*: ordained] or purveyed. May it please you, most sovereign lord, by the advice of your said full noble and right wise council, tenderly to consider the deceits and defaults aforesaid, daily found [*scored*: in such] in selling of such malt, and thereupon graciously to ordain that your said victuallers, the Brewers, may have 8 rase, that is to say 8 bushels of clean malt for the quarter, and that such malt as hereafter shall be put on sale be good and clean malt, or else that your said beseechers, will have more joy and buy their malt according to the measure, as they used to have and were accustomed to before this time, in recompense for the great dust and filth so continually found in such malt, any statute made to the contrary about this notwithstanding, and this for the love of God and in the way of charity.

[250] [f. 78v]
[*Latin*]
The names of those with sums for clothing pardoned

n Adam Copendale	3s. 6d.	**[251]**	
n Dederic Johnson	4s.	n Nicholas Muryell	8d.
n David Brownyng	2s. 8d.	n Nicholas Gommaylok	8d.
n Gilbert Botonne	4d.	n Nicholas Fuller	3s. 5d.
n Henry Grene	3s. 4d.	n Nicholas Mertonne	12d.
n Hugh Glene	½d.	n Peter Hayford	16d.
n Henry Rowe	8d.	n Philip Godfrey	12d.
n Henry Staple	2d.	n Peter Roos	16d.
n Henry Fereby	2d.	n Richard Aleyn	1d.
n Henry Wikkeston	5d.	n Robert Nikke	3s. 4d.
n Henry Bedell	2s. 1d.	n Randolph Mark	2s. 2d.
n John Masonne	8d.	n Robert Giles	8d.
n John Salter	2s. 2d.	n Roger Swanneffeld	10d.
n John Hopkyn	2d.	n Richard Lucas	2d.
n John Chapman	16d.	n Richard Shirewod	2s.
n John Caryonne	2d.	n Randolph Palmer	2s.
n John Reyner	5d.	n Robert Bullard	5d.
n John Newman	4d.	n Robert Walram	8d.
n John Stone	12d.	n Robert Pede	1d.
n John Brewstre	2s. 1d.	n Robert Dillawe	7½d.
n John Bedeford	13d.	n Robert Dorwell	12d.
n John Snell	2d.	n Robert Ketyng	12d.

[348] Made foul, defiled.

n John Frost	10*d.*	*n* Richard Carrowe	16*d.*
n John Humbre	8*d.*	*n* Richard Brynton by Kyllom	16*d.*
n John Pyken	2*d.*	*n* Richard Frepurs	2*s.*
n John Lenegro	1*d.*	*n* Roger Baronne	8*d.*
n John Bosevenan	13*d.*	*n* Simon Petevyn	8*d.*
n John Aleyn at the Crutched Friars	4*d.*	*n* Simon Herry	2*d.*
n John Yver	14*s.*	*n* Thomas Hancock	2*d.*
n John Riche de Fleet Street	2*d.*	*n* Thomas Pole	4*d.*
n John Reeffawe	2*s.* 3*d.*	*n* Thomas Hatcher	2*d.*
n John Wightmore	1*d.*	*n* Thomas Emond	2*d.*
n John Gibbes	22*d.*	*n* Thomas Aleyn	2*d.*
n John Sere	12*d.*	*n* Thomas Ayle	8*d.*
n John West	1*d.*	*n* Thomas Kyrtot	12*d.*
n John Dene	4*d.*	*n* Thomas Merssh	4*d.*
n John Bernewell	4½*d.*	*n* Thomas Bristowe	3*d.*
n John de Van	1*d.*	*n* Thomas Pensonne	8*d.*
n John Bugby	½*d.*	*n* Chareltonne	8*d.*
n John Southmede	8*d.*	*n* William Petevyle	2*d.*
n John Turveye	4*d.*	*n* William Payn	8*d.*
n John Lucas	1*d.*	*n* William Claysson	2*d.*
n John Lumbard	2*d.*	*n* William Canonne	8*d.*
n John Thomas	6*d.*	*n* William Best	1*d.*
n John Bayly	2*d.*	*n* William Boteler	12*d.*
n Jacob Itecombe	6*d.*	*n* William Bayly	12*d.*
n John Pamplionne	1*d.*	*n* William Ferrour Junior	20*d.*
n John Quyntyn	2*d.*	*n* William atte Well	1*d.*
n Ive Jacob	8*d.*	*n* William Grosse	2*s.*
n John Davy	2*d.*	*n* William Dowedale	1*d.*
n John Riche, tailor	6*d.*	*n* William Mascall	1*d.*
n John Geddenay	5*d.*	*n* William Herry	4*d.*
n John Goldryng	1*d.*	*n* William Rose	1*d.*
n Michael Tregononne	2*s.* 4*d.*	*n* William Geffray	2*d.*
		n William Baconne	½*d.*
		n William Style	4*d.*
		n William Andrewe	1*d.*
		n William Hill	1*d.*
		n William Pompe	5*d.*
		n William Frank	1*d.*
		n William Smalsho by J. Bedeford	2*s.* 2*d.*
		n William Bernard	4*d.*
		n William Rawlyn	8*d.*

Examined
Sum £5 15½*d.*

[f. 79r]

n Thomas Rodyer	–
n Thomas North	12*d.*
n Robert Squyere	4*d.*
n Will	–

[252]
Various vestments by gift and without payment

n Hugh Neel	34*s.* 8*d.*
n John Philippe	33*s.* 4*d.*
n Robert Smyth	34*s.* 8*d.*
n William Crane	26*s.* 8*d.*
n John Pekker, carpenter,[349]	25*s.*
n John Ryngesson	24*s.*
n William Porlond	22*s.* 6*d.*
n Gilbert, aletaker,	6*s.*
n John Boys	10*s.*
n John Hardy, cook,	6*s.* 8*d.*
n Richard Osbarn	5*s.* 8*d.*
n Robert Lynford	5*s.*
n Rose with W. P.[350]	5*s.*
n William Devenyssh	6*s.*
n William Ryparn	6*s.* 8*d.*

[*Added*: Robert Charletonne, sergeant, 4*s.*]
[*Added*: John Swypston 10*s.*]

Examined

£13 5s. 10d.

[*French*] This makes the total received in silver for clothing £29 0*s.* 2½*d.*

[253] [f. 79v]
[*French*] **The Ordinance for a Dinner called amongst us our Feast during this the second year of the reign of King Henry, the sixth after the Conquest** [1423–4].

The First Course	**The Second Course**
brawn with mustard	white mortrewes
cabbage in pottage	venison in broth
boiled chicken	cony with venison
swan	partridges with cocks
custard	large and small birds
	quince in pastry

The expenses of our said Feast in the same year
The Saturday
First, on the Saturday next before the Feast for Robert Smyth for oysters 6*d.*
Item for red herring baked   10*d.*

---

[349] John Pekker, carpenter, worked on Brewers' Hall but he proved expensive to hire and he failed to finish the work. Here he was given a livery gown by the Brewers, see J. Harvey, *Mediaeval Architects*, 230.
[350] Rose, servant of William Porlond, was granted this sum, probably for a livery hood. See **[243]**.

Item for 3 codling and 3 quarters of a halibut	6s. 2d.
Item for 1 conger	2s. 8d.
Item for 5 pike, 5 anguill and lampron	11s. 8d.
Item for 300 whelks	11d.
Item for herbs	1½d.
Item for mussels from William Porlond, clerk	5½d.

Sum 23s. 4d.

[254]
In the Pantry

First for cheat bread, payment for 2 quarters 2 bushels of flour at 17d., by John Philippe,	25s. 6d.
Item for white leavened bread	18d.
Item for bread called trencher bread,	10d.
Item for 3 bushels and half of coarse flour for the pastry at 16d.,	4s. 8d.
Item for bread bought on two occasions as appears plainly	17d.

Sum 33s. 11d.

In the Buttery

First for 1 hogshead³⁵¹ of red wine bought by W. Crane and paid by W. Porlond	26s. 8d.
Item for half a gallon white wine bought by H. Neel and paid by W. Porlond	4d.
Item for Romonty³⁵² bought by the said H. Neel and Hardy and Devenyssh on two occasions and paid for by W. P.,	6d.
Item for 1 barrel of good ale and 1 barrel penny ale by Robert Smyth	7s.
Item for 2 barrels of good ale by William Crane	9s. 4d.
Item for 2 barrels of good ale by John Philippe	9s. 4d.
Item for 1 barrel of good ale by Hugh Neel	4s. 8d.
Item for 6 dozen hanaps, new and white at 8d., bought by W. Porlond,	4s.
Item for 2 earthenware pots at 4d.,	8d.
Item for 2 barrels of sousing ale by John Philippe	2s.
Item for 1 kilderkin of penny ale by Hugh Neel	12d.
Item for tunnage³⁵³ of the hogshead of wine abovesaid 8d. & for portage of the same, 4d., in total	12d.

Sum 66s. 6d.

[255] [f. 8or]
In the kitchen

First for 1 boar, bought by John Philippe and paid for by William Porlond	15s.
Item for scalding the same and another given as a present, paid for by J. Philippe	16d.
Item for cabbages in pottage, 8 large, paid by W. Porlond	2s. 6d.

351	Large cask, approximately sixty-three wine gallons in 1423.
352	Sweet wine. Romeney.
353	Tax or duty upon casks or tuns of imported wine.

Item for 5 dozen marrow bones at 10s., and 2 gallons of fresh grease at 2s. 4d.,	12s. 4d.
Item for 2 rounds of beef	6d.
Item for 1 sirloin of beef	10d.
Item for half a sheep	10d.
Item for 6 pestles³⁵⁴ of pork,	16d.
Item for 6 neats tallow, guts and entrails	14d.
Item for 5 quince for meat in pastry	4s. 2d.
Item for 15 gallons of cream at 4d.,	5s.
Item for 2 gallons and half of honey at 16d.,	3s. 6d.
Item for 5 dozen marrow bones bought by Hardy, Cook, and paid for by W. Crane	10s.
Item for 6 ells of Schewescherclorh³⁵⁵ at	5d.
2 yards of Buttelcloth³⁵⁶ for strainers at	3d.
2 and a half ells³⁵⁷ of Brabant cloth at	7d.
8 ells of straight cloth at	4d.
2 ells of white Flemish cloth at	7½d.
and 3 ells of strait cloth at 4d. for hogsheads, hangings, aprons, strainers and necessaries for various offices bought by William Crane, 12d.,	9s. 4½d.
Item paid by W[illiam]³⁵⁸ for scalding the 2 boars abovesaid, for William Crane	4d.

Sum 68s. 2½d.

[256]
In Poultry

First for 7 dozen and 2 coneys at various prices paid by W. Crane & J. Philippe	16s. 5d.
Item for 24 cygnets at 4s.,	£4 16s.
Item for 3 dozen and 6 partridges at 5s., with 6d. rebated on payment	17s.
Item for 3 dozen and 6 woodcocks and plovers at 4s., 8d. rebated as before,	13s. 4d.
Item for 6 dozen large and great birds	3s. 4d.
Item for 24 dozen larks	10s.
Item for 8 dozen *puliynes*³⁵⁹ bought for 12s., and rebated on payment by 12d.,	11s.
Item for 700 eggs at 12d., 4d. rebated on payment,	6s. 8d.
Item for 12 capons bought by Hugh Neel and paid for by W. Porlond	6s. 2d.
Item for 12 capons bought by Robert Smyth	4s. 5d.

Sum £9 4s. 4d.

Sauces

First for 1 gallon and 1 quart mustard	5d.
Item for 1 gallon vinegar	4d.
Item for 1 gallon half vert juice	6d.

³⁵⁴	Forelegs.
³⁵⁵	Cheesecloth?
³⁵⁶	Butter cloth?
³⁵⁷	Brabant cloth. Ell: English measure of cloth, 45 inches.
³⁵⁸	Porlond.
³⁵⁹	Pullets?

Item for half a gallon ginger sauce	3*d.*
Item for half bushel *Beresflet* salt	6*d.*
Item for Salersalt³⁶⁰	3*d.*
Item for 1 peck onions	2½*d.*
Item for packthread for roasting	3*d.*
Item for green sauce	2*d.*
Item for 1 pint of honey	2*d.*
Item for 1 quart of neat oil	4*d.*

Sum 3s. 4½d.

[257] [f. 8ov]
The Scullery

First for 3 bushels of charcoal for the Monday at 2*d.*,	6*d.*
Item for 6 quarters of coal through William Porlond at 8½*d.*,	4*s.* 3*d.*
Item for 100 faggots	4*s.*
Item for [?] herbs to diverse persons	2*d.*
Item for 12 dozen pewter vessels, garnished beforehand for the feast at 6*d.*,	6*s.*
Item for 4 dozen chargers [*garnished*] beforehand as before	16*d.*
Item for 1 dozen plates garnished and 2 dishes garnished at 7*d.*,	21*d.*
Item to a pewterer for 2 dozen [?]sauces singly	5*d.*

Sum 18s. 5d.

Spices

First for 1 lb pepper	19*d.*
Item for 1 quarteron saffron	3*s.*
Item for half lb ginger in powder	9*d.*
Item for half lb canell in powder	14*d.*
Item for 1 quarteron of cloves and mace	7*d.*
Item for 12 lbs garden almonds	2*s.* 6*d.*
Item for 3 lbs raisins of Corinth	2*s.*
Item for 10 lbs dates	2*s.* 6*d.*
Item for 2 ounces sanders	2*d.*
Item for a half lb aniseed confit crisp	12*d.*
Item for 2 lbs sugar *casson*	2*s.*

Sum 17s. 3d.

[258]
The various costs and foreign payments³⁶¹

First to William Lent and his companions for an interlude with players	7*s.*
Item to William Devenyssh for his labour in the pantry	3*s.* 4*d.*
Item to the said William Devenyssh for the amendment of the dossers in the hall	12*d.*

---

³⁶⁰ Cellar salt?
³⁶¹ Payments outside the Brewers' usual circle.

Item to Rows, tailor, for the same *loneraigne* for 2 days[362]	12d.
Item to the said Rows for rings, tenterhooks, lyor,[363] blue thread, wire and other things at	8d.
Item to the same Rows for his labour in the pantry with Devenyssh	20d.
Item to John Hardy, Cook, and his companions for their labour in the kitchen	22s. 4d.
Item to John Dene for his labour in the buttery	20d.
Item to William Ryponne in the buttery	2s. 4d.
Item to Thomas Clerc, servant, in the pantry for his labour	12d.
Item to John Hill, porter, for various victuals & for his labour	10d.
Item to various *turnbrochers* for their labour	21d.
Item to 2 labourers in the kitchen for 1 day	4d.
Item to John Goodfelowe for 1 week before the feast and also afterwards for his labour	12d.
Item to a woman dish washer for her labour	3d.
Item to 3 women on the eve of the Feast for laying rushes and making the hall clean	3d.
Item to 1 labourer for various necessary work in the same place	3d.
Item for carriage of dung also by day	4d.
Item to the porter at our gate for his labour	12d.
Item to a water bearer for carrying water from the conduit for his labour	2s.
Item for 6 loads of Thames water in bouges	6d.
Item paid to Kingeston Sueys for our Feast for his reward	8d.
Item paid for rushes bought by Robert Smyth with carriage for 8 rounds etc.,	2s. 8d.
Item for 7 lbs cotton candle at 1½d., spent in various offices, with wax and handling	10½d.
Item for laundry of diverse napery after the Feast and for a certain breakfast beforehand	18d.
Item for [?hg] half a bushel of salt & water & for the pullets, good corn, and meat for the same preceding breakfast	22d.
Item for 3 birch brooms bought for the feast	1½d.

Sum 58s. 2d.

Sum total £23 13s. 6d. paid.

[259] [f. 81r]
[Latin]
The names of brothers and sisters and others present at our Feast in the said second year [1423–4] as appears in the following

Alexander Marcowe	16d.			
Agnes Bugge	12d.	**[260]**		
		Juliana Hatersete, widow,	12d.	
Baldewyne Hoper	16d.	Johanna the wife of John Amwell	12d.	
Dederic Johnson	16d.	Katherine Wyrgeyn	12d.	

---

362 Decoration or ordering?
363 Cloth from Lier in Flanders.

Henry Rows with his wife	2s.	Michael Tregononne with his wife	2s.
Henry Trobolans with his wife	2s.	Michael Eve with his wife	2s.
Henry Stapill	16d.	Margaret Burne	12d.
Henry Bedell	16d.		
Henry Boston, mason,	20d.	Nicholas Muryell	16d.
Henry Noble	14d.	Nicholas Agonmaylok	16d.
Hugh Glene	16d.		
		Peter Carpenter with his wife	2s.
John Ketyng with his wife	2s.	Peter Roos	16d.
John Fekenham with his wife	2s.	Peter Hayford	12d.
John Elcy with his wife	2s.	Peter Short	12d.
John Aston with his wife	2s.	Philip Godfrey	12d.
John Masonne with his wife	2s.		
John Riche de Fleet Street with his wife	2s.	Robert Ketyng with his wife	2s.
John Spenser with his wife	2s.	Robert Elkyn with his wife	2s.
John Pyken with his wife	20d.	Robert Hylton with his wife	2s.
John Luke with his wife	2s.	Robert Calowe, shearman, with his wife	2s.
John Turvey with his wife	2s.	Robert Nikke	16d.
John Bosevenen with his wife	2s.	Robert Walram	16d.
John Brewster with his wife	2s.	Robert Carpenter	12d.
John Humber with his wife	2s.	Robert Pede	16d.
John Hopkyn with his wife	2s.	Robert Mayhewe	15d.
John Spore	16d.	Robert Delowe	16d.
John Laurence	16d.	Richard Lucas with his wife	2s.
John Mabyle	16d.	Richard Aleyn with his wife	2s.
John Yver	16d.	Richard Frepurs	16d.
John Ser, glover,	16d.	Richard Harlowe	16d.
John Brook	16d.	Roger Baronne	16d.
John Bassett	12d.	Randolph Mark	16d.
John Caryonne	16d.		
John Stokes	16d.	Stephen Clean	16d.
John Stone	16d.	Stephen Roo	16d.
John Bedford	12d.	Simon Potekyn	12d.
John Wake	16d.		
John Riche de Wood Street	12d.	Thomas Hancok with his wife	2s.
John Serle	12d.	Thomas Grene with his wife	2s.
John Holbek	16d.	Thomas Godyng with his wife	2s.
John Parker	16d.	Thomas Emond	12d.
John Salter	12d.	Thomas Aleyn	15½d.
John Eylond	16d.	Thomas North	16d.
John Barneweld	16d.	Thomas Hatcher	12d.
John Quyntyn	12d.	Thomas Kyrtot	16d.
John Jacob	16d.		
John Hanslape	16d.	William atte Well with his wife	2s.
John Lumbard	16d.	William Smalsho with his wife	2s.
John Sharp, maltman,	16d.	William Baconne with his wife	2s.
Jacob Tolven	16d.	William Bayle with his wife	2s.
John Riche, tailor,	16d.	William Dowdale with his wife	2s.

William Ferrour Senior with his wife	2s.
William Grosse with his wife	2s.
William Canonne	12d.
William Eyre	16d.
William atte Wode	12d.
William Harry	12d.

[261] [f. 81v]
The names of those present at our Feast

William Rose	16d.
William Bodevyle	16d.
William Calston, plumber	16d.
William Ferrour Junior	16d.
William Rawlyn	16d.
William Termeday	14d.
William Pompe	16d.
Walter Colshull with his wife	2s.
The widow of William Ederiche	2s.
The wife of John Bate, fishmonger	16d.

The names of those present there and not paying
The Prior of the Augustinian Friars
Adam, rector of the church of All Hallows London Wall
Sir William Goodswayn, rector of the church of [*St Mary*] Woolnoth[364]
Sir Robert Steynton
Robert Smyth
Hugh Neel
John Philippe
William Crane
John Turner, shearman
The daughter of the wife of Robert Smyth
The daughter of Robert Smyth
A woman, servant with Agnes Bugge
John Burton
Wenge Dedellus, tailor
4 players with 3 minstrels
Gilbert, aletaker
Idonea, former servant of William Ederich
Thomas Driffeld

Sum total received for the feast
£8 6s. 10½d.

William Copwod, maltman,	16d.

[[*Latin*] Not entered.]

Pardons made to various persons for the tax for the feast

John Pyken	4d.
Simon Potekyn	4d.
John Salter	4d.
Agnes Bugge	4d.
Katherine Wirgeyn	4d.
Peter Short	4d.
John Bedeford	4d.
Robert Mayhew	1d.
Philip Godfray	4d.
Henry Noble	2d.
Johanna Ambewell	4d.
William Termeday	2d.
Thomas Aleyn	½d.

Sum of pardons for the feast 3s. 5½d.

---

[364]   Rector, St Mary Woolnoth 1417–28 (d. 1428–9). Hennessy, *London Clergy*, 314–15.

John Berkyng, Friar
The wife of William Crane
The wife of Robert Smyth
Thomas Donyngton, sergeant
The wife of Hugh Neel
William Pethin
Isabell Corniche, Fleming
John Pekker, carpenter
John Rynggsson
A certain glazier
Johanna Awmbele
Robert Tanner
John Swypstonne with his wife
William Hanyngton, tiler.
    Examined.

[262] [f. 82r]
The Account of R. Smyth, W. Crane, H. Neel and J. Philippe.

The names of the brothers and sisters paying their quarterage during the time of William Walderne being mayor of the city of London [1422–3] and the aforesaid Robert Smyth, William Crane, Hugh Neel and John Philippe were Masters of the craft, during the second year of the reign of King Henry, the sixth after the Conquest [1423–4].

Adam Copendale and Emma his wife	2s.	Henry Wykston, fishmonger,	12d.
		Henry Staple	12d.
Alexander Myles and Isabella his wife	2s.	Hugh Glene and Margaret his wife	2s.
Alexander Marcow	12d.	Hugh Neel and Emma his wife	2s.
Alan John and Johanna his wife	2s.		
		John Pyken and Alice his wife	2s.
Agnes Strattonne	12d.	John More at Aldersgate and	
Agnes Bugge	12d.	Cristiana his wife	2s.
Agnes Carletonne	12d.	John Randolf and Juliana his wife	2s.
Agnes the widow of Walter Riche	12d.	John Riche de Wood Street and Margaret his wife	2s.
Alice the widow of William John	12d.	John Frost and Alice his wife	2s.
Alice Hore	12d.	John Humber and Margaret his wife	2s.
Alice the widow of William Bolton	12d.	John Riche, tailor, and Alice his wife	2s.
		John Benge and Alice his wife	2s.
Baldewyne Hoper and Johanna his wife	2s.	John Brewster and Johanna his wife	2s.
		John Toke and Alice his wife	2s.
		John Holbek and Margaret his wife	2s.
Cristiana the widow of John Ballard	12d.	John Caryonne and Alice his wife	2s.
		John Philippe and Margaret his wife	2s.
		John Ketyng and Margaret his wife	2s.
Sir Adam Dalton, Rector	12d.	John Goldryng and Johanna his	
Sir Robert Steynton	12d.	wife	2s.

211

Dederic Johnson and Weveyn his wife	2*s.*	John Qwyntyn and Katherine his wife	2*s.*
Dionysia Barthorpe	12*d.*	John Elcy and Alice his wife	2*s.*
		John Eylond and Dionysia his wife	2*s.*
Elizabeth Colbrook	12*d.*	John Reyner and Agatha his wife	2*s.*
Emma Canonne	12*d.*	John Castonne and Agnes his wife	2*s.*
		John Masonne and Felicia his wife	2*s.*
Henry Trebolans and Elizabeth his wife	2*s.*	John Spenser and Margaret his wife	2*s.*
		John Salter and Johanna his wife	2*s.*
Henry Rous and Johanna his wife	2*s.*	John Warsoppe and Agnes his wife	2*s.*
Henry Lymber and Felicia his wife	2*s.*	John Lumbard and Margaret his wife	2*s.*
Henry Bedell and Alice his wife	2*s.*	John Stone and Agnes his wife	2*s.*
Henry Grene and Agnes his wife	2*s.*		
Henry Noble and Agnes his wife	2*s.*	John Tregelowe and Johanna his wife	2*s.*
		John Reeffawe and Juliana his wife	2*s.*
		John Broke and Cristiana his wife	2*s.*
		John Aston and Matilda his wife	2*s.*
		John Jacob and Alice his wife	2*s.*
		John William and Johanna his wife	2*s.*
		John Riche Junior de Fleet Street and Mathia his wife	2*s.*
		John Turvey and Margaret his wife	2*s.*
		John Russell and Alice his wife	2*s.*
		John Chapman and Juliana his wife	2*s.*
		John Wyghtmour and Johanna his wife	2*s.*

[263] [f. 82v]

John Basset	12*d.*	Morris Tranaill & Margaret his wife	2*s.*
John Southmede	12*d.*	Margaret the widow of John Thetford	12*d.*
John Pamplyonne	12*d.*		
John Kenaky	12*d.*		
John Gedeney	12*d.*	Nicholas Agomnaylok and Johanna his wife	2*s.*
John Snell	12*d.*		
John Lynne	12*d.*	Nicholas Fuller and Alice his wife	2*s.*
John Assh	12*d.*	Nicholas Muryell and Agnes his wife	2*s.*
John Ratford, glover,	12*d.*		
John Hardyng	12*d.*		
John Hardy, Cook,	12*d.*	Nicholas Merton for his wife	12*d.*
John Sonder	12*d.*	Nicholas Aleyn	12*d.*
John Serle	12*d.*		
John Hopken	12*d.*	Peter Carpenter and Katherine his wife	2*s.*
John de Dene	12*d.*		
John West	12*d.*	Peter Short and Alice his wife	2*s.*
John Mabyle	12*d.*	Peter Hayford and Matilda his wife	2*s.*
John Turnour, shearman,	12*d.*		
John Laurence	12*d.*	Peter Andrew	12*d.*
John Ryngesson	12*d.*	Peter Roos	12*d.*
John de Van	12*d.*		

John Lucas	12d.	Philip Godfrey	12d.
John Bronnyng	12d.		
John Sire, glover,	12d.	Richard Shirwode and Alice his	
John Bargonne	12d.	wife	12d.
John Bate	12d.	Richard Terill and Isabella his wife	2s.
John Bedford	12d.	Richard Lucas and Alice his wife	2s.
John Baily	12d.	Richard Carowe and Elizabeth	
John Hanslappe	12d.	his wife	2s.
		Richard Aleyn and Johanna his wife	2s.
Jacob Levegro	12d.	Richard Harlowe and Johanna his	
		wife	2s.
Johanna the wife of John			
Amwell, skinner,	12d.	Robert Elkyn and Cecilia his wife	2s.
Johanna Rothyng	12d.	Robert Smyth and Anna his wife	2s.
Johanna Horold, widow of John		Robert Pede and Alice his wife	2s.
Turmyn	12d.	Robert Nikke and Alice his wife	2s.
Johanna Awmbele	12d.	Robert Carpenter and Margaret	
		his wife	2s.
Idonea Hatton	12d.	Robert Delowe and Margaret his	
		wife	2s.
Juliana Hetersete	12d.	Robert Gyles and Johanna his wife	2s.
		Robert Hilton and Margaret his	
Michael Eve and Elizabeth his wife	2s.	wife	2s.
Michael Tregonnone	12d.	Robert Ketyng and Margery his	
		wife	2s.
		Robert Mayhew and Juliana his	
		wife	2s.
		Roger Ware and Alice his wife	2s.
		Roger Blissote and Matilda his wife	2s.
		Randolph Mark and Rose his wife	2s.

[264] [f. 83r]
R. Smyth, W. Crane, J. Philippe, H. Neel.

Richard Crosse	12d.	William Porlond and Dionisia, wife	2s.
Richard Bryntonne	12d.	William Bailly and Alice his wife	2s.
Richard Frepurs	12d.	William Botiller and Elizabeth	
		his wife	2s.
Robert Walram	12d.	William atte Wode and Katherine	
Robert Jewell, grocer,	12d.	his wife	2s.
		William Grosse and Katherine	
Roger Baronne	12d.	his wife	2s.
		William Harry and Agnes his wife	2s.
Simon Potekyn and Matilda his wife	2s.	William Rose and Johanna his wife	2s.
Simon Petesyn and Isabella his wife	2s.	William Ederich and Alice his wife	2s.
		William Dowdale and Johanna	
Simon atte Welle	12d.	his wife	2s.

Stephen Clean	12*d.*	William Claisson and Isabella his	
Stephen Roo	12*d.*	wife	2*s.*
		William Crane and Helena his wife	2*s.*
Thomas Hatcher and Margaret		William Ferrour Juniour and	
his wife	2*s.*	Agnes his wife	2*s.*
Thomas Grene and Matilda his wife	2*s.*	William Canonne and Elizabeth	
Thomas Merssh and Agnes his wife	2*s.*	his wife	2*s.*
Thomas Yole and Alice his wife	2*s.*	William Petevyle and Johanna	
Thomas Hancok and Dionisia his		his wife	2*s.*
wife	2*s.*	William Reponne and Margery	
Thomas Aleyn and Letitia his wife	2*s.*	his wife	2*s.*
Thomas Godyng and Margaret			
his wife	2*s.*	Walter Colshull and Alice his wife	2*s.*
Thomas Dewy and Agnes his wife	2*s.*		
Thomas Edmond and Sibille his		William Overton	12*d.*
wife	2*s.*	William Watford	12*d.*
Thomas Gratley and Margaret his		William Bacon	12*d.*
wife	2*s.*	William Illyng	12*d.*
		William Devenyssh	8*d.*
Thomas Ayle	12*d.*	William Andrew, hosteler,	12*d.*
Thomas North	12*d.*	William Bodevyle	12*d.*
Thomas Pensonne	12*d.*	William Termeday	12*d.*
Thomas Bristowe	12*d.*	William Belle	12*d.*
Thomas Martyn	12*d.*	William Bernard	12*d.*
		William Mascall	12*d.*
William atte Well and Alice, wife	2*s.*	William Pompe	12*d.*
William Rawlyn and Alice, wife	2*s.*		
William Frank and Cecilia his wife	2*s.*	Walter Glyn	12*d.*
William Ferrour Senior and			
Agnes, wife	2*s.*	**Sum of Quarterage for this year**	
William Bullok and Johanna, wife	2*s.*	**£15 11*s.* 2*d.***	
William Bracy and Alice, wife	2*s.*		
William Geffrey and Anna, wife	2*s.*	[*English*] **Arrears leviable**[365]	
William Payn and Elena his wife	18*d.*	Johanna the wife of John	
		Fekenham	12*d.*
		John Waghorn	12*d.*
		Thomas Howe, maltman,	12*d.*
		William Copwod, maltman,	2*s.*

[265] [f. 83v]		
[*English*]		
Arrears not leviable by the time of	John More in Holborn	2*s.*
the aforesaid Robert Smyth, William	John Bray, butcher	12*d.*
Crane, John Philippe and Hugh Neel	Richard Welde	12*d.*
	Thomas Jakes	12*d.*
	William Smalsho	2*s.*

---

[365] 'Levable', now obsolete.

[266]
Parcels of rent received for the tenement near our great gate for 2 years, during the time of the said Robert Smyth and his fellows

First from John Stafford for the term of Easter in the 10th year of the reign of
King Henry V [1422]   5s. 10d.
And for the term of St John the Baptist in the same year, the tenement was
void without a tenant
Item from John Hevyngham for the term of Michaelmas in the first year of
the reign of King Henry VI [1422–3]   5s. 10d.
Item from the aforesaid John Hevyngham for the term of Christmas the same
year [1422]   5s. 10d.
Item from the said John for the term of Easter the same year [1423]   5s. 10d.

Sum 23s. 4d.

And after the same term of Easter, on the 6th day of May in the year [*the first?* 1422–3]
of King Henry VI, the same tenement was made and ordained to be an almshouse
for the poor brothers and sisters of the craft and fraternity of the Brewers of London,
by a common assent, granted, that is, to wit, by Robert Smyth, William Crane, Hugh
Nell, John Philippe, Masters of the craft and fraternity at that time, and John Reyner,
William atte Wode, John Masonne, John Broke, William Smalsho, Thomas Hatcher,
Robert Carpenter, John Piken and William Ferrour the Elder. And the aforesaid
Robert Smyth paid of his own good £10 to divide the house into diverse chambers,
as for masonry, carpentry and daubing of diverse walls, with paving of the kitchen
and making of the stone wall for the reredos,[366] with making of a privy in the same
almshouse, and so all costs made at that time were paid by the said Robert, taking out
and excepting 2s. 6½d., which is from the common costs of the said craft, above the
aforesaid £10, and about the same parcels and in what manner they were spent, you
shall find them clearly on the seventh leaf after this as they are paid at this time.[367]

[267] [f. 84r]
The names of crafts and fraternities which hired our Hall during the said two years, with the sums of money that they paid

First from the Armourers, 4 times,	6s. 4d.	**The names of the persons who died in**
Item from the Fraternity of the		**these 2 years, for whom various sums**
Cross, twice,	3s. 8d.	**of money were given to the craft and**
Item from the Girdlers, 5 times,	5s.	**fraternity**
Item from the Clerks, 5 times,	6s. 2d.	
Item from the Barbers, 9 times,	10s.	John Thetford	20s.
Item from the Football Players,		William Ederiche	13s. 4d.
twice,	20d.	John Ballard	12d.

---

366 Stone backing of a fireplace or open hearth.
367 Chambers and Daunt thought that the last phrase was written in the same hand but in
darker ink, added a little later. Chambers and Daunt, *London English*, 147. The expenses
were listed further on, see **[288–301]**.

Item from the Coopers, twice,   4s. 6d.
Item from the Point-makers, 3 times   5s.
Item from the Ferrours, once, 12d.
Item from the Fraternity of the
Trinity, 4 times,   3s. 10d.
Item from the Yeomen of the
Cordwainers, once,[368]   3s. 4d.
Item from the Cooks, 3 times,   7s. 4d.
Item from the Butchers once,   12d.
Item from the Galoche makers,
once,   8d.
Item from the Smiths, once,   20d.
Item from the Foundours, once,   20d.
Item from the Glaziers, once,   12d.
Item from an Inquest of the
Wardmote, once,   4d.

Sum 64s. 2d. Examined.

John Moyle   20d.
Margaret Hiltonne   6s. 8d.
William Bolton   6s. 8d.

Sum 49s. 4d. Examined.

The names that have been entered, with their sums of money, who are freemen and brethren, under 1 sum in the same 2 years, and there are 20 of them as it shows afterwards

Dederik Johnson, Dutchman, at
the Hartshorn in Petty Wales   £4.
William Misterton at the
Katherine Wheel in Grub Street
without Cripplegate   20s.
John Pamplion at the Cock and
Star in Cornhill   20s.
Richard Stonham at the Ship
without Cripplegate   13s. 4d.
John de Van sometime at the Key
in Bassishaw   16s. 8d.

[268] [f. 84v]

Henry Stapill at the Chequer in East Cheap	10s.
John Warsoppe at the Ship near London Wall	20s.
William Dowdale at the Saracen's Head within Aldgate	13s. 4d.
Matys Adrianesson, beerman,[369] near St Katherine's, in part payment of £4	20s.
Peter Andrew at the Bell in Holborn	13s. 4d.
John Hopkyn at the Horse in Aldersgate Street	13s. 4d.
John Mabile at the Red Cock in the Poultry	16s. 8d.
John Bugby at the Swan in Aldersgate Street	13s. 4d.
Nicholas Mertonne at the Hart in St John Street	20s.
William Rose sometime at the Moon outside Bishopsgate	26s. 8d.
John West at the Cock near the Austin Friars	16s. 8d.
William Watford at the Lamb in Abchurch Lane	21s. 8d.
John Purley at the Key in Holborn	23s. 4d.
Jacob Tolvan at the Crane near St Nicholas Shambles	13s. 4d.
Thomas Walsh at the Hartshorn against [*St Katherine*] Christ Church	16s. 8d.

Sum £20 8s. 4d., of which to the Common Box £10 and so there is left clearly to the profit and to the costs of the Masters, Robert Smyth and his fellows, £10 8s. 4d.

---

[368]   A fraternity for younger men, newly free of apprenticeship, see Barron, *London in the Later Middle Ages*, 214.
[369]   This Dutch or Flemish 'beerman', as opposed to ale brewer, joined the craft and fraternity of Brewers of London.

[269]

The names that have been entered below are all freemen only during the said 2 years, with their sums of money paid, as it shows underneath

John Vevian at the Lily in Staining Lane, in part payment of 13s. 4d.,	6s. 8d.
John Nicoll at the Cup outside Ludgate	6s. 8d.
John Lacy at the Hand in Fleet Street near Temple Bar	20s.
Thomas Molton of Yaxley in the shire of Huntingdon	6s. 8d.
Thomas Smyth at the Garland outside Bishopsgate	13s. 4d.
John Elsy at the Popinjay in Fenchurch Street	10s.
Thomas Rodier at the Falcon in Aldersgate Street	11s. 8d.

[f. 85r]

John Bretaigne at the Snipe in East Cheap	13s. 4d.
John Godyng at the Pie in the Moor outside Cripplegate	10s.
Thomas Gilderedge, Master Brewer with Robert Swan	6s. 8d.
Thomas atte Hethe at the Basket in Fenchurch Street	13s. 4d.
John Jacow at the Swan in Bassishaw	13s. 4d.
John Bernewell at the Swan near Billingsgate	13s. 4d.
Ivy Jacow sometime at the Rose in White Cross Street	13s. 4d.
Henry Payne at the Garland in Wood Street	13s. 4d.
Robert Bernard at the Tankard upon the Tower Hill, in part payment of 13s. 4d.,	2s. 11d.
	Examined.

Sum £8 14s. 7d., of which to the common box 100s. and so there is left clearly to the profit and for the costs of the said Masters, Robert Smyth and his fellows, £3 14s. 7d.

[270]

The names written before are not entered at the Guildhall in this time	The names written before, and entered as brethren, refuse to pay their quarterage yearly	The names of those who have paid various amounts of money in part payment for their freedom and fraternity entry, and will pay no more
Matys Adriansson		
Thomas Walssh	William Misterton	
William Watford	Richard Stonham	
John Vevyan	Matis Adrianssonn	
Thomas Rodier		Matys Adrianssonn
		John Vevyan
John Lacy		Robert Bernard
Ivy Jacow		
J. Bernewell		
Robert Bernard		

[271]

The names of those entered as brethren during the last 2 years, with their sums of money paid, and of these there are 77 persons.[370]

Dederik Johnson, Dutchman
John de Van
Peter Andrew
John Bugby
William Rose & Johanna his wife
Jacob Tolvan

William Misterton
Henry Stapill
John Mabile
John Hopkyn
John West
Thomas Walssh with Johanna his wife

John Pamplionne
John Warsoppe & Anneys
Matys Adrianesson with Margaret his wife
Nicholas Mertonne with Agnes his wife
William Watford
Richard Stonham
William Dowdale with Johanna his wife
John Purley with Johanna his wife

[272] [f. 85v]

William Andrew at the Castle in Fleet Street	5s. 11d.
Richard Lucas with Alice his wife at the Horse Head in Bower Row	5s. 11d.
John Frost with Alice his wife at the Hartshorn without Newgate	6s. 8d.
Richard Carowe with Elizabeth his wife sometime at the Key in Holborn	6s. 8d.
John Hanselap at the Horse within Aldgate	6s. 8d.
Raff Marke with Rose his wife at the White Lion	6s. 8d.
Peter Short with Alice his wife at the Vine near Holborn Cross	6s. 8d.
John Bronnyng with Johanna his wife sometime at the Moon in Bishopsgate [*above the line*: Street]	6s. 8d.
Henry Wikstonne, with Thomesyne his wife, fishmonger,	6s. 8d.
John Bate, with Anneys his wife, fishmonger,	6s. 8d.
John Massy, draper, at the Three Nuns at the end of Sithebourne Lane	6s. 8d.
William Bullok with Johanna his wife, tapester,[371] at the Christopher in Fenchurch [*above the line*: Street]	6s. 8d.
Henry Rowe with Johanna his wife at the Two Keys without Bishopsgate	6s. 8d.
Robert Ketyng with Margery his wife at the Key in Coleman Street	6s. 8d.
William Franke with Cecily his wife at the *Colver* [*pigeon or dove*] in Fenchurch Street, in part payment of 6s. 8d.,	3s. 4d.
John Caston with Anneys his wife at the Crown without Cripplegate	6s. 8d.
Simon Petsyn with Isabell his wife at the Peahen in Bishopsgate Street	6s. 8d.
William Mascall at the Swan in Holborn in full payment	5s.
Thomas Walpooll with Johanna his wife, maltman, in part of payment of 6s. 8d.,	3s. 4d.
Simon atte Welle at the Hind without Cripplegate	6s. 8d.
William Rawlyn with Alice his wife at the Mill in St John Street	6s. 8d.
John Bedford at the Seven Stars in Smithfield in full payment	3s. 4d.

---

370 No sums of money were entered in this section. Seventy-six men were listed, thirty-seven with their wives, then Katherine Wirgeyn in her own right, and William Calston, plumber, who paid in lead.

371 Maker or weaver of figured cloth or tapestry, or a tapster, who drew ale for customers at the Christopher.

John Riche, tailor, with Alice his wife at the Ramb in Fleet Street	6s. 8d.
William Totewell with Isabell his wife at the Hartshorn in Southwark, in full payment	5s.

[273] [f. 86r]
R. Smyth, W. Crane, H. Nele, J. Philippe

Thomas Merssh, webber,[372] with Anneys his wife at the Harp in Tower Street, in part payment of 6s. 8d.,	3s. 4d.
John Fayreman with Johanna his wife at the Dragon without Bishopsgate	6s. 8d.
William Pompe at the Vine in the Riall	6s. 8d.
John Sharppe, maltman, in full payment	3s. 4d.
John Iver with Isabell his wife at the Rose near St Lawrence (of) Pountney	4s.
Thomas North sometime at the Bell without Aldgate in full payment	3s. 4d.
John Chercheseye, tailor, with Alice his wife at the Cock against the Friars Minor, in part payment of 6s. 8d.	3s. 4d.
William Hanyngtonne, tiler, in full payment	3s. 4d.
Henry Grene with Anneys his wife at Long Entry	3s. 4d.
John Gremesby at the Swan in Holborn	6s. 8d.
Richard Tyler, maltman, in full payment	3s. 4d.
Roger Awdymer, vintner, in Crooked Lane	3s. 4d.
John Bosvenonne at the Vine within Bishopsgate	5s.
Sir Adam Dalton, parson of All Hallows in the Wall	5s.
William Ferrour the Younger with Anneys his wife at the Bell in St Margaret Pattens Lane	5s.
John Spore, ferrour, dwelling in Wood Street	3s. 4d.
Thomas Ayle at the Eagle near St Bartholomew	6s. 8d.
Katherine Wirgeyn, the wife of William Termeday, at the Maid without Cripplegate	3s. 4d.
John Amwell sometime at the Cock at Ivy Lane end	6s. 8d.
Roger Ware with Alice his wife, pavior,[373] at the Cock within Aldgate	6s. 8d.
John Astonne near Holborn Bridge in the house formerly of John Stannton	6s. 8d.
Richard Herty with Alice his wife at the Dolphin near St Anne's	6s. 8d.
William Miles, maltman, with Maud his wife	6s. 8d.

[274] [f. 86v]

Alexander Marcowe with Anneys his wife at the Harp in Fleet Street	6s. 8d.
Sir William Goodswayne, parson of St Mary Woolnoth,	6s. 8d.
Henry Boston, mason, in full payment,	3s. 4d.
Master Richard Donyngton, Austin Friar, late prior of the same place,	6s. 8d.
John Cavendissh, with Alice his wife, broderer,	6s. 8d.
Richard Bulwik with Johanna his wife sometime at the Key outside Ludgate	6s. 8d.
Friar John Berkynge of the Austin Friars	6s. 8d.
Robert Calowe, shearman,	6s. 8d.
William Covele, goldsmith, sometime at the Ball in the Old Change,	6s. 4d.

---

[372] Weaver.
[373] One who lays paving.

William Calston, plumber, gave 1 cwt of new lead to the craft and fraternity for his entry[374]

Sum £15 13*s.* 10*d.* Of which to the common box for 77 persons £9 6*s.* 8*d.*, with 1 cwt of new lead, and so there is left clearly to the profit and to the costs of Robert Smyth and his fellows, £6 7*s.* 2*d.*

[275]
These are the names of those who were entered as Brethren during these 2 years and refuse to pay their quarterage

Thomas Walpole, maltman, with Johanna his wife
John Yver with Isabell his wife
John Chirchisseye, tailor, with Alice his wife
William Hanyngtonne, tiler
Henry Botston, mason
William Covele, goldsmith

[276]
The names of those who paid various parcels of money towards the reparation of our Hall during the said 2 years

John Mason 16*s.* 2*d.*, and the same John Masonne made at his own costs 2 paleytes[375] between the hall and the great gate, with all the timber, locks, keys and all the workmanship of carpentry for the said 2 paleytes

Maud Stanntone	13*s.* 4*d.*	John Brook	13*s.* 4*d.*	John Riche of	
Thomas Aleyn	12*s.*	Richard Aleyn	11*s.* 8*d.*	Wood Street	13*s.* 4*d.*
Dederik Johnsonne	10*s.*	Alexander Miles	10*s.*	Thomas Hatcher	10*s.*
Henry Trebolans	7*s.*	John Chapman	6*s.* 8*d.*	John Ketyng	9*s.*
				John Humber	9*s.*

[277] [f. 87r]
Robert Smyth, W. Crane, H. Nele, J. Philippe

John Rothyng	6*s.* 8*d.*	Roger Blissote	6*s.* 8*d.*	John Moore	6*s.* 8*d.*
John Russell	6*s.* 8*d.*	Roger Swanneffeld		John Reyner	6*s.* 8*d.*
William atte Welle	6*s.* 8*d.*		6*s.* 8*d.*	Raff Marke	6*s.* 8*d.*
Thomas Hancok	6*s.* 8*d.*	William Ferrour the		John Qwyntyn	6*s.* 8*d.*
Robert Hilton	6*s.* 8*d.*	Elder	6*s.* 8*d.*	William Ferrour	
Robert Calowe	6*s.* 8*d.*	William Payn	6*s.* 8*d.*	the Younger	6*s.* 8*d.*
Henry Rowe	3*s.* 4*d.*	Thomas Godyng	6*s.* 8*d.*	John Brewester	3*s.* 8*d.*
John Reffawe	3*s.* 4*d.*	John Fekenham	4*s.* 4*d.*	John Salter	3*s.* 4*d.*
William Eyre	3*s.* 4*d.*	Robert Elken	3*s.* 4*d.*	John Elcy	3*s.* 4*d.*
Davy Bronnyng	3*s.* 4*d.*	William Baily	3*s.* 4*d.*	William Herry	3*s.* 4*d.*

---

[374] 1 cwt or hundredweight of lead, 112 lbs. See [316] where this quantity was listed as being worth 8*s.*

[375] Perhaps palisades – fences of wooden stakes as partitions.

Adam Copendale	3s. 4d.	Henry Nobull	3s. 4d.	Roger Ware	3s. 4d.
John Lumbard	3s. 4d.	Walter Colshull	3s. 4d.	Richard Bulwik,	
John Piken	3s. 4d.	Richard		grocer,	3s. 4d.
Hugh Glene	3s. 4d.	Sherewode	3s. 4d.	John Serle	3s. 4d.
William Waas,		Alison Herty	3s. 4d.	Peter Short	3s. 4d.
baker	3s. 4d.	Master Richard		John Newman	3s. 4d.
Robert Pede	3s. 4d.	Donyngtonne	3s. 4d.	John Wightmore	3s. 4d.
Peter Carpenter	3s. 4d.	William Grosse	3s. 4d.	Johanna Holbek	3s. 4d.
Richard Harlowe	3s. 4d.	Sir Robert		William Petevile	3s. 4d.
Alex Marcowe	3s. 4d.	Steynton	3s. 4d.	Robert Carpenter	3s. 4d.
William Belle	3s. 4d.	John Stokes	3s. 4d.	John Lacy	3s. 4d.
John Norman	2s. 4d.	Roger Baronne	3s. 4d.	Simon Potekyn	2s. 4d.
John Lucas	2s.	John Carion	3s. 4d.	Thomas Kent	2s.
John Faireman	20d.	William Rose	3s. 4d.	John Laurence	2s.
John Hardyng	20d.	John Thomas	2s. 6d.	William Bernarde	20d.
John Warsoppe	20d.	Nicholas Goomnailok	2s.	Robert Bullard	20d.
John Riche at the		Robert Ketyng	2s.	William Illyng	20d.
Angel	20d.	William Dowdale	20d.	John Jacobb	20d.
		John Bedford	20d.		
		Baldewyne Hoper	20d.		
		Nicholas Fuller	20d.		

[278] [f. 87v]

Robert Giles	20d.	Robert Dorewell	20d.	Anneys Bugge	20d.
Henry Bedell	20d.	Wiliam Rawlyn	20d.	Simon Herry	20d.
John Riche, tailor,	20d.	John Kenaky	20d.	Thomas Penson	20d.
John Bronnyng	20d.	Thomas Kirtoth	20d.	Philip Godffrey	20d.
John Frost	20d.	John Stone	20d.	Robert Dellowe	20d.
William Claisson	20d.	William Franke	20d.	William Geffrey	20d.
John Barstonne	20d.	Henry Grene	20d.	Jacob Levegro	20d.
John Snell	20d.	William Reponne	20d.	John Brokford	16d.
John Aleyn	12d.	Nicholas Muriell	12d.	John de Van	12d.
Walter Glyn	12d.	Gilbert Botonne	12d.	William Bodevyle	12d.
John Bugby	12d.	Thomas Ayle	12d.	John West	12d.
Thomas Gratley	12d.	William Devenyssh	6d.		

And the aforesaid John Elcy gave to the reparation of the great window in the hall
3 quarterons and 1 lb of old lead to the value of 4s. ½d.
And Peter Hayford gave to the same reparation of the great window 118 lbs of old
lead to the value of 6s. 1d.

Sum £23 16s. 10d.

[279]
The names of those who gave of alms to the costs of the stained halling that hangs in our hall

John Turvey	4*d.*	William Ferrour		Henry Trebolans	4*d.*
Robert Hiltonne	4*d.*	the Elder	4*d.*	Peter Hayford	4*d.*
Hugh Neel	4*d.*	William Ederich	4*d.*	John Reyner	4*d.*
Robert Carpenter	4*d.*	John Masonne	4*d.*	John Salter	2*d.*
		Robert Smyth	4*d.*		

Sum 3*s.* 10*d.*

[280]
The names of persons who committed various trespasses, for which they paid fines to the craft of Brewers

Michell Tregononne	3*s.* 4*d.*
John Hopkyn	3*s.* 4*d.*
Thomas Boteler	5*s.*
Item received from money given by the Masters and the Searchers from fines that were made at the Guildhall	8*d.*

Sum 12*s.* 4*d.*

[281] [f. 88r]
R. Smyth, W. Crane, H. Nele, J. Philippe

Parcels of diverse goods sold, with torches made for the interment of King Henry V

First by William Porlond, clerk, 100 tiles at 8*d.*, with 1 cartful of tile shards at 12*d.*, sold by him,	20*d.*
Item from Hugh Neel for 1 torch that weighed 15 lbs. Item for another torch that weighed 13 lbs at 3*d.*,	7*s.*
Item from Robert Smyth for 1 torch weighing 13 lbs at 3*d.*,	3*s.* 3*d.*
Item from William Ferrour for 1 torch weighing 15 lbs at 3*d.*,	3*s.* 9*d.*
Item from John Salter for 1 torch weighing 14 lbs at 3*d.*,	3*s.* 6*d.*
Item from John Philippe for 1 torch weighing 14 lbs at 3*d.*,	3*s.* 6*d.*
Item from William Crane for 1 torch weighing 14 lbs at 3*d.*,	3*s.* 6*d.*
Item from William Ederiche for 1 torch weighing 14 lbs at 3*d.*,	3*s.* 6*d.*

Sum 29*s.* 8*d.*[376]

---

[376] The sum of 28*s.* for torch ends from the King's interment was recorded in the account of the King's funeral [224].

[282]

These are the names of Brewers of London who paid diverse sums of money to help to destroy the weirs in the Thames, so that the commonalty of the city of London should have more plentiful fish

John Snell	7½d.	William Boteler	8d.	Robert Pede	8d.
Richard Carowe	4d.	Richard West	4d.	Thomas Yole	8d.
Thomas Smalsho	4d.			John Holbek	4d.
John Gremesby	6d.	John Freeke	6d.	William Cowlee	4d.
John Hardyng	6d.	John Norman	4d.		
		Robert Dorwell	4d.		

[283] [f. 88v]

John Kenaky	5d.	William Cardell	8d.	John Baily	4d.
John Salman	4d.	John Basset	6d.	Roger Swanneffeld	12d.
Richard Herty	8d.	Hugh Glene	8d.	Gwy[378] Baker	8d.
Stephen Clean	6d.				
Richard Sherewode	12d.	John Thomas	4d.[377]	William Jordan	6d.
William Payn	12d.	Emma Canonne	8d.	Richard Stonham	8d.
Richard Mayhew	4d.	Richard Lucas	8d.	John Tregelowe	8d.
John Brownyng	4d.	John Dunche	4d.	John Lutonne	4d.
John Fayrman	6d.	Thomas North	4d.	Walter Glyn	4d.
Thomas Sore	4d.	Roger Baronne	4d.	John Heylond	6d.
William Termeday	4d.	Simon Poteken	6d.	John Salter	6d.
Henry Rows	6d.	William Marke	4d.	Michael Tregononne	8d.
William Barte	12d.	John Dawbere	2d.	John More	8d.
Richard Bryntonne	6d.			Morris Travaill	6d.
		William Riche	4d.	John Laurence	6d.
Austyn Hawkyn	6d.			Thomas Ayle	6d.
Michael Eve	6d.	John Fekenham	12d.	Katherine Pynchebek	2d.
Reynald Broke	4d.	Henry Grene	4d.	Richard Waltham	4d.
John Thomas	6d.	Simon Herry	4d.		
William Andrew	6d.	Henry Sadiller	6d.	Thomas of Kent	8d.
Walter Cook	6d.	Cristyan Ballard	8d.	Thomas Aleyn	12d.
John Hill	6d.	Richard Marchall	4d.	Richard Harlowe	8d.
John Randolff	6d.	John Trum	4d.	Thomas Merssh	6d.
Agneys Carleton	6d.	Alexander Marcow	6d.	Davy Bronnyng	8d.
Nicholas Fuller	4d.	Reynald Bewchamp	4d.		
John Stokes	6d.	John Riche	4d.	John South	6d.[379]
William Bullok	6d.	Noell Maryagek	4d.	Simon Petesyn	6d.
Robert Elkyn	8d.			William Boltonne	6d.
Adam Webbenbury	4d.	Robert Carpenter	8d.	John Humber	8d.

---

[377] Two men called John Thomas were recorded as paying different amounts.
[378] Guillaume or Guy?
[379] Possibly an incomplete entry for Southmede.

[284] [f. 89r]
R. Smyth, W. Crane, H. Neel, J. Philippe

Henry Bright	4d.	William Bernard	6d.	William Belle	8d.
William Bourne	6d.	Thomas Penson	5d.	Richard Kilsole	8d.
Baldewyne Hoper	5½d.	John Refawe	8d.		
John Chapman	2d.			Robert Smyth	12d.
John Shermanne	4d.	Henry Serle	4d.	Robert Tanner	6d.
William Misterton	4d.	John Essex	8d.	John William	8d.
William Petevile	2d.	Adam Copendale	6d.	Philip Dawe	4d.
Thomas Wirgeyn	6d.	Robert Ketyng	4d.		
Simon atte Welle	6d.			Johnette Rothyng	6d.
John Spenser	8d.	William Bracy	11d.	William Ederiche	12d.
John Swan,		Nicholas Kene	5½d.	John Stone	6d.
cordwainer	4d.	John Elcy	12d.		
Robert Delowe	4d.	Thomas atte Wode	12d.	John Reyner	8d.
Thomas Martyn	8d.	John Bate	8d.		
Simon Kyng	6d.	Simon Franke	4d.	William Crane	8d.
John More	4d.				
Richard Terell	6d.	Alexander Miles	8d.	William Herry	8d.
Thomas Aleyn[380]	4d.	John Grymmesby	2d.	Philip James	4d.
William Lonell	4d.				
Nicholas Muryell	6d.	John Brooke	12d.	William Smalsho	6d.
Thomas Wegge	4d.	John Merstonne	4d.		
Emond Disse	4d.	John Waghorn	4d.	John Massy	4d.
John Castonne	4d.	John Carionne	8d.		
John Aleyn	4d.			Thomas Hancok	6d.
Randolph Palmer	6d.	William Canonne	6d.	William Ferrour	8d.
Gilbert Botonne	4d.	Beatrix Tye	6d.	William Reponne	4d.
		Richard Crosse	4d.		
John Lucas	8d.			John Russell	12d.
Jacob Levegro	8d.	Nicholas		John Yver	6d.
Milicent Burgh	4d.	Goomnaylok	6d.	John Assh	6d.
Roger Ware	4d.	Robert Mailond	6d.		
Robert Walrarn	4d.				
John Parker	4d.				

[285] [f. 89v]

Richard Clerk	4d.	John Clerk	8d.	William Goodburgh	4d.
John Philippe	8d.				
Thomas Whityng	4d.	Nicholas Aleyn	6d.	Richard Aleyn	8d.
				Cristyan Bekeswelle	8d.
John Turvey	4d.	John Cole	4d.		
Henry Bedell	6d.	Stephen Bugge	8d.	William Illyng	4d.
Thomas Grene	8d.				
John More	8d.	Richard Frepurs	4d.	William Mymmes	8d.

---

[380] On the previous folio, a Thomas Aleyn gave 4d. **[283]**, so there were perhaps two men of that name.

Thomas Botelmaker	6*d.*	Jacob Ytacombe	2*d.*	John Brewster	4*d.*
Wiliam atte Wode	7*d.*				
Peter Carpenter	6*d.*	John Goldryng	6*d.*	Thomas Hatcher	8*d.*
				William Claissonne	8*d.*
William Fox	3½*d.*	William Grosse	6*d.*	John Horold	12*d.*
John Benge	6*d.*	John Erle	6*d.*	William Geffrey	6*d.*
John Jacob	6*d.*			Dederik Johnson	8*d.*
Roger Blissote	6*d.*	Margaret Thetford	12*d.*		
John Amwell	8*d.*			William Andrew	8*d.*
		John Aleyn	6*d.*	Robert Hilton	12*d.*
Robert Giles	6*d.*	John Ludlowe	4*d.*	Richard Spray	3½*d.*
				John Frensh	4*d.*
Stephen Roo	6*d.*	John Riche	12*d.*	John Frost	4*d.*
Alan John	4*d.*			John Newman	8*d.*
John Piken	8*d.*	Thomas Botiller	4*d.*	Peter Short	8*d.*
Richard Flete	6*d.*	Henry Trebolens	8*d.*	Henry Lymber	4*d.*
Robert Frank	6*d.*	Henry Wexen	6*d.*	John Stanntonne	12*d.*
		Thomas Godyng	8*d.*	Henry Basset	6*d.*
John Sturmyn	8*d.*	Hugh Neel	8*d.*	John Palmer	4*d.*
		Thomas Gratley	6*d.*	William Style	6*d.*
				William Eyre	4*d.*
				Robert Bullard	4*d.*
				John Bedford	4*d.*
				John Toke	6*d.*
				Richard Rowdonne	6*d.*
				William Baily	6*d.*
				Thomas Pothill	6*d.*
				John Gardyner	4*d.*

[286] [f. 90r]
R. Smyth, W. Crane, H. Nele, J. Philippe

William Knot	4*d.*	Juliane Hetersete	4*d.*	Thomas Emond	12*d.*
John Brokford	6*d.*			Peter Hayford	12*d.*
Walter Colshull	8*d.*	John de Lynne	6*d.*		
William Hill	3½*d.*	Robert Squyere	4*d.*		

Examined.

Sum £6 8*s.* 2*d.*

[287]
Of which was paid to Thomas Grene and to Roger Swanneffeld for their business and their travail rowing in a barge with the mayor from London to Staines, with victuals and reward given to them for their labour 13*s.* 4*d.*
Item given to John Masonne & to Robert Carpenter for their business and their travail being in a barge in the same company abovesaid, from London to Queenborough, with victuals and reward given to them for their labour 26*s.* 8*d.*
Item paid to the chamberlain of the Guildhall, the costs of 3 labourers to draw down and to destroy the said weirs in the aforesaid time, for 28 days at 2*s.*, 56*s.*

Item 1 groat of copper[381] received at that time that was of no value 4*d.*
And so there is left clearly underspent to the use of the commonalty to put in the common box 31*s.* 10*d.*

And for to have better knowledge as well of receipts for the expenses for the costs, and for the said weirs in the Thames, you shall find good mention made in a roll of parchment hanging in a purse of leather by this book.[382]
And as for the said 31*s.* 10*d.*, that is left clearly to the common profit, rehearsed and written before, this sum was delivered to the said common profit, as is mentioned in the aforesaid roll of parchment and also in the accounts of the aforesaid Robert Smyth and his fellows, 32*s.* Examined.

[288] [f. 90v]
These are the parcels that are spent and paid in the tenantry[383] outside the gate, to make the same tenantry into an almshouse for poor brothers and sisters of the craft and fraternity of Brewers of London, for which Robert Smyth paid £10 as is written before[384]

First for sawing of diverse pieces of timber	17*d.*
Item paid to Jankyn Pekker, carpenter, for all the workmanship as in carpentry, for he took it great, that is, to wit, to task,	40*s.*
Item paid to John Stok, timbermonger, for diverse timber bought from him for the same almshouse at diverse times,	42*s.*
Item for ale to the carpenters	1*d.*
Item for 400 oaken lathes at 8*d.*,	2*s.* 8*d.*
Item for 400 lathes of sappin[385] at 6*d.*,	2*s.*
Item to Nicholas Fuller for 1 and a half lbs of iron called stirrups	3*d.*
Item to Robert Cok, labourer, for half a day breaking a wall in the tenantry called the almshouse	1*d.*
Item to another labourer for 2 days,	4*d.*
Item to one John, labourer, for his labour for 5 days at 3*d.* the day,	15*d.*
Item in reward to the same labourer	1*d.*
Item to one Robert, dauber, for his daubing for 7 days at 4½*d.* the day, with his noonnchyns,	2*s.* 7½*d.*
Item to John Smyth, labourer, for 9 and a half days, the day 4*d.* with noonnchyns and reward given, to serve the same dauber,	3*s.* 3*d.*

[289] [f. 91r]

Item to one Peter, labourer, for 3 days and a half, the day 5*d.*,	17*d.*
Item to Robert Rowe, dauber, for 10 days and a half, the day 6*d.*, for daubing diverse walls,	5*s.* 3*d.*
Item for his noonnchyns to the same dauber	4½*d.*
Item to one John, labourer, for 1 day	4½*d.*

---

[381] A false groat which should have been made of silver.
[382] The parchment and purse have not survived.
[383] The property formerly let out to tenants.
[384] See [286].
[385] A kind of fir or pine.

Item for straw for the same daubing[386]	3d.
Item to John Smyth, labourer, for portage of tiles	1d.
Item to the aforesaid Robert, dauber, for 5 days in amending diverse defaults with daubing and other labour in diverse places of the same almshouse the day 5d.,	2s. 1d.
Item to the said Robert, dauber, for his labour in lathing and daubing for 3 days, the day 6½d., with his *noonnchyns*,	19½d.

Item for freestone[387] to the great door	2s.
Item for carriage of the same stone	3d.
Item to John Crowston, mason,[388] for 1 paas[389] containing 4 feet of hard stone for the foot of the door in the said almshouse	16d.
Item to Goldryng, mason, for 2 freestones with the work of masonry	4d.
Item paid for 1 freestone to the side of the said door	6d.
Item paid to Raff Worsted, hewer of freestone, for 7 days, the day 8d.,	4s. 8d.
Item for his *noonnchyns* on the aforesaid days with reward	2d.
Item to William Batte, mason, for 6 days and half, the day 8d.,	4s. 4d.
Item to John Wolde, mason, for 9 days, the day 8d.,	6s.
Item paid for ale with the masons, daubers and labourers	1d.
Item to 2 masons, the servants of Henry Botston, mason, for 2 weeks, to each mason by the week, 4s. 3d., with their *noonnchyns*, in the making of the walls of the privy and a wall called the reredos in the kitchen, with paving of the same kitchen	17s.
Item to William Walton, labourer, to serve the masons for 11 days, the day 5d.,	4s. 7d.
Item for 6 days to another labourer to serve the said masons, the day 5d.,	2s. 6d.

[290] [f. 91v]

Item for firming of the old privy in the almshouse	2s. 2d.
Item for 1 gutter of new lead to the same privy, weighing 27 lbs,	22d.
Item for making of 2 toise[390] of pavement to the same gutter of lead to keep the water out of the privy	16d.
Item for 1 cartful of gravel to the same work	4d.
Item given to Stephen Brewer to fetch stones for the paviors out of the little cellar for making the same pavement	4d.
Item for a half 100 and 18 paving stones for the kitchen of the said almshouse	5s. 6d.
Item for 100 and a half quarteron[391] of *Flaundrissh* tiles, price the 100, 12d., for the aforesaid kitchen,	13½d.
Item for carriage of the said stone and tiles	6d.

---

386 Daubing involved using straw for rough mortar or plaster.
387 Stone that can be sawn in any direction and readily shaped with a chisel, such as sandstone or limestone.
388 John Crowston or Croxton, master mason at the Guildhall from 1411. Harvey, *Mediaeval Architects*, 76.
389 A pack or team of asses, which carried or pulled the stone.
390 Toise or teyse. French lineal measurement equivalent to six square feet.
391 Presumably half of twenty-five.

Item to John Tenterden for 5,000 and a half and 200 of transom³⁹² price the
1,000 10*d*., 4*s*. 9*d*.
Item for twopenny nails, fourpenny nails, fivepenny nails and sixpenny nails, 3*d*.
Item for 100 of sprig nails³⁹³ for daubers 1*d*.
Item to the timber-monger of Wood Street for 200 of fivepenny nails 10*d*.
Item for 100 of fourpenny nails 4*d*.
Item for twopenny nails, threepenny nails, sixpenny nails, eightpenny nails, 15½*d*.
Item for 2 nails³⁹⁴ of lead for the foremast³⁹⁵ door of the almshouse for the
lock, clicket, and bolts of the same door 8*d*.

Item for 1 lock to a door with 1 staple and the setting on to a chamber of the
said almshouse 8*d*.
Item for 2 staples to the bolts of the middle door 1*d*.
Item for amending the clickets of diverse doors 1*d*.
Item for 1 lock to the kitchen door with 1 staple 6*d*.
Item for 3 new keys with the amendment of 3 locks to diverse doors 8*d*.

[291] [f. 92r]
R. Smyth, W. Crane, H. Nele, J. Philippe

Item for 1 lock and 1 staple with 3 keys to the chamber door of Robert Lynford 12*d*.
Item for 1 latch, 1 catch, 1 cramp³⁹⁶ to the aforesaid door 1*d*.
Item for 2 keys to the stair door of the almshouse 6*d*.
Item for a new clicket for the wife of the said Robert Lynford 3*d*.
Item for setting on of a lock with 1 staple, above the stair, to a chamber door
near Jonette Awmbele 2*d*.
Item for 1 hasp with 1 staple to the kitchen door 1½*d*.
Item for 1 cramp with 1 catch to the kitchen window 1*d*.
Item for amending of a lock to the door of the privy in a chamber of the said
almshouse 2*d*.
Item for 1 new key to the kitchen door 3*d*.
Item for amending of a lock in the dark chamber³⁹⁷ 2*d*.
Item for diverse hinges to windows and doors with 1 pair of garnets³⁹⁸ 15*d*.

Item for 9 loads of lime to the said almshouse 8*s*. 10*d*.

Item for 6 loads of sand to the making of all works in the said almshouse, at
5*d*., 2*s*. 6*d*.
Item for 5 loads of loam to the daubing in the same almshouse, at 4*d*. the load, 20*d*.

---

³⁹² Wood or stone for a cross-beam.
³⁹³ Small nails with small heads that would not show on the surface.
³⁹⁴ A measurement, now obsolete, or nails made of lead.
³⁹⁵ Foremost?
³⁹⁶ An iron bar with the end bent to a hook, a grappling iron. Perhaps 'a small metal bar
with bent ends to hold two pieces of masonry or timber together', Chambers and Daunt,
London English, 258.
³⁹⁷ Perhaps a dark closet used for food storage at Brewers' Hall.
³⁹⁸ A hinge with the upright part nailed to the support with the horizontal to the door or
shutter.

Item for carriage of 6 loads of robux unto the field, the load 3*d*.,	18*d*.
Item for 5 lbs of cotton candle in mornings and evenings, for carpenters, daubers and other labourers	7½*d*.
Item for 1 earthen pot to keep the water in for the privy in a chamber of the said almshouse	1*d*.

[292] [f. 92v]

Item for making a coal bin for the chamber of Jonette Awmbele and for amending a floor in another chamber with loam, for 2 days, the day 3*d*.,	6*d*.
Item to the timber-monger of Wood Street for 6 boards for diverse doors and to a pipe of the privy, with a window in the kitchen with 14 quarters³⁹⁹ for *poonchyns*⁴⁰⁰ and *stodes*⁴⁰¹ to serve to the aforesaid window and doors	8*s*. 2½*d*.

Examined.

Sum total £10 2s. 6½d.

[293]

**These are the parcels for a gutter above
the kitchen of the tenantry
now called the almshouse**

First for 2 quarters for the transoms in the said gutter	8*d*.
Item for 1 long board for the bottom of the same gutter	10*d*.
Item to 2 carpenters by 1 day, to each of them with their *nonsenches*, 8½*d*., for to make the aforesaid gutter,	17*d*.
Item for half a 100 and 16 lbs of new lead, the hundred 8*s*., for the same gutter, that amounts to	5*s*. 2*d*.
Item for the [ex]change of 103 quarterons of old lead, the hundred 16*d*., that amounts to	2*s*. 4*d*.
Item for portage of the old lead and new lead in and out	4*d*.

Sum 10s. 9d.

[294] [f. 93r]
R. Smyth, W. Crane, H. Nele, J. Philippe

**These are the parcels of timber and carpentry
for the making of a tresance sometime
called the cloister, between the great kitchen and the hall**

Item for 2 great puncheons of tree, the piece 12*d*.,	2*s*.
Item for 2 other puncheons, the piece 10*d*.,	20*d*.
Item for carriage of the same	2*d*.
Item for 4 transoms, price the piece 8*d*.,	2*s*. 8*d*.

---

³⁹⁹ Wood 4 inches wide by 2–4 inches thick, used as an upright stud or short cross beam in partitions.
⁴⁰⁰ Puncheon: A short upright supporting timber post. Perhaps door posts here.
⁴⁰¹ Studs. Wooden upright props or supports.

Item for the carriage thereof and for ale to the sawyers who sawed the same transoms — 1½d.

Item for 4 eaves boards in that same place where the cloister was beside the kitchen — 6d.

Item for a post to the gutter where the cloister was — 6d.

Item for a summer[402] to bear up the side formerly of the same cloister — 12d.

Item for carriage of another summer that John Philippe gave, to bear the other side of the same work — 2d.

Item to 3 carpenters for 2 days, each of them taking the day 8d., to make the same work, — 4s.

Item for their *noonchyns* every day, to each of them ½d., — 3d.

Examined.

Sum 13s. ½d.

[295]

These are parcels for paving between the great kitchen and the hall, where the cloister used to stand sometime, with parcels of solder and other things

Item for 4 carts full of gravel — 16d.

Item for the paving of 6 and a half toise in the place formerly called the cloister, each toise 8d., — 4s. 2d.

Item for the mending the grate at the head of the gutter that runs through the hall — 2d.

Item for 2 lbs of solder in the gutter over the parlour near the garden of Jonette Brigham — 12d.

Item for 1 faggot of wood to heat the irons for the same solder — ½d.

Examined.

Sum 6s. 8½d.

[296] [f. 93v]

These are parcels for tiling from the hall door inwards, for all the houses in our place were pointed new[403] as in tiling at this time, except for the body of the great hall

Item for 200 lathes — 16d.

Item for 4,000 tiles, price the thousand, 5s. 8d., — 22s. 8d.

Item for half a quarteron of roof tiles — 9d.

Item for 3 loads of sand, each load 6d., — 18d.

Item for 6 loads of lime — 6s.

Item for 5 pecks of tile pins, price the peck 1½d., — 7½d.

Item for 1,000 of roof nails — 12d.

Item for half a 1,000 of transom[404] — 5d.

Item for spiking nails — 3½d.

---

402 A horizontal load-bearing beam.
403 Repointed.
404 Transom-nails.

Item for board nails	1*d.*
Item for 1 tiler and his man for 29 days and a half in tiling, pointing, daubing diverse houses in the place and the tenantry, taking every day 12*d.*,	29*s.* 6*d.*
Item in a reward given for *noonchyns* to the same tiler and his man by all the time	3*d.*
Item paid for bearing of tile shards down into the cellar	2*d.*
Item paid to a labourer by a day, to make clean the place and to couch[405] the tile shards after the tilers and the carpenters, with his *noonchyns*	5½*d.*
Item to Robert Cook for the couching of the stones in the little cellar and amending of diverse things in our place	2*d.*
Item to a woman, to pick our place[406] of tile stones and sweeping of the kitchen cloister and of our yard	2*d.*
Item for ale to the same woman and to Robert Lynford and to William Porlond at the time of the sweeping of the said place	1*d.*
	Examined.

Sum £3 5*s.* 5½*d.*

[297] [f. 94r]
R. Smyth, W. Crane, H. Nele, J. Philippe

These are the parcels for a gutter above the hall in the tenantry now called the almshouse

First for 3 pieces of timber for transoms to the said gutter	6½*d.*
Item for threepenny nails, fourpenny nails, fivepenny nails, sixpenny nails,	6*d.*
Item given to a man for to help the carpenter in the said gutter and to couch up the tiles	1*d.*
Item for 3 boards to the bottom of the same gutter	10*d.*
Item for 3 boards to the sides of the said gutter	10*d.*
Item for half an estrich board to a window in the great chamber of the same tenantry	3½*d.*
Item to a carpenter for 4 days working in the same gutter and other things, taking the day with *noonchyns* 7½*d.*,	2*s.* 6*d.*
Item paid to 1 plumber[407] for working and taking up and setting again of the old lead in the same gutter with 2 lbs of solder	18*d.*
Item paid for 100 lathes to the tiling for the houses near the said gutter	8*d.*
Item for 3 sacks of lime	6*d.*
Item for lath nails	3½*d.*
Item for 1 quarteron of tiles	2*d.*
Item to 1 tiler by 1 day and a half in tiling of the aforesaid houses, taking each day with his *noonchyns* 8½*d.*,	13*d.*
Item for his servant by 1 day and a half, taking each day with his *noonchyns* 6*d.*,	9*d.*
Item for 1 load of loam for amending diverse defaults in the said gutter underneath	4*d.*

---

405 Perhaps to lay or bed the shards and the stones in the cellar.
406 Pick clean.
407 Originally one working with lead, but later one working with pipes for water in buildings.

[298] [f. 94v]

Item to a dauber for 1 day for the mending of aforesaid faults, with his *noonchyns*, taking .... 8½*d.*

Item paid to 1 servant by 1 day to the same dauber taking the day, with his *noonchyns*, ... 6½*d.*

Item for carriage of robux from the same gutter .... 1½*d.*

Item for 1 piece of new lead, weighing 26 lbs, to a gutter of the aforesaid tenantry, above the pentice[408] of a window .... 23*d.*

Item for lead nails to the same lead .... 1*d.*

Sum 14s. 3d.

[299]

These are the parcels for an almarie[409] that stands in the great kitchen

Item to the timber-monger of Wood Street for 17 quarters of timber .... 5*s.* 3*d.*

Item 216 feet of oaken boards and 2 boards of elm for shelves in the aforesaid almarie, 4*d.*, with a board of oak for a coal bin, 3*d.*, ... 8*s.* 9*d.*

Item for 4 estrich boards for the doors of the aforesaid almarie .... 2*s.*

Item for 8 garnets .... 10*d.*

Item for 2 other garnets, price .... 3*d.*

Item for 200 and a half of fourpenny nails .... 10*d.*

Item for 300 and a half of threepenny nails .... 10½*d.*

Item 5 locks with 3 keys and 5 rings, price the lock with the ring, 6*d.*, ... 2*s.* 6*d.*

Item for ale given to the carpenter .... 1*d.*

Item to a carpenter by 8 days, for making of the same almarie, taking the day with his *noonchyns* 8½*d.*, ... 5*s.* 8*d.*

Item paid to the same carpenter for his labour about the buying of timber and boards .... 2*d.*

Examined.

Sum 27s. 2½d.

[300] [f. 95r]
R. Smyth, W. Crane, H. Nele, J. Philippe

These are parcels of a hen coop that stands in the yard,
towards which John Philippe gave all the great timber that belongs thereto

Item for 1 lb of cotton candle for the carpenters and tilers .... 1½*d.*

Item for 1 load of lime .... 12*d.*

Item to 1 tiler for 2 days working above the coop, taking the day 7*d.*, ... 14*d.*

Item to his servant for 2 days taking the day 5*d.*, ... 10*d.*

Item for their *noonchyns* .... 2*d.*

Item for 1 peck of tile pins .... 1½*d.*

---

408 A sloping roof extending from above the window.
409 Cupboard or storeroom.

Item to a carpenter for 5 and a half days in the month of October, the first year of King H[enry] VI [1422], taking the day 8*d.*, 3*s.* 8*d.*

Item for 9 days to the same carpenter in the month of December in the said year, taking the day 7*d.*, 5*s.* 3*d.*

Item to one Robert Cook, labourer, for his labour in breaking of a wall for the foundement[410] of the same coop, with other labour which was in the place, in nailing and other things, 5*d.*

Item for ale to the aforesaid carpenter 1*d.*

Item for ale to the said Robert Cook and to Robert Lynford 1*d.*

Item for 100 & a half elm boards at 2*s.* 8*d.* the hundred, 4*s.*

Item for 200 & a half fourpenny nails, 10*d.*, for 100 threepenny nails, 3*d.*, for half a 1,000 roof nails, 6*d.*, for 100 small nails, 1*d.*, for 100 twopenny nails 2*d.*, for 6 pairs of *potents*[411] at 1½*d.* the pair, 9*d.*, 2*s.* 7*d.*

Item for 6 estrich boards, the piece 6*d.*, 3*s.*

Item for 6 troughs to the coop for to keep in meat and drink for the poultry 2*s.*

Item for 8 hooks of iron for the said troughs, the piece 1*d.*, 8*d.*

[301] [f. 95v]

Item for 6 hasps and 12 staples, price of each hasp with 2 staples 1*d.*, 6*d.*

Item for nails to the said hooks for the troughs 1*d.*

Item for 12 old boards bought from Robert Lynford, price the piece 1*d.*, 12*d.*

Item for an eaves board to the same coop 8*d.*

Item to a labourer for making of a bench[412] to the foot of the same coop with mortar and tile shards, to defend water from the aforesaid coop, 4*d.*

Examined.

Sum 27*s.* 9*d.*

[302]

This is a copy of an indenture of the covenants to amend our hall as it shows, for it was on the point at this time of falling down for default of reparation

This indenture[413] made between Robert Smyth, William Crane, John Philippe, and Hugh Neell, citizens and Brewers of London and Masters of the same craft on that one part, and John Pekker, carpenter of Cambridge on that other part, witnesses that the aforesaid John Pekker has covenanted and undertaken to the said Masters to work and amend certain works of carpentry within the hall of the said craft of Brewers, in the parish of Our Lady [*St Mary*] of Aldermanbury within the said city of London, that is, to wit, that the same John Pekker shall gather together the raisings[414] of the same hall and strengthen and amend the south side of the said hall sufficiently and honestly as belongs to the work of carpentry, the which raisings shall be sufficiently bound with two great beams within the same hall; and also the same

410 Foundation.
411 Stays or supports.
412 Perhaps a stand or ledge to prevent flooding.
413 This copy of an indenture was not punctuated, being a legal document. Modern punctuation has been added to make this document more intelligible.
414 A beam, plank or piece of timber.

John Pekker shall make a bay window in the south side of the same hall, after the space assigned to it within the same hall by the said Masters, like and in the same

[303] [f. 96r]
R. Smyth, W. Crane, H. Nele, J. Philippe

form of work of carpentry for the bay windows in the new corner rent of the Charterhouse in Cornhill of London, with 6 bays, as it is in the same rent, with a vault to be made by the same carpenter underneath the same window in the said Brewers' Hall, and also the same carpenter shall make two other plain windows, each window of 2 bays, in the same south side with lintels above, filled in the head of the same window honestly as it befalls[415] to the work of carpentry, and if the same John Pekker through the said works of carpentry in his default breaks or impairs any works of tiling and daubing, or of any other work within the same hall, then the same John Pekker at his own costs and expenses, shall sufficiently make and amend the same defaults so by him or by his workmen broken or impaired, with the stuff thereto belonging, and leave it in as good state or better than it was before. The which works shall be truly done, ended, and performed in the manner before rehearsed, sufficiently ably and honestly as belongs to the work of carpentry between this and the 14th of August next coming after the date of these indentures, without any further tarrying.

[304]
The same John Pekker will find at his own costs and expenses for the same works, two great beams bound with 4 braces and 4 postels[416] and two great posts and a groundsel[417] and all other timber that shall belong to the said bay window and to the other two windows, with workmanship of carpentry and the carriage thereof unto the aforesaid hall of Brewers. For which works sufficiently to be performed in the manner and form declared before, the aforesaid Masters shall give and pay to the aforesaid John Pekker £10 of sterling, of which the same John Pekker shall be paid on the day of the making of these indentures £5 into his hands, and when the said carpenter has plainly ended and performed the said works in the manner and form before declared, then he shall be paid the other £5 in full payment of the aforesaid £10, and also it is accorded between the aforesaid parties that when the said works

[305] [f. 96v]
be fully ended and performed in the form rehearsed before, then it shall be lawful for the aforesaid John Pekker to have to his own use and to carry out such timber as is left from the said works from his bringing to the use of the said works, without any gainsaying or letting[418] from any man, and the aforesaid Masters and their successors shall warrant and save the same John Pekker and all his [*workmen*] from harm from the craft of Carpenters[419] within the city of London: as for the said works to be made and performed in the manner and form specified before, and furthermore

---

[415] Or 'is fitting'.
[416] Pillar or post, doorpost or gatepost.
[417] Ground-sill: foundation timber to carry a superstructure.
[418] Hindering.
[419] Pekker was from Cambridge [302] so the Carpenters of London might be angered by his appointment.

this present indenture witnesses how the aforesaid John Pekker and John Pekker, citizen and vintner of London[420] by their obligation are beholden and bound to the aforesaid Robert Smyth, William Crane, John Philippe, & Hugh Neell in £20 of sterling, to be paid [on] the 14th day of August next coming, as is more plainly contained in the same obligation. Nevertheless the same Robert, William, John Philippe & Hugh for them and for their successors [as] Masters of the same craft for the time, being willing and granting by this present [indenture] that, if the said John Pekker, carpenter, on his part well and truly holds and performs all the covenants and conditions rehearsed before and declared in the manner aforesaid, then that obligation of £20 will be held for nought and of no value, and else[421] stand in his strength and virtue, and how the same Robert, William, John Philippe, and Hugh by their obligation are beholden and bound to the said John Pekker, carpenter, in £20 of sterling to be paid on the aforesaid 14th day of August, as is more plainly contained in the same obligation. Nevertheless, the said John Pekker, carpenter, wills and grants by this indenture that, if the same Masters on their part hold and perform all the covenants rehearsed in the manner aforesaid, then this obligation of £20 in which the said Masters are bound to the said John Pekker carpenter will be held for nought and else stand in his strength and

[f. 97r]
R. Smyth, W. Crane, H. Nele, J. Philippe

virtue. In witness of which things the parties aforesaid to these indentures sonderly[422] have put their seals.
Written at London on the 8th day of June in the year of the reign of King Henry the Sixth after the Conquest the first [1423].

[306]
And as touching the aforesaid bay window that the said John should have made, after the example of the window in the rent of the Charterhouse in Cornhill: for as much as Robert Smyth and his fellows, with other good counsel, understanding and considering that the said window in Cornhill should have hung upon the hall and have drawn the hall downward, therefore the said Robert and his fellows did make new covenant with the same John Pekker, for to make a bay window that should underset[423] the said hall, after the example of the bay window that is in the inn of the earl of Warwick,[424] by the side of the hall in the said inn. For which workmanship and timber of the bay window, as it stands now here in this place at Brewers' Hall, the same John Pekker has 26s. 8d. more than his covenant was first in the aforesaid indenture, as the same indenture makes mention, and so his covenant was for to have in all £11 6s. 8d. for to make all the workmanship of carpentry, finding the timber thereto for the said bay window, with all other covenants that the aforesaid indenture makes mention of, as it is now made and shows at this time, for the which

420 Brother of John Pekker, carpenter [309].
421 Otherwise.
422 Separately, individually, in turn.
423 Support, prop up.
424 Warwick Inn, Warwick Lane, St Sepulchre was owned by the Beauchamp family and stood just to the south of Newgate, on the west side of Warwick Lane. *Map of Tudor London.*

workmanship and timber of the said hall and window, the aforesaid John Pekker did receive all the parcels written underneath by an indenture made

[f. 97v]

Between the said John and Robert Smyth and his fellows, as it shows in the parcels following, and this is a copy of the same indentures parcel by parcel as it was received. Examined.

[307]
Parcels of payment received by John Pekker, carpenter

First the aforesaid John Pekker, carpenter, received by the hands of W. Porlond on the 24th day of June in the year the first of the reign of King H[enry] VI [1423]   £5.

Item received from the aforesaid William on the 2nd day of August next ensuing   13s. 4d.

Item received from the same William, the 6th day of August   12d.

Item received from the aforesaid William Porlond, the 6th day of September in the year the second of the reign of King Henry VI [1423]   6s.

Item received by the hands of John Philippe   26s. 8d.

Item received by the hands of Robert Smyth   12d.

Item received by the hands of William Porlond on the 7th day of September in the year the second [1423]   8d.

Item received by the hands of W. P. the 16th day of September   4d.

Item paid for 2 days to labourers by the aforesaid William   3s.

Item paid to one James Carpenter, the 12th day of September in the same second year [1423]   55s.

Item paid by the aforesaid W. Porlond for meat and drink to the said John Pekker and his workmen   21s. 9d.

Item paid to John Pekker by the hands of W. P. the 20th day of September   7s.

Item paid by the same W. P. to Gille Carpenter in Cornhill   36s. 8d.

Item paid by the same W. Porlond for 2 pieces of timber bought from John Stok, carpenter,   3s.

Item paid by Rose, the servant of the aforesaid William, the 2nd day of October, the year the second [1423]   4d.

Item paid by the aforesaid W. P. the 3rd day of October to John Pekker by the commandment of Robert Smyth   6s. 8d.

[308] [f. 98r]
R. Smyth, W. Crane, H. Neele, J. Philippe

Item paid by the aforesaid William the 14th day of October to John Pekker   4d.

Item paid by the aforesaid William to a dauber and his man for 8 days,   8s. 8d.

Item paid by the aforesaid William for the hiring of a ferne[425] with carriage of the same,   16d.

Item for 2 cartfulls of loam   8d.

Item for 1 cartful of sand   5d.

---

[425] Windlass, hoisting machine.

Item for 400 laths	2s. 8d.
Item for 1 load of lime	12d.
Item for 4 estrich boards to the lintels of the 2 windows in the hall	2s.
Item for lathnails, transom, sprigg and roof nails,	4s. ½d.
Item paid by the aforesaid William to John Pekker the 6th day of November in the year the second [1423]	6s. 8d.
Item paid by the aforesaid William for *pelers*[426] to the said 2 windows in the hall	15d.
Item paid in reward given to the same John Pekker by the hands of Robert Smyth in the last payment	26s. 8d.

Sum £16 18s. 1½d.

And not withstanding all the parcels of money that the said John Pekker received, as it is declared before, more than his covenant was, the aforesaid Robert Smyth and his fellows gave to him a gown cloth of the livery of the Brewers' craft at that time, at their own costs and not of the common good of the said craft, which gown stood[427] them at 16s. and more, for it was of 4 yards of ray and 3 yards of cloth of colour.

And also this is to wit that John Pekker, carpenter and John Pekker, vintner of London, are written in the aforesaid indenture, and by the same writing of the said indenture, it shows that John Pekker, vintner was bound

Examined.

[309] [f. 98v]

for John Pekker, carpenter, brother to the said vintner, for to hold and perform all the covenants that the said indenture makes mention of, and the said John Pekker, vintner, would not seal the said indenture nor the obligation, nor be *borwe*[428] nor be bound for the said John Pekker, carpenter, neither by word nor by scripture, wherefore Robert Smyth and his fellows, masters at that time did deliver by indentures all his payment of money to John Pekker, carpenter, as is declared before; and the same John Pekker, carpenter made no work of carpentry beside his covenant at Brewers' Hall, but only the pentice that is on the side of the said hall, notwithstanding all the parcels of money that he received, as is written before, more than his covenant was at the beginning.

Examined.

[310]

Parcels of stone and with workmanship of masonry to the *gronselyng*[429] of the hall and the bay window

First paid for 1 load of chalk with the carriage of the same	2s.
Item for 11 feet of Ashlar stone[430]	23d.

426 Shutters, curtains, pillars, or handles to pull windows? Spelt as 'pilers' on the next page.
427 Cost.
428 Act as security, guarantor.
429 Ground-sill: timber foundation for superstructure, used here as a verb.
430 Square hewn stone for building.

Item for 3 carts full of stone, price the load 2s. 8d.,	8s.
Item 16 feet of stone of Kent[431] to the windows of the great cellar	5s. 4d.
Item paid for carriage of ragstone	10d.
Item paid for carriage of 1 load of the aforesaid stone of Kent,	3d.
Item to a mason for 19 days at 8½d. the day with *noonchyns*,	13s. 5½d.
Item to a labourer for 19 days at 5½d. with his *noonchyns*,	8s. 8½d.
Item for 5 loads of lime and 4 sacks, at 12d. the load,	5s. 8d.

Sum 46s. 2d.

[f. 99r]

[311]
R. Smyth, W. Crane, H. Nele, J. Philippe

Parcels of daubing upon the said bay window with amending of other defaults in diverse places

First to a dauber for 3 days with his *noonchyns* at 7½d. the day,	22½d.
Item to his servant by the same 3 days at 5½d. with his *noonchyns*,	16½d.
Item for straw to the work of the said daubers at diverse times	4d.
Item for 200 laths of beech bought from Carpenter in the Riall, with 2 quarters of timber	23d.
Item for 2 loads of sand, the load 5d.,	10d.
Item for 4 loads of loam, the load 4d.,	16d.
Item for 2 lbs (of cotton) of cotton candle for the masons, carpenters and daubers, for mornings and evenings in the month of October,	3d.

Sum 7s. 11d.

[312]
Parcels of tiling in diverse places as it shows underneath

First to a tiler and his servant for 1 day, with their *noonchyns*, upon the north side of the hall,	13d.
Item for half a hundred tiles to the same repairs	4d.
Item to the same tiler for 2 days in tiling of diverse defaults made by John Pekker the carpenter upon the sides of the hall, the day 7½d. with his *noonchyns*,	15d.
Item to a labourer for the said 2 days, at 5½d. with his *noonshyns*,	11d.
Item paid for tile pins to the said works	1½d.

Sum 3s. 8½d.

---

[431] Kentish stone was clearly available for purchase in London at this time.

[313]
Nails to the said works of daubing and tiling

First 3,300 transom for daubing work, the 1,000, 10*d*.,   2*s*. 9*d*.

[f. 99v]
Item for 700 roof nails for tiling work, price   10*d*.
Item for twopenny nails, fourpenny nails, fivepenny nails and sixpenny nails,   5*d*.
Item 200 sprig nails 2*d*. Item for rackhooks[432] 1*d*. Item for tenterhooks ½*d*.,   3½*d*.

Sum 4*s*. 3½*d*.

[314]
Timber, nails, garnets,[433] laths, boards, legs,[434] estrich boards, in amending the side of the hall and the bay window, with the making of a pentice on the side of the said hall and amending the windows of the same hall.

First for 100 oak laths, 9*d*. Item for another 100 laths of beech 7*d*.,   16*d*.
Item for 6 quarters of timber for pilers to the windows in the hall and for sails[435] to the same windows above and beneath   2*s*. 2½*d*.
Item half a hundred sprig nails 5*d*., item for 100 nails 5*d*., item for another 100 nails 5*d*., for the same works   15*d*.
Item for twopenny nails, threepenny nails, fourpenny nails, sixpenny nails and eightpenny nails,   14*d*.
Item for 2 boards to the *leves*[436] of the same windows because they were too narrow,   9*d*.
Item half a hundred and 18 feet of boards instead of laths upon the bay window next to the lead[437]   2*s*. 2*d*.
Item for 1 board to the same window beneath, to keep the earth from the timber,   4*d*.
Item for a pair of garnets to the 2 windows of the cellar,   8*d*.
Item for 9 legs to the pentice that is without [*above the line*: in the yard] on the side of the hall   9½*d*.

[f. 100r]
Item for 15 estrich boards to the said pentice at 6*d*.,   7*s*. 6*d*.
Item for carriage of the same boards   4*d*.

Sum 18*s*. 6*d*.

432   Rack hooks and tenterhooks were hooked or right-angled nails or spikes, set along a tenter in a close row to hold cloth firmly, or metal hooks from which things were hung.
433   Cross garnets: hinges with the upright part nailed to the support and the horizontal to the door or shutter.
434   Perhaps 'supports'.
435   Amount of projection from a surface. Possibly shutters.
436   Perhaps for raising or opening the windows?
437   Perhaps 'under the lead roof', Chambers and Daunt, *London English*, 259.

[315]

Parcels paid to labourers against the first breaking of our hall for the work of carpenters with other parcels

First given to a labourer for carriage of old loam of the wall in the hall when
it was first broken, with his *noonchyns*   5½d.
Item to a labourer for making clean our hall against the amendment of the
said hall for the carpenters' work   6d.
Item for carriage of rushes, and dung that was in the same hall,   3d.
Item to a woman for to help to shake the said rushes out of the dust   2d.
Item in reward given for *hayres*[438] to stop out the sun in the great window for
diverse crafts and fraternities   2d.
Item for 101 lbs of new iron work to our hall, that is to wit, dogs,[439] bolts and
nails to the same at 1¾d.,   14s. 8¾d.
Item for 1 quarter-board[440] for various pentices near the coupe[441] upon the bay
window,   8d.
Item in reward to Crowston, the Master Mason of the Guildhall, for the
oversight of our works,   20d.

Examined.

Sum 18s. 7¾d.

[316] [f. 100v]

Parcels of lead to cover the bay window

First for 1,103 quarterons 4 lbs of new lead to the said bay window at 8s.,   £4 14s. 3d.
Item for the working of 103 quarterons and 19 lbs of old lead given by
Peter Haiford and John Elcy, at 16d.,   2s. 6½d.
Item 28 lbs of solder at 6d.,   14s.

Sum £5 10s. 9½d.

of which is abated by William Calston, plumber, for his entry into the
fraternity of Brewers of London 1 cwt of new lead, given by the same
William, the price 8s., and so there is clearly received by the said William
Calston   £5 2s. 9½d.[442]

---

438   Coarse fabric such as sackcloth.
439   Clamp or grappling iron for holding a log to be hoisted or sawn. Chambers and Daunt,
       London English, 259, suggested 'dognails', with heads sticking out on one side. Dognail:
       nail with solid, slightly countersunk head, large nail with head projecting on one side,
       a strong square spike with flat point and hooked head.
440   Used in carpentry and shipping, wood extended around a ship's quarters. Perhaps timber
       with a rounded edge for a sill.
441   Perhaps cope, covering. Chambers and Daunt, *London English*, 259, suggested 'a quarter
       board for several pentices near the iron grating on the bay window.'
442   See **[274]** for Calston's fraternity entry.

Glass to the same bay window

First 171 feet of glass to the said bay window at 8*d*.,	£5 14*s*.
Item in reward given to the said glazier by covenant	6*s*. 8*d*.
Item paid for nails to the said glazier	12*d*.

Sum £6 20*d*.

Iron work to the same bay window

First for the making of 80 *sowdelettes*[443] of iron for to stay the glass in the said bay window at ½*d*.,	3*s*. 4*d*.
Item for the making of 16 lockets[444] of iron to the same window at 1*d*.,	16*d*.
Item for 38 new *sowdelettes* for the said window and to the window that John Swepston did make in the side of the hall,	2*s*. 4*d*.

Sum 7*s*.

[317]

    Money given [*above the line*: in reward] **to various sergeants of** [*above the line*: the] **mayor for their labour to the profit of the craft** [*scored*: for to be good friend to our craft]

First to John Combe	3*s*. 4*d*	Item to Robert Charleton	10*s*.
			Examined.

[f. 101r]

[*Latin*: which was made before][445]

Item to Hastynge	5*s*.	Item to Rawlyn, sergeant,	3*s*. 4*d*.
Item to Richard Davy	8*d*.		
		Item to John Crewse	12*d*.

Item to a Taker of the King's for to suffer our carpenters still in our work at Brewers' Hall[446]	16*d*.

Sum 24*s*. 8*d*.

[318]

Parcels paid at the Interment of King Henry V

First to 8 torchbearers at the interment of the said king	4*s*.
Item for portage of 8 gowns of white cloth for the same torchbearers from the Guildhall to Brewers' Hall	1*d*.

Sum 4*s*. 1*d*.

---

[443] Perhaps iron to support glass in the window, similar to leading.
[444] Locket: horizontal bar, usually of iron, to support glass in a window.
[445] This is a continuation of expenses from the King's funeral [220–2]. John Combe was common sergeant at arms or common crier, 1417–60, and John Hastings was the mayor's esquire or sword bearer, 1421–6, see Barron, *London in the Later Middle Ages*, 365–6.
[446] Payment to avoid conscription of the carpenters into the King's army.

Costs of a Barge

Item for hiring a barge on the day that William Walderne, mayor of London, [1422–3] took his charge at Westminster in the first year of King Henry VI [1422–3]   6s. 8d.
Item for meat and drink to the bargemen of the same barge   2s.

Sum 8s. 8d.

Diverse gifts

Item to John Carpenter, clerk of the Guildhall for 1 purse given to the said John,   2s. 9d.
Item to the said John, in reward given for diverse evidence that he delivered out of the Guildhall to the Masters of the craft,   6s. 8d.
Item in reward given to the clerks of the said John Carpenter, for to have a copy of the Coopers' marks of London447   12d.

Examined.

Sum 10s. 5d.

[319] [f. 101v]
Diverse costs made as it shows underneath

First 69 lbs of iron for grates to the windows of the great cellar, 1½d. ¼d. the lb,   10s. 1d.
Item for 5 estrich boards to the cellar of the bay window at 6d.,   2s. 6d.
Item for the half part of 1 pair of indentures made between John Pekker, carpenter, and the Masters of Brewers' craft,   8d.

Sum 13s. 1d.

Diverse parcels paid for making clean our hall against the coming of crafts and fraternities to our hall, in the time of reparation of the said hall

First to a labourer for cleansing of our hall and gathering of chips out of the said hall and also of dust, with strewing of rushes and setting of tables in the aforesaid hall, against the feast of the Barbers, with other occupations,   5½d.
Item to the same labourer, and to a woman, for the cleansing of the hall after the said Barbers and against the work of the carpenters,   2d.
Item for half a burden448 of rushes against the feast of the same Barbers   2d.
Item for trashes449 and nails against the feast of the Cooks   1½d.
Item to a labourer by 1 day for making clean of our hall against the feast of the Cooks   5d.
Item to another labourer for helping of the said works   3d.
Item for making clean the hall and the kitchen with water after the said Cooks   5d.
Item to a woman in helping of the said occupation   1d.

447 *Cal. Letter-Book, I*, 237.
448 Burden or load carried by animal or man, used as a measure of quantity.
449 Trash-nails for fixing scenery for revels.

Item to another labourer by 1 day in making clean of the hall and other
diverse things against the feast of the Armourers   5½d.

[320] [f. 102r]
Item given to a woman for to help to the same works   1d.
Item for nails, that is, to wit, fourpenny nails, against the same feast of [*the*]
Armourers,   1d.
Item for carriage of dung after the Armourers, Glaziers, and Clerks,   1d.
Item to John Smyth for cleansing of our place, with carriage of timber, tiles
and tile shards, for 2 days,   4d.
Item to 2 women for their travail in helping to make clean the hall against
our feast day, with their meat,   6d.
Item given to Olde Stephene for making clean of the place with washing
[*above the line*: gutters] of the same place, and for carriage of timber and
other things into the great cellar against our feast day,   6d.
Item to a labourer for 1 day against the feast of All Saints, after the working
of masonry, in making clean of the place,   5½d.

Sum 4s. 7d.

[321]
   **Diverse parcels paid for certain necessary things bought as it shows
   underneath**

First for washing of a towel to an altar,   1d.
Item for a lattice that stands in the window of the great chamber at end of
the great counter,   8d.
Item for a little lattice with 2 small garnets that stands in the chamber over
the oven in the kitchen,   4d.
Item for 2 garnets to the falling boards⁴⁵⁰ at doors of the pantry and buttery, 8d.
Item for amending of a clicket to the great gate and for amending of a lock
with 2 rings to the doors in the hall and to the entering of the great chamber,
with the amending of the lock to the hall door,   4½d.
                                                                        Examined

[322] [f. 102v]
Item paid for 4 yards of black cloth, price 3s. 4d. the yard, for William
Porlond, clerk, for the interment of King Henry V, late king of England,   13s. 4d.
Item for 2 latches, 2 catches, 2 cramps, with nails and working of the same
to the door of the chamber over the oven in the kitchen, with amending
of the door of the withdrawing chamber in the great chamber, and with
amending and working of a ring to the parlour door, with amending of a
latch for 1 window in the hall,   8d.
Item for 3 days to Robert Cook for making of hangings for diverse things
in the almarie in the great kitchen, with amending of diverse stools, and
daubing of 2 holes, that is, to wit, 2 windows in the kitchen above the

---

⁴⁵⁰   Boards fixed to the wall that could be folded down to rest on supports and form a table.

243

almaries, so that the rain should not enter in, with making of pins to the windows in our place, with amending of other various things, 12*d.*

Item for 6 lbs of new iron to amend the old spit, 12*d.*

Item for an old stall to set ale upon 3*d.*

Item for boat hire the last day of August, in the obit of King Henry V, from Westminster to London, 8*d.*

Item for 1 rope to the bucket of the well, with the occupation to 1 labourer to fasten the rope to the same bucket, and for other things, the which had fallen in the aforesaid well, 10*d.*

Item paid for a new key to the buttery door 3*d.*

Item to John Pekker for 2 estrich boards 12*d.*

Item to a text-writer for the writing of names of the brethren and sisters in the table 6*d.*

Item to a limner for the illuminating of the letters in the same table 2*d.*

Item for an amendment of 1 piece of iron to the head of the gutter that runs under the hall 4*d.*

[323] [f. 103r]

Item to paviors for levelling with gravel of the yard so that water should not stand still in the said yard, 9*d.*

Item for the setting on of a stock-lock⁴⁵¹ for the door of the great cellar, with 1 staple, 2*d.*

Item 2 hasps, 4 staples for diverse doors in our place 4*d.*

Item to Robert Cook for portage of tiles and tile shards and stones at certain times, 3*d.*

Item to Olde Stephene in amending and cleansing our place, with delving⁴⁵² of stones in the almshouse, dressing of timber in the great cellar and washing of doors and windows and diverse boards, 4½*d.*

Item for mail of habergeons⁴⁵³ to our halling ½*d.*

Item to Robert Cook for washing with lime the walls of Jonette Brygham⁴⁵⁴ 6*d.*

Item for 2 boards bought to make benches for various herbs in the yard, 12*d.*

Item for working of the same, with carriage of dung and earth, 2*d.*

Item for 1 new key for the flail⁴⁵⁵ of our great gate, with the mending of the same lock, 4*d.*

Item paid to the raker of Bassishaw for carriage of robux from the Guildhall unto Brewers' Hall⁴⁵⁶ 2*d.*

Item for 1 board, with the working of the same board between 2 forms, to the high table, 4*d.*

Item for nails to Jankyn Tenterdene and other things to the hen coop, 4*d.*

⁴⁵¹ A lock enclosed in a wooden case, usually on an outer door.
⁴⁵² To dig, hide in the ground.
⁴⁵³ A sleeveless coat of mail or scale armour. The Armourers used Brewers' Hall for their feast, [319]–[320], which might explain this decoration. Chambers and Daunt, *London English*, 260, suggested that rings of [old?] armour were used to fasten the halling [painted cloth or tapestry] in the hall.
⁴⁵⁴ A resident, tenant, or a neighbour.
⁴⁵⁵ A swing bar for a gate.
⁴⁵⁶ Perhaps rubble was needed for building work at Brewers' Hall.

Item for 3 clickets to the almshouse, with 1 key to the almaries in the kitchen,   12*d.*
Item for 4 lbs of old lead   1½*d.*

Sum 28*s.*

Examined

[324] [f. 103v]

The costs of the bins in the pantry

First for 4 boards for the covering of the bins in the pantry   5*d.*
Item to John Goodfelawe for his labour of 2 days in making and covering of
the aforesaid bins in the pantry, and for making and amending of the hooks
in the hall for hanging of the dosser and costers with the hanging of the
costers in the parlour, taking the day with his meat 5*d.*,   10*d.*
Item for nails and hooks to the aforesaid bins and other things,   5*d.*

Sum 20*d.*

[325]

**Hoops to diverse vats and tubs with other reparations to the same, and
brooms bought at diverse times**

First for hoops to diverse vats and tubs with amending of the same without
and within,   7½*d.*
Item for 2 hoops to 1 kimnel[457]   2*d.*
Item for 1 bar to the bottom of a tub, with the amendment of another tub   2*d.*
Item for 3 new hoops with 1 piece of timber to the bottom of the great vat   3½*d.*
Item for 3 new hoops to 2 tubs   2½*d.*
Item for 6 hoops to 3 vats and to various tubs   6*d.*
Item for bottoming of 1 tub with boards and pitching of the aforesaid vats
and tubs,   2*d.*

[f. 104r]
Item for 1 hoop to a tub, with 1 board for the bottom of a vat,   1½*d.*
Item for (an) mending of 1 long vat with pitch,   1*d.*
Item for cutting of a hogshead with 2 hoops & 2 bars to the same, for to
make 2 tubs,   4*d.*
Item for brooms bought at diverse times, of brush and broom,   5*d.*

Examined.

Sum 3*s.* 1*d.*

[326]
And as touching a dosser, 2 costers for the hall, with 1 coster stained for the parlour,
it is made mention of in the accounts, the which accounts are written afterwards in
this book.[458] For all the parcels that were received and paid in the time of the said

---

457   Tub used for brewing.
458   See **[334]–[356]**.

Robert Smyth, William Crane, Hugh Neell and John Philippe were written plainly
and shortly[459] in their accounts with diverse sums, as it shows.

And other sums, that have many parcels upon them, have been declared here in this
book, parcel by parcel; and other sums have not been declared nor written here,
because they have been shortly declared in the same accounts, as it shows, by the
aforesaid dosser and costers.[460]

And as for wax to the interment of King Henry V, it is written before in this book
and in the same accounts shortly.[461] And also of a present that was given to William
Walderne when he was last mayor of London, it is written before in this book and in
the same accounts.[462] And furthermore, as touching the costs of the weirs[463] in [*the*]
Thames, done and paid in the time of the said William Walderne, mayor of London,
you shall find [*them*] shortly written in the same accounts. And all other things that
have been paid from duty yearly, that is, to wit: for various hoods given, fees to various
persons, trentals, ink and paper and parchment, salary to priest & clerk, alms given to
various persons, wax[464] in the chapel, offering, rewards to various clerks of churches,
Holy bread, and rose garlands for quit rent: of all these, mention was made in each of
the accounts of all the Masters, in times before said, as it shows there, openly written to
those persons who will have understanding and knowledge thereof.[465]   Examined.

[327] [f. 104v]
**The ordinance of a dinner with all the parcels thereof, in the Tuesday, the feast
of the decollation of Saint John [*the*] Baptist,[466] in harvest, in the year of King
Henry VI the second [29 August 1424], the day of accounts of Robert Smyth,
William Crane, John Philippe and Hugh Neell.**

The First Course
Numbles[467] to pottage
Pheasants stewed with a syrup
Swan with chawdron[468]

The Second Course
Cream of almonds in pottage
Cony
Pigeon
Dowcettes

The costs of the same dinner

First in bread,	2*s.* 10*d.*
Item for 1 kilderkin of good ale	2*s.* 4*d.*
Item for 1 kilderkin of three-halfpenny ale	22*d.*
Item for 8 gallons and 1 quart of red wine	4*s.* 1*d.*

---

459 In the sense of 'briefly'.
460 See [354].
461 See [281], [346], [354].
462 See [227].
463 See [163]–[164].
464 'Bex', in the manuscript: 'wax' or 'box'?
465 The clerk did not wish to write out costs again here and believed that he had already
recorded them. The masters clearly had their own records of accounts, which have not
survived.
466 The beheading of John the Baptist, which was commemorated on 29 August.
467 Animal entrails, especially deer, part of the back and loins of a hart.
468 Sauce with chopped entrails and spices.

Item for 4 gallons and 1 pottle with 1 pint of white wine[469]	18½*d.*
Item for 6 swans, 3*s.* 4*d.* apiece,	20*s.*
Item for 4 dozen pigeons, the dozen 10*d.*,	3*s.* 4*d.*
Item for 15 conies	3*s.* 9*d.*
Item for 14 pullets	4*s.* 1*d.*

Item in expenses for a supper at *Hole Boole* in East Cheap,[470] the day of the aforesaid accounts, 18*d.*

Item in expenses of 1 dinner made in East Cheap at the said *Hole Bole*, the day of the interment of King Henry Vth,	19½*d.*
Item for 100 eggs	8*d.*
Item for 3 geese	21*d.*
	Examined.

[328] [f. 105r]

Item for calves' *gadres*[471]	10*d.*
Item for 16 marrowbones	2*s.*
Item for 1 dish of butter	2½*d.*
Item for onions	2*d.*
Item for 2 gallons of cream	8*d.*
Item for 1 peck of coarse flour	4½*d.*
Item for water in tankards	4*d.*
Item for baking of 2 conies	3*d.*
Item for white suet	2*d.*
Item for roasting of a cony	1*d.*
Item for 1 quart & 1 pint of vinegar	1*d.*
Item for 1 quart & 1 pint of white honey	6*d.*
Item for salt	1½*d.*
Item for baking of a goose	4*d.*
Item to 2 *tornebrochers*	4*d.*
Item for hiring of spits	4*d.*
Item for 1 cream cloth	6*d.*
Item for 1 quarter of coals bought at Baynard's Castle	8*d.*
Item for the portage of the same coals	1*d.*
Item for 16 faggots	8*d.*
Item to 1 Minstrel called Percivale	4*d.*
Item for the hiring of pewter vessels	6*d.*
Item given in reward for 1 cloth to the dresser, to the wife of Robert Lynford,	1*d.*
Item for 1 wiping cloth for the pewter vessels	1*d.*
Item for washing of napery	6*d.*
	Examined.

[329] [f. 105v]

Item for carriage of dung	1*d.*
Item to Thomas Bourne, Cook,[472] for his travail, 6*s.* 8*d.*	£3 6*s.* 3½*d.*

---

469 A slip of paper with 'white wyne' written on it has been pasted over 'wyhte white wyne'.

470 Le Hole Bole or Bull, Honey Lane, Cheap ward. Harben, *Dictionary*, 304.

471 Testicles, livers?

472 Bourne was not the usual Brewers' cook. Payments for the cooking of conies and a goose suggest that this did not happen at Brewers' Hall on this occasion.

First for 4 lbs of almonds, 8*d*., 2 lbs of dates, 5*d*.,   13*d*.

Item for 1 lb and half of raisins of Corinth, 7*d*., half quarteron of cloves, 4*d*.,   11*d*.

Item for 1 ounce of mace, 2*d*., half an ounce of saffron, 5*d*.,   7*d*.

Item for half a lb of white sugar, 6*d*., 1 quarteron of red *dragge*473 and white *frise* 6*d*.,   12*d*.

Item for pepper 7*d*., 1 quarteron of ginger 5*d*.,   12*d*.

Item for 1 quarterons and half of *canell*   13*d*.

Sum £3 11*s*. 11½*d*.

[330]

In the same day that the aforesaid Robert Smyth and his fellows made their accounts, by a common assent of the persons written afterwards, the Masters at that time with others who had been Masters before that time, who were there present in that day; in that day it was granted to William Porlond, clerk of Brewers' craft at that time, 40 shillings by year more than any clerk had before the same time from the said craft. For all the clerks before that time took no more than 40*s*. by year for their salary, with other casualties.474 And the said William had no more by 5 years but 40*s*. by year, wherefore the Masters, with other good counsel, considered that the same William was profitable and busy to do the common

Examined

[f. 106r]

profit of the same craft, they granted to him 40*s*. by the year more than any clerk had before that time, with all other casualties and advantages. So that the said William did take £4 by year after that time, beginning at Christmas next following [1424], to receive the first payment of 20*s*. by the quarter, and so forth afterwards in each quarter.

[331]

> **These are the names of the Masters at that time, with other persons who had been Masters before that time and were present and heard the said accounts of Robert Smyth and his fellows**

| John Masonne | Thomas Hatcher | John Broke | Henry Trebolans |

Masters of the said craft of Brewers of London at that time475

Robert Smyth	William Crane	Hugh Nell	John Philippe
John Ketyng	John Reyner	John Riche	John Pyken
John Basset	Peter Hayforde	Robert Hiltonne	Robert Carpenter
William Ferrour	William atte Wode	Alan Brett	

---

473 Possibly dredge: sweetmeat containing a seed or grain of spice, or a preparation made with spices, and froise or fryes, pancake containing bacon.

474 Casual or incidental charge or payment.

475 Mason, Hatcher, Broke and Trebolans were the new masters, elected in autumn 1423 or 1424. Smyth, Crane, Neel (Nell) and Philippe had been masters 1421–23, see *Cal. Letter-Book, I*, 287. Their accounts were heard at this feast on 29 August 1424. Hayford

[332]

These are the names of those who were at dinner with the persons written before, on the day of the said accounts

The prior of the Freres Austyns	Sir Robert Steynton	Thomas Driffeld		
John Salter	Three of the wives of the said Masters	John Humber		
Friar John Berkynge	Peter Carpenter	Richard Aleyn	Robert Nikke	
William Belle	Henry Payn	William Ferrour the Younger		
William Repon	John Spore	William Pethin	John Ryngesson	J. [*above the line*: James] Mogonne, poulter.

[333] [f. 106v]

These are the names of the persons that were prayed[476] to the same dinner on the day of the said accounts, but were not present at the said dinner, and neither did they hear the same accounts.

Adam Copendale	Alexander Miles	Davy Bronnynge	John Chapmanne
John Qwyntyn	Richard Sherwode	Richard Welde	Thomas Grene
William Petevile	William atte Welle	John Caryon	John Spencer
Roger Awdymer	William Calstonne	John Russell.	

[334] [f. 107r]

Robert Smyth, William Crane, John Philippe, Hugh Neele

These are the same accounts, as it shows openly afterwards

[*Latin*] **The account of Robert Smyth, William Crane, John Philippe and Hugh Neel, Masters of the craft of Brewers and the fraternity of the Holy Trinity in the church of All Hallows beside London Wall, of all receipts & expenses to the use and profit of the said craft and fraternity, from the feast of All Hallows in the year of the reign of King Henry V the 9th until the same feast in the year of the reign of King Henry VI, the second, that is, for two whole years [1421–3],[477] William Porlond at that time being common clerk of the said craft and & fraternity.**

Remaining in the common box

---

was a Master in 1406, atte Wode, Reyner and Ferrour from 1418–19, Hylton, Pyken and Carpenter from 1419–21, see Appendix I.

476 Invited.

477 1 November 1421 to 1 November 1423.

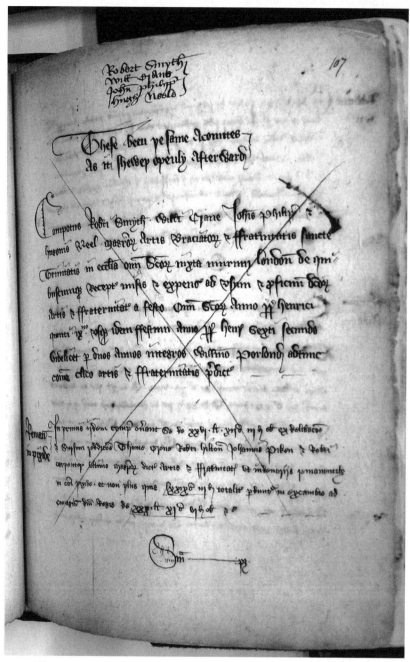

Figure 10. GL MS 5440 The Brewers' Book, folio 107r. Entries in
Latin and English on the same page. © The Brewers' Company.

First the same accountants take over the sum of £26 12s. 3½d. from the deliberations and surplus rendered by Thomas Grene, Robert Hilton, John Piken and Robert Carpenter, last Masters of the said craft and fraternity, so that in money [*this sum*] remains in the common box and no more, because 79s. 3d. in all was lost in the exchange to the coinage of the said King, from the total of £30 11s. 6½d.

Examined.

Sum as appears

[335] [f. 107v]
Rent from the tenement

And of 5s. 10d. received for rent of the tenement beside the gate for the term of Easter in the year of the said reign of the said King Henry V the 10th.[478]
And other rents for the same tenement for the term of St John the Baptist in the same year: nothing was received for lack of a tenant.
Then 17s. 6d. from the rent of the said tenement for the terms of St Michael, the Nativity of Our Lord and Easter from then on following
And other rents to come from the said tenement in future were nothing, because by the consent and assent of the Masters and commonalty, it was agreed that the tenement was to be transformed into an almshouse for the poor brothers and sisters of the said fraternity being sustained by alms.
And the reparations for the abovesaid house in total were undertaken by Robert Smyth, one of the 4 Masters abovesaid and a few others besides

Examined.

Sum 23s. 4d.

[336]
Hire of the Hall
[*Latin and English*]
And of 6s. 4d. received from the Armourers for occupying the hall 3 times altogether
And of 3s. 8d. received from the Fraternity of the Holy Cross for occupying the same hall twice
And of 4d. received from the Jury of an Inquest for occupying as above, once
And of 5s. received from the Girdlers for occupying as above, 5 times
And of 6s. 2d. received from the Parish Clerks of London, occupying as above, 5 times
And of 10s. received from the Barbers for occupying as above, 9 times
And of 20d. received from the Football Players for occupying, twice
And of 4s. 6d. received from the Coopers for occupying as above, twice
And of 5s. received from the Point-makers for occupying as above, 3 times
And 12d. received from the Ferrours for occupying as above, once.
And of 3s. 10d. received from the Fraternity of the Holy Trinity for occupying as above, 4 times
And of 3s. 4d. received from the yeomen Cordwainers for occupying as above, once
And of 7s. 4d. received from the Cooks of London for occupying as above, 3 times

---

[478]   See **[266]** where the same rents were listed.

And of 12*d*. received from the Butchers of London for occupying as above, once
And of 8*d*. received from the Galoche makers for occupying

[337] [f. 108r]
as above, once.
And of 20*d*. received from the Smiths for occupying as above, once
And of 20*d*. received from the Founders for occupying as above, once
And of 12*d*. received from the Glaziers for occupying as above, once

Examined
Sum 64*s*. 2*d*.

[Latin]
Quarterage
And of £30 4*s*. 11*d*. received from the brothers and sisters of the said fraternity, that is, for the said 9th year and 10th year of the reign of the said King Henry V [1421–2 and 1422], £14 13*s*. 9*d*., in the time of Robert Chichele being mayor of London [1421–2], and £15 11*s*. 2*d*. during the first year of the reign of King Henry VI [1422–3] William Walderne then being mayor of the said city [1422–3].

Sum as appears

[338]
Testamentary Legacies

And of 49*s*. 4*d*. received from various people, that is
For the soul of John Thetford 20*s*.
For the soul of William Ederich 13*s*. 4*d*.
For the soul of John Balard 12*d*.
For the soul of John Moyle, skinner, 20*d*.
For the soul of Margaret, the wife of Robert Hilton, 6*s*. 8*d*., and
For the soul of William Bolton 6*s*. 8*d*.

Sum as appears

[339]
Admission to the Freedom

And of £11 13*s*. 4*d*. received from 35 men admitted to the freedom of the craft of Brewers during the time of this account, that is
Dederic Johnson, Ducheman
William

Examined.

[f. 108v]
Misterton
John Pamplionne
John Vivean
Richard Stonham
John Nicoll
John de Van

252

Henry Stapill
John Lacy
John Warsoppe
Thomas Meltonne
William Dowdale
Matthias Adriannesson
Peter Andrew
John Hopkyn
John Mabile
John Elcy
John Bugby
Nicholas Merton
William Rose
Thomas Rodier
John West
John Bretaigne
John Godyng
Thomas Gilderedge
Thomas atte Hethe
William Watford
John Jacow
John Bernewell
John Purley
Ivy Jacow
Jacob Tolvan
Henry Payn
Thomas Walsh
& Thomas Smyth
That is, from each of them, 6s. 8d.

And John Swepston, sergeant in the city, and John Westmestote, serving in the said county of Ware were admitted into the freedom of the said craft and paid nothing.

Sum as appears

[340]
Entry of Brothers

And of £12 13s. 4d. received from the entry of 76 brothers during the time of this account, that is from:
Dedric John-son, Ducheman
William Misterton
John Pamplionne
Richard Stonham
John de Van
Henry Stapull
John Warsoppe with Agnes his wife
William Dowdale with Johanna his wife
Peter Andrew
John Mabile

253

Mathias Adrianneson with Margaret his wife
John Bugby
John Hopkyn
Nicholas Merton with Agnes his wife
William Rose with Johanna his wife
John West
William Watford
John Purley with Johanna his wife
Jacob Tolvan
Thomas Walsh with Johanna his wife
William Andrew
Richard Lucas with Alice his wife
John Frost with Alice his wife
Richard Carrowe with Elizabeth his wife
John Hanslape
Randolph Marke with Rose his wife
Peter Short with Alice his wife
John Bronnyng with Johanna his wife
Henry Wikkeston with Thomasina his wife
John Bate with Anya his wife
John Massy

Examined

[341] [f. 109r]
William Bullok with Johanna his wife
Henry Rows with Johanna his wife
Robert Ketynge with Margery his wife
William Frank with Cecilia his wife
William Covele
John Caston with Agnes his wife
Simon Petessyn with Isabella his wife
William Mascall
Thomas Walpole with Johanna his wife
Simon atte Welle
William Rawlyn with Alice his wife
John Bedford
John Riche, tailor, with Alice his wife
William Totewell with Isabella his wife
Thomas Merssh with Agnes his wife
John Faireman with Johanna his wife
William Pompe
John Sharpe, maltman
John Iver with Isabella his wife
Thomas North
John Chercheseye, tailor, with Alice his wife
William Hanygnton [*above the line*: tiler]
Henry Grene with Agnes his wife
John Gremesby
Richard Tiler, maltman
Roger Awdymer [*above the line*: vintner]

John Bosvenon
Sir Adam Dalton
William Ferrour Junior with Agnes his wife
John Spore
Thomas Ayle
Katherine Wirgen
Johanna the wife of John Amwell, skinner
Roger Ware with Alice his wife
John Aston
Richard Herty with Alice his wife
William Miles, maltman, with Matilda his wife
Alexander Marcowe with Agnes his wife
Sir William Goodswayn, [*above the line*: parson]
Henry Boston, mason
Master Richard Donyngton of the Augustinian Friars
John Cavendissh with Alice his wife
Richard Bulwik with Johanna his wife
Friar John Berkyng &
Robert Calowe, shearman

That is, from each 3s. 4d.

And from William Calston, plumber, for entry into the said fraternity, 100 lbs of lead, at the value of 8s.

Sum – as appears

[342]

Collection made for the reparation of the Hall and Windows
[*Added*: Received from the persons written below, that is, the sum from each person towards our hall and said windows]
And of £23 16s. 10d. received from various persons towards the reparation of our Hall, that is:
From John Mason 16s. 2d.
And on their part for the palisade between the hall and the gate, from each part with keys, locks and all the work pertaining to it:
Matilda the widow of John Stannton
John Broke and John Riche of Wood Street.

Examined.

[343] [f. 109v]
Who each paid 13s. 4d. & Thomas Aleyn at 12s. & Richard Aleyn at 11s. 8d.
Thomas Hatcher, Dedric Johnson and Alexander Miles each at 10s.
& John Ketyng and John Humber both at 9s.
& Henry Trebolans at 7s.

& John Chapman, John Rothyng, Roger Blissote, John More at Aldersgate, John Russell, Roger Swanneffelde, John Reyner, William atte Welle, William Ferrour at the Maid, Randolph Mark, Thomas Hancok, William Payn, John Quyntyn, Robert

Hilton, Thomas Godyng, William Ferrour at the Bell and Robert Calowe, shearman, 17 persons each at 6s. 8d.

John Fekenham at 4s. 4d. John Brewester at 3s. 8d.

& Henry Rowe, Robert Elkyn, John Salter, John Reeffawe, William Bayly de Smithfield, John Elcy, William Eyre, Henry Noble, William Henry, David Brownyng, Walter Colshull, Roger Ware, Adam Copendale, Richard Sherewode, Johanna the wife of Richard Bulwik, grocer, John Lumbard, Alice Herty, John Serle, John Piken, Master Richard Donyngton, Augustinian Friar, Peter Short, Hugh Glene, William Grosse, John Newman, a baker de Wood Street, Sir Robert Steynton, John Wightmore, Robert Pede, John Stokes, Johanna[479] Holbeke, Peter Carpenter, Roger Baronn, William Petevile, Richard Harlowe, John Carionne, Robert Carpenter, Alexander Marcowe, William Rose, William Lacy and William Belle – 40 persons each at 3s. 4d.

[344]
& John Thomas at 2s. 6d.
& Simon Potekyn and John Norman each at 2s. 4d.
& Nicholas Gomnaylok, Thomas Kent, John Lucas, Robert Ketyng and John Laurence, 5 persons, each at 2s.
& John Fayreman, William Dowdale, William Bernard, John Hardyng, John Bedford, Robert Bullard, John Warsoppe, Baldewyne Hoper, William Illyng, John Riche at the Angel, Nicholas Fuller, John Jacob, Robert Giles, Robert Dorewell, Agnes Bugge, Henry Bedell, William Rawlyn, Simon Herry, John Riche, tailor, John Kenaky, Thomas Penson, John Bronnynge, Thomas Kirtot, Phillip Godfrey, John Frost, John Stone, Robert Delowe, William Claissonne, William Frank, William Geffray, Henry Grene, Jacob Lonegro, John Barston, John Snell and William Reponne – 35 persons at 20d.

& John Brokford at 16d.
& John Aleyn at the Crutched Friars, Nicholas Muriell, John de Van, Walter Glyn, Gilbert Botonne, William Bodevile, John Bugby, Thomas Ayle, John

Examined

[f. 110r]
West, Thomas Gratley, 10 persons each at 12d.

William Devenyssh at 6d.
And the abovesaid John Elcy gave towards the repair of the hall windows 3 quarters and 1 lb of lead to the value of 4s. ½d.
Peter Haiford gave to the same repairs 118 lbs of lead to the value of 6s. 1½d.

Sum as appears

[479] The abbreviation suggests Johanna rather than John. John Holbek's wife was listed as Margaret at this time. Johanna Holbek also appeared earlier **[277]**.

[345]
Diverse Alms

And of 3s. 10d. received from diverse alms given on the said day of accounts by
Thomas Grene and his associates, and that is from
John Turvey, William Ferrour at the Cony, Henry Trebolans, Robert Hiltonne,
William Ederich, Peter Hayford, Hugh Neell, John Masonne, John Reyner, Robert
Carpenter and Robert Smyth, 11 persons each at 4d.
And John Salter at 2d.

Sum as appears

[346]
Sales made

And of 20d. received from William Porlond, clerk, for the price of 100 tiles at 8d.
and 1 cartful of tile shards at 12d. sold by him
And of 28s. received from Hugh Neel, Robert Smyth, William Ferrour, John Salter,
John Philippe, William Crane and William Ederich for the price of 112 lbs wax
bought by them and remaining after the burial of our lord King Henry V, late King
of England, price the lb, 3d.

Sum 29s. 8d.

[347]
Fines for transgressions with fines in the Guildhall

And of 11s. 8d. received from fines for transgressions against the craft of Brewers,
that is, from Michael Tregononne 3s. 4d., & John Hopkyn 3s. 4d., and from Thomas
Boteler 5s.
And of 8d. received from the Searchers of the craft for fines made in the Guildhall

Sum 12s. 4d.

[348] [f. 110v]
Of money remaining from a certain tax made for the weirs

And of 32s. received from William Porlond, clerk, that remains in money from
a certain tax levied during the time of William Cambrigge, mayor of the city of
London [1420–1], that is, in the year the 9th of the reign of King Henry V [1421–2]
for destroying the weirs in the river Thames, by the order of the said King and on
behalf of the said mayor and made in full Parliament.
The last money was spent by Thomas Grene & his associates between London &
Staines on the one part, and by John Mason and his associates on the other, between
London & Queenborough in the city of the said mayor.
[*above the line*: in the present leaf plainly declared]
[*scored*: As is plainly written in a certain roll of parchment made before].

Sum as appears

257

Sum total received £115 15s. 4½d. From which money there remains in the common box £26 12s. 3½d.

[349]
Alms given

for which the aforesaid Masters seek allowance for alms given to Stephen Lalford for the terms of St John the Baptist in the year of the reign of King Henry V the 10th and the terms of St Michael and the Nativity of our Lord in the year of the reign of King Henry VI the first, from the outset, for certain causes now past, taking by term 5s., total 15s., during the time of this account.

By agreement alms were given to Robert Lynford, another almsman, as above, that is, for the terms of St John the Baptist, St Michael, the Nativity of our Lord, Easter, St John the Baptist, St Michael, the Nativity of Our Lord, that is, for 7 terms in the time of this account, 35s.

Alms given to Johanna Cole, a woman in alms, for the term of Easter in the 10th year of the reign of Henry V and at that time dying, that is for one term during the time of this account 7s. 7d.

And by agreement alms were given to Johanna Awmbele, a certain woman in alms taking alms by quarter as above, that is, for the said two whole years during the time of this account 60s. 8d.

Sum 118s. 3d.

Examined

[350] [f. 111r]
Bread, wine and wax in the Chapel

And in bread and wine spent in the fraternity Chapel for the holy altar and made ready there, used in the time of the abovesaid account, 4s.
And for 17 lbs and a half of new wax made at diverse prices and 30 lbs of old wax at diverse prices during the time of this account, 10s. 9d.
And in amending a certain old cope in the same, that is, in weaving the wool, with either dyeing or staining, with completion during the time of this account 8s. 6d.
And in amending a window in the said Chapel during the time of this account 6d.

Sum 23s. 9d.

[351]
Stipends

and in the stipend of Sir Robert Steynton, chaplain of the said fraternity, taking £6 13s. 4d. yearly, that is for the said time of this account £13 6s. 8d.

And in the customary stipend or fee, to William Porlond, clerk of the said craft and fraternity, taking 40s. per annum, that is, for the time of this account £4.[480]

Sum £17 6s. 8d.

[352]
Customary Payments

and in money paid to the rector of the church of [*St Mary*] Aldermanbury for his oblations, at 3s. 4d. per annum, that is for the said time, 6s. 8d.
And to the parish clerk of the same church, taking 12d. the year by custom, for the said time, 2s.
And for holy bread at 4d. yearly, that is for the said time of this account, 8d.
And in the price of 2 rose garlands for the quitrent of our hall for 2 years, that is, in the time aforesaid, 4d.
And to the parish clerk of the church of All Hallows [*London Wall*] abovesaid,[481] at 12d. the year, that is, for the time of this account, 2s.

Sum 11s. 8d.

[353]
Reparations

And paid for timber & carpenters for the said hall and window at £16 18s. 1½d.
To the mason and dauber & their servants for their labour, stone, loam, and lime for diverse parcels for filling, £4 19s. ½d.
For glass with workmanship £6 20d.
For lead with workmanship at 102s. 9½d.
For iron tools with workmanship 7s.

In total for reparations to the hall and for new windows made there the total is £33 8s. 7½d.

Sum – as appears

Examined

[f. 111v]
Reparations

And in money paid for timber, carpentry, tiles and all filling for the cloister between the hall and kitchen at £4 4s. 7½d.
Timber, planks, bolts, carpentry and other materials, spent for le chapon house,[482] newly made, 27s. 9d.
Diverse repairs and amendments in the tenement beside the gate 14s. 3d.

---

480 This was before Porlond's pay rise took effect: see **[330]**.
481 All Hallows church was not in fact mentioned above, although the fraternity and chapel were.
482 Hen house.

Timber, tables, bars, keys, carpentry and other things for the cupboard in the kitchen, 27s. 2½d.
The storeroom below the guest room 11s. 4d.
In total during the time of the aforesaid account £8 5s. 2d.

Sum as appears

[354]
[*scored*: Cust] **Necessary Expenses**

And paid for one dosser with 2 costers of colour green and ruby, each with weaving and staining with the Holy Trinity and 3 images of the same in adoration as plainly appears, 100s.
Customary payment made for a coster in the parlour with weaving and staining in two colours and staining with 3 images and their scriptures as appears there, 48s. 8d.
Wax bought for the exequies of the Lord King Henry V, 51s. 8d.
A certain present made 37s.
A customary payment made by William Crane and his associates concerning weirs, 36s. 8d.
Reward made to diverse sergeants and to a certain taker of the lord King, with Crewse the esquire of the mayor at diverse times by the sheriffs, 24s. 8d.

Reward made to diverse sergeants and to a certain taker of the lord King, with Crewse the esquire of the mayor at various times, 24s. 8d.

Money paid for reparations to the almshouse, the last sum of £10 paid by Robert Smyth and 2s. 6½d.
And for torch bearers, barges hired and other sums and diverse payments made in diverse ways and times, 73s. 9d.
In total during the time of this said account £18 14s. 11½d.

Sum as appears

[355]
Clothing Given
And in the price of 3 hoods given to 3 various people, that is to Sir Robert, chaplain of the fraternity, William Pethin and Thomas Donyngton, sergeant, each at 5s., total 15s., during the time of this account

Sum as appears

Examined

[f. 112r]
Fees and in fees to Thomas Donyngton, sergeant at the chamber of the Guildhall, taking 6s. 8d. yearly, for 2 years for the time of this account, 13s. 4d.

Sum as appears

[356]
Trentals

And for trentals for various brothers and sisters of the fraternity, that is: David Soys, Richard Neweman, William Robard, Cecilie Parker, John Sonman, John Rothyng, Margaret Setyngborne, John Thetford, John Ballard, William Bolton, Richard Rowdon, Nicholas Kene, Margaret formerly the wife of Robert Hilton, Matilda formerly the wife of John Philippe, Johanna Cole, William Bracy, John Stannton and William Ederiche, for the souls of the said 18 who have died during the time of the said account and the time of the account of Thomas Grene and his associates, and who were admitted[483] in this way and 2*s.* 6*d.* was paid for each, 45*s.*

Sum as appears

Parchment, paper & ink

and for the price of parchment, paper and ink spent by William the clerk of the said craft and fraternity for the time of the account abovesaid, 4*s.*

Sum as appears

Sum total of expenses and outgoings £89 6*s.* 5*d.*

And there remains in the hands of the Masters thus in the said box for the common store £26 8*s.* 11½*d.*
And thus from the box decreased in the time aforesaid 3*s.* 4*d.*
And the aforesaid 4 Masters, desiring to improve and in no way decrease, in all things, for the said commonalty and their box, paid with money in their own hands towards the repairs of the company hall and the making of windows 100*s.*, that is 25*s.* each. And thus there is in the box £31 5*s.* 7½*d.*
And in increase from their time £4 16*s.* 8*d.*

Examined.

[f. 112v is blank]

[357] [f. 113r]
[English]
John Mason, Thomas Hatcher, John Broke, Henry Treybolens

In the year of the reign of King Henry VI the second [1423–4] William Crowmere [*was*] mayor of London [1423–4], the which William was a good [*man*] of governance for all the commonalty of the city and all the city was well pleased with him and also he was a good man and a loving to the craft of Brewers, and in his year he did no dis-ease[484] to the said craft, nor would he receive any gifts nor rewards from the same craft in all his time, but he thanked the Masters of the craft

---

483   Their names would have been entered on the fraternity bede-roll and then trentals of
       thirty masses and prayers for their souls would be offered.
484   Disquiet.

goodly[485] with all his heart for their good proffer that they made to him as for to have given him gifts. And also he thanked them as much as though he had received them and he made promise to be a good friend to them during all his year, and so he was.

John Mason, Thomas Hatcher, John Broke and Henry Trebolans [*were*] Masters of the said craft of Brewers in the said year and the same Masters chose Searchers of the said craft for their time, that is to wit: Peter Carpenter, William Belle, William Ferrour the Younger and John Humber.

[358]

The names of Brewers who had barrels and kilderkins which were not sealed with the Cooper's mark, in the time of the said William Crowmere mayor of London [1423–4]

Henry Stapull has 1 kilderkin that is not marked in the house of Julyane, huckster, dwelling in the alley under the shaft[486] in Cornhill.

Examined.

[f. 113v]

Thomas Smyth at the Garland without Bishopsgate has 1 kilderkin not marked in the house of John Cordewaner at the Lily in Lombard Street

Richard Clerk at the Swan in Bassishaw has 1 kilderkin not marked, against the Guildhall gate in the house of a huckster in Bassishaw

John Philippe has 1 kilderkin not marked, in the same place

Thomas Hatcher at the Cup beside Wool Quay has 1 kilderkin not marked in the house of Simon Seman, alderman

Simon Petesyn at the Peahen in Bishopsgate Street has 1 kilderkin not marked, found in Cornhill upon the shoulders of his servants.

Horold at the Cross in Tower Street has 1 barrel not marked, found upon the shoulders of his servants

Felton at the Lamb in Mart Lane has 1 barrel not marked, found in the high street upon the shoulders of his servants.

Thomas Boteler at the Helm in Cornhill has 1 kilderkin not marked at the house of Thomas Goldsmyth in Gracechurch Street

Robert Rose near the Dolphin in the parish of St Magnus has 1 kilderkin not marked, and he will not tell [*the searchers*] to whom it belongs, and the same Robert and his wife, Foowle, disputatiously reproved the Wardens of the craft that were at that time

Richard Stonham at St Julian beside the Bars in Aldersgate Street, against John Tregelowe, has 1 kilderkin not marked in the house of John Mogen, poulter, in Cornhill.

[359]

Malt that was forfeited in the market by the Masters and the Wardens in the time of the said mayor

First of John Sharppe,   2 quarters   of John Tyler,   2 quarters

---

[485]   Kindly.
[486]   The maypole shaft outside St Andrew Undershaft church.

[f. 114r]

Of Thomas Cokkeshed	1 quarter	of Ayleward or else called Aylewin	1 quarter		
Of Robert Sharnebroke of Hoddesdon	1 quarter	of Richard Carter of Barnet	1 quarter		
of Danyell	2 quarters	of Grene	1 quarter	of a man of South Mimms	1 quarter

[360]

These are the persons that sold their ale without measure in the time of the said William Crowmere, mayor, which persons made various fines, as it shows afterwards

[*Latin*: quie amen Clerk [?] quem deus …]⁴⁸⁷

Thomas Kent at the Basket beside Billingsgate			1 k.
John Gremesby at the Kings Head	1 k	Robert Rauff, huckster, near the same place	1 k.
Robert Shadde near the said place	1 k	Mongeonne, huckster,	1 k.
The wife of Trevelias	1 k.	Maud Rose beside the Dolphin near St Magnus	1 kilderkin
John of Lynne at the Three Nuns beside the Stocks			1 barrel
Item at the Long Entry	1 barrel	Item at the Seven Stars	1 barrel
Item at the Red Cock	1 k.	Margaret, huckster, at the Austin Friars' gate	1 k
Item at the White Cock	1 barrel	Johanna Langton against the gate of the Taylors	1 k.

Buyles, huckster, in the alley at Gracechurch Street in the parish of St Peter in Cornhill   1 k.

Bradeweye at the Malt market in Gracechurch   1 k.

Paddeswikk, grocer,	1 k.	Hans, Dutchman, at the Green Gate in Pudding Lane	1 k.

William Hacomblene, grocer, in a cellar beside the Seven Stars in (the) Poultry,   1 k

John Blostmer at the [*above the line*: Cony in] Conyhope Lane   1 k.

Bienvenu, dwelling in the Scalding Alley in (the) Poultry   1 k.

John Leke at the Lamp in Fleet Street   1 k.

---

⁴⁸⁷ The meaning is unclear.

The wife of Robert Cordewaner, huckster, in Showe Lane against the Castle,   1 k.
Katherine Badeston in Elden Lane in the parish of St Martin at Ludgate[488]   1 k.

Examined

[f. 114v]
[English]
A servant that dwells with Baldok, the wax chandler, against the wardrobe of
the King's beside Baynard's Castle   1 k.
John Aleyn, Brewer, at the Cock near the Crutched Friars   1 k.
Roger Blissote at the Swan near St Nicholas Shambles   1 barrel

[361]
Foreign ale forfeited in the time of the aforesaid mayor, W. Crowmere

Alis Martyn, the wife of a baker in the parish of St Katherine of Christ Church
against the Well at the end of the wall of the prior of Christ Church,[489] has 1 k. of
foreign ale, forfeited
Gace dwelling against the Butchers at the end of Ivy Lane has 1 barrel of foreign ale,
forfeited
The wife of Robert Cordewaner, huckster, in Showe Lane against the Castle has 1 k.
of foreign ale, forfeited
The servant with Baldok, wax chandler against the wardrobe of our Lord King
beside Baynard's Castle has 1 k of foreign ale, forfeited
A foreigner dwelling at the Lattice against the joiner in Hosier Lane beside Watling
Street upon the west side, has 1 k of foreign ale, forfeited

[362]
**In this year was received from John Beterden, chamberlain of the Guildhall, for
the quarter part of the fines made and raised from the persons written before
for diverse defaults, as it is shown above, 18s. 2½d.**

Item received from the sheriffs of London at that time for the quarter part of the malt
that was arrested because it was not carried to the plain market at Gracechurch to be
sold, but it was sold by sample, and therefore the owners of the said malt made fines
to the same sheriffs of London, from which fines the craft of Brewers received the
quarter part for their own part, that is to wit, 6s. 8d.

[f. 115r]
And all the aforesaid money that was received from the said chamberlain and
sheriffs was spent on a dinner made on the Monday after Passion Sunday in the
year of the reign of King Henry VI the third [2 April 1425] for the most worshipful
persons of the Brewers' craft at that time. And to the costs of the aforesaid dinner,
beside the same money that was received from the chamberlain and the sheriffs,
Frere John Berkyng paid to the same dinner 5s., Sir Robert Steynton, priest, paid

---

488   Part of Warwick Lane, St Martin Ludgate.
489   Holy Trinity Priory, a house of Augustinian canons. A well is shown on the *Map of
Tudor London*. The capital W for Well here might suggest an inn or tavern.

to the said dinner 3s. 4d., William Porlond, the common clerk of the Brewers' craft 3s. 4d.

Peter Carpenter, William Belle, William Ferrour the Younger and John Humber, each of these persons paid 20d., 6s. 8d.

Sum 43s. 2½d.

[363]

These are the parcels of the same dinner

First for bread	2s. 1d.	Item for flour	10d.
Item for good ale and three-halfpenny ale	3s. 10d.	Item for diverse sauces	4½d.
		Item for onions and salt	1d.
		Item for herbs	½d.
Item for 9 gallons of wine and 1 quart	6s. 2d.	Item for coals	14½d.
Item for spices	2s. 2½d.	Item for 12 faggots of wood	6d.
Item for eels	22d.	Item for 20 tankards of water	4d.
Item for green fish	6d.	Item for washing of napery	3d.
Item for whelks	2s.	Item paid to Minstrels	12d.
Item for sturgeon	5s.	Item paid to [*above the line*:	
Item for fresh salmon	10d.	John] Hardy, Cook, for his travail,	2s.
Item for mussels	2d.	Item to William Repon, butler,	6d.
Item for 1 pickerell[490]	16d.	Item for carriage of dung out of	
Item for plaice	3s. 4d.	the place	2d.
Item for halibut	2s. 8d.		
Item in pike and eels	17s. 9d.	Item to the porter for keeping of	
Item in stockfish[491]	2d.	the gate	2d.
Item for portage of the said fish	6d.	**Sum 57s. 10d.**	
		Examined	

[364] [f. 115v]
Quarterage of Crowmere [1423–4]

Alexander Marcowe and Agneys his wife	2s.	Sir William Goodswayn, parson of St Mary Woolnoth	12d.
Alexander Myles and Isabell his wife	2s.	Sir Adam Dalton, parson of All Hallows in the Wall,	12d.
Aleyn Brett for his arrears	9s. 2d.	Sir Robert Steynton	12d.
Adam Copendale [*Latin*: for himself][492]	12d.	Dederik Johnson and Weveyn his wife	2s.
Anneys Stratton	12d.	Dionyse Barthorpe	12d.
Anneys Bugge	12d.		
Anneys Carletonne	12d.	Elizabeth Colbrook	12d.

490 Young pike.
491 Cod and other fish split and dried in the open air without salt.
492 Copendale was married to Jonette, then Emma, last mentioned at **[262]**. Here the scribe added that Copendale paid only for himself. His wife, unnamed, was recorded again at **[412]**.

Anneys, the wife of William Render,	12*d.*
Alice, sometime the wife of William John,	12*d.*
Alice, sometime the wife of John Benge,	12*d.*
Alice, late the wife of W. Ederich,	12*d.*
Alice Hore	12*d.*
Alice, late the wife of William Bracy,	2*s.*
Baldewyne Hoper and Johnete, his wife,	2*s.*
Cristiane sometime the wife of J. Ballard,	12*d.*

Emma Canonne	12*d.*
Henry Trebolans and Elizabeth his wife	2*s.*
Henry Wixstone and Thomasine his wife	2*s.*
Henry Rowe and Johanna his wife	2*s.*
Henry Bedell and Alice his wife	2*s.*
Henry Noble and Anneys his wife	2*s.*

[365] [f. 116r]

Henry Grene and Anneys his wife	2*s.*	John Holbek and Margaret his wife	2*s.*
Henry Lymber and Felise his wife	2*s.*	John Jacob and Alice his wife	2*s.*
Henry Staple	12*d.*	John Bate and Anya his wife	2*s.*
Hugh Neel and Emma his wife	2*s.*	John Hardyng and Anneys his wife	2*s.*
Hugh Glene and Margaret his wife	2*s.*	John Bosvenon and Alice his wife	2*s.*
		John Barston [*Latin*: for himself]	8*d.*
John Piken and Alice his wife	2*s.*	John Lumbard and Margaret his wife	2*s.*
John Elcy and Alice his wife	2*s.*	John Wyghtmore and Isabelle his wife	2*s.*
John Brooke and Cristiane his wife	2*s.*	John William and Johanna his wife	2*s.*
John Frost and Alice his wife	2*s.*	John Mason and Felice his wife	2*s.*
John Eylond and Denyse his wife	2*s.*	John Ketynge and Margaret his wife	2*s.*
John Astonne and Maud his wife	2*s.*	John de Van and Katheryne his wife	2*s.*
John Humber and Margaret his wife	2*s.*	John Stone and Anneys his wife	2*s.*
John Goldrynge and Johanna his wife	2*s.*	John Reyner and Agatha his wife	2*s.*
John Tregolowe and Johanna his wife	2*s.*	John Chapman and Juliane his wife	2*s.*
John Randolf and Juliane his wife	2*s.*	John Caryon and Alice his wife	2*s.*
John Riche, tailor, and Alice his wife	2*s.*	John Quyntyn and Katherine his wife	2*s.*
John Riche of Wood Street and Margaret his wife	2*s.*	John Caston and Agnes his wife	2*s.*
John Riche the Younger and Mathie his wife	2*s.*	John Fayreman and Johanna his wife	2*s.*
John Brewester and Johanna his wife	2*s.*	John Purley and Johanna his wife	2*s.*
John Spenser and Margaret his wife	2*s.*	John Reeffawe and Juliane his wife	2*s.*
John Toke [*Latin*: for himself]	12*d.*	John Philippe and Margaret his wife	2*s.*
John Salter and Johanna his wife	2*s.*	John Cavendissh, broderer,	12*d.*
John Russell and Alice his wife	2*s.*	John Basset	12*d.*
		Friar John Berkynge	12*d.*
		John Snell	12*d.*
		John Pamplion	12*d.*

John Lynne	12*d.*
John Bedford	12*d.*
John Hardy, Cook,	12*d.*
	Examined

[366] [f. 116v]

John Assh	12*d.*	Johanna Horold	12*d.*
John Turnour	12*d.*	Johanna Rothyng	12*d.*
John Bargonne	12*d.*	Johanna the wife sometime of	
John West	12*d.*	Alan John	12*d.*
John Sere, glover,	12*d.*	Johanna Amwell	12*d.*
John Gremesby	12*d.*	Johanna Awmbele	12*d.*
John Mabile	12*d.*	Idonye Hatton	12*d.*
John Hanslape and Lettice his wife	2*s.*	Julyan Hetersete	12*d.*
John Kenaky	12*d.*		
John Gedeney	12*d.*	Katherine Wirgeyne	12*d.*
John Ratford	12*d.*		
John Sonder	12*d.*	Michael Tregononne	12*d.*
John Serle	12*d.*	Michael Eve, Elizabeth [*Latin:*	
John Southmede	12*d.*	his wife, for 2 years]	4*s.*
John Warsoppe	12*d.*		
John Waghorn	12*d.*	Margaret Thetford	12*d.*
John Massy	12*d.*		
John Spore, ferrour,	12*d.*	Nicholas Gomnailok and Johanna	
John Bugby	12*d.*	his wife	2*s.*
John Hopkyn and Alice his wife	2*s.*	Nicholas Fuller and Alice his wife	2*s.*
John Luke	12*d.*	Nicholas Mertonne and Agnes	
John Laurence	12*d.*	his wife	2*s.*
John Bronnyng and Johanna his		Nicholas Muriell and Agnes his	
wife	2*s.*	wife	2*s.*
John Baily	12*d.*	Nicholas Aleyn	12*d.*
John More and Cristiane his wife	2*s.*	Peter Carpenter and Katherine	
John Gibbes	12*d.*	his wife	2*s.*
John Sharppe, maltman,	12*d.*	Peter Short and Alice his wife	2*s.*
John William in Southwark &		Peter Haiford & Maud his wife	2*s.*
Alice his wife	2*s.*	Peter Roos	12*d.*
		Peter Andrew	12*d.*
Johanna the wife of John			
Fekenham, for 2 years,	2*s.*	Philip Godfrey	12*d.*

[367] [f. 117r]

Robert Elkyn and Cecily his wife	2*s.*	Roger Baronne	12*d.*
Robert Ketynge and Margery his		Roger Awdymcr, vintncr,	12*d.*
wife	2*s.*		
Robert Delowe and Margaret his		Raff Mark and Rose his wife	2*s.*
wife	2*s.*		
Robert Miles, maltman, and		Simon Petesyn and Isabell his wife	2*s.*
Margery his wife	4*s.*	Simon atte Well	12*d.*

Robert Carpenter and Margaret his wife	2s.	Stephen Clean	12d.
Robert Pede and Alice his wife	2s.	Stephen Roo	12d.
Robert Mayhew & Juliane his wife	2s.		
Robert Nikke and Alice his wife	2s.	Thomas Hatcher & Margaret his wife	2s.
Robert Gyles and Johanna his wife	2s.	Thomas Hancok and Denyse his wife	2s.
Robert Hilton and Margaret his wife	2s.	Thomas Dewy and Agnes his wife	2s.
Robert Smyth and Anya his wife	2s.	Thomas Grene and Maud his wife	2s.
Robert Walram	12d.	Thomas Aleyn and Lettice his wife	2s.
Robert Jewell for 2 years	2s.	Thomas Emond and Sibile his wife	2s.
Robert Fordam	12d.	Thomas Merssh and Anneys his wife	2s.
Robert Lynford	12d.	Thomas Godyng and Margaret his wife	2s.
Richard Sherewod and Alice his wife	2s.	Thomas Gratley and Margaret his wife	2s.
Richard Carowe and Elizabeth his wife	2s.	Thomas Yole and Alice his wife	2s.
Richard Aleyn and Johanna his wife	2s.	Thomas Walssh and Johanna his wife	2s.
Richard Herty and Alice his wife	2s.	Thomas Smyth and Alice his wife	2s.
Richard Lucas and Alice his wife	2s.	Thomas atte Wode	6d.
Richard Harlowe and Johanna his wife	2s.		
Richard Bulwik and Johanna his wife	2s.		
Richard Tiler, maltman,	12d.		
Richard Donyngton	12d.		
Richard Brynton	12d.		
Richard Frepurs	12d.		
Roger Ware and Alice his wife	2s.		
Roger Blissote and Maud his wife	2s.		

Examined.

[368] [f. 117v]

Thomas Ayle	12d.	William Totewell and Isabell his wife	2s.
Thomas Penson	12d.		
Thomas Howe	12d.	William Miles, maltman, and Maud his wife	2s.
Thomas Martyn	12d.		
Thomas North	12d.		
Thomas Bristowe	12d.	William Andrewe, hosteler,	12d.
		William Bernard	12d.
William atte Welle and Alice his wife	2s.	William Watford	12d.
William Baily and Alice his wife	2s.	William Illyng	12d.
William Payne and Elene his wife	2s.	William Mascall	12d.
William Dowdale and Johanna his wife	2s.	William Baconne, butcher,	12d.
		William Termeday	12d.
William Rawlyn and Alice his wife	2s.	William Pompe	12d.
		William Bodevile	12d.

William Boteler and Elizabeth his wife	2s.	William Hanyngton, tiler,	12d.
William Claisson and Isabelle his wife	2s.	William Calstonne, plumber,	12d.
		Walter Glyn	12d.
William Frank and Cecily his wife	2s.	Walter Colshull and Alice his wife	2s.
William atte Woode and Katherine his wife	2s.		
William Crane and Elene his wife	2s.		
William Ferrour the Elder and Anneys his wife	2s.		
William Grosse and Katherine his wife	2s.		
William Ferrour the Younger and Anneys his wife	2s.		
William Bullok and Johanna his wife	2s.		
William Harry and Agnes his wife	2s.		
William Canonne and Elizabeth his wife	2s.		
William Porlond and Denyse his wife	2s.		
William Petevile and Johanna his wife	2s.		
William Geffrey and Anya his wife	2s.		
William Belle and Florence his wife	2s.		

Sum £17 15s. 5d.

Examined.

[369] [f. 118r]
These are the parcels for a dinner made on the 7th day of May in the year the third of the reign of King Henry VI [1425] to various persons of Brewers' craft, at which dinner each person paid 6d.
Sum total received at that time in Brewers' Hall for the same dinner   57s. 9d.
[*French*: to whom is …]

The First Course
Beef stewed in a syrup, goose and capon roasted

The Second Course
2 chickens in a dish, 1 endorred,[493] pigeons roasted, dowcettes

In the buttery and pantry

First for white bread and trencher bread and 3 pecks of fine flour	7s. 10d.
Item 1 barrel and a kilderkin of good ale	7s.
Item 2 barrels of three halfpenny ale	7s. 3d.
Item for 1 kilderkin of penny ale	12d.
Item for red wine, that is to wit, 35 gallons,	23s. 4d.
Item for 2 dozen earthen pots	8d.
Item for 4 dozen cups	2s. 4d.

493   Glazed with egg yolk and saffron.

Item to William Devenyssh, panter,   16*d.*
Item to William Reponne, butler,   12*d.*

Sum 51*s*. 9*d*.

In the kitchen

First for 2 points[494] of beef with certain ribs and 8 fillets of veal and 1 sirloin
of beef,   8*s*. 11*d.*
Item 4 dozen and 2 geese   29*s*. 2*d.*
                                                                       Examined.

[370] [f. 118v]
Item 4 dozen capons   17*s.*
Item 8 dozen chickens   13*s*. 4*d.*
Item 9 dozen and 1 (of) pigeons   10*s*. 2*d.*

Item 2 dozen of marrowbones & a half,   5*s*. 4*d.*
Item for carriage of venison   4*d.*
Item 400 eggs   2*s*. 4*d.*
Item for 2 dishes of butter   8*d.*
Item for portage of beef and other things   6*d.*
Item for herbage   3½*d.*
Item for 5 gallons of cream   20*d.*
Item for pulling[495] of pigeons   2*d.*
Item to the *tornebrochers*   9*d.*
Item to John Hardy, Cook,   10*s.*
Item to a water bearer   10*d.*
Item for 4 quarters of coals   2*s*. 4*d.*
Item for faggots   13*d.*
Item for wiping cloths   2*d.*

Sum £5 5*s*. ½*d*.

Diverse necessaries

First for a burden of rushes in the hall   4½*d.*
Item for washing of diverse napery   12*d.*
Item for 8 dozen of pewter vessels   20*d.*
Item for carriage of dung   2*d.*
Item to a porter   2*d.*
Item to one Stephen for diverse labour   4*d.*
Item for tares and barley for the poultry   2½*d.*
Item for blanderelles[496]   8*d.*

Sum 4*s*. 7*d*.

[494] Not found. Chambers and Daunt, *London English*, 261, suggested 'joints taking the leg all together'.
[495] Plucking.
[496] A variety of apple.

270

[371] [f. 119r]
Sauce

First for 1 peck of salt and a half,	4*d.*
Item for 1 pottle and 1 pint of honey	10*d.*
Item for garlic and onions	7*d.*
Item for 3 quarts of verjuice	3*d.*
Item for packthread	½*d.*

Sum 2*s.* ½*d.*

Spices

Item half lb of pepper	10½*d.*
Item for 1 quarteron of saffron	3*s.*
Item for 1 quarteron of powder of ginger	6*d.*
Item for 1 quarteron of powder of canell	8*d.*
Item for 3 lbs of raisins of Corinth	18*d.*
Item for 5 pounds of dates	15*d.*
Item for half a quarteron of cloves	5*d.*
Item for half a quarteron of mace	4*d.*
Item for half lb of sugar	8*d.*
Item for powder of sanders	2*d.*
Item for half a pound of powder of ginger and canell	14*d.*

Sum 10*s.* 6½*d.*

Sum total of the aforesaid dinner £8 13*s.* 11½*d.*

Of which was received from diverse persons that were present at the same dinner, as it is written before, 57*s.* 9*d.* And so the same Masters, John Mason, Thomas Hatcher and their fellows paid clearly of their proper good £5 16*s.* 2½*d.*

[f. 119v is blank]

[372] [f. 120r]
In the year of King Henry VI the third [1424–5], John Michell was mayor of London, [1424–5] the which John was a good man and meek and soft to speak with. To the which John Michell, by a common assent of the craft of Brewers, after the said John was chosen mayor of London, before he took his oath at Westminster, we gave him an ox, price 21*s.* 2*d.*, and a boar, the price of 30*s.* 1*d.* And so in the time and the year of the same John mayor of London, he did no harm nor dis-ease to the said craft of Brewers, but he charged the Masters of the same craft that they should ordain to make good ale for the King's people and that no man should have cause to complain to the same John Michell, mayor, about Brewers' craft. John Mason, Thomas Hatcher, John Broke and Henry Trebolans [*were*] Masters of the said craft of Brewers in the same year. Peter Carpenter, William Belle, William Ferrour the Younger and John Humber [*were*] Searchers of the same craft in the said year.

[373]

These are the persons who sold their ale without measure, in the time of the said John Michell, mayor, the which persons made diverse fines, as it shows afterwards

The wife of John Austyn, tailor, beside the Ram's Head in Conyhope Lane	1 k.
John Stone at the Rose in the Old Jury	1 k.

[f. 120v]

The huckster at the cellar underneath St Thomas of Acre	1 k
John Baily at the Swan in Pissing Lane	1 k
Agnes Grene at the Pewter Pot in Ironmonger Lane	1 k
Dalamar Cosermaker[497] against a cellar in St Lawrence Lane	1 k
Elene the wife of Bridges, the goldsmith,	1 k
The wife of Janyn at the end of Gutter Lane	1 k
Alice Brayn	1 k
John Assh at the Christopher near St Martin le Grand	1 k
James Tolvan at the Crane near St Nicholas Shambles	1 k
Margarete Wortwiffe	1 k
John Brewester at the Pannier in Paternoster Row	1 k
Luce Chaundell	1 k
John Bron and the huckster at the Ball in the Shambles	2 barrels

[374]

Foreign Ale forfeited in the time of the aforesaid Mayor John Michell

John Sonder in the parish of the Whitechapel has 2 k of foreign ale in the house of John Tookman, Cook

The same John Sonder has 3 k of foreign ale in the house of Simond Moysaunt beside St Helens

A brewer at the Hammer in the parish of Whitechapel has 1 k of foreign ale in the house of William Welton against St Katherine Colman.

[375] **[f. 121r]**

Vessels unsealed in the time of the said mayor John Michell

Thomas Macchynge has 1 quart pot that is not sealed
Robert Pakkar has 1 k not sealed
A point-maker at the cellar in St Lawrence Lane has 1 quart pot not sealed
Alice Gayton at the Swan in Old Fish Street has 1 quart pot and 1 k not sealed
Margaret Wortwiff has 1 k that is not sealed
William Andrewe at the Horse Head without Newgate has 1 barrel not sealed in the house of Thomas Warwik, woodmonger, beside the Broken Wharf
Robert Bullard at the Swan in Smithfield has 1 k not sealed.

---

[497] Perhaps a maker of costers (hangings), or a costermonger, who sold fruit from a barrow.

[376]
In this year was received of John Beterden, chamberlain of the Guildhall, for
the fourth part of the fines made and raised from
the persons written before, for diverse defaults, as it is shown above   9s. 1½d.
The which money, by motion of William Belle, was given to the reparation of the
almshouse, as it shows in the accounts of John Mason, Thomas Hatcher, John Broke
and Henry Trebolans.

[377] [f. 121v]
First from John Gladewyne and Robert Chamber, 1 piece of murrey
containing 17 yards at 3s. 5d. the yard,   58s. 1d.
Item from the same John Gladewyne and Robert Chamber, 1 piece of murrey
containing 17 yards, price the yard 2s. 10d.,   48s. 2d.
Item from Robert Chambre and John Gladewyne 1 cloth of murrey
containing 36 yards & a half, price the yard 3s. 4d.,   £6 12d. Pardoned 8d.
Item from John Gladewyne and Robert Chamber 8 yards & a half of murrey
at 3s. 2d.,   26s. 11d.
Item 1 cloth of murrey containing 11 yards bought from the same John
Gladewyne and Robert Chamber, price the yard at 4s. 4d.,   36s. 8d.

Sum £14 10s. 10d.

Examined.

Item from John Gedeneye for 2 cloths of murrey, each cloth containing
38 yards & a half at 3s. 8d.,   £14 2s. 4d.
Item from the said John Gedeneye for 1 cloth of murrey containing 33 yards
at 3s. 8d.,   £6 12d.

[378] [f. 122r]
Item from the same John Gedeneye for 1 cloth of murrey engrained
containing 24 yards at 6s. 6d.,   £7 16s.

Sum £27 19s. 4d.

Examined.

Item from Raff Holond 1 piece of murrey containing 4 yards and a half, price
the yard 3s. 8d.,   16s. 6d.
Item from Clement Lyffyn 1 cloth of murrey containing 14 yards and
1 quarter, price the yard 3s. 4d.,   47s. 6d.
Item from Richard Skernyng 1 cloth of murrey containing 24 yards and a
half, price the yard 4s. 4d.,   £4 20d.
Item from Thomas Porter, draper, for 1 cloth containing 33 yards of murrey,
price the yard 3s. 8d.,   £6 4d. Pardoned 8d.
Item from Richard Sutton for 1 cloth of murrey containing 23 yards of
murrey, the yard at 3s. 8d.,   £4 4s. 4d.
Item of John Haltonne for 3 yards of murrey, price the yard at 3s. 10d.,   11s. 6d.

Sum £18 22d.

Examined.

Item from Nicholas Cowbrege of Bristol 1 cloth of murrey containing
22 yards and a half, price   59s. 8d.
Item from the same Nicholas 4 cloths, of which 3 each of 24 yards & 1 of
23 yards of murrey,   £13 3s. 10d.

Sum £16 3s. 6d.

Examined.

[379] [f. 122v]
Item of Robert Tetersale, draper, 24 cloths of ray, each cloth containing
200 rays, taking out and except for 18 rays wanting in all the said cloths, the
price of each cloth 46s. 8d., abated and forgiven 5s.,   £55 15s. Pardoned 5s.

Sum as appears

Examined.

Item to John Turnour, shearman, for the shearing of cloth of colour and rays,   40s.
Item to Robert Calowe, shearman, and to another shearman, for shearing 13
cloths,   25s. 8d.
Item in [?] draft, good silver and good ale[498]   5d.

Sum 66s. 1d.

Sum total of cloth of murrey 443 yards 3 quarters
Rays 4,782 rays
Money £135 16s. 7d.
Examined.

[380] [f. 123r]
Alan Brett 36 rays 3 yards of murrey   26s. 8d.
Alexander Miles 38 rays 3 yards of murrey   28s.
Alexander Marcow 29 rays 2 yards 1 quarter and half quarter of murrey   22s. 10d.

Adam Smyth 9 rays 3 quarters of murrey   6s. 8d.
Adam Copendale 1 yard 1 quarter half quarter of murrey   8s.

Agnes Carleton 1 yard of murrey   5s.

Baldewyne Hoper 28 rays 2 yards of murrey   22s.

Sir Adam Dalton, parson of All Hallows in London Wall, 4 yards & 1 quarter
murrey   18s. 8d.
Sir Robert Steynton 4 yards 1 quarter of murrey   17s.

Dederik Johnson 40 rays 3 yards of murrey   30s.

---

498   For Raff Hollond **[378]**, see Matthew Davies, 'Holland, Ralph (d. 1452), tailor and
      alderman of London', *ODNB*. The entry 'drauft, godsilver and good ale' probably
      accounted for ale and money given to the shearmen. I am grateful to Dr John Oldland
      for this suggestion.

Davy Bronnynge 37 rays 3 yards of murrey | 27s.

[Gr]499 Elizabeth Colbrok 1 yard of murrey engrained | 8s.
Edmond Bosvenonne 9 rays half a yard half quarter of murrey | 6s. 8d.

Gebon Aletaker 8 rays half a yard & 1 nail of murrey | 6s.

[381] [f. 123v]
Henry Trebolans 38 rays 5 yards of murrey | 34s. 8d.
[Gr] Item 2 yards of murrey engrained | 16s.
Henry Payne 34 rays 2 yards & a half of murrey | 25s. 8d.
Henry Grene 38 rays 3 yards murrey | 28s.
Henry Rowe 26 rays 2 yards & half quarter of murrey | 21s.
Henry Stapill 36 rays 2 yards 3 quarters of murrey | 26s. 4d.

Hugh Neell 28 rays 2 yards 3 quarters & a half of murrey | 24s.
Hugh Glene 36 rays 2 yards 3 quarters of murrey | 26s. 8d.

Henry Bacy500 8 rays half yard half quarter of murrey | 6s.
Henry Bedell 8 rays half yard half quarter of murrey | 6s.
Henry Noble 10 rays 3 quarters of murrey | 7s. 4d.
Henry Fereby 9 rays 3 quarters of murrey | 6s. 8d.
Henry Wixtone 8 rays half yard of murrey | 6s.
Henry Lymber 8 rays half yard of murrey | 6s.

Sum Rays 521 Examined.
Murrey cloth 53 yards 3 quarters half quarter & 1 nail Examined.
Murrey engrained 3 yards Examined.
Money £23 12s. 10d. Examined.

John Mason 48 rays 5 yards of murrey | 36s. 8d.
[Gr] Item for 1 yard & 3 quarters of murrey engrained | 14s.
John Broke 38 rays 5 yards of murrey | 34s. 8d.

[382] [f. 124r]
[Gr] Item for 4 yards of murrey engrained for hoods to the said John Broke
& his wife, to Thomas Harford and Hugh Warde | 32s.
John Salter 34 rays 2 yards & half of murrey | 25s. 8d.
John Philippe 36 rays 3 yards of murrey | 27s. 4d.
John Piken 32 rays 2 yards & half & half quarter of murrey | 24s.
John Humber 38 rays 3 yards of murrey | 28s.
John Reyner 34 rays 2 yards 3 quarters & half quarter of murrey | 26s. 8d.
John Fekenham 11 rays 4 yards 3 quarters & half quarter of murrey | 24s. 6d.
[Gr] Item 2 yards & 1 nail of murrey engrained for hoods | 16s. 6d.
John Kenaky 36 rays 2 yards 3 quarters murrey | 26s. 8d.
John Hopkyn 26 rays 2 yards of murrey | 20s.

499 'Gr' denoted the more expensive engrained murrey cloth.
500 Bracy?

John Bedford 30 rays 2 yards & 1 quarter of murrey	23s.
John Thomas 36 rays 2 yards 3 quarters of murrey	26s. 8d.
John William 36 rays 2 yards 3 quarters of murrey	26s. 8d.
John Tregelowe 32 rays 2 yards & 1 quarter of murrey	24s.
John Carionne 30 rays 2 yards & 1 quarter half quarter of murrey	23s.
John Danyell, maltman, 38 rays 2 yards & half of murrey	26s. 8d.
John Fairman 38 rays 3 yards of murrey	28s.
John Hardynge 26 rays 2 yards of murrey	20s.
John Hanslape 36 rays 3 yards of murrey	26s. 8d.
John Dunche 32 rays 2 yards & half of murrey	24s.
John Warsoppe 28 rays 2 yards 1 quarter of murrey	22s.
John Riche of Wood Street 38 rays 3 yards of murrey	28s. 8d.
John Ketynge 4 yards & half & half quarter of murrey with 9 rays	28s.
John Aleyn 34 rays 2 yards 3 quarters of murrey	25s. 8d.

[383] [f. 124v]

John Parker 34 rays 2 yards & half of murrey	25s. 8d.
John Spenser 26 rays 2 yards of murrey	20s.
John Chapman 31 rays 2 yards of murrey	20s.
John Stone 34 rays 2 yards & half of murrey	25s. 8d.
John Bentele 30 rays 2 yards & 1 quarter of murrey	22s. 8d.
John Bosvenon 34 rays 2 yards & half murrey	25s. 8d.
John Newman the Elder 36 rays 2 yards & half murrey	26s. 8d.
John Pamplion 28 rays 2 yards & half quarter of murrey	22s.
John Brewester 28 rays 2 yards & half of murrey	22s.
John Elcy 38 rays 3 yards of murrey	28s.
John Bugby 28 rays 2 yards & half quarter of murrey	22s.
John Russell 36 rays 2 yards 3 quarters of murrey	26s. 8d.
John Turnour, shearman, 8 rays 2 yards & half of murrey	10s. 2d.
John Frost 32 rays 2 yards 1 quarter half quarter of murrey	24s.
John Bassett 36 rays 3 yards of murrey	26s. 8d.
John Withmore 36 rays 2 yards & half of murrey	25s. 4d.
John Riche the Younger 26 rays 2 yards of murrey	20s.
John Langford, maltman, 34 rays 2 yards & half of murrey	25s. 4d.
John Reeffawe 32 rays 2 yards 3 quarters of murrey	22s.
John Lumbard 28 rays 2 yards & half quarter of murrey	22s.
John Ryngesson 26 rays 2 yards & 1 quarter & half quarter of murrey	15s. 3d.
John Lacy 28 rays 2 yards of murrey	22s.
John Qwyntyne 8 rays 4 yards of murrey	23s. 4d.
John Sharppe, maltman, 34 rays 2 yards & half & half quarter of murrey	26s. 8d.
John Smyth of Gamlingay 26 rays 2 yards & 1 quarter of murrey	21s.

[384] [f. 125r]

John Jacow 9 rays 3 quarters of murrey	7s.
John Mabile 9 rays half yard half quarter of murrey	8s.
John Laurence 9 rays half yard half quarter of murrey	7s.
John Bronn, cooper, 8 rays 3 quarters of murrey	5s. 4d.
John de Dene 9 rays 3 quarters of murrey	6s. 8d.
John Sere, glover, 7 rays half yard half quarter of murrey	6s.
John Bernewell 11 rays 3 quarters half quarter & 1 nail of murrey	8s.

276

John Eylond 7 rays half yard of murrey	5s. 6d.
John Goldrynge 9 rays half yard & half quarter of murrey	6s. 8d.
John Killom 8 rays half yard & half quarter of murrey	6s.
John Moris 9 rays 1 yard & half & half quarter of murrey	11s. 8d.
John Newman at the Austin Friars 9 rays half yard half quarter of murrey	6s. 8d.
John Newman the Younger 8 rays half yard half quarter of murrey	6s.
John Jacob 10 rays 3 quarters of murrey	7s. 4d.
John de Kent, cooper, 9 rays 3 quarters of murrey	6s. 8d.
John de Lynne 9 rays 3 quarters of murrey	7s. 4d.
John Purley 1 yard & 1 quarter of murrey	6s.
John Wilde 8 rays half yard half quarter of murrey	6s.
John Bretaigne 7 rays half yard & 1 nail of murrey	5s. 6d.
John Blostmere 9 rays 3 quarters of murrey	6s. 8d.
John Randolff 1 yard of murrey to his wife	5s.
John Southmede 8 rays half yard of murrey	6s.
John Snell 8 rays half yard of murrey	6s.
John Gremesby 8 rays half yard of murrey	6s.
John Bronnynge 9 rays half yard half quarter of murrey	6s. 8d.
John Astonne 1 yard & half of murrey	8s.
John Norman 8 rays half yard of murrey	6s.

[385] [f. 125v]

John Hobek 9 rays half yard half quarter of murrey	6s. 8d.
John Assh 9 rays half yard half quarter of murrey	6s. 8d.
John Luke 10 rays 3 quarters of murrey	7s. 4d.
John Sheffeld, fletcher, 10 rays 3 quarters of murrey	7s. 4d.
John Davy 8 rays half yard half quarter of murrey	6s.
John Baily 9 rays half yard half quarter of murrey	6s. 8d.
John Sonder 9 rays 3 quarters of murrey	7s.
John West 8 rays half yard half quarter of murrey	6s.
John Caston 8 rays half yard half quarter of murrey	6s. 8d.
John Took 9 rays half yard half quarter of murrey	6s. 8d.
John Barston 10 rays 3 quarters of murrey	7s. 4d.
John Wake 8 rays half yard half quarter of murrey	6s. 8d.
John William 8 rays half yard half quarter of murrey	6s.
John Bewchamppe 8 rays half yard half quarter of murrey	6s. 8d.
John Riche, tailor, 7 rays half yard & 1 nail of murrey	6s.
John Waghorn 9 rays half yard half quarter of murrey	6s. 8d.
John Serle 6 rays half yard of murrey	5s.
John Woodleff, maltman, 9 rays 3 quarters of murrey	6s. 8d.
John Hardy, Cook, 9 rays half yard half quarter of murrey [*above the line*: & 1 nail]	5s.
Inglezard Snaith 8 rays half yard half quarter of murrey	6s.

Sum of Rays 1,889 Examined.
Murrey cloth 166 yards, half, half quarter Examined.
Murrey engrained 7 yards 3 quarters 1 nail Examined.
Money £78 10s. 1d. Examined.

[386]

James Ytecombe 28 rays 2 yards and half quarter of murrey	22s.
James Tolvan 30 rays 2 yards of murrey	22s. 8d.
James Mogonne, poulter, 8 rays half yard half quarter of murrey	6s. 8d.

[f. 126r]

[Gr] Leonell Power 4 yards of murrey engrained	32s.
Michell Tregononne 10 rays 3 quarters of murrey	9s.
Michell Eve 8 rays half yard half quarter of murrey	6s.
Mustell the younger, maltman, 7 rays half yard half quarter of murrey	6s.
Nicholas Goonmailok 30 rays 2 yards 1 quarter of murrey	23s.
Nicholas Muriell 28 rays 2 yards 1 quarter of murrey	22s.
Nicholas Fuller 28 rays 2 yards of murrey	22s.
Nicholas Mertonne 10 rays 3 quarters of murrey	7s. 4d.
Philippe Godfray 7 rays half yard of murrey	5s. 6d.
Peter Carpenter 36 rays 3 yards of murrey	26s. 8d.
Peter Short 1 yard of murrey	5s.
Peter Andrew 8 rays half yard half quarter of murrey	6s.
[Gr] Peter Haiford 10 rays 3 quarters of murrey engrained	12s.

Sum of Rays 248 Examined.
Murrey cloth 19 yards half quarter Examined.
Murrey engrained 4 yards 3 quarters Examined.
Money £11 13s. 10d. Examined.

[387]

Robert Carpenter 26 rays 2 yards of murrey	20s.
Robert Smyth 36 rays 3 yards of murrey	26s. 8d.
Robert Ketynge 26 rays 2 yards of murrey	20s.
Robert Mayhew 32 rays 2 yards 3 quarters of murrey	24s.

[f. 126v]

Robert Giles 34 rays 2 yards 3 quarters of murrey	20s.
Robert Elkyn 38 rays 3 yards of murrey	28s.
Robert Pede 36 rays 2 yards 3 quarters of murrey	26s. 8d.
[Gr] Robert Caterton 1 yard & half of murrey engrained	12s.
Robert Miles, maltman, 7 rays half yard 1 nail of murrey	5s. 6d.
Robert Asshborne 10 rays 3 quarters of murrey	7s. 4d.
Robert Charletonne, sergeant, 1 yard 1 quarter of murrey	4s. 6d.
Robert Goneld 9 rays half yard half quarter of murrey	6s. 8d.
Robert Walram 9 rays half yard half quarter of murrey	6s. 8d.
Robert Fordam, maltman, 7 rays half yard half quarter of murrey	6s.
Robert Nikke 9 rays half yard half quarter of murrey	6s. 8d.
Robert Calowe, shearman, 7 rays half yard & 1 nail of murrey	6s.
Robert Cristophore, fruiterer, 8 rays half yard half quarter of murrey	6s.
Robert Dorewell 8 rays half yard half quarter of murrey	6s. 8d.

Richard Lucas 40 rays 3 yards & 1 quarter of murrey	30*s.*
Richard West 32 rays 2 yards & 1 quarter of murrey	23*s.* 6*d.*
Richard Aleyn 40 rays 3 yards of murrey	28*s.* 6*d.*
[Gr] Item 1 yard of murrey engrained to his wife	8*s.*
Richard Bulwik, grocer, 1 yard of murrey to his wife	5*s.* 8*d.*
Richard Terrell 8 rays half yard half quarter of murrey	6*s.*
Richard Kilsole 7 rays half yard & 1 nail of murrey	5*s.*
[Gr] Item half yard half quarter of murrey engrained to his wife	5*s.*
Richard Tailour 8 rays half yard half quarter of murrey	6*s.*
Richard Herlowe 8 rays half yard half quarter of murrey	6*s.*

[388] [f. 127r]

Richard Waltham 1 yard & half of murrey	7*s.* 6*d.*
Richard Gerveys 10 rays 3 quarters of murrey	7*s.* 4*d.*
Richard Bever, brewersman,[501] 1 yard of murrey	5*s.*
Richard Osbarne 1 yard of murrey[502]	3*s.* 8*d.*
Richard Bryntonne 9 rays 3 quarters of murrey	7*s.*
Richard Carowe 8 rays half yard & 1 nail [*of murrey*]	6*s.*
Richard Fulke 9 rays 3 quarters of murrey	6*s.* 8*d.*
Richard Frepurs 6 rays half yard of murrey	5*s.*
Richard Tiler 8 rays half yard half quarter of murrey	6*s.*
Richard Sherewod 11 rays 3 quarters of murrey	10*s.*
[Gr] Richard Herty 1 yard half quarter of murrey engrained to his wife	9*s.*
Roger Blissote 28 rays 2 yards & 1 quarter of murrey	22*s.*
Roger Ware 28 rays 2 yards of murrey	22*s.*
Roger Lamelyn 8 rays half yard half quarter of murrey	6*s.*
Roger Baronne 9 rays 3 quarters of murrey	7*s.*
Roger Swanneffeld 8 rays half yard half quarter of murrey	10*s.*
Raff Palmer 38 rays 3 yards half quarter and 1 nail of murrey	28*s.*
Raff Marke 9 rays half yard half quarter of murrey	6*s.* 8*d.*
Reginald Trewyle outside Temple Bar 9 rays half yard half quarter & 1 nail of murrey	6*s.* 8*d.*
Stephen Clean 28 rays 2 yards of murrey	20*s.* 8*d.*
Stephen Roo 8 rays half yard half quarter of murrey	6*s.*

[389] [f. 127v]

Simon Herry 8 rays half yard half quarter of murrey	6*s.* 8*d.*
Simon Petesyne 10 rays 3 quarters of murrey	7*s.* 4*d.*

501   Bever was later described as a servant to Thomas Hancok, **[446]**. He had no rays here, so was perhaps not yet a freeman of the craft.
502   Richard Osbarn was not a brewer: he was the clerk to the chamber. See **[86]**.

Simon atte Welle 8 rays half yard half quarter of murrey 6s.
Simon Franke, fishmonger, 1 yard of murrey to his wife 5s.

Sum of Rays 705 Examined.
Murrey cloth 61 yards and half and half quarter Examined.
Murrey engrained 4 yards & 1 quarter Examined.
Money £29 16s. 7d. Examined.

[390]
Thomas Hatcher 50 rays 5 yards of murrey 38s. 4d.
[Gr] Item 1 yard 3 quarters of murrey engrained for hoods 14s.
Thomas Driffeld 4 yards 1 quarter of murrey 16s.
Thomas Hancok 38 rays 2 yards 3 quarters of murrey 27s. 4d.
Thomas Grene 36 rays 3 yards of murrey 26s. 8d.
Thomas Aleyn 36 rays 2 yards 3 quarters of murrey 26s. 8d.
Thomas Ayle 34 rays 2 yards & half of murrey 25s. 8d.
Thomas Kirtoth 34 rays 2 yards 1 quarter and half quarter of murrey 25s. 4d.
Thomas Godyng 28 rays 2 yards of murrey 20s. 8d.
Thomas Smyth 28 rays 2 yards of murrey 21s. 8d.
Thomas Yole 28 rays 2 yards half quarter of murrey 22s.

Thomas atte Hethe 8 rays half yard half quarter of murrey 6s.
Thomas Gremesby, baker, 8 rays half yard half quarter of murrey 6s.
Thomas Walsh 10 rays 3 quarters of murrey 7s. 4d.
Thomas Multonne 8 rays half yard and 1 nail of murrey 6s.

[f. 128r]
Thomas Bronn 8 rays half yard & 1 nail of murrey 6s.
Thomas Mersh 10 rays 3 quarters of murrey 7s. 4d.
Thomas Donyngton, sergeant, 1 yard 1 quarter of murrey 4s. 7d.
Thomas Moris 9 rays half yard half quarter of murrey 6s. 8d.
Thomas Hille, maltman, 9 rays half yard half quarter of murrey 6s. 8d.
Thomas Howe, maltman, 8 rays half yard half quarter of murrey 6s. 8d.
Thomas Maltonne 8 rays half yard half quarter of murrey 6s. 8d.
Thomas Mariott 8 rays half yard half quarter of murrey 6s.
Thomas Sebarne, maltman, 7 rays half yard half quarter of murrey 6s.
Thomas atte Wode 8 rays half yard half quarter of murrey 6s.
Thomas Gratley 7 rays half yard half quarter of murrey 6s.
Thomas Cokeshede, maltman, 7 rays half yard of murrey 6s.
Thomas Dewy 8 rays half yard half quarter of murrey 6s.
Thomas Penson 8 rays half yard half quarter of murrey 6s. 8d.

Sum of Rays 451 Examined.
Murrey cloth 40 yards & half & half quarter Examined.
Murrey engrained 1 yard 3 quarters Examined.
Money £18 16s. 11d. Examined.

[391]
William Porlond 9 yards 1 quarter of murrey to himself & his wife 33s. 11d.
William atte Woode 38 rays 2 yards half quarter of murrey 24s.

[Gr] Item half a yard & half quarter of murrey engrained	5s.
William Crane 37 rays 2 yards 3 quarters half quarter of murrey	29s. 8d.

[f. 128v]

William Belle 36 rays 3 yards of murrey	26s. 8d.
William Ferrour the Younger 38 rays 3 yards of murrey	28s.
William Ferrour the Elder 36 rays 3 yards of murrey	26s. 8d.
William Herry 36 rays 2 yards & half of murrey	26s. 8d.
William Grosse 42 rays 3 yards & half of murrey	31s.
William Baily 33 rays 2 yards & 1 quarter of murrey	24s.
William Canonne 27 rays 2 yards of murrey	24s. 4d.
William Dowdale 30 rays 2 yards & 1 quarter of murrey	22s. 8d.
William Payn 38 rays 3 yards & 1 quarter of murrey	28s. 8d.
William Hert of Ware 32 rays 2 yards & 1 quarter & half quarter of murrey	24s.
William Pompe 36 rays 2 yards 3 quarters of murrey	26s. 8d.
William Petevile 31 rays 2 yards & half of murrey	23s.
William Hill 34 rays 2 yards & half & half quarter of murrey	24s.
William Boteler 28 rays 2 yards & half quarter of murrey	22s.
William Geffray 24 rays 2 yards of murrey	19s.
William Fish 34 rays 2 yards & half of murrey	25s. 4d.
William Bodevile 34 rays 2 yards & half & half quarter of murrey	26s. 8d.
William Claisson 36 rays 4 yards of murrey	31s. 8d.
Walter Colsull 32 rays 2 yards & half of murrey	24s.

[Gr] William Calston, plumber, 10 rays 3 quarters of murrey engrained	10s.
William Boterfeld, cooper, 8 rays half yard half quarter of murrey	6s.
William Bernard 7 rays half yard of murrey	6s. 8d.

[392] [f. 129r]

William Pethin 9 rays half yard half quarter & 1 nail of murrey	5s.
William Devenyssh 8 rays half yard half quarter of murrey	5s.
[Gr] William Story, grocer, 13 rays 1 yard of murrey engrained	11s.
William Illynge 9 rays half yard half quarter of murrey	6s. 8d.
William Termeday 10 rays 3 quarters of murrey	7s. 4d.
William Eyre 10 rays 3 quarters of murrey	7s. 4d.
Item 1 yard of murrey to his wife	5s.
William Miles, maltman, 7 rays half yard & 1 nail of murrey	5s. 6d.
William Franke 8 rays half yard half quarter of murrey	6s.
William Cokreth 8 rays half yard half quarter of murrey	6s.
William Longe 8 rays half yard of murrey	6s.
William Rawlyn 10 rays 3 quarters of murrey	7s. 4d.
William Mascall 9 rays half yard half quarter of murrey	6s. 8d.
William Lyndesay 8 rays half yard of murrey	6s.
William Watford 7 rays half yard of murrey	5s. 8d.
William Reponne 9 rays half yard half quarter of murrey	6s. 8d.
William Stile 7 rays half yard half quarter of murrey	6s.
William Vevian 8 rays half yard and 1 nail	6s.
William Gore, maltman, 8 rays half yard and 1 nail	6s.
William Copwode 8 rays half yard half quarter of murrey	6s.
William Mulso 8 rays half yard half quarter of murrey	6s.

William Petiver 8 rays half yard half quarter of murrey   6s.

[393] [f. 129v]
William Robert 8 rays half yard half quarter of murrey   6s.
William Bacon, butcher, 8 rays half yard and 1 nail of murrey   6s.
Walter Glyn 8 rays half yard half quarter of murrey   6s.
Walter Behethelen 10 rays 3 quarters & 1 nail of murrey   8s.

Sum of Rays 951 Examined.
Murrey cloth 82 yards & half quarter Examined.
Murrey engrained 2 yards 1 quarter half quarter Examined.
Money £38 17d. Examined.

Sum total delivered of

Rays 4,765 Examined.
Murrey cloth 424 yards & 1 nail Examined.
Murrey engrained 23 yards 3 quarters half quarter & 1 nail Examined.
Money £200 11s. 8d. Examined.

[394] [f. 130r]
To the right worshipful and discreet mayor and aldermen of the city of London:
Your servants, all the Brewers, citizens of the same city, beseech meekly and
charitably for the common profit

for as much as (where) about in the first year and second year of King Henry IV
[1399–1401], progenitor of our Liege Lord now, [*it*] was unduly used [*accustomed*]
by diverse persons, servants, officers of the said city to take toll and custom for
the goods, merchandise, victuals belonging to the citizens of the same city, carried,
brought on ships, carts or horse, at all ports of the said city, against the liberties of
the same city.
(There) [*Then in*] the third year of the reign of the said King Henry IV [1401–2],
a supplication was put to John Shadworth, then mayor, [1401–2] and the worthy
aldermen of the said city at that time, comprehending that all the citizens of the
same city, from that time forward, might be quit of all manner of toll and custom
by [*scored:* of mayor the said 4th year of the] all the king's power, as well on this
side of the sea as on the other side, after the form and effect of the king's charters
thereof, granted and confirmed to them from ancient time.
Wherefore [*on*] the 12th day of May in the said 3rd year of the reign of King
Henry IV [1402] abovesaid in the Guildhall of the same city, summoned by the
said mayor, Maiken [Matthew] Suthworth, recorder, William Venour and William
Fremelyngham sheriffs, John Hadley, John Hende, William Stanndonne, Richard
Whytyngton, Thomas Knolles, John Frannceys, John Walcote, John Wodecok,
William Parker, William Bramtonne, William Askham, John Warner, Thomas
Willford, John Wakelee, William Walderne, Thomas Polle and Thomas Fawconer,
then aldermen, and by that time a notable number of worthy commons of the same
city, chosen from all the wards and summoned there, it was accorded, granted and
fully affirmed and to be entered [*in*] the books of record in the said Guildhall, and so
to be entered in a book soon after, so that no manner of citizen of the said city
from that time forward, should pay any toll or custom at the ports of the said city

for their proper goods, merchandise or victuals, although [*whether*] the said goods, merchandise or victuals were brought to the same city or carried to the same upon horse, ships, boats or carts belonging to strangers, and so that the same strangers should be quit of all manner of toll and custom at every port of the same city for their horse, ships, boats and carts, such said goods, merchandise or victuals of the said citizens so carrying; and moreover your said beseechers meekly beseech you to consider that aliens dwelling near to the city brew [*scored*: their] beer and sell it to retail within the same city as freely as any of the said citizens that are at lot and all other charges of the said city do [*sell*] their ale and other victuals, against the liberty of the said city and [*to the*] derogation⁵⁰³ of the common profit to the chamber of the said city, as it seems to them.

Also moreover, where it was wont to be used by good and notable diverse ordinances ordained for the common profit and ease of the said city that no servant of Brewers' craft shall serve by week nor by day but

[395] [f. 130v]
by the whole year, the chief Brewer taking for his salary for the year 4 marks,⁵⁰⁴ with meat, drink and clothing and his advantages, and the second Brewer 40s. by year, with meat, drink and clothing and his advantages, upon certain penalty thereof ordained.

And now by confederacy [*scored*: confedered other] made among the said servants of Brewers' craft, they will not serve but by the week or by the day all only, or else take too outrageous a salary, to great hindering of the said citizens, Brewers, and hindering to the commons, in as much as they may not duly keep their course of brewing to serve their customers, in default [*because of*] of such confederacies. Wherefore like it to your high [*scored*: and noble] purveyed⁵⁰⁵ and noble discretion, to rule, govern and ordain such comenable and sufficient remedy upon these matters aforesaid, for ease and common profit, that the said beseechers thereby may also be eased and [*have*] remedy, for God's love and in way of charity.
[*To the right are some symbols: four with three dots and a long tail, possibly a symbol of the Trinity, and three pairs of dots, one above the other, two with lines to the right, one with lines to the left. There is a sketched figure, with a striped gown and a two-pointed hat*]

[396] [f. 131r]
Quarterage of John Michell [1424–5]

Alexander Miles and Isabell his wife	2s.	Sir Adam Daltonne	12d.
		Sir Robert Steyntonne	12d.
Alexander Marcow and Anneys his wife	2s.	Sir William Goodswayn	12d.
		Emma Canonne	12d.
Adam Smyth and Margery his wife	2s.	Elizabeth Colbroke	12d.
		Friar John Berkynge	12d.
Alice Edericge	12d.		

⁵⁰³ Taking away.
⁵⁰⁴ A mark was worth 13s. 4d., so 53s. 4d.
⁵⁰⁵ Ordained.

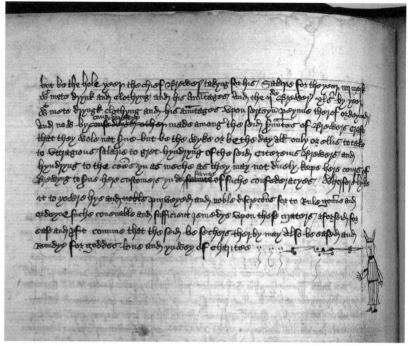

Figure 11. GL MS 5440 The Brewers' Book, folio 130v.
Clerk's doodle showing a figure in a two-pointed hat
and striped gown. © The Brewers' Company.

Alice Benge	12*d.*	Gilbert Botonne	12*d.*
Alice Hore	12*d.*		
Alice late the wife of William		Henry Payne and Anneys his wife	2*s.*
atte Welle	12*d.*	Henry Fereby and Cecily his wife	2*s.*
Alice late the wife of William		Henry Lymber with Felise his wife	2*s.*
John	12*d.*	Henry Grene and Anneys his wife	2*s.*
		Henry Stapill	12*d.*
Anneys Bugge	12*d.*	Henry Wixton	12*d.*
Anneys Carletonne	12*d.*	Henry Bedell	12*d.*
Anneys Rendre sometime the		Henry Bracy	12*d.*
wife of Walter Riche	12*d.*	Henry Rowe and Johanna his wife	2*s.*
		Henry Trebolans and Elizabeth	
Baldewyne Hoper and Johanna		his wife	2*s.*
his wife	2*s.*		
Cristiane More	12*d.*		
Cristiane Ballard	12*d.*		
Dederick Johnson and Weveyn			
his wife	2*s.*		
Denise Barthorpe	12*d.*		

[397] [f. 131v]

Hugh Neell and Emmote his wife	2s.	John Barstonne	16d.
Hugh Glene and Margaret his wife	2s.	John Broke and Cristiane his wife	2s.
		John Russell and Alice his wife	2s.
John Eylond and Denise his wife	2s.	John Sere, glover	12d.
John Killom and Maud his wife	2s.	John Riche the younger and	
John Riche, tailor, and Alice his wife	2s.	Mathie his wife	2s.
John Piken and Alice his wife	2s.	John Ketynge and Margaret his wife	2s.
John Qwyntyn and Katherine his wife	2s.	John Turvey and Margaret his wife	2s.
John Spenser and Margaret his wife	2s.	John Astonne and Maud his wife	2s.
John Took and Alice his wife	2s.	John Sowthmede	12d.
John Frost and Alice his wife	2s.	John Bassett	12d.
John Wightmore and Isabell his wife	2s.	John Goldrynge and Johanna his wife	2s.
John Reyner and Agatha his wife	2s.	John Massy	12d.
John Stone and Anneys his wife	2s.	John Luke	12d.
John Hanslape and Lettice his wife	2s.	John Lynne	12d.
John Holbek and Margaret his wife	2s.	John Newman	12d.
John Serle	12d.	John Newman the Younger and Betonne his wife	2s.
John Laurence	12d.	John Warsoppe	12d.
John Bretaigne	12d.	John Jacob and Alice his wife	2s.
John Sharppe	12d.	John Child and Katherine his wife	2s.
John Salter and Johanna his wife	2s.	John Mabile	12d.
John Bosvenonne and Alice his wife	2s.	John Fekenham and Johanna his wife	2s.
John Thomas and Johanna his wife	2s.	John Blostmere	12d.
John Jacow and Alice his wife	2s.	John Philippe and Margaret his wife	2s.
John Kenaky	12d.	John Danyell	12d.
John Purley and Johanna his wife	2s.	John Waghorn	2s.
John Fairman	12d.	John Turnour	12d.
John Pamplionne	12d.	John Bargonne	12d.
John Bate and Anya his wife	2s.	John Bentele and Margery his wife	2s.
		John William and Johanna his wife	2s.

[398] [f. 132r]

John Mason & Felise his wife	2s.	James Ytecombe	3s.
John Brewster & Johanna his wife	2s.	James Tolvan & Anneys his wife	2s.
John Champman & Juliane his wife	2s.		
John Spore	12d.	Juliane Hetersete	12d.
John Reffawe & Juliane his wife	2s.		
John Hardy	12d.	Johanna Rothyng	12d.
John Bugby	12d.	Johanna Horolde	12d.
John Snell	12d.	Johanna Awmbele	12d.
John Riche in Wood Street & Margaret his wife	2s.	Johanna late the wife of Alan John	12d.
John Carionne & Alice his wife	2s.	Johanna Amwell	12d.
John Hardynge & Anneys his wife	2s.		
John Randolff & Julyane his wife	2s.	Katherine de Van	2s.

John Caston & Anneys his wife	2s.	Michael Tregononne	12d.
John Gremesby	12d.		
John Bedford	12d.	Margaret Thetford	12d.
John Assh	12d.		
John West	12d.	Nicholas Merton & Anneys his wife	2s.
John Parker	12d.	Nicholas Muriell & Anneys his	
John Sonder	12d.	wife	2s.
John Ratford, glover,	12d.	Nicholas Aleyn	12d.
John Newman at the Austin Friars	12d.	Nicholas Fuller & Alice his wife	2s.
John Hopkyn & Alice his wife	2s.	Nicholas Goonmailok & Johanna	
John Elcy & Alice his wife	2s.	his wife	2s.
John Humber & Margaret his wife	2s.		
John Lumbard & Margaret his wife	2s.	Peter Short & Alice his wife	2s.
John Cavendissh, broderer,	12d.	Peter Hayford & Maud his wife	2s.
John Smyth	12d.	Peter Roos	12d.
John Tregelowe [&] Johanna his		Peter Andrew	12d.
wife	2s.	Peter Carpenter & Katherine his	
		wife	2s.
		Phillip Godfray	12d.

[399] [f. 132v]

Richard Aleyn and Johanna his wife	2s.	Roger Blissote and Maud his wife	2s.
Richard Harlowe and Johanna his		Roger Swanneffelde and Idonea	
wife	2s.	his wife	2s.
Richard Gerveys and Emote his		Roger Baronne	12d.
wife	2s.		
Richard Herty and Alice his wife	2s.	Simon Frank and Elizabeth his wife	2s.
Richard Lucas and Alice his wife	2s.	Simon Petesyn and Isabell his wife	2s.
Richard Carowe and Elizabeth		Simon Herry and Elizabeth his wife	2s.
his wife	2s.	Simon atte Welle	12d.
Richard Tiler	12d.		
Richard Sherewode and Alice his		Stephen Roo	12d.
wife	2s.	Stephen Clean	12d.
Richard Bulwik and Johanna his			
wife	2s.	Sibile the wife of Alan Brett[506]	12d.
Richard Frepurs	12d.	Thomas Ayle	12d.
Richard West	12d.	Thomas Pensonne	12d.
Richard Bryntonne	12d.	Thomas Godyng and Margaret	
Master Richard Donyngtonne,		his wife	2s.
friar,	12d.	Thomas Hancok and Denise his	
Robert Elkyn and Cecile his wife	2s.	wife	2s.
Robert Smyth and Anya his wife	2s.	Thomas Dewy	12d.
Robert Giles and Johanna his wife	2s.	Thomas Gremesby and Johanna	
Robert Pede and Alice his wife	2s.	his wife	2s.
Robert Asshbourne	12d.	Thomas atte Hethe and Anneys	
Robert Walram	12d.	his wife	2s.

[506] Usually listed as Isabel.

Robert Ketynge and Margery his wife	2s.	Thomas Grene and Maud his wife	2s.
Robert Fordam	12d.	Thomas Bronn and Anneys his wife	2s.
Robert Calowe, shearman, and Maud his wife	2s.	Thomas Merssh and Anneys his wife	2s.
Robert Goneld	12d.	Thomas Gratley and Margaret his wife	2s.
Robert Nikke and Alice his wife	2s.	Thomas Nonnseglos	12d.
Robert Mayhew and Juliane his wife	2s.	Thomas Aleyn and Lettice his wife	2s.
Robert Jewell	18d.		
Raff Marke and Rose his wife	2s.		

[400] [f. 133r]

Thomas Smyth & Alice his wife	2s.	William Illynge	12d.
Thomas Yole & Alice his wife	2s.	William Petyver & Marion his wife	2s.
Thomas Multonne & Margaret his wife	2s.	William Dowdale & Johanna his wife	2s.
Thomas Moris & Cecile his wife	2s.	William Andrew	12d.
Thomas Kirtoth	12d.	William atte Woode [&]	
Thomas Howe	3s.	Katherine his wife	2s.
Thomas Bristowe	12d.	William Belle & Florence his wife	2s.
Thomas Walissh & Johanna his wife	2s.	William Geffray & Anya his wife	2s.
Thomas Martyn	12d.	William Baily & Alice his wife	2s.
Thomas Hatcher & Margaret his wife	2s.	William Crane & Elene his wife	2s.
		William Robert	12d.
		William Bullok & Johanna his wife	2s.
William Ferrour the Elder [&] Anneys his wife	2s.	William Boteler	12d.
William Petevile & Johanna his wife	2s.	William Termeday & Katherine his wife	2s.
William Lyndesay & Margery his wife	2s.	William Canonne & Elizabeth his wife	2s.
William Baconne, butcher,	12d.	William Ferrour the Younger & Anneys his wife	2s.
William Grosse & Katherine his wife	2s.	William Pompe	12d.
William Watford	12d.	William Rawlyn & Alice his wife	2s.
William Porlond [&] Denyse his wife	2s.	William Franke & Cecile his wife	2s.
William Stile	12d.	William Cokreth	12d.
William Bernard	12d.	William Hill	12d.
William Payn & Elene his wife	2s.	William Bodevile	12d.
William Eyre & Anneys his wife	2s.	William Cardell	6d.
William Totewell & Isabell his wife	2s.	William Herry & Anneys his wife	2s.
William Claissonne & Isabell his wife	2s.	William Copwod & Isabell his wife	8s.
		Walter Glyn	12d.
		Walter Colsull and Alice his wife	2s.
		Walter Behethelen	12d.

[401] [f. 133v]
[*English*]
Money paid by William Rawlyn, Thomas Smyth and Nicholas Mertone in the 20th day of November the year the 17ᵗʰ for our sovereign lord the King [1438] at the hall of Brewers, to each man half his sum, as it shows afterwards[507]

[*Damaged*: [?] Delivered Half]
First John Humber £12 10d. ½d. ¼d.
Paid for the costs 6s. 4d.
Received £12 4s. 4d. ½d. ¼d.
John Abbesse £15 10s. 11½d.
Paid for costs 7s. 10d.
Received £15 3s. 1d. ½d. ¼d.
Benet Maly 13s. 6½d.
Paid for costs 4d.
Received through Abbesse 13s. 2½d.
Thomas Remy £3 8s. 3d. ½d. ¼d.
Paid for costs 20d.
Received £3 6s. 7d. ½d. ¼d.
William Herry £4 15s. 11¼d.
Paid for the costs 2s. 5d.
Received through John Smyth £4 13s. 6¼d.
Adam Turvyng £12 4s. 6d. ½d. ¼d.
Paid for costs 6s. 1d.
Received through Nicholas Mertone £11 18s. 5½d. ¼d.
William Rawlyn £32 19s. 4d. ¼d.
Paid for costs 16s. 6d.
Received £32 2s. 10¼d.
Philip Porcell £3 15s. 3½d.
Paid for costs 22½d.
Received £3 13s. 5d.
Thomas Smyth £24 4s. 10d.
Paid for costs 12s. 2½d.
Received £23 12s. 7½d.
William Cornmongere 20s. 1d.
Paid for the costs 6d.
Received 19s. 7d.
Richard Moore, tailor, £4 8s. 2½d.
Paid for costs 2s. 3d.
Received £4 5s. 11½d.
William Payn 43s. 9d.
Paid for costs 13d.
Received 42s. 8d.
William Ferrour Senior £5 19s. 5d. ½d. ¼d.
Paid for costs 3s.

[507] This formerly blank page was used to record money lent by some Brewers in 1438. The money was probably connected with acquisition of the Brewers' royal charter. Rawlyn was one of the masters 1437–8 (f. 272r, see Part 2 of the Brewers' Book). The amounts recorded have been reproduced faithfully here, despite apparent errors.

Received £5 16s. 5d.
John Brook £6 7d.
Paid for costs 3s.
Received £5 17s. 7d.
Thomas Cokeshed £11 3s. 5½d.
Paid for costs 5s. 7d.
Received £10 17s. 10d.
William Downyng, cooper, 44s. 2½d.
Paid for costs 13d.
Received through Porlond 43s. 1d.
Thomas Whyte £16 18s. 9d. ½d. ¼d.
Paid for costs 8s. 4d.
Received £16 10s. 6d. ½d. ¼d.
Nicholas Mertone £20 9s. 4d.
Paid for costs 10s. 3d.
Received £19 19s. 1d.
John Davy £14 8s. 11d. ½d. ¼d.
Paid for costs 7s. 3d.
Received £14 20d. ½d. ¼d.
John Salter £4 17s. 5½d.
Paid for costs 2s. 6d.
Received £4 14s. 11½d.

[402] [f. 134r]

First course	The Second Course
Brawn with mustard	Venison in broth
Browet tuskan[508] to pottage	Pheasant roasted
Wood doves stewed	Venison roasted
Swan roasted	Partridge and cocks
Chickens baked	Doucettes

The Third Course
Pears in syrup
Great birds and larks together
Fritters with a bake-meat

On the Saturday

First for baked herring	17d.
Item in green fish	4s. 7d.
Item for mussels	2d.
Item 12 pike	15s.
Item 3 congers	7s.
Item 1 codling	14d.

---

508 Broth of boiled meat juice. Tuskan: a pottage of pork or chicken, or meatballs, served in a seasoned and coloured broth. See Constance B. Hieatt, comp. and ed., *The Culinary Recipes of Medieval England* (Totnes, 2013), 77. I am grateful to Martha Carlin for this reference and for discussion of this recipe.

Item 600 whelks	3s.
Item in herbs	4d.

[403] [f. 134v]

Item for wardens and custards	2s. 5d.
Item for portage of pikes	1d.

Sum 35s. 2d.

Pantry

First 2 quarters of cheat-bread and rounds, of which 2 quarters and 3 bushels of rounds,	20s.
Item for white sourbread	12s.
Item for mayn French [*bread*]	3s. 9d.
Item for trencher bread 2s. 4d., of which trencher bread 10d. is abated for the aforesaid cheat	18d.
Item for 2 bushels of mayn flour, price the bushel 18d.,	3s.
Item for 3 bushels of coarse flour, the bushel 15d.,	3s. 9d.

Sum 44s.

Buttery

First for red wine bought at the Eagle in Cheap	20s. 7d.
Item 1 hogshead of red wine	44s. 4d.
Item for tonnage of the said hogshead	2d.
Item for carriage of the same hogshead	8d.
Item for 7 barrels of good ale, price the barrel 5s.,	35s.
Item 4 barrels of three halfpenny, ale price the barrel 3s. 9d.,	15s.
Item 1 barrel of sousing ale to the brawn	12d.
Item 1 barrel of penny ale	2s. 6d.
Item for ale to the servants who travailed about various occupations or [*else*] the ale in the buttery were *tarned*509	5d.
Item for hiring of earthen pots	23d.
Item for 8 dozen cups, the dozen 7d.,	4s. 8d.

Sum £6 5s. 3d.

[404] [f. 135r]
Kitchen

First for 2 boars with 1 shoulder of brawn and the portage	22s.
Item paid to a labourer for the seething of the said brawn	3d.
Item for meat to the said labourer	2d.
Item for 8 dozen marrow bones	4s.
Item for brokemary	16d.
Item for carriage of the said bones and brokemary510	8d.
Item for 4 loins of pork and half	2s. 5d.
Item for 17 fillets of pork and half	16d.

---

509   Would have been turned sour.
510   Broken marrow bones?

Item for 1 quarter of beef	3*s.* 3*d.*
Item for 5 gallons of grease	6*s.* 8*d.*
Item for 1 dozen of neats	3*s.* 4*d.*
Item for blood and that belongs thereto	4*d.*
Item 14 gallons of cream	4*s.* 8*d.*
Item for mutton	12*d.*
Item for 9 ells of linen cloth for aprons for the cooks, price the ell 4½*d.*,	3*s.* 4½*d.*
Item for 1 ell of cloth for the Master Cook	7½*d.*
Item for 2 strainers	6*d.*
Item for portage of fish and flesh	6*d.*
Item for wiping cloths	10*d.*
Item for 3 great stewing pots	6*d.*

Sum 55*s.* 10*d.*

Poultry

First 32 swans at 4*s.* 4*d.*,	£6 18*s.* 8*d.*
Item 64 pheasants at 11*d.*,	58*s.* 8*d.*
Item 108 partridges and cocks at 4*d.*,	36*s.*

[405] [f. 135v]

Item 106 plovers at 3*d.*,	26*s.* 6*d.*
Item 11 dozen wood doves, the dozen at 18*d.*,	16*s.* 6*d.*
Item 36 dozen great birds, the dozen at 6*d.*,	18*s.*
Item 14 dozen larks at 3*d.*,	3*s.* 6*d.*
Item 8 dozen finches the dozen at 2*d.*,	16*d.*
Item 56 conies at 2½*d.*,	11*s.* 8*d.*
Item 6 dozen pullets, the dozen 2*s.*,	12*s.*
Item 1100 eggs at 10*d.*,	9*s.* 2*d.*
Item 44 capons, the piece at 6*d.*,	22*s.*
Item 6 geese, price the piece 8*d.*,	3*s.*

Sum £17 16*s.* 11½*d.*[511]

Sauce

First 1 bushel and half of salt, price the bushel 8*d.*,	12*d.*
Item 3 gallons of honey & half, price the gallon 16*d.*,	4*s.* 8*d.*
Item 2 gallons vinegar and 1 quart, price the gallon 3½*d.*,	8*d.*
Item 1 gallon mustard and 1 quart, price the gallon 6*d.*,	7½*d.*
Item for 1 pottle of ginger sauce and 1 quart, price the pottle 4*d.*,	6*d.*
Item for 1 gallon verjuice and 3 quarts,	6*d.*
Item for oatmeal	2*d.*
Item for onions	5*d.*
Item for 10 lbs candles, price the lb 1½*d.*,	15*d.*
Item for pack thread	4*d.*

Sum 10*s.* 1½*d.*

511 There are no halfpennies in the sub totals, so perhaps some discount was given. The sub total for the geese should be 4*s.*, so perhaps a digit has been erased.

Scullery

First for 15 quarters of charcoal, price the quarter 7*d*.,	8*s*. 9*d*.
Item for 100 faggots	3*s*. 8*d*.

[406] [f. 136r]

Item paid to the pewterer in Cheap for hiring 5 dozen chargers⁵¹² at 4*d*.,	20*d*.
Item to the same pewterer for 8 dozen garnished vessels at 8*d*.,	4*s*. 10*d*.
Item to the said pewterer for 18 lbs of pewter vessels lost and stolen, at 3*d*.,	4*s*. 6*d*.
Item for hiring 16 dozen garnished of pewter vessels to W. P. at 5*d*.,	6*s*. 8*d*.
Item for 2 platters and 5 saucers lost at the same feast	20½*d*.

Sum 31*s*. 9½*d*.

Spices

First 2 lbs & a half quartron of pepper, powder and whole, price the lb 20*d*.,	3*s*. 6½*d*.
Item saffron, 1 quarteron & half and 1 ounce price the lb 13*s*.,	5*s*. 10*d*.
Item for powder of cinnamon, 1 lb,	2*s*. 8*d*.
Item for ginger, 1 lb,	2*s*.
Item for cloves, half lb,	20*d*.
Item for mace, half lb,	20*d*.
Item sanders 1 quarteron & half a quarteron,	4½*d*.
Item raisins of Corinth 6 lbs, the pound 5*d*.,	2*s*. 6*d*.
Item sugar casson⁵¹³ 3 lbs, the lb 8*d*.,	2*s*.
Item sugar fine, 5 lbs, the lb 16*d*.,	6*s*. 8*d*.
Item almonds of Valencia 20 lbs, the lb 2*d*,	3*s*. 4*d*.
Item flour of rice, 8 lbs, the lb 4*d*.,	2*s*. 8*d*.
Item powder aniseed 1 lb,	4*d*.
Item caraway in comfit, 1 lb,	2*s*. 4*d*.
Item aniseed in comfit plain,	12*d*.
Item 24 lbs of dates	2*s*.
Item 8 lbs raisins of Malaga the lb 2*d*.,	16*d*.

Sum 41*s*. 11*d*.

[407] [f. 136v]
Diverse Costs

First to Hugh Sharpe for his travail in the buttery	12*d*.
Item to the keeper of the cupboard	20*d*.
Item to William Devenysh, panter,	3*s*. 10*d*.
Item to Thomas Borne, porter,	16*d*.
Item to William Gerveys in the pantry	8*d*.
Item to Thomas Clerk, brasier, in the pantry	8*d*.
Item John Orgon in the parlour	8*d*.
Item to Henry Taverner in the chamber above the parlour	8*d*.
Item to Thomas Clerk of Coleman Street in the great chamber	8*d*.
Item to Richard Fraunceys in the hall	8*d*.

---

⁵¹² Platters for food, or vessels for liquid.
⁵¹³ Possibly a shapeless loaf of fine sugar.

Item to *turnebrochers* in the Sunday & Monday	3s. 4d.
Item to a turner of guts	1d.
Item for water by the tankards 20d.	
Item to William Cokreth for 4 pipes of water at 2d.,	8d.
Item to John Hardy, Cook and his servants	30s.
Item to the said John for carriage of brass pots and spits	6d.
Item for 7 burdens of rushes and the carriage	2s. ½d.
Item given to 2 brewersmen for carrying vats and kimnels to the house of John Phillipe and to William Cokreth	1½d.
Item for carriage of a table & 1 pair of trestles to the house of John (of) Mason	2d.
Item for hiring of timber, tables and trestles from Thomas Brighte of Wood Street, with carpentry to make the hale[514] in the yard	4s. 8d.
Item to John Houghton for 6 days to help to make the said hale with other occupation of making of tables and trestles, the day 4d.,	2s.
Item to Olde Stephen in reward to make clean the place against the feast day and after the said feast, also with bearing of gowns and hoods, for his reward in all	12d.

[408] [f. 137r]

Item for carriage of stools, tables and forms from Brewers' Hall into [the] timber yard of Thomas Brighte, carpenter,	2d.
Item for loading away of 4 loads of dung by William Cokreth[515] at 2d.,	8d.
Item for 3 hurdles to the larder house	9d.
Item to Jonette Moyne for 1 stool lost	2d.
Item for diverse iron work to the hale	12d.
Item paid to John Danyell & William Bodevyle, maltmen, for venison	8s. 7d.
Item paid to the players	7s.
Item to 2 minstrels, Blind William & his fellow	12d.
Item paid at the house of John Brooke for 1 dinner	18d.
Item for washing of 3 board cloths diapered[516] with 4 cloths, long, plain, old & new, the piece 3d.,	21d.
Item for 10 pieces of board cloth in the 2 chambers and in the hall the piece at 2d.,	20d.
Item for the washing of 2 sanaps new, the piece 1d.,	2d.
Item for the washing of a long towel diapered	2d.
Item for 2 towels diapered in the porch	2d.
Item for 2 sanaps long in the parlour	2d.
Item 4 sanaps in the great chamber	2d.

Sum £4 2s. 6d.

Sum total of this Feast £38 4s. 2d.

514 Perhaps decorative panels for the hall, elsewhere described as 'halling', or simply the hall.
515 Cokreth was not recorded before this as the raker.
516 Linen or silk fabric woven with a repeated pattern of figures or geometrical designs.

[409]

Alan Brett with his wife	2s.	Agnes Bugge	12d.
Adam Smyth	16d.	Alice the widow of John Benge	12d.
Alexander Marcow	16d.	Baldewyne Hoper	16d.

[410] [f. 137v]

Cristiane More	12d.	John Lumbarde	16d.
Dederik Johnson with his wife	2s.	John Parker	16d.
Edmund Bosvenonne with his wife	2s.	John Assh with his wife	2s.
Edmund Cok, bookbinder, with		John Aleyn with his wife	2s.
his wife	2s.	John Eylond	16d.
		John Hopkyn with his wife	2s.
Henry Bracy	16d.	John Leche	16d.
Henry Rowe with his wife	2s.	John Hardynge	16d.
Henry Wixtone	16d.	John Wilde	16d.
Henry Grene with his wife	2s.	John Purley	16d.
Henry Stapill	16d.	John Gremesby	16d.
Henry Payn with his wife	2s.	John Piken	12d.
Henry Fereby	16d.	John Philippe with his wife	20d.
		John Bentele	16d.
Hugh Warde	12d.	John Fayreman with his wife	20d.
Hugh Glene	16d.	John Bedewelle	16d.
Hugh Neel with his wife	2s.	John Holbek with his wife	2s.
		John Pamplion with his wife	2s.
John Blostmere with his wife	2s.	John Warsoppe	16d.
John Chapman with his wife	2s.	John Thomas	12d.
John Castonne with his wife	2s.	John Bosvenon with his wife	2s.
John Sere, glover,	16d.	John Humber with his wife	20d.
John Spenser	16d.	John Langford, maltman,	16d.
John Ketynge with his wife	2s.	John Hanslape with his wife	2s.
John Fekenham with his wife	2s.	John Reeffawe	12d.
John Spore	16d.	John Salter	16d.
John Davy	16d.	John Tornour, shearman, with his	
John Jacow	16d.	wife	2s.
John Nicholl	16d.	John Golderynge	16d.
John Riche the younger with his		John Mabile	16d.
wife	2s.	John Laurence	12d.

[411] [f. 138r]

John Brewester with his wife	2s.	Peter Carpenter with his wife	2s.
John Riche without Cripplegate	12d.		
John Reyner	12d.	Richard Carowe with his wife	2s.
John Carion	16d.	Richard Aleyn with his wife	2s.
John Aston with his wife	2s.	Richard Gerveys with his wife	16d.
John Russell with his wife	2s.	Richard West	16d.
John Qwyntyn with his wife	2s.	Richard Lucas with his wife	2s.
John Jacob with his wife	2s.	Richard Sherewod	12d.
John Stone	16d.	Richard Frepurs	16d.
John Elcy with his wife	2s.		

John Killom	16*d.*	Robert Smyth with his wife	2*s.*
John Riche, tailor,	16*d.*	Robert Carpenter with his wife	20*d.*
John Sowthmede with his wife	2*s.*	Robert Ketynge with his wife	2*s.*
John Dunche	16*d.*	Robert Pede with his wife	2*s.*
John Lynne	16*d.*	Robert Elkyn with his wife	2*s.*
John Bernewell with his wife	2*s.*	Robert Nikke	16*d.*
John Sonder	16*d.*	Robert Bullard with his wife	2*s.*
John Morys with his wife	2*s.*	Robert Mayhew	15*d.*
John Danyell	16*d.*	Robert Calow	16*d.*
		Robert Cristophore with his wife	22*d.*
Jacob Tolvan with his wife	2*s.*		
		Roger Swanneffeld with his wife	2*s.*
Julyane Hetersete	12*d.*	Roger Blissote with his wife	2*s.*
		Roger Baronne	16*d.*
Johanna Amwell	12*d.*		
		Raff Palmer with his wife	2*s.*
Katherine de Van	12*d.*	Raff Marke with his wife	2*s.*
Mustell, maltman,	16*d.*	Raff Trewyle with his wife	2*s.*
Michael Tregononne with his wife	2*s.*	Simon Herry	16*d.*
		Simon at Welle	16*d.*
Margaret Thetford	12*d.*		
Nicholas Merton with his wife	2*s.*		
Nicholas Muriell	16*d.*		

[412] [f. 138v]

Stephen Clean	16*d.*	William Boterfeld, cooper,	12*d.*
Stephen Roo	16*d.*	William Bodevile	16*d.*
		William Petevile	16*d.*
Thomas Harford	12*d.*	William Eyre with his wife	2*s.*
Thomas Grene with his wife	2*s.*	William Longe	16*d.*
Thomas Kirtoth with his wife	2*s.*	William Belle with his wife	2*s.*
Thomas Morys	16*d.*	William Robert	16*d.*
Thomas Ayle with his wife	2*s.*	William Ferrour the Younger	
Thomas Smyth	16*d.*	with his wife	2*s.*
Thomas atte Hethe	16*d.*	William Vevian with his wife	2*s.*
Thomas Mershe	16*d.*	William Rawlyn	16*d.*
Thomas Hancok	16*d.*	William Miles, maltman,	12*d.*
Thomas Alfrend, cooper,	16*d.*	William Gore, maltman,	16*d.*
Thomas Cokeshed	8*d.*	William atte Woode with his wife	2*s.*
William Fissh with his wife	2*s.*	William Story, grocer, with his wife	2*s.*
William Termeday with his wife	2*s.*	William Calston, plumber,	16*d.*
William Baconne with his wife	2*s.*		
William Ferrour the Elder with		The wife of Adam Copendale	8*d.*
his wife	2*s.*	The wife late of James Knyght	12*d.*
William Dowdale with his wife	2*s.*	The wife of William Claisson	12*d.*
William Grose with his wife	2*s.*		
William Baily with his wife	2*s.*	Walter Colshill with his wife	2*s.*

William Lyndesay	16d.	Walter Behethelen	16d.
William Canonne	16d.	Walter Glyn	16d.
William Cokrede	16d.	**Sum £12 17s. 1d.**	
William Crane	12d.	Examined.	
William Pompe	16d.		
William Hille with his wife	2s.	[*Guests at the Brewers' feast c. 1425*]	
William Herry	16d.		
William Hert of Ware	16d.	Agnes the servant with Agnes Bugge	
		Sir Adam Dalton, parson	
		Wissygnsete, the chief lord of the fee[517]	

[413] [f. 139r]

2 servants with John Brook
2 women with Thomas Hatcher and the daughter of the said Thomas
Friar John Berkynge
The daughter of Henry Rowe
Geven, aletaker, with his wife
The wife of John Spore
John Turvey
John Ryngesson
John Wynge
Langtonne of the Counter
Master Richard Donyngton, the prior of the Austin Friars
The Provincial of the Austin Friars

The parson of [*St Mary*] Woolnoth
The parson of [*St Mary*] Woolchurch
James Mogonne, poulter
James Ytacombe with his wife
Thomas Donyngtonne
William Pethin
The brother of William Pompe
The wife of John de Dene
A stranger with Henry Somer[518]
A stranger with John Broke of Gray's Inn
John Skynner called Caponherst with his wife
John Stephene
Leonell Power
The widow in the almshouse of the Taylors with her servant
The 4 wives of the Masters of the craft.

Examined.

[414] [f. 139v]
Reparations

First paid to John, plasterer, for making of the said femerell[519] upon the hall, taking in great — 35s.

Item paid for timber and nails for the same work — 5d.

Item paid for the vane that stands upon the same femerell — 1s. 6d.

Sum 37s. 1d.

---

[517] Landlord to whom taxation was due.
[518] Perhaps Henry Somer, chancellor of the exchequer from 1410 for twenty-nine years, also keeper of the exchange and mint at the Tower. J. L. Kirby, 'Somer, Henry (d. 1450), administrator', *ODNB*. See [445] and [452]. For Leonell Power, see R. Bowers, 'Power, Lionel (c.1375x80–1445), composer', *ODNB*.
[519] Structure typically dome-shaped, with lateral ventilation openings on roof over a hall or kitchen.

[f. 140r]

The Painting of the Bay Window

First paid for the painting of the same window, taken in great,	20s.
Item for crests to the said window	18d.
Item for stopping of the crevices to the same window	8d.
Item for boards to the pentice of the same window	12d.
Item for nails to the same window	4d.
Item for 1 board to make *sconchons*520	2d.
Item to a carpenter for making the same pentice for 1 day and a half at 8½d.,	13d.
Item for varnishing of the same window	8d.

[Clerk's note: ame, followed by another m and 3 minims]

Sum 25s. 5d.

[415]

The making of the doors to the buttery and pantry with amending of other necessary things in the place

First for 1 pair of hinges with hooks for the buttery door, weighing 4 lbs and a half,	9d.
Item for half a hundred board nails	2d.
Item for half a hundred seam-nails521	1½d.
Item for 1 pair of hinges with hooks to the pantry door, weighing 5 lbs and a half,	11d.
Item for seam-nails	½d.
Item for 2 latches with the *paraill*522	4d.
Item for 1 quarteron of board nails	1d.
Item for spiking-nails	½d.
Item for 2 bolts with the *paraill* to the doors of the pantry and buttery	4d.
Item for half a hundred *grapnails*523	1d.
Item for 1 lock staple to the buttery door	1d.

[416] [f. 140v]

Item for 2 small staples to the said doors for the bolts	½d.
Item for 1 pair of potens garnets for the dresser in the kitchen	4d.
Item for 1 pair garnets to the same dresser	3d.
Item for nails to the hen coop and in other places	2d.
Item for amending of diverse locks to the doors before written, with amending of diverse locks to the almaries in the great kitchen	6d.
Item for 2 small staples	1d.
Item for 1 hinge to the door of the little cellar	5d.

---

520 Sconce: candlestick with a shade to protect the flame from wind.
521 Nails for fastening overlapping edges, with the end of the nail clinched to form a rivet. A further payment without any quantity was noted below.
522 Perhaps the outer trim.
523 Nails or 'grapnels' – implements for grasping.

Item for 5 boards of oak and elm to the shelves in the buttery, whereof
2 boards for the dresser in the kitchen   12*d.*

Item for 4 quarters, whereof 3 in the buttery to make shelves, and in the
kitchen by the hall door to serve the dresser, with a foot to the board of the
said dresser, and timber to brackets to the doors of the pantry and buttery,
with timber for brackets to the said shelves in the buttery   8*d.*

Item to a carpenter for 3 days in cutting of the said doors with the making of
the same and also making of the shelves in the buttery, with the making of
boards to the dresser, the day 8*d.*,   2*s.*

Sum 8*s.* 5*d.*

The Glazing of 2 glass windows in the side of the hall

First for 45 feet of glass to the 2 windows in the side of the said hall at 11*d.*,   41*s.* 8½*d.*

Sum as appears

[417] [f. 141r]

First to a smith for a caas[524] of iron to the lesser window in the parlour   20*d.*

Item to the glazier for the setting in of the glass in the said caas   8*d.*

Item to iron work to the greater window in the parlour, that is to say garnets,

    3*s.* 4*d.*

Item for setting in of the glass in the same iron work   10*d.*

Item to the glazier for setting in the sign of Thomas Yole   8*d.*

Item for setting in of the name of John Russell   4*d.*

Item for 1 mending of a little piece of glass in the bay window that was broken   2*d.*

Item to the glazier for setting in of the glass in the iron work of the 2 borders
in the hall with the making of diverse signs in diverse glass windows   3*s.*

Item to a smith for the making of ironwork to the same 2 borders   2*s.* 4*d.*

Item for surmounts of iron to the same windows   20*d.*

Item for the making of a bar of iron to the great window in the parlour for a
hanging lock   4*d.*

Item for a lock to the same window   3*d.*

Item for 1 hanging lock to the whetstone at the hall door   3*d.*

Sum 15*s.* 6*d.*

    Examined

[418] [f. 141v]

**Parcels of a stone wall called the reredos in the great kitchen, with amending a
wall in the little cellar, and in the roll of accounts of the said Masters the said
reredos and the wall in the little cellar are in a sum of £11 5*s.* 6½*d.*, with 13
parcels and 13 sums thereto, as it shows afterwards by the said parcels.**

First to a dauber and his man by 1 day to break the wall of the said great
kitchen and to dress the loam and keep it together with lathing of the said
wall, for the work of masonry went up by the same wall within the said
kitchen   13*d.*

---

[524]   Perhaps casing, surround, frame or casement.

Item to Goldynge, mason, for making the wall called the reredos in the same
great kitchen, which he took in great, finding lime, stones and chalk, with all
workmanship to the same,   £4 2d.

Item to John Houghtonne for 12 days & a half in daubing and mortaring
of the wall of the said kitchen without, and dressing and amending of the
almarie in the said kitchen, with amending of diverse other defaults in
diverse places, with making of giftes⁵²⁵ and shelves in the little cellar, with his
meat, in the day 6d.,   6s. 3d.

Item for half of 1,000 tiles called brick, with the carriage of the same brick,
to amend a wall in the said cellar,   3s. 4d.

Item to Richard Goldynge, mason, for 4 days working in the great kitchen
upon the hearth and paving of the same kitchen, with making of the wall in
the little cellar with tile called brick, the day 8½d., with noonchyns,   2s. 10d.

Item for 1 cartful of sand to the said Goldynge for same works   4d.

Item to Thomas Balame, labourer, for 6 days to serve the same mason and
for to void robux out of the kitchen and out of the place, the day 5½d., with
noonchyns,   2s. 9d.

Item to the said Thomas for 3 days in voiding of the robux with a barrow,
out of the place next to our kitchen and also out of our place, the day 5d.,   15d.

Item for the carriage of 9 carts full and a half of robux and earth out of the
place next to the great kitchen and out of the great place of Brewers' Hall at
2½d.,   2s.

Item for 3 dogs of iron, to diverse beams in the great kitchen, weighing
12 lbs & a half, with nails, price the pound 2d.,   2s. 1d.

[419] [f. 142r]

Item to John Peressonne lime-burner for 2 loads of lime to the said work   22d.

Item for 2 lbs of cotton candle to the works in the little cellar of masonry, in
the mornings and evenings, and to diverse works of carpentry and daubing,   3d.

Item for 2 quarters of new timber bought from Thomas Brighte in Wood
Street to the shelves in the little cellar   4d.

Item to 1 labourer by half a day to help John Houghtone in casting of loam   2½d.

Item for 2 days and a half to 2 carpenters for driving in of the side of the
kitchen and undersetting of the same   3s. 4d.

Item for 1 beam in the same kitchen to bind the 2 sides together   10d.

Item for blocks and *clavys*⁵²⁶ and hiring of the shores⁵²⁷ and cutting of the same
shores   2s.

Item for noonchyns to the same carpenters by the said 2 days and ½,   2d.

Item for 100 of *hortlaths*⁵²⁸   8d.

Item for 2 days work of a carpenter working 1 plate above the stone wall   16d.

Item for the plate of the same wall   12d.

Item for 1 quarter of timber to amending the almarie in the kitchen   3d.

Sum £5 14s. 3½d.

---

⁵²⁵   Resting place. A similar meaning to shelf.
⁵²⁶   Perhaps bolts, from the Latin *clavis*.
⁵²⁷   Timber props to support a building undergoing repairs.
⁵²⁸   Some kind of lath, thin strips of timber for roof tiles or plaster. Short lath perhaps?

[420]

Parcels paid to John Houghtone, labourer, for carpentry and daubing with other costs as it shows afterwards

First to the said John Houghtone, labourer, for 2 days working in amending of the great windows in the almshouse for they would not shut nor unshut, and for daubing of the new window in the house sometime of Rose,[529] with carpentry of a *shettynge*[530] made in the same house, for the ground was too low at that time, with the making of forms at the great gate for the porters and for other men to sit upon, the day with his *noonshyns* 6½*d.*, 13*d.*

[f. 142v]

Item paid to John Houghtone for 6 days in amending of the paleys[531] and covering of the locks of the said palays and making of a pan for fire with boards and tiles, to Johanna Awmbele, and hanging of a window in one of the almshouses and beam filling[532] of the hall with loam and stones and also beam filling of the end upon the side of a chamber over the parlour, so that smoke should not enter into the said chamber, at 6*d.*, 3*s.*

Item for a [?]cover[533] to the aforesaid fire pan 1*d.*

Item for 5 old boards to make the aforesaid pan 4½*d.*

Item to another labourer by 1 day & a half in amending of a chimney in the great chamber and in amending of a femerell upon the almshouse 9*d.*

Item to the same labourer by 1 day in amending of 2 gable walls upon the almshouse in daubing with loam and mortar 6*d.*

Item to John Houghtone, labourer, for 1 day in daubing within the roof by the side of the great kitchen for to keep out the smoke of the chamber over the parlour, 6*d.*

Item to John Houghtone, labourer, for 2 days in parting the almarie in the great kitchen with boards of poplar and the making of a window in the buttery, with amending of the chimney in the parlour 12*d.*

[421]

Item to the said John Houghtone for the making of hanging for ladders in the privy house with amending of diverse defaults in stopping of holes in the pantry, with amending of a gutter in carpentry over the kitchen door in the almshouse, with the making of a cupboard in the great chamber and the making of the hanging of a lavabo[534] for washing of hands in the said chamber, by 2 days & a half at 6*d.*, 15*d.*

Item to the same John Hougtone for 2 days in amending of the coop for the poultry with the making of hooks to the same coop for the doors of the said coop, and amending of diverse defaults in the little chamber of the almshouse against

---

529 This may be Rose, Porlond's servant. She did not occur again in the book.
530 Shutters or 'shutting' or a raised floor?
531 Storehouse or cellar, fence of pales or enclosure, yard, enclosed by a palisade.
532 Plastering, filling empty space.
533 Cr or Gr in the manuscript, perhaps short for couvre or cover.
534 Basin.

the coming of Thomas Draycote, broiderer,[535] with amending of the chimneys in the parlour and making of pins to the windows in the place, with other diverse occupations in the same place

[422] [f. 143r]

And the making of diverse small pieces of lead upon the pentice in the side of the new bay window, with amending of the paleys in the yard, at 6*d.*,	12*d.*
Item to the said John, labourer, for 1 day amending of a window to the great cellar with new garnets and making of perches[536] for napery in the pantry and buttery with amending of other small things by the same day,	6*d.*
Item to the same John for amending of the wall near Jonette Moyne as in carpentry, and with tile, stone and mortar, and with amending of the forms outside the great gate,	6*d.*
Item to the said John Houghtone by 1 day & a half to make a window with a lattice in the pantry, with the setting of a board and various shelves in the said pantry	9*d.*
Item to the same John for 2 days in amending the head of a gutter that runs under the hall floor, with other various works in the almshouse and in other places, with paving of diverse holes in the great kitchen, at 6*d.*,	12*d.*
Item to the same John for 8 days, with his meat, at 6*d.*, in making of windows in the dark chamber near the privy in the almshouse, with daubing near the same dark house and making of shelves, forms, trestles and stools, with amending of a stair of the great cellar, with other occupation in the same cellar,	4*s.*
Item for various nails with a hinge to the same window of the said dark chamber	14*d.*

Sum 17s. 5½d.

[423]

> **The making of the chamber that was broken with thunder, as it shows afterwards**

First to 1 new rafter & to the carpenter for setting up of the same rafter, and with his working,	14*d.*
Item to a tiler for 2 days tiling upon a chamber that was broken with thunder, with amending of other defaults upon the houses, the day 8½*d.*, with his *noonchyns*,	17*d.*
Item to 1 servant for the same 2 days in helping with the same works at 6½*d.*,	13*d.*
Item for 1 x 100 of laths	8*d.*
Item for half a peck of tile pins	1½*d.*
Item for 3 roof tiles to the same	2*d.*

---

535 Draycote was either moving into the almshouse or using the chamber for his trade. He was not recorded as a brewer nor as a fraternity member at this time, so he may have been a tenant rather than an almsman.

536 Storage for table linen?

[f. 143v]

Item for sprig nails	1*d*.
Item for 2 x 100 & 1 quarteron of new tiles at 7*d*;	15½*d*.
Item for 1 cartful of sand	5*d*.
Item for ale given to the said carpenters and to the tilers	2*d*.
Item for carriage of robux and dung out of the same chamber	3*d*.
Item to a dauber for 2 days in making the gable wall of the said chamber at 7*d*.,	14*d*.
Item to a servant for to help the same dauber	4*d*.

Sum 8*s*. 4*d*.

[424]
Amending a kitchen by our place for dread of fire

First for a little quarteron of timber to make rafters	1½*d*.
Item for 100 laths of oak	8*d*.
Item for 1 cartful of loam	4*d*.
Item for carpentry, to a man, and for daubing of the roof of the said kitchen by 3 days at 6*d*.,	18*d*.
Item [*to*] Old Stephen for helping to serve the carpenter and the dauber	1*d*.
Item for straw to the said work	½*d*.
Item for 2 x 100 tiles at 8*d*.,	16*d*.
Item for 3 roof tiles	2½*d*.
Item for roof nails, sprig nails, with other nails	6½*d*.
Item for 2 sacks of lime and sand	4½*d*.
Item to a tiler and his man for the third part of a day in tiling of the said kitchen	8*d*.
Item for half x 100 tiles to the side of the buttery to keep the ground sill from rotting and to amend the cloister by our great kitchen	4*d*.

Sum 6*s*. 2½*d*.

[425]
Parcels of tile and [*payments*] to the tiler for tiling in various places

First to a tiler and his man by 1 day in the month of November the year the third of King Henry VI [1424], to make a barge[537] upon the capon house to save the boards from water, with amending a default of tiling [*at the*] chamber end,	13*d*.

[f. 144r]

Item for half x 100 & half a quarteron of tiles to the said barge of the capon house and to amend the house of Johnette Awmbele in the almshouse	5*d*.
Item for 1 x 100 tiles to the said almshouse upon various houses	8*d*.
Item to a tiler by half a day to make & amend the same houses	4*d*.
Item to a tiler & his servant by 1 day to amend a gutter between the house of Russe[538] & the little chamber that is over the buttery, with carpentry of the said gutter of the same tiler	12*d*.

---

[537]   A stand, layer of tiles, or roof, as a barrage against water?
[538]   A neighbour, John Russe: see **[432]**.

Item for 1 quarteron of tiles to the same tiler	*2d.*
Item for timber to the same bottom of the said gutter	*3d.*
Item to a tiler and his servant by 3 days, the day 12*d.*, upon the hall & upon the almshouse and in setting in of various chimneys	*3s.*
Item for 3 hundred of new tiles to diverse works & chimneys, to stop with, after the making of the said chimney in the almshouse and in other places,	*21d.*
Item to William Ferrynge, tiler, for shutting in of a chimney as in tiling in the almshouse by 1 day, & his man,	*12d.*
Item to another tiler & his man for 1 day tiling about the femerell of the hall and in various places	*14½d.*
Item for 6 roof tiles for to cover with chimneys & summer upon the hall roof by the new femerell	*4½d.*

Sum 11*s.* 3*d.*

[426]
Parcels of loam, lime and sand that served to diverse works

First for 1 cartful of loam to the beam filling in the hall with the chamber over the parlour	*4d.*
Item for 1 load of lime that served to the chamber that was broken with thunder, in tiling & daubing, and to amend the capon house	*12d.*
Item for 5 sacks of lime to diverse works in tiling & daubing	*8d.*
	Examined

[f. 144v]

Item for diverse works in the place, 3 loads of loam, price the load 4*d.*,	*12d.*
Item for 2 loads of sand to serve in various works [*scored*: to the said] price at 5*d.*,	*10d.*
Item to John Peresonne for 1 load of lime in various places	*12d.*
Item to John Riche for 4 loads of loam, of which given by the said John Riche, 2 loads of the said lime,	*8d.*
Item for 2 sacks of lime that served about the femerell of the hall and in various places	*4d.*
Item for 1 sack of lime to wash with the dark chamber by the privy in the almshouse	*2d.*

Sum 6*s.*

[427]
Parcels of locks, keys, clickets, laths and latches

First for 1 lock with a staple to the door of a tenant called Johnette Bromle,[539] with one new key,	*9d.*
Item for 1 lock to the middle kitchen door in the alley of the almshouse	*6½d.*
Item for 5 new keys to the privy door of the almshouse at 2½*d.*,	*12½d.*
Item for 1 new clicket to the foremost door of the almshouse	*3d.*

---

539   She is recorded as a tenant rather than an almswoman here.

Item for 2 crooked latches, 2 cramps 2 catches, 2 hooks upon the paleys in
the yard, 2 latches, 2 cramps, 2 catches to the doors of the almshouse, with 1
new key to the door in the kitchen of the said almshouse,   11*d.*
Item for amending of a lock to the buttery door and for amending of a lock
to the great chest in the buttery, with amending of a clicket lock to the great
gate and for amending of a lock to the pantry door,   6*d.*
Item for amending of 1 lock to the privy door in the almshouse   1½*d.*
Item for a new lock with a key to the chamber of John Turvey in the said
almshouse   6*d.*
Item for 1 new key to the woodhouse door in the place   3*d.*
Item for 2 new keys to the 2 kitchen doors in the almshouse   7*d.*

Sum 5*s.* 5½*d.*

Examined

[428] [f. 145r]
Hoops to diverse vats and tubs with brooms and nails

First for various hoops to diverse vats and tubs   2*s.* 8½*d.*
Item for various brooms of birch and broom   7½*d.*
Item for nails, tenterhooks, garnets, door hooks, lead nails, lattice nails,
transom nails, padlocks, hasps & staples with rings for doors   7*s.* 6½*d.*

Sum 10*s.* 10½*d.*

[429]
The ceiling of the pantry, with iron to the corbe[540] of the well and the making of the same, with the costs of a counter in the hall, with carrying out of dung as it shows afterwards

First to John Houghton for 13 days working as in carpentry and daubing of
the works, the day 6*d.*, with his meat,   6*s.* 6*d.*
Item for old iron, with the making of the same iron to the well   16*d.*
Item for red lead, molten, and coal   6½*d.*
Item for 2 x 100 laths to the ceiling of the said pantry   8*d.*
Item for diverse boards for windows with shelves in the same pantry, with
diverse quarters, legs and fillets in the same pantry to the said windows and
shelves   20*d.*
Item for sprig nail, twopenny nails, threepenny nails, fourpenny nails and
half x 100 sixpenny nails,   14*d.*
Item for 1 pair of garnets to the counter in the hall   4*d.*
Item for 1 lock to the said counter   6*d.*
Item for carriage of dung that was in a chamber of the almshouse and in the
coop of the great place   1½*d.*

Sum 12*s.* 10*d.*

---

540 Corbel: projection from a wall of stone, iron or timber to support a superincumbent
     weight.

[430]
Amending of our halling with mail and hooks

First given to a tailor by 1 day for his labour in amending the hooks, with setting on of the mail541 upon the hanging for the

[f. 145v]

hall and for the parlour	5½d.
Item given to Thomas Evesham in helping of the same work	2d.

Sum 7½d.

[431]
Payment for various and small parcels

First for washing of 2 albs and towels with setting on of the orphreys542 to the same albs,	4d.
Item for 2 forks and 2 troughs for daubing	4d.
Item for 2 old stools and a little board bought of one Johnet in Bassishaw	2d.
Item for 1 old counter that stands in the bay window	6d.
Item for dressing of a piece of iron to hold up the transom in the hall	4d.
Item for 2 old boards to the chamber of Robert Lynford	4d.
Item to a smith for amending diverse surmounts to 2 windows in the almshouse	4d.
Item for carriage of lead upon the eaves of the capon house	1d.
Item for carriage of a gutter of lead that stands by the door of the kitchen of the almshouse within the paleys	2d.
Item given in reward to a carpenter for making ready a board above the said gutter so that the plumber should the better line the lead to be [?]current543	1d.
Item bought from Vevyan the Armourer, diverse boards, small and great, to keep the ground sill of our buttery from rotting	5d.
Item for boards with fillets for shelves in the pantry	11½d.
Item for carriage of 200 [*lbs?*] lead from the house of Thomas Emonde to the house of the plumber in St Clement's Lane	2d.
Item to John Turvey for diverse occupation in our place at diverse times as in labour	12d.
Item to Lemyngton for helping with the said occupation	8d.
Examined	

[432] [f. 146r]

Item for 2 boards bought from the mother sometime of Vevyan the Armourer	2d.
Item paid for amending the hammer of the great gate	1d.
Item for 6 poplar boards to depart with the almarie in the great kitchen, in the middle of the said almarie	15d.
Item for diverse legs of the said almaries	4½d.
Item for 3 transoms in a gutter that is between John Russe and our buttery	3d.

---

541 Rings for chain mail. W. H. Black, who compiled the manuscript volume, The Brewers' Company Extract of Minutes 1418–40, GL MS 5441, in 1830, suggested that mail meant netting here.
542 Gold embroidery.
543 'Leyne ye led to be corannt.' To encourage the flow of water?

Item for carriage of dung that was in the pantry where the bread bin sometime stood	*1d.*
Item for carriage of dust and rushes after the making of the new femerell above the hall roof	*1d.*
Item for carriage of a torch from the house of Denyse Barthorppe into the church of All Hallows in the Wall	*½d.*
Item paid for wharfage of a carre[544] that brought 2 burdens of rushes to our hall against the Feast of the Cooks	*½d.*
Item for 1 new shovel	*4d.*
Item for the hemming of a green cloth and making of the same, which lies upon the counting board in the hall	*3d.*
Item for 1 old chest to serve for a moulding board	*7s.*
Item for the hemming of 4 new board cloths with 2 sanaps new, against the feast day	*4d.*
Item for carriage of 2 loads of robux out of the almshouse after the making of the new chimneys	*6d.*
Item for small hooks with small staples to make the lattice window in the pantry	*2d.*
Item given to a plumber's man for amending of a pipe of lead to the privy in the almshouse	*½d.*
Item for amending of 2 tables with trestles	*20d.*
Item to a carpenter for making of a quarter of timber at the foot of the cupboard that stands against the doors of pantry and buttery	*1d.*
Item given to a servant of a tiler for making clean of diverse gutters in our place	*½d.*
Item for wine and ale in counselling with the Recorder of London and with various men of law for making rent secure to our craft by testament, and for the carrying of the Mass books that Robert Mayhewe gave, from the house of the said Robert to our Hall	*16d.*
[*Latin*: which missals were given by Robert Mayhewe].	

[433] [f. 146v]

Item for dressing of an old dog of iron the which is in the great kitchen	*3d.*
Item for various pieces of timber bought from Alison, sometime the wife of Stephen Brewer	*8d.*
Item for 2 new lattices in the pantry	*16d.*
Item for amending of a lattice in the great chamber, with amending of 2 other lattices in the chamber over the parlour,	*6d.*
Item for 1 burden of rushes	*4d.*
Item for paving and amending a gutter to the privy of the almshouse	*5d.*
Item for carriage of earth and dung	*4d.*
Item for the making 5 hen troughs with plates of iron	*8d.*
Item for 1 lb of cotton candle to make with the dark chamber in the almshouse	*1½d.*
Item to John Stafford of the Guildhall for drawing of a bill out of English into French and for the writing of the said bill	*2s.*

Sum 26s. 7½d.

---

[544] Cart.

[434]
Parcels paid to one Old Stephen labourer and sometime brewersman for various occupations

First to the said Old Stephen for his travail in amending with timber of the stair in the buttery, with making clean of the cellar and amending of other things — 2*d.*
Item given to Old Stephen for making clean of the kitchen after the Smiths and 2 quarter days of the Brotherhoods of the Trinity and Clerks — 2*d.*
Item given to the said Stephen for to help to make the kitchen clean and ready against the Feast of Cooks, and other occupations — 1*d.*
Item given to the same Old Stephen in reward for delving of stones in the almshouse and carriage of the same stones to the cellar, with making clean and washing of the kitchen after the Coopers, — 2*d.*

Sum 7*d.*

First to the glazier for the setting of a greyhound in the glass window for William Copewod — 12*d.*

Sum as appears.

Examined.

[435] [f. 147r]
Bread and wine for 2 years
First for bread and wine to our priest for 2 years, spent in our chapel at the church of All Hallows in the Wall — 4*s.*

Sum as appears

First for 2 elm boards for the same window, the piece 3*d.*, — 6*d.*
Item for a pew with board for the stall — 4*d.*
Item for legs and fillets — 4*d.*
Item to a carpenter for the work of the same window — 10*d.*
Item for 1 pair of garnets to the said stall — 3*d.*
Item for nails to the same windows — 3*d.*

Sum 2*s.* 6*d.*

[436]
The making of the chamber of John Turvey in the almshouse with the making of other things in the same place

First for sawing of a transom, with ale given to workmen — 2*d.*
Item paid for a rib of beef to Robert Smyth and Hugh Nell, to make the said Robert Smith well-willed to deliver old timber to make with the same chamber, — 3*d.*
Item for carriage of 2 loads of timber and boards — 8*d.*
Item to John Houghtonne for 1 day to load the cart with the same timber and unload it — 6*d.*
Item to another labourer by half a day to help to load the same timber — 3½*d.*

| Item for carriage of boards | 2*d.* |
| Item for ale with Robert Smyth | ½*d.* |

Item for 2 dogs of iron to bind the gable wall in the almshouse, from flying outwards,[545] with nails, 15*d.*

Item to a carpenter for 12 days in making of a chamber in the said almshouse, the day at 8*d.*, 8*s.*

[437] [f. 147v]

Item for *noonchyns* to the said carpenter	7*d.*
Item for 1 piece of timber in the wall by the great gate	12*d.*
Item to a dauber and his man for daubing of the same wall	6*d.*

Item for carriage of 4 pieces of timber from the house of John Masonne unto Brewers' Hall, with ale, in all 2½*d.*

Item for carrying of 3 pieces of timber from the house [*of*] Richard Tailor without Aldgate unto Brewers' Hall 2*d.*

| Item for 1 piece of timber to Goldynge, mason | 2*d.* |

Item paid to 2 carpenters for 1 day making of a little loft in the said chamber of John Turvey, 15*d.*

| Item for 1 new piece of timber in the said little loft | 8*d.* |

Item paid to Jankyn Tenterden, ironmonger, for nails, garnets, hooks, and other things of iron work that served to the new chamber of John Turvey, and to a loft made in the said chamber, and in other places, 11*s.* 4*d.*

Sum 27*s.* 2½*d.*

[438]

The making of 5 chimneys in diverse chambers of the almshouse, with other costs in the said chambers

First paid to John, plasterer, for making of 2 chimneys of plaster in 2 chambers, 26*s.* 8*d.*

Item for 3 x 100 nails to the mantel sides and with reward given to the said plasterer 15*d.*

Item paid to John Goldynge, mason, for the making of 3 chimneys of lime and stone, in great, 58*s.* 2*d.*

| Item for carriage of 4 cartfulls and a half of robux | 10*d.* |

Item for 7 quarters of timber, the piece 1½*d.*, to the wall between the rent of Elsyngspital, sometime the parsonage of Aldermanbury,[546] and the aforesaid almshouse, 9*d.*

[439] [f. 148r]

| Item for 1 board under the chimney by the said rent of Elsyngspital | 10*d.* |

---

545 To prevent this.
546 The former parsonage of St Mary Aldermanbury, rented out by Elsyngspital, the hospital founded by William Elsyng. It became an Augustinian house, one of whose canons served as curate for St Mary Aldermanbury. See Bowtell, Elsyngspital, III, 264.

Item to a carpenter for 2 days with 2 hours work before the masonry and after the masonry of the said chimneys	18*d.*
Item for 1 x 100 laths to the said wall	8*d.*
Item for crests of plaster to the said 3 chimneys	2*s.* 6*d.*
Item to a dauber and his man by 3 days with their *noonchyns* in daubing of walls and making of floors in the almshouse after the making of the said chimneys	4*s.* 2*d.*
Item given to Old Stephen for making clean of diverse in the said almshouse	8*d.*
Item to a dauber for 1 day and a half for making of floors and diverse defaults in the chamber with the privy	8*d.*
Item to John Houghtonne for 2 days and a half in amending, with carpentry, of a long beam in the midst of the chamber with the privy in the almshouse, and other diverse in the almshouse	15*d.*
Item to a smith for making meet the surmounts to the window of Thomas Draycote, broiderer,	3*d.*
Item for 2 dogs of iron weighing 11 lbs, in the chamber of John Turvey, at 2*d.* each,	22*d.*
Item for [a] piece of timber to the said window of Thomas Draycote	4*d.*
Item to John Houghton for 3 days and a half in amending of floors, with making of a lattice & daubing of a wall, with the ceiling of the chamber of Thomas Draycote, at 6*d.*,	21*d.*
Item to Thomas Carpenter of Wood Street[547] for diverse quarters & boards, with 100 laths for the almshouse	20*d.*

Sum £5 5*s.* 9*d.*

The making of a little loft in the chamber sometime of Alison Brewer in the said almshouse

First to John Houghtonne for 3 days in making of a little loft in the said chamber, with the nailing of dogs of iron in the same chamber and in the kitchen, the day with his meat at 6*d.*,	18*d.*
Item for 3 pieces of new timber to the said loft,	10*d.*
Item for 14 lbs of new iron to the said dogs at 2*d.*,	2*s.* 4*d.*
	Examined

[440] [f. 148v]

Item for 100 sixpenny nails	6*d.*
Item for half x 100 fivepenny nails	2½*d.*
Item for 1 pennyworth of sixpenny nails	1*d.*
Item for 100 & a half of fourpenny nails	7*d.*
Item for half x 100 twopenny nails	1*d.*
Item for half x 100 twopenny nails	1*d.*[548]
Item for 2 x 100 sprig nails	2*d.*

Sum 6*s.* 3½*d.*

---

[547] Usually he was called Thomas Bright, carpenter, of Wood Street.
[548] This item was entered twice but counted only once in the total.

[441]
Parcels of lead and solder

First for the changing of 2 x 100[549] of old lead, some to the pentice on the side
of the hall & some to the pipe at the kitchen door of the almshouse and some
to the corbe of the well, at 16*d*., 2*s*. 8*d*.
Item for 1 quarteron and 14 lbs of new lead to the said pentice, pipe and corbe, 3*s*.
Item for 6 lbs of solder to the said pipe and to the corbe of the well at 6*d*., 3*s*.

Sum 8*s*. 8*d*.

Examined.

[442] [f. 149r]
> **The names that are entered with their sums of money are freemen and
> brethren, under one sum in the same 2 years, and of them there are 13
> persons, as it shows afterwards**

John Gybbes sometime dwelling in St John Street	20*s*.
William Cokreth at the Axe in Aldermanbury	26*s*. 8*d*.
Richard Tailor at the Key without Aldgate, in part of payment of 26*s*. 8*d*.,	16*s*. 8*d*.
Inglezard Snayght at the Tankard, upon the Tower Hill	40*s*.
Walter Bohethelon at the Cock near Holborn Cross	20*s*.
Martyn Nonnseglos at St Andrew Cross in Holborn, with Anneys his wife, in part payment of 26*s*. 8*d*.,	20*s*.
Adam Smyth at the Swan near Billingsgate in part payment of 26*s*. 8*d*.,	20*s*.
William Petyver at the Ram's Head in Fenchurch Street	23*s*. 4*d*.
Richard Gerveys at the Cock in Crooked Lane	26*s*. 8*d*.
Thomas Bronne at the Ship in Tower Street	23*s*. 3*d*.
William Vevyan at the Axe in St John Street	26*s*. 8*d*.
John Bentele at the Dragon in Bishopsgate Street	26*s*. 8*d*.
Will Longe at [*the*] Peacock in Aldersgate Street	23*s*. 4*d*.

[443]
> **The names that are entered here [*are*] all only freemen by the said 2 years, with
> their sums of money that they paid, as it shows underneath**

William Hood, sometime servant with John Broke, at the Seven Stars near the Stocks	6*s*. 8*d*.
John Sprotley, vintner, at the King's Head in Wood Street	20*s*.

[f. 149v]

Henry Bracy at the Bell in Philpot Lane	20*s*.
Edmund Bosvenonne at the White Leg in Fleet Street	26*s*. 8*d*.
Nicholas Doffeland at the Swan near Lothbury Bridge	23*s*. 4*d*.
Thomas Grene the Younger sometime at Long Entry near the Stocks	20*s*.
Richard Tolle at the Key in Bassishaw	26*s*. 8*d*.
John Eyre at the Sickle near Holborn Cross in full payment of 20*s*. for his freedom,	17*s*. 8*d*.

---

549   Pounds or pieces.

Waryn Fowler, servant with Robert Carpenter at the Cock in Bishopsgate
Street   13s. 4d.

John Gybbes	William Cokreth	Richard Tailor
Inglezard Snayght	Walter Behethelen	Martyn Nonnseglos with
Adam Smyth	William Petyver	Anneys his wife
Thomas Bronne	William Vevian	Richard Gerveys
	William Longe	John Bentele

Robert Fordam, maltman,	6s. 8d.[550]
Thomas Smyth with Alice his wife at the Garland outside Bishopsgate	6s. 8d.
Richard Fulke, maltman,	8s. 4d.
John Bugby at the Swan without Aldersgate	3s. 4d.
Richard Flete, capmaker, [*with*] Anneys his wife at the Fleur de Lys in Fenchurch Street	6s. 8d.
Henry Payne with Anneys his wife at the Garland in Wood Street	6s. 8d.

[444] [f. 150r]

John Childe with Katherine his wife at the Swan in Old Fish Street	6s. 8d.
John Bretaigne with Alice his wife at the Snipe in East Cheap	6s. 8d.
William Style at the Unicorn without Newgate	6s. 7d.
Roger Swanneffeld at the Two *Stolpes* near Baynard's Castle	6s. 8d.
John Newman the Younger with Botonne his wife at the Lily in Staining Lane	6s. 8d.
John Smyth maltman of Gamlingay	10s.
Thomas atte Hethe with Anneys his wife at the Basket in Fenchurch Street	10s.
John Thomas with Johanna his wife at the Eagle in Gracechurch Street	5s. 10d.
John Jacowe with Alice his wife at the Swan in Bassishaw	6s. 8d.
William Fissh with Anneys his wife at the Axe without Aldgate	5s.
Thomas Gremesby, baker, with Johanna his wife at the Chequer in Fenchurch Street	6s. 8d.
Henry Fereby with Cecile his wife at the Horn in the parish of St Giles	6s. 8d.
John Nicholl at the Cup without Ludgate	6s. 8d.

[445]

Robert Asshbourne at the Hind in Fenchurch Street	6s. 8d.
John Parker at the Angel near the Queenhithe	6s.
Jacob Tolvan with Anneys his wife at the Crane near St Nicholas Shambles	6s. 8d.
William Middelcote, carrier of sand, in the parish of St Giles in Holborn	6s. 8d.
John Newman the Elder at the Ram near Holborn Cross	6s. 8d.
William Michell at the Hartshorn in the parish of All Hallows the Less [*the Little*] in Thames Street	6s. 8d.
Thomas Nonnseglos at the Bishop, or else the Bishop's Head, outside the Bars in Holborn	6s. 8d.
Thomas Kirtoth at the Lion in Wood Street	6s. 8d.
William Lyndesay with Margaret his wife at the Bolt and the Ton in Fleet Street	6s. 8d.

[550]   These are probably fraternity entry fees, which were usually 6s. 8d.

Jacob Ytecombe at the Cony in Cony Hope Lane	6s. 8d.
John Bernewell with Emma his wife at the Swan in Billingsgate	10s.
Thomas Dryffeld sometime at the George in Coleman Street	3s. 4d.
Leonell Power, clerk and singer near the church of St George in Pudding Lane	6s. 8d.
Robert Caterton, clerk with Henry Somere	6s. 8d.
John Aleyn with Johanna his wife at the Cock near Crutched Friars	6s. 8d.
William Robert at the Bell in Coleman Street	6s. 8d.
William Boterfeld, cooper,	6s. 8d.

[446] [f. 150v]

John Danyell, maltman,	5s.
John Bronne, cooper,	6s. 8d.
Thomas Harford, clerk of the Exchequer, with Alice his wife,	3s. 4d.
Hugh Warde, clerk of the said Exchequer	3s. 4d.
William Story, grocer, with Johanna his wife,	6s. 8d.
John Cheffeld, fletcher, at Lamp within Newgate	3s. 4d.
Thomas Mariot, whitetawyer, by London Wall, with Maud his wife	6s. 8d.
John Bedewell, whitetawyer, by London Wall, with Cecily his wife	6s. 8d.
Thomas Hill, maltman, at the Cock near the end of Secoll Lane without Newgate	20s.
Richard Bever, servant with Thomas Hancok,	6s. 8d.
James Mogonne, poulter,	6s. 8d.
Robert Cristopher, fruiterer, with Johanna his wife,	6s. 8d.
Thomas Alfrend, cooper,	6s. 8d.
Edward Cok, stationer in Paternoster Row	3s. 4d.
William Gore, maltman,	6s. 8d.
Roger Lamelyn with Constance his wife at the Bell outside Aldgate	6s. 8d.

[447]

William Hill with Cristiane his wife at the Cock in Coleman Street	6s. 8d.
William Eyre with Anneys his wife at the Black Horse in Fleet Street	6s. 8d.
Simon Herry with Elizabeth his wife at the Bear in St Clement's Lane	6s. 8d.
Thomas Multonne with Margaret his wife, at the Hartshorn outside Aldgate	6s. 8d.
John Killom with Maude his wife at the Skimmer [*Skomour*] in Birchin Lane	6s. 8d.
Robert Goneld at the Pannier near the Queenhithe	6s. 8d.
Simon Franke with Elizabeth his wife at the Key near the Broken Wharf	6s. 8d.
John Newman at the Vernacle near the Austin Friars	5s. 10d.
John Fekenham at the Harp in St Clement's Lane	3s. 4d.
Thomas Moris with Cecily his wife at the Bell near the Queenhithe	6s. 8d.
William Was, baker,	5s.
John Norman with Anneys at [*blank*] near Baynard's Castle	4s. 4d.
Reynalde Trewyle at Christopher without Temple Bar	5s. 4d.
William Mulso, maltman,	5s.

[448] [f. 151r]

John Woodleff, maltman	6s. 8d.
Thomas Cokeshede, maltman,	6s. 8d.
John Langforde, maltman,	6s. 8d.
Richard Kilsole with Alice his wife at the Cock near St John Zachary	6s. 7d.

John Morris at the Key in St John Street   6s.
John Blostmere at the Star near Crooked Lane   5s.

[449] [f. 151v]

First course	Second course
Brawn with mustard	Blanche mortrewes
frumenty with mutton	Cony roasted
partridge stewed	plovers roasted
pheasant roasted	great birds with small
chickens baked	*dowcettes* with quince baked.

Costs of the same Dinner[551]

Pantry

First for white bread	2s. 10d.
Item for trencher bread	4d.
Item for 5 pecks of flour	15d.

Sum 4s. 5d.

Buttery

Item for red wine	7s. 8d.
Item for 2 kilderkins of good ale, price	5s.
Item for 1 k of three halfpenny ale	22d.
Item 1 k of penny ale	15d.
Item for 1 dozen of white cups	8d.

Sum 16s. 5d.

Kitchen

Item for 3 pieces of brawn	4s.
Item 200 quinces	2s.
Item 30 marrowbones, price	3s. 9d.
Item 1 sirloin of beef, price	13d.
Item 1 loin of pork	5d.
Item 3 fillets of pork	3d.
Item 5 breasts of mutton, price	10d.
Item 1 pottle of grease, price	8d.
Item 3 gallons of frumenty	6d.

[450] [f. 152r]

Item 6 gallons of milk	6d.	Item sanders	2d.
Item 2 gallons of cream	8d.	Item sugar half lb	9d.
		Item Almonds *jardons* 4 lbs & a half	13d.
Sum 14s. 8d.		**Sum 7s. 5d.**	

---

551   No date was recorded for this dinner, perhaps 1424–5?

Poultry

Item 1 swan, price	3s. 8d.
Item 14 pheasants at 12d.,	14s.
Item 33 partridges at 4d.	11s.
Item 4 dozen plovers & 3 at 3d.,	12s. 9d.
Item 22 dozen of birds at 1½d.,	2s. 9d.
Item 34 chickens, the dozen at 18d.	4s. 3d.
Item 200 eggs at 9d.,	18d.
Item 1 goose, price	6d.
Item 15 conies at 2½d.,	3s. 1½d.
Item paid to the poulter in reward	7½d.

Sum 54s. 2d.

Sauce

Item for salt	2½d.
Item for 3 quarts honey	12d.
Item for 1 quart vinegar	1d.
Item for 1 quart verjuice	1d.
Item 1 pot of mustard	1d.
Item for onions	½d.
Item for pack thread	½d.
Item for 1 lb of candle	1½d.

Sum 20d.

Spicery

Item for 1 quarteron and 1 ounce of powder of pepper	6½d.
Item for 1 ounce & a half of saffron	21d.
Item for 1 quarteron of cloves and mace	11d.
Item for 1 quarteron of ginger and canell	10d.
Item 3 lbs of dates	9d.
Item raisins of Corinth 1 lb & a half	7½d.

Costs

Item paid at the Greyhound in East Cheap the day of reckoning with Mogonne, poulter, for wine, bread and fish	22d.
Item for 1 burden of rushes	4d.
Item paid to the *turnbrochers*	6d.
Item to William Devenyssh, panterer,	8d.
Item to William Repon, butler,	6d.
Item to John Hardy, Cook,	6s. 8d.
Item to John Howtonne, porter of the gate,	2d.
Item for 20 tankards of water	5d.
Item for carriage of dung	3d.
Item for washing of 3 board cloths with 1 cloth diapered,	10d.
Item to John Hardy, Cook, for diverse portage of fish and flesh, with spits, pots and pans,	6d.
Item for the washing of 4 sanaps long with 1 long washing towel	10d.
Item for the washing of 1 towel diapered of 6 yards that served before meat, and 2 sanaps with wardnapes[552] for the ewery	2d.
Item for 1 long sanap to the board in the parlour	2d.
Item for meat cloths in the hall with 1 cloth to the second table in the parlour	3d.
Item for 19 faggots of wood	9½d.

Sum 14s. 10½d.

Examined. **Sum total of the dinner £5 13s. 7½d.**

---

[552] Wardnape: A wooden or metal mat placed under dishes to protect the tablecloth. Ewery: Room where ewers of water, basins, table linen and towels were kept.

[451] [f. 152v]

John Fekenham
Henry Trebolans
John Ketynge
Robert Smyth
John Masonne
Alan Brett
John Qwyntyn
Robert Mayhew
John Gedeney
William Bodevyle
John Humbere

William Crane
Hugh Nell
John Broke
John Reyner
John Salter
Thomas Grene
Leonell Power
Henry Payn
Robert Caterton, clerk
James Mogonne
Will Story, grocer

William Ferrour the Elder
Robert Carpenter
Thomas Hatcher
John Philippe
John Riche of Wood Street
William Belle
Thomas Driffeld
Robert Nikke
William Ferrour the
Younger
John Barston
John Turvey

[452]

Richard Sherewod
Richard Aleyn
John Turnour, shearman

John Pyken
John Russell

The Parson of All Hallows
William Calstone, plumber

Henry Somer
John Burveyn
Sir Raff, priest[553]
Thomas Harford

Friar John Whetby
Thomas Howe, maltman
Cotton, draper
Hugh Warde

2 sergeants of law
1 stranger
Selow the man of law
Sherox with Henry Somer

The Master of Cornhill

[453] [f. 153r]
John Masonne, Thomas Hatcher, John Broke, Henry Trebolans, Wardens by 2 years

> [*Latin*] **The account of John Masonne, Thomas Hatcher, John Broke and Henry Trebolans, Masters of the craft of Brewers and the fraternity in the church of All Hallows beside London Wall, and of their receipts and expenses to the use and profit of the said craft and fraternity, from the feast of the said All Hallows in the second year of the reign of King Henry VI [1423] until the same feast in the fourth year of the same King [1425], that is for two whole years, as appears, William Porlond then being common clerk of the aforesaid craft and fraternity.**

Remaining in the Common Box

First the same accountants discharge themselves of £31 5s. 7½d., from the deliberations of Robert Smyth, William Crane, John Philippe, and Hugh Neel, last Masters of the said craft and fraternity, which remains in money in the common box.

Sum as appears

---

553 Possibly Ralph Mymne, from Elsyngspital, who was later the curate for St Mary Aldermanbury church. Bowtell, Elsyngspital, 306.

315

Rent of the Tenement

And of 7s. 11d. received from rent of the tenement beside the gate by our hall, at the time of this said account

Sum as appears

[454]
Hire of the Hall

[*Latin and English*]
and for 4s. received from the fraternity of St Cross for the hall, and for 12d. received from

[f. 153v]
the fraternity of St John[554]
And 2s. from the Armourers
And of 8s. 8d. received from the Clerks
And of 12d. received from the Penny Brotherhood
And 5s. 10d. received from the Barbers
And of 2s. 8d. received from the Pinners
And of 5s. 4d. received from the Founders
And of 2s. received from les Players at Football
And of 2s. 8d. received from the Cooks
And of 4s. 6d. received from the Coopers
And of 6s. 4d. received from the Cutlers
And of 4s. 4d. received from the Point-makers
And of 18d. received from the Girdlers
And of 3s. 10d. received from the fraternity of the Holy Trinity
And of 20d. received from the Waxchandlers
And of 8d. received from William Herry, brewer
And of 2s. received from the Smiths

Sum 60s.

[455]
Quarterage with Arrears of Quarterage
And of £36 2s. 7d. received from the brothers and sisters that is, for the time of this account.
And of arrears, that is, from Alan Brett 9s. 2d. And from William Copwode 6s.

Sum £36 17s. 9d.

---

554   Names in Latin have been translated. Some French pronouns were used.

316

Testamentary Legacies

And of 40s. received from various, that is, for the soul of Dionysia Barthorppe,
13s. 4d.
And from the executors of William atte Welle 13s. 4d.
And from the executors of Robert Hilton 13s. 4d.

Sum as appears

[456]
Admissions to the Freedom

And of £7 6s. 8d., received from 22 men admitted to the freedom of the craft of
Brewers during the time of this account, that is from:
John Gybbes
William Cokreth
Richard Tailor
Inglezard Snayth
Walter Behethelen

[f. 154r]
Martin Nonnseglos
Adam Smyth
William Petyver
Richard Gerveys
Thomas Bronne
William Vevian
John Bentele
William Longe
John Sprotley
Henry Bracy
Edmund Bosvenonne
Nicholas Doffeland
Thomas Grene Junior
Richard Tolle
John Eyre
Warin Fowler
William Hood
That is, from each of them, 6s. 8d.

Sum as appears

[457]
Entry of Brothers

And of £14 received from the entry of 84 brothers during the time of this account, that
is from: John Blostmere, John Gibbes, William Cokreth, Richard Tailour, Inglezard
Snayth, Walter Behethelen, Martin Nonnseglos, Adam Smyth, William Petyver, Richard
Gerveys, Thomas Bronne, William Vevian, John Bentele, William Longe, Robert
Fordam, maltman, Thomas Smyth, Richard Fulke, maltman, John Childe, Richard

317

Flete, capmaker, Henry Payn, John Bretaigne, William Style, Roger Swanneffeld, John Newman Junior, John Smyth, maltman, Thomas atte Hethe, John Thomas, John Jacowe, William Fish, Thomas Gremesby, baker, Henry Fereby, John Nicholl, Robert Asshbourne, John Parker, Jacob Tolvan, William Middelcote, John Newman Senior, Thomas Nonnseglos, Thomas Kirtoth, William Lyndesay, Jacob Itecombe, John Bernewell, Thomas Driffeld, Leonell Power, clerk, Robert Caterton, clerk, John Aleyn, William Robert, William Boterfelde, cooper, John Danyell, John Bronne, cooper, Thomas Hertforde, Hugh Warde, William Story, grocer, John Cheffeld, fletcher, Thomas Mariot, John Bedewell, Thomas Hille, maltman, Richard Bever, Jacob Mogonne, poulter, Robert Cristopher, Thomas Alfrende, cooper, Edmund Cok, stationer, William Gore, maltman, Roger Lamelyn, William Hille, William Eyre, Simon Herry, Thomas Multonne, John Killom, Robert Goneld, Simon Franke, John Newman, vintner, John Fekenham, Thomas Morys, William Michell, William Was, baker,

[f. 154v]
John Norman, Reginald Trewyle, William Mulso, maltman, John Wodleffe, maltman, Thomas Cokeshede, maltman, John Langforde, maltman, Richard Kilsole, John Moris, from each of them, 3s. 4d.

Sum as appears

[458]
[Latin]
Collection made for the repair of the Hall and for glass to the window of the said Hall

And of £7 14s. received from various persons towards the repair of the Hall and window, that is, from John Pamplionne 3s. 4d., Nicholas Goonmailok 20d., Friar John Berkynge 20d., William Watforde 20d., William Cokreth 20d., John Hopkyn 2s., John Riche in Fleet Street 20d., John Bugby 20d., Nicholas Muriell 20d., Jacob Tolvan 20d., Thomas Yole 6s. 8d., William Canonne 2s., William Baconne, butcher, 20d., John Weste 12d., John Bedford [blank], Henry Nobull 20d., John Aleyn 20d., John Tregelowe 20d., William Boteler 20d., John Mabile 3s. 4d., Stephen Clean 20d., Walter Colshull 3s. 4d., Cristiana More 6s. 8d., Emma Canonne 20d., Katherine de Van 4d., John Burveyn 20d., the wife of Thomas Emond 6s. 8d., the wife of Richard Burgate 8d., the wife of John Davy 20d., William atte Wode 6s. 8d., Thomas Boteler 12d., John Kenaky 20d., John Parker 12d., John Waryn 20d., John Dunche 12d., John Tooke 3s. 4d., John Waghorne 12d., Michael Eve 20d., Roger Awdymer 6s. 8d., Richard Harlowe 20d., Peter Heyforde 20d., Alice Ederiche 20d., John Refawe 20d., John Salter 20d., John Elcy 20d., John Russell 3s. 4d., Matilda Stanntone 3s. 4d., Richard Lucas 3s. 4d., Stephen Clean 20d.,555 Thomas Kebull 2s. 4d., William Ferrour Senior 3s. 4d., Anna Smyth 12d., Margaret Thetford 12d., Thomas Dewy [blank], Robert Pede 4s. 4d., John Broke 5s., Henry Trebolans 5s., Peter Carpenter 3s. 4d., Robert Elkyn 3s. 4d., William Belle 3s. 4d., William Copwode 5s. 4d., Thomas Aleyn 3s. 4d.

Sum as appears

555 Clean either gave twice or was listed twice here.

318

[459] [f. 155r]
Collection of money for repairs of the Almshouse

And of £6 4s. 2d. received in alms from various men, that is, from John Russell
13s. 4d., Margaret Thetford 20d., Alice Ederiche 3s. 4d., Alexander Myles 3s. 4d.,
Richard Harlowe 20d., Robert Lynforde 3s. 4d., Robert Smyth & his associates 21s.,
from the quarter part of fines at the Guildhall 9s. 1½d., from John Broke from the
goods of Richard Tyler 12d.; of alms sought from outside the craft towards repair of
the almshouse £3 6s. 4½d.

Sum as appears

[460]
Fines for transgressions
And of 11s. received from fines for transgressions against the craft, that is, from John
Kenaky 20d., William Grosse 20d., William Robert 12d. Thomas Godynge 5s., John
Tregolowe 20d.

Sum as appears

**Sum total received £109 7s. 1½d. From which money there remains in the
common box
£31 5s. 7½d.**

[461]
Alms
And from which the aforesaid Masters seek allowance for alms given to Robert
Lynforde for the terms of Easter,[556] the Nativity of St John the Baptist in the year the
second of the reign of King Henry VI [1424] and for the term of St Michael in the
year of the reign of the same King the third [1424], for each term 5s. Sum 15s. To the
same Robert

[f. 155v]
For the terms of the Nativity of our Lord, Easter and St John the Baptist in the year
of the same King the third [1424–5]
And St Michael and the Nativity of our Lord in the fourth year [1425–6] for each
feast 7s. 7d.
Sum 37s. 11d.

And to Johanna Awmbele for the time of this account £3 8d.

Sum £5 13s. 7d.

[462]
Bread, wine with wax in the Chapel
And in bread and wine for two years, 4s.

---

556 Easter: 23 April 1424; the Nativity of St John: 24 June 1424; and St Michael: 29 September
1424.

And for 16 lbs of new wax and 3 quarters at 6*d.*, Sum 8*s.* 4½*d.*
And for the making of 37 lbs of old wax 17½*d.*
And for the changing of 19 lbs of old wax 20*d.*

Sum 15*s.* 5*d.*

[463]
Stipends
And in salary to Robert Steynton, chaplain of the said fraternity, £6 13*s.* 4*d.* by the
year, that is, for the time of this account, £13 6*s.* 8*d.*
And in agreed salary to William Porlond, clerk to the aforesaid fraternity for the
terms of Easter & St John the Baptist in the second year [1424] and for the term of
St Michael in the 3rd year [1424], for each term, 10*s.*, that is 30*s.*
And in salary to the same William for the terms of the Nativity of Our Lord, Easter
and the Nativity of St John the Baptist in the 3rd year [1424–5] and St Michael and
the Nativity of Our Lord in the 4th year [1425–6], for each feast, 20*s.*, £5[557]

Sum £19 16*s.* 8*d.*

Customary payments
And in money paid to the Rector of the church of Aldermanbury for his oblations by
the year, 3*s.* 4*d.*, that is, for the time of this account 6*s.* 8*d.*
And to the clerk of the same church by the year 12*d.*, for the said time 2*s.*
And for holy bread 4*d.* by the year, for the said time 8*d.*
And for the price of 2 rose garlands for rent of the Hall for the said time 5½*d.*
And to the clerk of the parish of All Hallows abovesaid, 12*d.* by the year, for the
time of this account 2*s.*

Sum 11*s.* 9½*d.*

[464] [f. 156r]
Donations
And in the present of a boar, given to John Michell, price 30*s.* 1*d.*
And in one gift to the same John, agreed and given, price 21*s.* 2*d.*
And to John Charltonne, sergeant, 3*s.* 4*d.*

Sum 54*s.* 7*d.*

Reparations above the hall and below
And 37*s.* 1*d.* paid for the making of a femerelle, made new, above the hall roof, with
all apparatus
And paid for a picture in the window of the said hall with other costs towards the
same 25*s.* 5*d.*
And in costs made over the doors to the pantry & buttery 8*s.* 5*d.*
And in glass for the windows in the hall 41*s.* 8½*d.*

---

557   Porlond's salary was doubled [330], to £4 a year in 1423–24.

And in windows in the parlour and hall, with diverse surmounts 15s. 6d.

Sum £6 8s. 1½d.

[*Added*: Here appear things made before]

[465]
Reparations to other houses
And for making the wall called the reredos in the great kitchen with amending a wall in the little cellar
And in carpenters, tilers, daubers, with tiles, laths, loam, lime, sand, lead, locks, clickets, dogs of iron, hoops, timber, tables & other costs made in various houses, that is the said hall and almshouse

Sum £11 5s. 6½d.

Reparations made in the Almshouse
And 2s. 6d. paid for making windows beside the gate of the almshouse
And 27s. 2½d. for making a new chamber in the said almshouse, apart from timber from a table given by Robert Smyth and John Masonne
And £5 5s. 9d. paid for the making and costs of 5 chambers
And 6s. 3½d. paid for the making and

[f. 156v]
costs for the solar called the little loft in one chamber of the said house
And 8s. 8d. for new lead with changing the old lead and various pounds of sand

Sum £7 10s. 5d.

[466]
Rewards given
And in the price of 3 rewards given to 3 persons, that is, to Sir Robert Steynton, chaplain to the said fraternity, price 5s.
And to Thomas Donygtonne, sergeant, 4s. 7d.
To William Pethin, aletaker, 4s. 9d.

Sum 14s. 4d.

Fees
And in fees to Thomas Donyngtonne, sergeant of the chamber of the Guildhall, taking by year 6s. 8d., for the said time 13s. 4d.

Sum as appears

Trentals
And in trentals for diverse brothers and sisters, that is: William Smalsho, Thomas Emonde, Margaret Riche, John More, William atte Well, Robert Hiltonne, John Benge, & Dionysia Barthorppe, for each, 2s. 6d.

Sum 20s.

Parchment, paper and ink

And for parchment, paper and ink, spent during the aforesaid time, 4*s*.

Sum as appears

Sum total of expenses and allowances £57 7*s*. 9½*d*.

**And remaining in the hands of the Masters so that there is
in the said box to the common treasury £51 19*s*. 4*d*.
Of which is received in the said common box as above £31 5*s*. 7½*d*.
And the aforesaid accountants give this sum to the
increase of the common box abovesaid
£20 13*s*. 8½*d*.**

SELECT GLOSSARY

Alien non-English resident in the city of London.

Almarie storage cupboard.

Burden of rushes, load carried by animal or person, used as a measure of quantity.

Casualty casual, incidental charge or payment.

Chaffure, chaffer: trade.

Charger platter for food.

Clicket latch of a door or gate.

Comenable convenient, appropriate.

Commonalty, commonality, the people of a city or company.

Coster ornamental hanging for a wall.

Cramp iron bar with the end bent to a hook, a grappling iron.

Dark chamber at the hall and almshouse, room without light, perhaps a cellar for food storage.

Dauber a plasterer, one who covers walls with mortar or clay.

Diaper linen or silk fabric woven with a repeated pattern of figures or geometrical designs.

Dosser ornamental cloth used as a wall hanging or for covering a seat or altar.

Doucettes, dowcettes, dowset, sweet baked egg custard tart containing any of varied ingredients: herbs, spices, nuts, fruit, meat, sweet custard or sweetened meat pie.

Drawk wild grass growing as weed among corn.

Engrained superior cloth dyed with 'grain' (a costly granular dyestuff made from the kermes insect), used for livery gowns and hoods.

Estrich board timber from Norway or the Baltic.

323

Ewery room where ewers of water, basins, table linen and towels were kept.

Falling boards fixed to the wall, boards which could be folded down to rest on supports and make a table.

Fanon or maniple, strip of cloth suspended from left arm near wrist as part of Eucharistic vestments.

Femerell ventilation structure, typically dome-shaped with lateral openings on roof over hall or kitchen.

Fime dung.

Foreigner in London, a non-resident who is English but not free of the city.

Forestall to buy up goods before they come to market.

Garnet hinge with the upright part nailed to the support and the horizontal to the door or shutter.

Ground-sill ground plate, foundation to carry a superstructure.

Halling tapestry or painted cloth for the walls of a hall.

Hanap drinking vessel of no certain measure, to be supplied by brewers for drinking purposes, whilst ale was to be sold in sealed measures.

Hogshead large cask, approx. 63 wine gallons in 1423.

Hosteler one who receives guests, innkeeper.

Huckster retailer who walks through the streets selling food, drink, or small goods from a basket. Applied to women, but sometimes men, also.

Kiddle dam or weir in a river with nets to trap fish.

Kimnel, kemelyn, tub used for brewing.

Lampron river lamprey.

Lath narrow strip of wood used as the base for tiles or plaster.

Leche Lumbard sliced meat with eggs, fruits, spices, in jelly.

Limners illuminators of text.

Mail metal rings for chain mail.

Manchet fine quality wheaten bread.

Select Glossary

Mortrewes thick white pottage of chicken, pork or fish, ground and boiled.

Murrey a purple red colour, like that of the mulberry, for livery cloth.

Nail a nail's breadth, measurement used in livery lists.

Neats cattle.

Noonchyns, nonsheng, nuncheon, nonsshyns, noonnchyns, nonsenches, a drink or snack taken in the afternoon.

Numbles, nombles, animal entrails, especially deer, part of back and loins of a hart.

Orphrey gold embroidery.

Ostler stableman or groom at an inn, also a variation of hosteler

Packthread strong cord for tying bundles.

Paleys fence of pales or enclosure, yard, surrounded by pales.

Panter household officer who supplied the bread and had charge of the pantry.

Peck measure of dry goods, a quarter of a bushel.

Pentice structure extending from the side of a building, with a sloping roof.

Pipe large container for liquids, containing approximately 2 hogsheads, 63 wine gallons or 477 litres.

Postel pillar, post, doorpost.

Potens garnet a crosspiece or T bar.

Pottle pot or tankard containing half a gallon.

Puncheon short upright supporting timber post.

Quart a quarter of a gallon, 2 pints.

Quarter (length) wood 4 inches wide by 2 to 4 inches thick used as an upright stud or short crossbeam in partitions.

Quarter (weight) of malt, 8 bushels.

Quarterage payment made quarterly, a subscription. The clerk entered the quarterage payments annually in this book but may have collected the money quarterly.

Quarteron a quarter in weight or measure, mostly for dry goods, such as a quarter of a hundredweight of tiles.

Rays striped cloth used for livery gowns and hoods, accounted for by the number of rays.

Recognizance bond.

Regrater one who buys commodities, food, to resell at a profit.

Reredos in a kitchen, a masonry backing for a fireplace.

Robux waste material, debris, refuse.

Sanap cloth runner placed over a tablecloth to keep it clean.

Sanders sandalwood, used in cooking.

Saucery the department of a household entrusted with the preparation of sauces.

Seam-nail nail for fastening overlapping edges, with the end clinched to form a rivet.

Shearmen shearers of woollen cloth.

Sprig nail nail with a small head, or no head.

Standard swan or coney (rabbit), served in an upright or standing position.

Stranger not a native of London, non-resident in a town, outsider.

Summer horizontal load-bearing beam, supporting girders or joists.

Tallage toll or customs duty.

Tallow hard fat from around the kidneys of animals, used for suet and candles.

Text-writer A professional writer of text-hand.

Teyse, toise, lineal measurement equivalent to 5 or 6 square feet.

Tharnes entrails.

Transom crossbeam to carry a superstructure, lintel.

Trash-nails for fixing scenery or the stage for revels, at the Brewers' Feast.

Trencher bread loaves made of coarse flour. The slices were used as disposable plates.

Trental a set of 30 requiem masses.

Tresance cloister, corridor, here referring to a passage linking the Brewers' almshouse to their main hall.

Tunnage tax or duty levied upon wine imported in casks or tuns.

Turnbrochers turnspits.

Verjuice, vertjuice, sour juice of unripe grapes or crab apples.

Wardnape wooden or metal mat placed under dishes at table to protect the tablecloth.

Weir barrier or dam placed across a river to restrain water.

Worts greens and leafy herbs.

APPENDIX I

LIST OF MASTERS OF THE CRAFT AND FRATERNITY OF BREWERS, 1406–25

Source: The Brewers' Book, by paragraph numbers, unless otherwise stated

Dates	Masters	*Calendar of Letter-Books of the City of London, I,* 51.	Wardens and Searchers if recorded
7 December 1406	Nicholas Stratton, Thomas Bristowe, Peter Hayforde, Richard Rowden		Wardens: John More, John Davy, John Wyghtmore, William atte Wode
1416/17–1418	John Thetford, Thomas Emond, Walter Riche, Henry Lymber	39, 40, 42.	
1418–19	William atte Wode, William Ederich, John Reyner, William Ferrour the Elder	1, 3, 22, 28, 38, 40, 41, 42, 55, 56, 73, 109, 177	
1419–21	Thomas Grene, Robert Hylton, John Pyken, Robert Carpenter	22, 38, 55, 60, 63, 66, 73, 97, 98, 109, 139, 143, 145, 147, 148, 150, 163, 176, 177, 188, 195	73, 97: Searchers or Wardens: William atte Wode William Ferrour, Thomas Hatcher, John Salter, Thomas Emond, John Mason, William Crane, William atte Welle, John Chapman, John Lumbard, William John. John Peken

1421–23	Robert Smyth, William Crane, Hugh Neel, John Philippe	22, 112, 199, 208, 209, 217, 219, 222, 226, 234, 247, 262, 264, 266, 268, 269, 273, 277, 281, 284, 286, 291, 294, 297, 300, 303, 305, 308, 311, 326, 327, 330, 331, 334, 453, 459 *Cal. Letter-Book, I*, 287. sworn 20 Nov 1421.	208: Searchers: William Ferrour, John Salter, Peter Carpenter, William Petevyle
1423–25	John Mason, Thomas Hatcher, John Broke, Henry Trebolans	331, 357, 371, 372, 376, 453	357, 372: Searchers: Peter Carpenter, William Belle, William Ferrour the younger, John Humber.

APPENDIX II
LIST OF NAMED PROPERTIES
IN WILLIAM PORLOND'S
BREWERS' BOOK, PART I

The names of brewhouses recorded in Porlond's book refer to the signs that they displayed. Such signs were commonly used on substantial commercial establishments, such as public inns (hotels) and taverns (which sold wine, and sometimes ale and beer as well). Some brewhouses (commercial breweries) and large alehouses (neighbourhood drinking houses) may also have had signs. In the list below, locations beginning 'St' are London parishes. Names of streets and parishes are those used in the Directory in the *Map of Tudor London*. The numbers refer to paragraph numbers.

Angel, 14, 277, 344
Angel, Bishopsgate, St Ethelburga, 204
Angel in Fleet Street, 100, 203
Angel near Queenhithe, St Michael
    Queenhithe, 98, 445
Angel and le Ball, St Andrew Holborn,
    202
Axe, Aldermanbury, 442
Axe, outside Aldgate, 76, 444
Axe in St John Street, 442

Ball in Old Change 141, 274
Ball, St Nicholas Shambles, 79, 373
Basket, beside Billingsgate, 75, 141, 201,
    360
Basket, le Cross, Cheap, 74
Basket, Fenchurch Street, All Hallows
    Staining, 22, 269, 444
Bear, St Clement's Lane, 98, 447
Bell, beside Aldersgate, St Anne, 2, 100
Bell, outside Aldgate, 273, 446
Bell, outside Bishopsgate, 98
Bell, Coleman Street, 445
Bell, Fenchurch Street, St Dionis, 200
Bell, Holborn, St Andrew Holborn, 79,
    119, 268

Bell, Philpot Lane, 443
Bell, [Bull?] near Queenhithe, 78, 447
Bell, Red Cross Street, St Giles
    Cripplegate, 22, 126
Bell, near St John, 121
Bell, St Margaret Pattens Lane, 98, 273
Bell called Savage's Inn, Fleet Street,
    122, 200
Bell, unspecified, 145, 209, 343
Bell and Dolphin outside Bishopsgate,
    Bishopsgate Street, 77
Bishop, or the Bishop's Head, outside
    the Bars in Holborn, 445
Black Horse, Fleet Bridge, Fleet Street,
    229, 447
Blossoms Inn, 228
Bolt and Ton, Fleet Street, 445
Bradwey le Horne, Gracechurch Street,
    73
Bull, le, Billingsgate, 75
Bull, Queenhithe, 78

Cardinal's Hat, Billingsgate, 76
Cardinal's Hat beside the hospital of
    St Mary Bethlehem or St Mary
    outside Bishopsgate, 123

330

334

Tavern, Gracechurch market, 95
Three Kings outside Aldgate, 77
Three Legs, St Dunstan in Fleet Street, 125
Three Nuns, the corner of, Sithebourne Lane, St Mary Woolnoth, 78, 118, 122, 272
Three Nuns, beside the Stocks, 360
Trump, the, Cheap, 141, 200, 228
Two Keys, outside Bishopsgate, 272
Two Nuns, outside Aldgate, 201
Two Staples, near Baynard's Castle, at Paul's Wharf, St Benet, 93, 444

Unicorn, Lombard Street, 55
Unicorn without Newgate, 444
Unicorn, St Nicholas Olave, 229

Vernacle in la Barbican, 123
Vernacle, St Bartholomew the Less, 98, 146

Vernacle near the Augustinian Friars, 447
Vine within Bishopsgate, 273
Vine, Holborn Cross, 272
Vine, in la Riole, 109, 273

Well, at end of the wall of Holy Trinity [Christ Church] Priory, 361
Welshman, outside Ludgate, 118
Wheatsheaf [*Glene*], Coleman Street, 119
Wheatsheaf [*Glene*], beside Queenhithe, 96
White Bear, St Andrew Holborn, 79
White Bull, Smithfield, 141
White Cock, 360
White *Colver,* [pigeon or dove] le, Fleet Bridge, 141
White Cross outside Cripplegate, 100
White Leg, beside Fleet Bridge, in Fleet Street, 80, 109, 200, 443
White Lion, St Thomas the Apostle, 200, 272

INDEX OF PEOPLE AND PLACES

The Index is to the main text only and not to the Introduction. Crafts have
been indexed under their modern name unless there is no modern equivalent.
Names of streets and parishes are those used in the *Map of Tudor London*.
Brewhouses, taverns and inns have been listed separately in Appendix II.
Numbers refer to paragraph numbers.

Austyn, John, tailor, 373
  wife of, 373
Awdre (Awdree), John, sheather, 14, 23,
    24, 137
Awdymer, Roger, vintner, 235, 243, 273,
    333, 341, 367, 458
Awmbele (Ambele), Johanna (Jonette),
    almswoman, 132, 196, 261, 263,
    349, 366, 398, 461
  chamber of, 291, 292, 420, 425
Ayle, Thomas, 17, 25, 35, 37, 114, 158, 174,
    176, 202, 211, 214, 245, 251, 264,
    273, 278, 283, 368, 390, 399, 412
  wife of Thomas, 35, 37, 174, 176, 412
Ayleward or Aylewin, 359

Bacon (Bakon), William, butcher, 8, 18,
    35, 69, 113, 114, 134, 160, 197, 211,
    246, 251, 259, 264, 368, 393, 400,
    412, 458
  wife of, 259, 412
Badeston, Katherine, 360
Bailey, 75, 78, 140
Bailly (Bayly), Alice, wife of William,
    260, 264, 368, 400, 412
  John, 5, 13, 68, 96, 115, 132, 154, 195,
    209, 240, 250, 263, 283, 366,
    373, 385
  [–], maltman, 206
  Peter, of Broxbourne, Herts., 206
  Robert, 201
  William, 3, 8, 18, 44, 69, 114, 134, 135,
    159, 196, 201, 211, 246, 251,
    260, 264, 277, 285, 343, 368,
    391, 400, 412
Baker, Gwy, Guillaume 283
  Katherine, huckster, 141
  at St Katherine Christchurch, 361
  of Wood Street, 343
Bakers, 26
Balame, Thomas, labourer, 417
Baldok, of New Alley, Cornhill, wax
    chandler, 74, 201, 360, 361
  servant of, 360, 361
Ballard (Balard), Cristiana (Cristyan),
    wife, widow, of John, 6, 23, 132,
    136, 195, 209, 262, 283, 364, 396
  John, 6, 14, 23, 68, 130, 132, 136, 145,
    195, 209, 215, 262, 267, 338,
    356, 364

Barber, unnamed, Candlewick Street,
    St Mary Bothaw, 125
  unnamed, St Mary Aldermary, 126
Barbers, 27, 163, 178, 267, 319, 336, 454
Barbican, 123, 230
Barbour, John, 140
  Matthew, 140
  wife of, 118
  Robert, porter, 172
Bardolf, John, shipman, Leaden Porch,
    140
Barentyn, Drew (Drugo), goldsmith,
    mayor [1398–9] [1408–9], 49, 120,
    208
Bargeman, Nicholas, 78, 140
  wife of, 140
Bargemen, 318
Bargonne, Agnes (Anneys), 23, 137
  John, tallow chandler, 23, 137, 138,
    155, 210, 214, 263, 366, 397
Barnet, Herts., 2, 93, 134, 146, 206, 359
Baronne (Baron, Baroun), Roger
    (Richard), 7, 16, 80, 118, 133, 158,
    196, 211, 243, 251, 260, 264, 277,
    283, 343, 367, 388, 399, 411
  wife of, 80
Bars, Aldersgate Street, 121, 230, 358
  Bishopsgate, 124
  Holborn, 445
  St Giles Cripplegate, 79
  Temple, 125, 225, 269, 388, 447
Barston (Barstonne), John, 239, 278,
    344, 365, 385, 397, 451
Barte, William, 69, 283
Barthorpe (Barthorppe), Denise
    (Dionysia, Dionyse), wife, widow,
    4, 20, 131, 195, 209, 262, 364, 396,
    432, 455, 466
  John, 131
Barton, Ralph, skinner, sheriff [1418–19],
    1
Basill, [–], corser, horse dealer, 228
Basing Lane, 2
Basket makers, 27
Basset, Agnes, wife of Henry, 209, 212
  Henry, 80, 98, 100, 152, 174, 179, 180,
    209, 212, 285
  John, 3, 13, 34, 44, 68, 132, 135, 153,
    195, 209, 238, 259, 263, 283,
    331, 365, 383, 397

212, 243, 263, 277, 285, 343,
360, 367, 388, 399, 411

Blostmer (Blostmere), John, 154, 360,
384, 397, 410, 448, 457
wife of, 410

Bocking, Essex, 150

Bodevyle (Bodevile), William, maltman,
8, 18, 35, 108, 134, 159, 174, 197,
211, 246, 261, 264, 278, 344, 368,
391, 400, 408, 412, 451

Bokelond, John, 2

Bolton (Boltonne), Alice, wife, widow,
of William, 115, 211, 262
John, maltman, 206
John, of Yorkshire, 128
William, 8, 18, 69, 115, 134, 159, 174,
197, 200, 211, 214, 262, 267,
283, 338, 356

Bookbinders, 26

Bordel, 92

Borne, Thomas, porter, 407

Boston (Botston), Henry, mason, 259,
274, 275, 289, 341
servants of, 289

Bosvenon (Bosvenonne, Bosevenan),
Alice, wife of John, 259, 365, 397,
410
Edmund, 380, 410, 443, 456, 457
wife of, 410
John, 238, 250, 259, 273, 341, 365,
383, 397, 410

Boteler (Botelere, Botteler, Botiler),
Elizabeth, wife of William, 211,
213, 264, 368
John, mercer, sheriff [1419–20], 55,
79, 108, 109, 126, 147
Thomas, 3, 17, 22, 69, 126, 134, 135,
159, 181, 196, 200, 203, 211,
280, 285, 347, 358, 458
servant of, 203
Walter, 69
William, 3, 18, 44, 76, 114, 134, 135,
159, 197, 204, 211, 213, 246,
251, 264, 282, 368, 391, 400,
458

Botelmaker, Thomas at Cock, Ludgate,
78, 80, 285

Boterfeld, William, cooper, 391, 412,
445, 457

Botle, William, hosier, 119

Boton, Botonne, Gilbert, 2, 43, 67, 121,
150, 162, 236, 250, 278, 284, 344,
396

Bottlemakers (Botelmakers), 27

Bourne, Thomas, cook, 330
William, at Pie in the Moor, 100, 160,
174, 180, 211, 212, 214, 284

Bower Row, Ludgate, 108, 272

Bowyer, Flexmer, 175

Bowyers, 26

Boys, John, chapman, 240, 252

Brachell, Simon, 200

Bracy (Bacy), Alice, wife, widow of
William, 8, 35, 197, 211, 264, 364
Henry, 381, 396, 410, 443, 456
William, 8, 18, 35, 69, 149, 159, 197,
211, 264, 284, 356, 364

Bradeweye, [–], at the maltmarket, 360

Bradmore, Alice at Bradwey le horne, 73

Bragour, John, Smithfield, 108
Richard, ostler, at the Ram,
Smithfield, 108

Brampton (Braunton, Bramton), Alice,
120
William, stockfishmonger, sheriff
[1394–5], 50, 53, 394

Brasiers, 27

Bray, Alice, wife of William, 134
John, butcher, 5, 13, 31, 113, 132, 154,
197, 209, 215, 265
William, 134, 144

Brayn, Alice, 373

Bread Street, 73, 75, 141, 142, 201

Bret (Brette, Brett), Alan, 4, 20, 131, 144,
149, 197, 331, 364, 380, 399, 409,
451, 455
Isabella (Sibille), wife of Alan, 4, 20,
131, 197, 399, 409

Bretaigne, Alice, 444
John, 269, 339, 384, 397, 444, 457

Brewer, Alice, huckster, 120
Geoffrey (Galfrid), foreigner, 205
Henry, foreigner, at the Ship, Temple
Bar, 125
Quentin, 141
Steven, 290, 433

Brewers of London
Accounts of craft and fraternity, 41,
177 [1419–21], 330–56 [1421–3],
453–65 [1423–5]

343

Bronnyng (Brownyng), Davy, David,
11, 25, 67, 151, 236, 250, 277, 283,
333, 343, 380
Johanna, 272, 340, 366
John, 98, 154, 174, 179, 240, 263, 272,
278, 283, 340, 344, 366, 384
Broochmakers (makers of spits), 27
Brook (Broke), Cristiana, wife of John,
195, 198, 209, 262, 365, 382, 397
John, 5, 12, 34, 67, 88, 114, 132, 141,
144, 145, 153, 174, 195, 198,
209, 228, 237, 259, 262, 266,
276, 284, 331, 341, 342, 357,
365, 372, 376, 381, 382, 397,
401, 408, 413, 443, 451, 453,
458, 459
servants of, 413
Broxbourne, Herts., 206
Brynton (Bryntonne), Richard, 7, 20, 68,
133, 158, 196, 211, 251, 264, 283,
367, 388, 399
Buckinghamshire, 93, 207
Buckle makers, 27
Bugby, John, 239, 250, 268, 271, 278,
339, 340, 344, 366, 383, 398, 443,
458
Bugge, Agnes (Anneys), 4, 11, 36, 131,
174, 195, 209, 259, 261, 262, 278,
344, 364, 396, 409, 412
servant of, 261, 412
Stephen, 69, 285
Bullard, Robert, 158, 243, 251, 277, 285,
344, 375, 411
wife of Robert, 411
Bulle, Margaret, huckster, Barbican, 123
Bullok, Johanna, tapster or tapester, wife
of William, 264, 272, 341, 368,
400
Margaret, 77
William, 264, 272, 283, 341, 368, 400
Bulwik, Johanna, wife of Richard,
grocer, 274, 341, 343, 367, 387,
399
Richard, grocer, 274, 277, 341, 343,
367, 387, 399
Burgate, Richard, wife of, 458
Burgeys, [–], maltman, 146
Burgh (Birgh), Adam (Ade), 133
Millicent (Milen), widow of Adam,
6, 20, 133, 181, 196, 284

Burlesters (sellers of victuals), 26
Burne, Margaret, 260
Burton, John, 175, 261
Burveyn, John, 452, 458
Bury, Margaret, huckster, 204
Bussh, William, 69
Butchers, 27, 267, 336
in Ivy Lane, 361

Calowe (Calowe, Calow), Maud, 260,
399
Robert, shearman, 234, 260, 274, 277,
341, 343, 379, 387, 399, 411
Calston (Calstonne), William, plumber,
261, 274, 316, 333, 341, 368, 391,
412, 452
Cambridge, 93, 96, 206, 302
Cambrigge (Camnbrigge, Cauntbrigge),
William, grocer, mayor [1420–1],
88, 138, 139, 143, 145, 147, 150,
163, 180, 195, 348
Candlewick Street, 2, 79, 125, 200, 201
Cannterbury, John, cooper, 128
Canonne (Canon), Elizabeth, wife of
William, 211, 213, 264, 368
Emma (Emmote), 4, 20, 131, 195, 209,
236, 262, 283, 364, 396, 458
John, 68, 96
William, 8, 18, 36, 69, 114, 134, 159,
197, 211, 213, 246, 251, 260,
264, 284, 368, 391, 400, 412,
458
Canterbury, 129
rent of the prior, 201
Caponherst, see Skynner
Cardell, William, 8, 18, 35, 119, 120, 130,
134, 159, 174, 197, 211, 283, 400
wife of, 35
Cardmakers, 27
Carleton, Agnes, 67, 181, 195, 209, 262,
283, 364, 380, 396
Carletonne, Johanna, 5, 20, 132
Carowe (Carrowe, Carrewe), Elizabeth,
263, 272, 340, 367, 399, 411
Richard, 99, 179, 243, 251, 263, 272,
282, 340, 367, 388, 399, 411
Carpenter
Gille, 307
[–], in la Riole, 311
James, 307

Crowmere (Crowmer), William, draper,
mayor [1413–14] [1423–4], 205,
357, 358, 360, 364
rent of, 205
Crowser, Thomas, 23, 137, 138
Crowston (Croxton), John, Master
mason at Guildhall, 289, 315
Crutched Friars, Friars of the Holy
Cross, 13, 77, 141, 204, 205, 250,
341, 344, 360, 445
fountain of, 141
Cryour, [–], at Newgate, 74
Curriers, 26
Cutlers, 26, 454

Dalton, Adam, parson, rector of All
Hallows, 35, 175, 236, 261, 262,
273, 341, 364, 380, 396, 412, 452
Dalygood, John, of Ickleton, Cambs., 206
Danyell, John, maltman, 359, 382, 397,
408, 411, 446, 457
Dauber, Robert, [Rowe?], 288, 289
Daubers, 188, 189, 191, 193, 288, 289,
290, 291, 298, 308, 311, 353, 418,
423, 424, 439, 465
servants of, 188, 193, 298, 308, 311,
353, 418, 423, 437, 439
David, [–], wife of, in Honey Lane, 73
Davy, John, 99, 153, 174, 176, 179, 240,
250, 385, 401, 410, 458
wife of, 458
Laurence, 23
wife of, 23
Richard, sergeant of mayor, 317
Dawbere, John, 283
Dawe, Philip, 284
Dedellus, Wenge, tailor, 261
Dellowe (Delowe, Dellewe, Dillawe),
Margaret, 211, 212, 263, 367
Robert, 100, 114, 174, 180, 211, 212,
243, 251, 260, 263, 278, 284,
344, 367
Dene, John de, 32, 136, 156, 172, 196,
198, 210, 239, 250, 258, 263, 384,
413
wife of, 413
Denton, William, cordwainer, 77
Devenyssh, Devenysh, William, panter,
tailor, 18, 19, 23, 24, 28, 33, 47,
113, 137, 138, 149, 160, 162, 172,

175, 186, 197, 198, 211, 215, 246,
252, 254, 258, 264, 278, 344, 369,
392, 407, 450
wife of, 175
Dewy, Agnes, 196, 198, 211, 264, 367
Thomas, 7, 21, 134, 196, 198, 211, 264,
367, 390, 399, 458
Dikson, Nicholas, Baron of the
Exchequer, 71
Disse, Edmund, 98, 150, 174, 176, 179,
284
Distaff Lane, 100
Doffeland, Nicholas, 443, 456
Dolphyn, John, maltman, 71, 93
Donyngton (Donyngtonne), Richard,
prior of the Augustinian friars,
274, 277, 341, 343, 367, 399, 413
Thomas, sergeant at Guildhall, 17,
47, 115, 159, 186, 194, 245, 261,
355, 356, 390, 413, 466
Dorwell, Dorewell, Robert, 158, 230,
243, 251, 278, 282, 344, 387
Double (Dowble), Johanna, 137
John, 23
Dowdale (Dowedale), Johanna, 260,
264, 271, 340, 368, 400, 412
William, 114, 246, 251, 260, 264, 268,
271, 277, 339, 340, 344, 368,
391, 400, 412
Dowgate, 3, 75, 78, 80, 141, 200
Dowhete, Thomas of Hoddesdon, Herts.,
93
Downyng, William, cooper, 401
Draper, Alice, at Horse Head,
St Sepulchre, 141
of Salisbury, 161
Drapers, 26, 161, 162, 220
Draycote, Thomas, broiderer, 421, 439
Drewe, hosteler, 207
Driffeld (Dryffeld), Thomas, 82, 114, 144,
261, 332, 390, 445, 451, 457
Dunche (Donche), John, 14, 25, 76, 115,
153, 174, 283, 382, 411, 458
Dyers, 27, 163
Dyers, Alice wife of Richard, 140
Richard, custodian of Billingsgate
wharf, 140

East Cheap, 2, 74, 96, 162, 168, 200, 201,
268, 269, 327, 444, 450

Grub Street, 79, 109, 123, 202, 267
Guildhall
  Attorney at, 36
  Books of record, 53, 394
  Brewers summoned to, 40, 81, 82–3,
    85–7, 89, 165, 217
    imprisoned in ward of
      chamberlain, 219
  Building work, 90, 194, 219, 323
  Clerk at, see Stafford, John
  Fines imposed upon Brewers and
    servants by chamberlain, 73,
    104, 110, 205, 207, 228, 230, 347
  Fines money returned to Brewers,
    126, 147, 181, 208, 231, 280,
    362, 376, 459
  Gate, 118, 358
  Ward of the chamberlain, 219
Gurney, [–], maltman, 95
Gutter Lane, 142, 203, 229, 373
Gyldesborough (Gyldysborough,
  Gyldesburgh), Alice, wife of
  Robert, 78, 118, 122
  Robert, 118
Gyles (Giles, Gilys), Johanna, 7, 133,
  196, 210, 263, 367, 399
  Robert, 7, 16, 69, 115, 133, 157, 196,
    210, 242, 251, 263, 278, 285,
    344, 367, 387, 399

Haberdashers, 26, 178
Hackney, Middx., 2
Hacombelane, William, grocer, 360
Hadlee (Hadley, Handle), John, grocer,
  mayor [1379–80], 49, 50, 53, 394
Haltonne, John, 378
Hamond, [–], of West Mill, 93
Hampton, John, servant of sheriff, 207
Hancok (Hancook, Hankcok), Dionysia
  (Denys, Dionisia), 174, 196, 198,
  211, 260, 264, 367, 399
  Thomas, 3, 17, 35, 44, 69, 134, 135,
    159, 174, 196, 198, 211, 245,
    251, 260, 264, 277, 284, 343,
    367, 390, 399, 412, 446
Hans, Dutchman, 360
Hanslap (Hanselap, Hanslappe), John,
  240, 259, 263, 272, 340, 366, 382,
  397, 410
  Lettice, 366, 397, 410

Hanwell, Austyn, 67
Hanyngtonne, William, tiler, 261, 273,
  275, 341, 368
Hardell, Ellis (Elias), 4, 11, 67, 131, 136
Hardy, John, cook at Brewers' Hall, 5,
  13, 19, 28, 33, 39, 40, 113, 132, 148,
  155, 162, 172, 197, 201, 210, 215,
  239, 252, 254, 255, 258, 263, 363,
  365, 370, 385, 398, 407, 450
Hardyng, Agnes, 365, 398
  John, of Holborn, 68, 100, 153, 180,
    210, 212, 239, 263, 277, 282,
    344, 365, 382, 398, 410
Harested, [–], mercer, 193
Harford, Alice, wife of Thomas, clerk,
  446
  Thomas, clerk of the Exchequer, 382,
    412, 446, 452, 457
Harlowe (Herlowe), Johanna, 7, 133, 196,
  211, 263, 367, 399
  Richard, capmaker and brewer, 7, 16,
    68, 114, 133, 158, 174, 196, 201,
    211, 243, 260, 263, 277, 283,
    343, 367, 387, 399, 458, 459
Harlyng, Katherine, 77
Harpers, 33, 112, 149
Hastynge, [John], sergeant of the mayor,
  [1421–6], 317
Hatcher (Atcher, Hawcher, Haccher),
  Margery, Margaret, wife of
  Thomas, 7, 23, 137, 138, 211, 213,
  264, 367, 400
  Thomas, 7, 17, 23, 35, 73, 82, 108, 115,
    126, 127, 134, 137, 138, 144, 149,
    158, 174, 196, 211, 213, 245, 251,
    260, 264, 266, 276, 285, 331,
    343, 357, 358, 367, 371, 372,
    376, 390, 400, 413, 451, 453
  daughter of Thomas, 413
  women, guests of, 413
Hatfelde, John, 23, 137
Hatters, 27
Hatton, Idonea (Idoyne, Ideyne, Idonia),
  wife of Roger Swannefelde, 5, 20,
  132, 196, 210, 263, 366
Haverill, John, 14
Hawkyn (Hawell, Hawkon, Hanwell),
  Austyn (Augustin), 67, 202, 229,
  283

363

St Christopher, 96
St Clement, East Cheap, 2
St Clement's Lane, 77, 98, 431, 447
St Dionis Backchurch, Fenchurch Street,
 3, 146, 200, 201, 207
St Dunstan in the East, Thames Street,
 2, 137, 201
St Dunstan in the West, Fleet Street, 74,
 80, 119, 125
St Ethelburga, 78, 204
St George Eastcheap, Pudding Lane, 445
St George's Bar, 224
St Giles Cripplegate, 2, 22, 79, 121, 122,
 123, 126, 155, 202, 203, 444
St Giles, Holborn, 445
St Gregory by [St] Paul's, 200, 207, 229
St Helen, Bishopsgate, 74, 140, 374
St James Garlickhithe, inn of the church,
 75
St John Street, 98, 118, 119, 230, 268,
 272, 442, 448
 vicinity of, 121, 123
St John Zachary, 80, 448
St Julian beside the Bars, Aldersgate
 Street, 358
St Katherine Christchurch or Cree, 76,
 123, 268, 361
St Katherine Coleman, 373
St Katherine, hospital, 201, 268
St Lawrence Jewry, 228
St Lawrence Lane, 203, 373, 375
St Lawrence Pountney, 125, 145, 273
St Lawrence, unspecified, bellringers
 of, 178
 fraternity of St John at, 178, 454
St Magnus, 73, 75, 224, 358, 360
St Margaret Pattens, 2, 3, 229
 Lane, 98, 273
St Margaret, Friday Street, 80, 118
St Margaret, Westminster, churchyard,
 224
St Martin Ludgate, 140, 360
 clerk of, 140
 wife of clerk, 140
St Martin Orgar, 79, 140
St Martin Outwich, inn of, 123
St Martin the Grand, 98, 100, 228, 373
St Martin, unspecified, 77
St Mary [or St Gabriel] Fenchurch, 140,
 201, 203

St Mary Aldermanbury, Our Lady of
 Aldermanbury, 46, 184, 302, 352
 Parish clerk, 46, 184, 352, 463
 Parsonage, 438
 Rector, 46, 184, 352, 463
St Mary Aldermary, 2, 96, 119, 120, 126
St Mary Bethlehem, hospital and priory,
 123
St Mary Bishopsgate, hospital, 123, 124
St Mary Bothaw, 125
St Mary Colechurch, 3, 96
St Mary Gracechurch, inn of church, 140
St Mary Magdalen, 78, 203
 chief clerk, 119
St Mary Somerset, 75, 76, 77, 204
St Mary Woolchurch, 2, 55, 228
 parson, 413
St Mary Woolnoth, 122
 parson, rector, 261, 274, 341, 364,
 396, 413
St Michael Bassishaw, 119, 203
St Michael Cornhill, 3, 79
St Michael Crooked Lane, 202
St Michael Huggin Lane, 3
St Michael le Querne, 2, 3, 79, 141, 202
St Michael Queenhithe, 3, 98
St Mildred Bread Street, 75, 118
St Mildred Poultry, 202
St Nicholas Cole Abbey, 2, 3
St Nicholas Olave, 229
St Nicholas Shambles, 2, 3, 73, 75, 79,
 119, 120, 122, 141, 142, 203, 228,
 268, 360, 373, 445
 fountain, 73, 228
 market, 75, 79, 228
St Pancras, 88, 108
St Paul's Cathedral, 224
 canon of, 141
 rent of, 78
St Peter the Poor, Broad Street, 200
St Peter, Cornhill, 200, 201, 203, 360
St Sepulchre, 2, 78, 119, 124, 126, 141,
 200, 202, 228
St Swithin, Candlewick Street, clerk of,
 2, 43
St Swithin's Lane, 77, 119
St Thomas Acre, 373
St Thomas the Apostle, 200
Salisbury, Sarum, Wilts., 11, 150, 161, 162
Salman, John, 283

Swepston (Swypston), John, sergeant,
239, 252, 261, 316, 339
wife of, 261
Swyffte, [–], weaver, wife of, 78
Sybbe, John, of Barnet, Herts., 206
Sybill, at Crown, 77
Sylke, Isabel, 23, 137
Thomas, 23, 137
Symond, Agnes, 23, 137
John, 23, 137
Syon, Agnes, at Holborn Cross, 74
Syre, John, 114
Syward, Isabella, widow of Vincent, 23,
137, 138, 195, 198, 215
Vincent, 23, 137, 138, 195, 198

Tablemakers (tablet makers), 26
Tailor (Tailour), Richard, 387, 437, 442,
443, 456, 457
Taker of the King's, 317, 354
Tallowchandlers (Tallwchanndeleres),
27, 163
Tanner (Tannere), Robert, 7, 16, 34, 69,
116, 133, 145, 157, 196, 210, 243,
261, 284
Tanners, 26
Tannton (Tawnton), Alice, huckster, 120,
205
Tapicers (makers of tapestry), 27
Tapster, at George, Smithfield, 141
Tatersale (Tattersale, Tattersall,
Tetersale), Robert, draper, sheriff
[1422–3], 10, 220, 234, 379
Taverner, Henry, 407
Tawyers, 118
Taylors' Company, Almshouse, 413
Craft, 26, 360
Gate, 360
Widow and her servant in the
almshouse, 413
Temple Bar, 125, 225, 269, 388, 447
Gate, 125
Tenterden (Tenterdene), John (Jankyn),
ironmonger, 290, 323, 437
Termeday, Katherine, formerly Wirgeyn,
273, 400, 412
William, husband of Katherine, 3, 18,
35, 44, 114, 134, 135, 160, 174,
197, 211, 247, 261, 264, 273,
283, 368, 392, 400, 412

Terrill (Terrell, Tirell, Tyrell), Isabella, 7,
20, 133, 196, 210, 263
Richard, 7, 20, 122, 133, 158, 196, 210,
243, 263, 284, 387
Tewkesle (Tewkeslay), Richard, clerk to
sheriffs' accountant, 97, 207
Text-writer, 322
Thakworthe, John, foreigner, 205
Thames, 78, 163, 258, 282, 287, 326, 348
Thames Street, 2, 23, 75, 100, 121, 125,
132, 136, 137, 140, 141, 145, 200,
204, 229, 230, 445
Cross, 141
Thebawde (Tewbawde), John, 78, 140
widow of, 140
Thetford, John, former master of
Brewers' craft, 5, 12, 34, 39, 42,
56, 68, 70, 72, 81, 130, 132, 144,
196, 215, 263, 267, 338, 356
Margery (Margaret), widow of John,
5, 132, 174, 175, 196, 210, 263,
285, 366, 398, 411, 458, 459
Thomas, Johanna, wife of John at Eagle,
397, 444
John, 155, 179, 240, 250, 277, 283,
344, 382, 397, 410, 457
John, brewer, at Hartshorn, Fleet
Street, St Bride's, 80, 202
John, at Eagle, Gracechurch Street,
98, 444
John, tailor, at Hartshorn, Fleet
Street, St Bride's, 68, 96, 146
[–], wife of, 78
Tilers, 189, 190, 192, 193, 296, 297, 300,
312, 423, 424, 425, 465
servant, 190, 192, 193, 296, 297, 300,
312, 423, 424, 425, 432
Timber-monger of Wood Street, 290,
292, 298
Toke, Took, Alice, 132, 135, 195, 209,
262, 397
John, 14, 44, 68, 116, 132, 135, 153,
174, 195, 207, 209, 239, 262,
285, 365, 385, 397, 458
Tolle, Richard, 443, 456, 458
Tolvan (Tolvan, Tolnan), Alice, Anneys,
398, 411, 445
Jacob, James, 240, 259, 268, 271, 339,
340, 373, 386, 398, 411, 445,
457, 458

LONDON RECORD SOCIETY

President: The Rt. Hon. The Lord Mayor of London

Chairman: Professor Caroline M. Barron, MA, PhD, FRHistS
Hon. Secretary: Dr Helen Bradley
Hon. Treasurer: Dr Penny Tucker
Hon. General Editors: Professor Clive Burgess†, Professor Jerry White

The London Record Society was founded in December 1964 to publish transcripts, abstracts and lists of the primary sources for the history of London, and generally to stimulate interest in archives relating to London. Membership is open to any individual or institution. Prospective members should apply to the Hon. Membership Secretary, Dr Penny Tucker, Hewton Farmhouse, Bere Alston, Yelverton, Devon, PL20 7BW (email londonrecordsoc@btinternet.com).

The following volumes have already been published:

1. *London Possessory Assizes: a Calendar*, edited by Helena M. Chew (1965)
2. *London Inhabitants within the Walls, 1695*, with an introduction by D. V. Glass (1966)
3. *London Consistory Court Wills, 1492–1547*, edited by Ida Darlington (1967)
4. *Scriveners' Company Common Paper, 1357–1628, with a Continuation to 1678*, edited by Francis W. Steer (1968)
5. *London Radicalism, 1830–1843: a Selection from the Papers of Francis Place*, edited by D. J. Rowe (1970)
6. *The London Eyre of 1244*, edited by Helena M. Chew and Martin Weinbaum (1970)
7. *The Cartulary of Holy Trinity Aldgate*, edited by Gerald A. J. Hodgett (1971)
8. *The Port and Trade of Early Elizabethan London: Documents*, edited by Brian Dietz (1972)
9. *The Spanish Company*, edited by Pauline Croft (1973)
10. *London Assize of Nuisance, 1301–1431: a Calendar*, edited by Helena M. Chew and William Kellaway (1973)
11. *Two Calvinistic Methodist Chapels, 1748–1811: the London Tabernacle and Spa Fields Chapel*, edited by Edwin Welch (1975)

All titles in the series are available from
Boydell and Brewer; please contact them for further details,
or see their website, www.boydellandbrewer.com